Praise for *Paradise Now*

"Uncommonly smart and beautifully written . . . [Chris] Jennings's sure grasp never falters. The result is a triumph of scholarship and narration: five stand-alone community studies and a coherent, often spellbinding history of the United States during its tumultuous first half-century. . . . Although never less than evenhanded, and sometimes deliciously wry, Jennings writes with obvious affection for his subjects. To read *Paradise Now* is to be dazzled, humbled and occasionally flabbergasted by the amount of energy and talent sacrificed at utopia's altar. But then, as Jennings so memorably puts it, 'Anyone nuts enough to try building heaven on earth is bound for a hell of his own making.'"

—*The New York Times Book Review*

"[An exemplar] of historical reconstruction . . . vividly bring[s] to life the ecological sensitivity, inclusiveness, and egalitarianism that inspired so many in early America . . . [Chris Jennings] has a gift for the striking phrase."

—*The New Yorker*

"In light of current social movements, there is some value in resurrecting the rich and otherwise obscure history of American utopianism—in reminding the world that the United States, exterminator of utopias abroad, has also been a fertile progenitor of them at home. . . . Jennings reconstructs vividly the 'exercises' to which the utopians subjected themselves, a mix of extravagant fantasy and practical experiment that fueled their idealism. . . . The long-dead dreamers of the nineteenth century may yet enjoy their resurrection."

—*Bookforum*

"Writing an impartial, respectful account of these philanthropies and follies is no small task, but Mr. Jennings largely pulls it off with insight and aplomb. Indulgently sympathetic to the utopian impulse in general, he tells a good story. His explanations of the various reformist credos are patient, thought-provoking [and] entertaining."

—*The Wall Street Journal*

"As a tour guide, [Chris Jennings] is thoughtful, engaging and witty in the right doses. . . . He makes the subject his own with fresh eyes and a crisp narrative, rich with detail. . . . In the end, Jennings writes, the communards' disregard for the world as it exists sealed their fate. But in revisiting their stories, he makes a compelling case that our present-day 'deficit of imagination' could be similarly fated."

—*San Francisco Chronicle*

"Chris Jennings is a natural storyteller, and his *Paradise Now,* a five-part chronicle of America's nineteenth-century utopian dreamers and doers, is the most clear-eyed, sympathetic, and inspiring account I've read of this vital chapter in American history in decades. What sort of future do we want? The Shakers, Owenites, Fourierists, Icarians, and Oneidans asked and answered the question, each group in its own way. Chris Jennings prods his readers to ask the question again—for ourselves."

—MEGAN MARSHALL, Pulitzer Prize–winning author of
Margaret Fuller: A New American Life

"Jennings knows how to tell a story and has the intellectual range to recover both the weirdness and wisdom of America's brief bout with Utopian illusions and ideals."

—JOSEPH J. ELLIS, Pulitzer Prize–winning author of
The Quartet: Orchestrating the American Revolution, 1783–1789

"In a perfect world, work will be irresistibly pleasurable. Women will have equal rights. Money and property will be shared, as will spouses. Or maybe sex won't be allowed at all? Even better! And once the ice caps melt, the sea will taste like lemonade. Bliss! With good humor, a lively style, and a deep knowledge of the historical scholarship, Chris Jennings tells the goofy, heart-breaking tale of nineteenth-century Americans who believed they could bring about heaven on earth, and managed to live out futures that the rest of us haven't yet reached."

—CALEB CRAIN, author of *Necessary Errors*

"Despite marked differences separating these utopian movements, Jennings prizes in all of them their distinctive—and utterly American—optimism in facing a future in which their adherents believed they would usher in a glorious new social order. . . . Readers who resent the constraints of a barren realism will value this deep-probing inquiry into the quest for new social possibilities."

—*Booklist* (starred review)

"Jennings proves an able guide to these groups. [His] comprehensive research makes for absorbing reading as he shows how different people attempted to find perfection and how they failed or succeeded."

—*Kirkus Reviews*

PARADISE NOW

PARADISE NOW

The Story of American Utopianism

Chris Jennings

RANDOM HOUSE

NEW YORK

2017 Random House Trade Paperback Edition

Copyright © 2016 by Chris Jennings

Published in the United States by Random House, an imprint
and division of Penguin Random House LLC, New York.

RANDOM HOUSE and the HOUSE colophon are registered
trademarks of Penguin Random House LLC.

Originally published in hardcover in the United States by Random House,
an imprint and division of Penguin Random House LLC, in 2016.

LIBRARY OF CONGRESS CATALOGING-IN-PUBLICATION DATA
Jennings, Chris.
Paradise Now / Chris Jennings
pages cm
Includes bibliographical references and index.
ISBN 978-0-8129-8389-0
ebook ISBN 978-0-8129-9371-4
1. Utopias—United States—History.
2. Communitarianism—United States—History.
3. National characteristics, American.
I. Title.
HX653.J46 2016
307.770973—dc23
205008149

Printed in the United States of America on acid-free paper

randomhousebooks.com

2 4 6 8 9 7 5 3 1

Book design by Dana Leigh Blanchette
Title-page image: © iStockphoto.com

For Tauba Auerbach

We can leave it to the literary small fry to solemnly quibble over these phantasies, which today only make us smile. . . .

—FRIEDRICH ENGELS ON THE UTOPIANS
OF THE NINETEENTH CENTURY

Contents

DARK DAY

The sun became black as sackcloth of hair, and the moon
became as blood. . . .

—REVELATION 6:12

At noon, darkness spread across the sky. It was the nineteenth of May
1780, a Friday. On the rolling pastureland of western New England,
sheep and cows lay down one by one in the damp grass. As the darkness
became total, finches and warblers quieted and returned to their roosts.
Above the white pines and budding oaks, bats stirred. Mistaking day for
night, they took wing.

The fratricidal war for American independence was grinding into its
fifth year. A week earlier, the Continental army had surrendered the
smoldering port of Charleston to the British navy after more than a
month of heavy shelling. In New England, with so many young men off
fighting, gardens went unplanted and the wheat grew thin.

For many colonists the war with Great Britain aroused a stolid nationalist piety, a consoling faith in "the sacred cause of liberty"—the belief that providence would guide the rebels to victory and that the fighting itself constituted an appeal to heaven. But in the hilly border-land between New York and Massachusetts, the anxiety and austerity of the long conflict inspired frenzied revival meetings. This was the New Light Stir, an aftershock of the Great Awakening of radical Prot-estantism that had coursed through New England in the 1740s. From makeshift pulpits, the New Light evangelists shouted an urgent mille-narian message: These are the Latter Days; the Kingdom is at hand.

Standing at the crack of American independence, these backwoods Yankees believed that they were living the final hours of history. It is written: He will come back and the righteous will be delivered from sin for a thousand years of earthly peace and happiness. The New Lights believed that the time had come and that their small revivals, held in fields and cowsheds, would trigger the return of Christ and the millen-nium of heaven on earth. Looking up from their plows and their milk-ing stools, these hill-country farmers scanned the horizon for signs of His approach.

In this atmosphere of millennial anticipation—days of "war and ru-mors of war"—the sudden midday blackness was an indisputable sign of the times. As New England and eastern New York were plunged into total darkness, nervous farmers lit smoky, fat-smelling candles just to eat their lunch or read a few lines of scripture. Lacking telegraphy, they were left to assume that the unnatural darkness had enveloped the whole globe. "People [came] out wringing their hands and howling, 'the Day of Judgment is come,'" recalled a young rebel fifer. Nobody could say for sure when or if the blackness would pass and the light return.

A doctor in New Hampshire tried to get an empirical grip on the situation. "A sheet of white paper held within a few inches of the eyes," he wrote by candlelight, "was equally invisible with the blackest velvet." Others turned to familiar stories for illumination. The black sky echoed the plague of darkness that God summoned over pharaoh's Egypt. Or it was a reprise of the midday eclipse that supposedly occurred while

Christ hung suffering on Calvary.* Even in the rational precincts of the Connecticut legislature, the sudden blackness stirred apocalyptic thinking. When the darkness forced the House of Representatives in Hartford to adjourn, Colonel Abraham Davenport stayed at his desk and asked that candles be brought into the statehouse. If the Day of Judgment was at hand, he said, he wished to be found at his work.

Near dawn the next day, the moon finally came out. A day past full, it shone red.

A month before the darkness, Talmadge Bishop and Reuben Wright, a pair of New Light revivalists from New Lebanon, New York, were walking west along a wooded footpath just north of Albany. Passing through a remote territory known as Niskeyuna, they happened upon a low, boggy homestead. Hoping to rest their feet and cadge some food, they knocked on the door of the rough, two-story cabin. Inside, they were surprised to discover a crowd: five men and seven women, living together in the small building. These were the Shaking Quakers, a raggedy sect from Manchester, England, gathered around a short, forty-four-year-old mystic named Ann Lee.

Lee, whom her followers addressed as "Mother," invited the travelers in. Bishop and Wright lived nearby, but they had never heard any mention of these people. The Shakers had been in the area for six years, but they had maintained a low profile. They had good reason. The Hudson River, which linked British-controlled Canada and the forts of the Adirondacks to the vital port in New York City, was of great strategic importance. The surrounding Hudson Valley was a hotbed of royalist counterrevolution. Improvised rebel militias were on hair-trigger guard against Tory sabotage. It was a dangerous place to have your commitment to the Revolution questioned. In this paranoid atmosphere, Lee and her followers had kept their eccentric faith and Mancunian accents to themselves.

---

* The eclipse is mentioned in Matthew, Mark, and Luke, the three "synoptic Gospels."

The Shakers fed the two travelers while Mother Ann explained her unusual gospel. She told the men that the millennium they and other New Lights had been furiously calling down from heaven had already begun. Its promised life of sinless perfection was free for the taking.

The next morning, Bishop and Wright hurried back across the Hudson to New Lebanon. They brought their tale of an ethereal, blue-eyed woman living in the wilderness to their minister, a popular New Light revivalist named Joseph Meacham. Meacham, a tall, grave young man who had left the Baptist Church to preach the new millenarian faith, had been leading revival meetings in New Lebanon for most of the past year. In the barn of a wealthy convert, he would whip his congregation to great heights of spiritual excitement. As he called out the good news of the coming paradise and the need for immediate surrender to the Holy Spirit, his audience trembled, stamped their feet in the straw, and let loose flurries of glossolalia.

The kinetic enthusiasm of Meacham's revival could not hold. His message, like the message of other revivalists throughout New York and New England, was one of bated anticipation: Paradise or Apocalypse is imminent. But nothing happened. The fall of 1779 closed into winter; winter opened onto spring; and still the world had not ended. The New Lights had been primed for cataclysm: fire from the sky, the Son of Man swinging a golden sword, the descent of the holy city of New Jerusalem. Instead, the long, hard days of spring planting started up again. Having screamed their millenarian faith until they were hoarse, many New Lights felt adrift.

After hearing Bishop and Wright's account of the woman called Mother, Meacham dispatched his friend Calvin Harlow to investigate. A few days later, Harlow returned to New Lebanon, spellbound. Meacham himself then set out on foot for Niskeyuna. And that is when the sky went black.

In her cabin in Niskeyuna, Ann Lee interpreted the "Egyptian darkness" as a divine signal that the time had come to open her gospel to the people of the New World.* When Meacham walked up the trail, Lee greeted him warmly. She said she had been expecting him.

Sitting with Shakers in their cramped cabin, Meacham quizzed them about their claim to have discovered the true nature of salvation. Had they really triumphed over sin? How was it possible that they were led, against the unambiguous teachings of Saint Paul, by a woman?† Something in the serene eloquence of their responses convinced Meacham that he was among a godly people. He converted that day. Mother Ann anointed him her "first-born son in America."

Following the lead of their impressive young pastor, other New Lights from across the Hudson made the trip to Niskeyuna to sit with Lee. They came from New Lebanon and also from the nearby Massachusetts towns of Pittsfield and Hancock. After six years of living in poverty and obscurity, the Shakers opened their small home to all comers.

Within a decade, thousands of Americans regarded Ann Lee, the scrawny daughter of a Manchester blacksmith, as the Second Coming of Christ. Eventually, more than twenty thousand people across much of the United States would live in the society she founded. The vision Mother Ann offered them, of an immaculate New World Zion—an austere, celibate, communistic paradise—inspired wave upon wave of Americans to come, as they liked to say, "out of the World."

The opening of the Shaker gospel in the weeks after what came to be called the Dark Day represents the start of a remarkable chapter in the history of the United States: a long, sunny season of American utopianism.

---

* Fire scarring on trees in Algonquin Provincial Park now indicates that the mysterious darkness of May 19, 1780, was caused by enormous wildfires in Ontario.
† Women, wrote Paul, stand in relation to men as men stand in relation to the church and the church stands in relation to God, as natural subordinates. (1 Cor. 11)

PARADISE NOW

INTRODUCTION

Man-Made Millennium

> A map of the world that does not include Utopia is not even worth glancing at. . . .
>
> —OSCAR WILDE

The dream of utopia is eternal. We walk through this world imagining another, better existence. Sometimes that perfected life is thought to be waiting on the far side of death, or on a remote island, or in the green shade of prehistory. Sometimes we imagine a flawless society right here, just a few years hence. Occasionally, people set their vision in brick and mortar—they frame the buildings of utopia, write out its customs, furnish its rooms, and try to move in.

No moment in history or place on the globe has been more crowded with utopian longing and utopian experimentation than the United States in the middle of the nineteenth century. Countless people on both sides of the Atlantic believed that a new and wondrous society was about to take form in the American wilderness. It was a time when the imminence of paradise seemed reasonable to reasonable people.

This surge of utopian energy came out of the confluence of two ideas, one mystical and ancient, one rational and modern. The first is the Judeo-Christian proposition that history is bookended by golden ages. In the beginning, God planted a garden in the East. And with it was planted the half-remembered dream of a bountiful, property-free existence in the orchards of Paradise, a life uncorrupted by capitalism, technology, or even pants. Scriptural history begins in a garden, but it ends in a metropolis—the gleaming, prefab city of New Jerusalem that God will lower down to us at the time of the millennium, the thousand-year reign of heaven on earth. All human existence—history, time, suffering—is just the hard distance between these two utopias, a long but finite exile from paradise.

The second idea, dating back to the seventeenth century, is that the human race is advancing ineluctably toward a perfection of our own making.* The intellectual triumphs of the Enlightenment—Newtonian physics, astronomy, rationalism, chemistry—all seemed to point toward the possibility that the universe is one big mechanism, as elegant and soluble as an equation. Thanks to the scientific method and the semi-miraculous power of Reason, humankind will eventually discover the obscure but predictable calculus—the *science*—beneath every phenomenon, even the muddled scrum of human affairs. A genuine science of society will not just be descriptive, telling us when and why people act the way they do, it will allow us to change how people act, to fix every social problem. The basic assumption was this: As knowledge deepens and old superstitions fade, the world will become more comfortable, more just, and more happy. Progress without end, amen.

This impression of endless and inevitable progress had particular force during the opening decades of the nineteenth century. Republicanism had taken firm root in the New World, and it was starting to

---

* Francis Bacon is the most notable proponent of this view, but it was general in the thinking of the time. The original title for Descartes's *Discourse on Method* (1637) was *The Plan of a Universal Science to Raise Our Nature to Its Highest Degree of Perfection.*

germinate in western Europe. New technologies of mass production augured a future in which scarcity would become a dim legend. New ideas crossed the globe with startling speed. To many, it felt as though history itself, like a hot-fired steam engine, were gathering momentum.

For horizon-scanning millenarians, this same sense of historical velocity and the uneasiness that was its constant attendant fueled the impression that things were coming to a head, that the End was nigh. Some combined the two strands of thought. The new faith in limitless, human-driven progress merged with the old faith in an imminent golden age. Perhaps human genius—manifested in new ideas, buildings, machines, and social institutions—would be the lever by which the millennium of fraternity and abundance was activated. New Jerusalem was coming, but it would not be winched down from above. It would be built from the ground up, by planners and engineers.

In Europe, this type of thinking was amplified by the vast, silent presence of the North American continent. Looking west across the Atlantic, European visionaries saw a wide-open wilderness, sparsely populated and loosely governed by liberal institutions. Through the rosy lens of millenarian optimism, the New World looked like a blank slate, blessedly removed from the ancient tangle of European principalities and churches. On the "fresh, green breast of the new world," as F. Scott Fitzgerald called it, any future might be inscribed. This sense of a clean start was woven into the keenest hopes of the American Revolution. "We have it in our power to begin the world over again," wrote Thomas Paine in 1776. "A situation, similar to the present, hath not happened since the days of Noah until now."

The notion that history, like the sun, travels east to west has been around since the Middle Ages. Under this theory, civilization began in the East (in "a garden eastward in Eden") and has been westering steadily across the face of the earth toward some unknown apocalypse. This view of things had obvious appeal to theologians and cartographers perched on the western limit of the known world. Later, when

people began to suspect that the earth is a globe, some claimed that the
End would come when we arrived back at the location of the beginning, when some Christian explorer macheted his way through the
jungle and arrived back at the Tree of Life. This was certainly Captain
Columbus's view as he probed the eastern fringe of the New World in
search of Eden.* The presence of a large indigenous population only
added to this European impression of Edenic innocence. Even for those
who did not see North America as the literal historic location of
Paradise—and there were plenty who did—the virginal continent
seemed inherently Edenic. Sailing west from Liverpool was like traveling back in time. "Thus in the beginning," wrote John Locke in 1690,
"all the world was America."

To people steeped in this conception of time and space, the New
World in the West looked to be the inevitable staging ground for the
final dispensation of history. Many early Anglo settlers sincerely believed that North America, conveniently hidden from Christendom
until the Reformation had gained traction, was destined to be ground
zero for the millennium.

In the nineteenth century, secular-minded Europeans took a surprisingly similar view. They claimed that the final chapter of history, the top
rung on the ladder of progress, would play out in the New World. In
Berlin, Hegel lectured that the United States was "the land of the future." It was there that "the burden of world history shall reveal itself."
North America was not just an expanse of plains and mountains; it was
a messiah made of land: the locus and guarantor of all redemption.
The most optimistic observers hoped that post-Enlightenment man,
with all of his newfound cleverness—his sudden zeal for steam engines,
hygienic tenements, the scientific method, and equality—finally had a
chance to get things right, to build paradise.

---

* Columbus wrote, "God made me the messenger of the new heaven and the new
earth, of which he spoke in the Apocalypse of Saint John after having spoken of it
by the mouth of Isaiah; and he showed me the spot where to find it."

All Things New

The spread and evolution of these ideas can be tracked through the rise and fall of five communalist movements that flourished during the busy golden age of American utopianism. These groups do not represent the sum total of that era's utopian experimentation, let alone American utopianism in general. At least one hundred experimental communities were founded in the United States during the nineteenth century and countless more since. But, taken together, these five interconnected groups represent the high-water mark of an intellectual impulse that has flowed through the American experiment since day one, an impulse that may now be near its lowest ebb.

The idea of a New World utopia was born in the fever dream of religious revelation and the waking nightmare of early industrialization. Led by the prophet Ann Lee, the Shakers decided that the Second Coming had already happened and that it was up to them to build the perfect earthly society: a whitewashed stronghold for the dawning millennium. To construct their Zion—a federation of tidy, communistic villages—the Shakers invented a new type of society from scratch, scorning the most fundamental and sacrosanct building blocks of Western civilization. In Zion there would be no property, no family, no sex. Women and men would be equal. Labor would be worship. And the individual would dissolve entirely into the collective.

By the 1820s, the Shakers had established prosperous villages throughout most of the settled regions of the United States. Inspired by their success, secular utopians took up the idea that small, planned communities might be the ideal mechanism with which to remake the world. In 1824, the Welsh socialist and textile magnate Robert Owen, a student and admirer of the Shakers, came to the Indiana frontier. In the village of New Harmony, Owen hoped to build a rationalist, communist utopia that he called the New Moral World. He would raise a "parallelogram," a palatial building in which thousands of people of every class could live and work in peace, abundance, and total equality. At New Harmony and a dozen smaller communities, the Owenites hoped to prove that property and religion were all that stood between humanity and a glorious future in a man-made paradise.

In 1840, a decade after the dramatic collapse of Owen's grand experiment, with the Republic in the doldrums of its first major depression, a New Yorker named Albert Brisbane began publicizing the doctrines of the French social theorist Charles Fourier. Like the Shakers and the Owenites, Fourier believed that the road to paradise lay in the establishment of small, cooperative villages. Fourier claimed that the right kinds of social institutions could unleash the powerful forces of human passion and usher humanity toward its true destiny: an orgiastic global utopia that he called Harmony. To hasten the ascent into Harmony, Fourier proposed building enormous complexes called "phalansteries," in which groups of precisely 1,620 people would live and work. Like Owen's parallelogram and the Bible's New Jerusalem, Fourier's phalanstery was essentially an entire city contained in a single building, a high-tech Versailles for the people. Once the era of Harmony commenced, Fourier prophesied, every human impulse, even the most taboo sexual predilection, will be satisfied and rendered productive. Abundance will prevail; mosquitoes will go extinct; friendly whales will tow our ships; and the oceans, tinctured by "boreal fluid" from the melting arctic icecap, will taste like lemonade. Fourier's ideas, broadcast daily on the front page of the *New-York Tribune,* the country's bestselling newspaper, spread fast. By the end of the 1840s, twenty-nine Fourierist "phalanxes" had been founded in the United States. Most were half-cocked, underfunded ventures that folded quickly. Others fared better. The longest lived was the North American Phalanx in New Jersey. The most famous was the Brook Farm Phalanx in Massachusetts, home to some of the illuminati of the New England literary renaissance.

In 1848, as the Fourierist phalanxes were falling apart and Europe erupted with republican uprisings, a fresh infusion of French utopianism arrived in the Port of New Orleans under the leadership of a Parisian radical named Étienne Cabet. In the mid-1840s, Cabet, known to his devoted followers as "Papa," was the leading communist in France. He preached a mystical strain of socialism in which Christ was celebrated as the first communist. The artisans who formed his base of support called themselves "Icarians" after the fictional people described in *Travels in Icaria,* Cabet's hugely successful utopian romance novel. Under Cabet's semimessianic leadership, several hundred French Icarians crossed the Atlantic to build the techno-communist utopia of Icaria in the Trinity River valley of east Texas, where Robert Owen had helped them secure cheap land. The community in Texas ended in disaster, but the determined Icarians went on to build colonies in Illinois, Missouri, Iowa, and California.

While the Shakers, Owenites, Fourierists, and Icarians all had intellectual roots in Europe, the most remarkable and, by many measures, the most successful utopian venture in United States history was entirely homegrown. New York's Oneida Community thrived for three decades under the brilliant and mostly benign autocracy of John Humphrey Noyes, a Dartmouth- and Yale-educated prophet of "Perfectionism," "Bible Communism," and free love. Like the Shakers, the Perfectionists believed that the prophesied millennium had already commenced, that they were freed from sin, and that it was up to them to commence building the perfect earthly society. To do so, they discarded institutions they deemed anti-Christian, such as the nuclear family, monogamy, and private property. Underwritten by several highly successful manufacturing enterprises, the Perfectionists lived a comfortable, intellectually rich life in a sprawling brick mansion in the spiritually turbulent Burned-over District of central New York. While earlier utopians often stumbled over their own rigid visions of the perfect society, Noyes and his followers lived in a state of constant social experimentation. To avoid the pitfalls of their forebears, the Perfectionists studied the strengths and follies of the Shakers, Owenites, Fourierists, Icarians, and others. On their beautifully manicured estate they championed gender equality, a novel form of birth control, and a unique method of group therapy. They also practiced "complex marriage," a carefully regulated system by which almost any woman in the commu-

nity could have sex with almost any man. In their final decade, they
initiated a program of eugenics to breed the ultimate citizen, the perfect
Perfectionist for the dawning millennium.

These five groups were guided by five different visions of utopia, yet
they generally regarded one another as fellow travelers. They exchanged
letters, newspapers, and visits. From time to time, Owenites became
Shakers; Fourierists moved to Icaria; or Perfectionists joined Fourierist
phalanxes. Despite their divergent views on sex, pleasure, and religion,
they mostly shared a basic set of (then) radical values that put them at
odds with the ascendant values of Jacksonian America. They all believed that men and women are more or less equal, that financial competition is morally corrosive, and that material equality is a precondition
of a just society. To their fellow citizens, the various utopians looked to
be part of a single, loosely defined movement. More significant, they all
shared the basic premise of utopianism: that the society in which they
lived required a total overhaul. Utopianism may be a species of optimism, but it is always born of discontent. Every utopia, whether it remains on the page or takes shape in brick and mortar, reveals the
anxieties and disappointments of its author(s). "The great utopians,"
wrote the historians Frank and Fritzie Manuel, "have all borne witness
to their anger at the world, their disgust with society."

Utopia is diagnostic. Suffering yields hope, and each particular shade
of hope is colored by the particulars of the suffering. The plow-broken
serf places his utopia on the rock-candy mountain, where hammocks
swing between sandwich trees and rivers run with beer. The harried,
well-fed urbanite puts her utopia in an arcadia of primitive farmwork.
The nineteenth-century utopians shared a common anxiety about the
rising specter of industrial capitalism, a then novel system that seemed,
to them, to lay waste to everything in its path while offering as its sole
compensation cheap goods and a few private fortunes. Rather than
blaming technology itself, the utopians sought to hitch the remarkable
new engines of mass production to a higher purpose. They could not
believe that something as unsavory—for many of them, as *irreligious*—as

competition was going to be the foundation of modern society. They refused to accept that "Cash Payment," as Thomas Carlyle wrote in 1843, was destined to be "the sole nexus of man with man."

The various utopians all agreed that society was rotten and that for the first time in history, the means to perfect it—through human ingenuity, divine providence, or both—were at hand. Even more than the scale of their ambition, the thing that set them apart from the other reformers of their day, the thing that really earns them the designation *utopian*, was their method. Rather than trying to improve the world in any of the usual ways—through electoral politics, prayer, propaganda, civil disobedience, armed insurrection—they intended to catalyze a global revolution by building a working prototype of the ideal society. Once a model of the new system is up and running, they believed, its example will be so compelling that it will be replicated ad infinitum. In short order, the new system will blanket the earth, spread entirely by the force of its own evident perfection. As the Owenite turned anarchist Josiah Warren wrote, the new ideas "only needed to be seen in their beautiful and consistent symmetry to be at once approved and adopted." This was how the utopians intended to trigger the man-made millennium. "The only practical difficulty," wrote Robert Owen, "will be to restrain men from rushing too precipitously" into the new paradise.

The word *utopian*, when used in reference to communal experimentation, is partly a matter of style. As Justice Potter Stewart said of pornography, you know it when you see it. The usual roster of American utopias is long and shifting, encompassing everything from small, back-to-the-land hippie communes to artists' colonies to architectural experiments to austere sects of religious separatists. The five movements chronicled here fit within a narrower definition. The Shakers, Owenites, Fourierists, Icarians, and Oneida Perfectionists all labored under the very specific belief that small communistic societies could trigger a new and perfected existence across the entire globe. While these communities often resembled their less ambitious counterparts, their hopes, and therefore their rhetoric, set them apart. They did not wish merely to

take leave of a fallen world or retreat into a pious enclave. They intended to lead the charge into a new and wholly transformed future.

This narrower, grander definition of the term *utopian* comes mostly
from those tireless coiners of terminology Karl Marx and Friedrich Engels. They used the designation *utopian-socialist* to classify a group of thinkers
who preceded them historically and whose socialism they found fundamentally bourgeois (because its aspirations were the aspirations of the
bourgeois and because it depended upon the largesse of private donors).
To populate this dubious intellectual category, Marx and Engels named
names: Robert Owen, Charles Fourier, Étienne Cabet.* Marx and Engels
sought to distinguish the theories of these "utopian socialists" from their
own brand of self-styled "scientific socialism." Mocking Fourier, Owen,
and Cabet in a single breath, *The Communist Manifesto* memorably scoffs
at the "dream of . . . founding isolated [Fourierist] 'phalansteres,' of establishing [Owenite] 'Home Colonies,' of setting up [Cabet's] 'Little
Icaria'—duodecima editions of the New Jerusalem—and to realize all
these castles in the air they are compelled to appeal to the feelings and
purses of the bourgeois." Beneath this condescension was a grudging
respect, evidenced by the great quantity of ink that Marx and Engels
spent upon their analysis of utopian socialism.† They granted that the
utopians had accurately diagnosed society's chief ailments—economic
competition and private ownership of the means of production—and
correctly determined that an extreme cure was required.‡ Besides, as Eric
Hobsbawm wrote about the relationship between Team Marx and the
utopians, "Even revolutionaries like to have ancestors."

---

* Henri de Saint-Simon also makes the list, but his ideas, unlike those of Owen, Fourier, and Cabet, had little impact on community building in the United States.
† In volumes 1 and 2 of the old official Soviet edition of the *Selected Works of Marx &
Engels*, there are twenty references to Robert Owen alone, some of them extensive.
‡ Ironically, the final station of Marx's historical progression—pure stateless
communism—looks an awful lot like the utopias of Owen, Cabet, and Fourier. As the
critic Edmund Wilson put it, "Though Marx had pointed out the naïveté of the utopias of his socialist predecessors, the prospect of the future he invoked, with its more
abundant flowings of the springs of cooperative wealth, was still itself rather utopian.
He had simply thrust the happy consummation a little farther off into the future."

———

Today, when these castles in the air warrant mention it is usually to underscore the extravagant "enthusiasms" of the middle nineteenth century. The utopians are remembered as little more than the crazy froth at the crest of a general wave of Jacksonian optimism. The sheer scale and folly of their expectations—the wrongheadedness of Owen's geometric paradise or Fourier's lemonade sea—are indeed baffling. We occupy the future about which they dreamed and we can plainly see that it looks nothing like their imaginings. A certain type of observer even seems to find reassurance in their failure: those self-proclaimed realists who keep watch over every sally into utopia, awaiting the moment when, as Mary McCarthy put it, "some practical joker . . . called 'human nature'" shows up to spoil the picnic.[*]

Yet the tens of thousands of Americans who lived in these communities were not fools. To be sure, in an era thick with cranks and faddists, the utopias sheltered more than their share. But the majority of the communitarians were intelligent, hardworking people. They came from every denomination and every social class. Significantly, unlike the utopian communalists of other eras, they were not primarily young people. They were blacksmiths and farmers, journalists and lawyers, tailors and scientists, teachers and clergymen. A few of them were among the most articulate and prescient reformers of their day. After their respective sojourns in utopia, many went on to illustrious careers elsewhere. They may have been dreamers, but they did their dreaming out loud, with their dollars, their arms, and their time. They tried to manifest their impractical visions with great practical skill.

It is not news that they failed. If they hadn't, we would be living in a communist paradise, flying about in Icarian hot-air balloons or spending four-day weekends at grand, state-organized Fourierist orgies. The

---

[*] While skimming an anthology of utopian literature, Saul Bellow's Augie March marvels at "what comfort some have that the negligible is upheld and all other greater effort falls on its face."

immediate reasons for their failure are mostly mundane. They bought too much land and went bankrupt; they bought too little land and went bankrupt; their buildings burned down; they got so rich that they feared letting in new members. Often the children of the founding generation wanted to see something else of the world. Sometimes the communards quarreled over doctrine. Sometimes they simply got sick of one another. The close quarters and shared chores of rural communalism make equanimity difficult. As the trustees of the doomed Nashoba Community learned, "That which produces in the world only common-place jealousies and every-day squabbles, is sufficient to destroy a community."

Mostly they failed because the utopians ceased to believe that paradise was waiting for them just around the corner. Breaking ground in the wilderness and building a new society from zero is incredibly hard work. As long as the colonists believed that their dream might be realized, they labored with heroic energy, gladly bearing immense hardships. At their best, they worked with an inspiring sense of solidarity, laboring, as Étienne Cabet wrote, "as one man, afire with dedication and enthusiasm." When the faith slipped, the wind spilled from their sails.

These serial failures have become the most potent legacy of the communal utopias. Many observers read the history of experimental utopianism as one long cautionary tale, told in a series of dismally repetitive chapters, about the hazards of radical adventurism. The failure of the nineteenth-century utopians to produce even one enduring society cannot be ignored, but neither is it the whole story. Questions about why these communities formed in the first place and what they were like during their relatively brief lives can be just as instructive as the mechanics of their ultimate self-destruction.

For better or worse, the utopian visionary sets out to remake the world by reordering life's most basic features. The base unit of utopian thinking is not the individual or even the community; it is the day. One of the most consistent features of utopian literature is the description of the typical citizen's typical day—a blow-by-blow accounting of how he or she wakes up, eats breakfast, dresses, rides to work aboard some new-fangled conveyance, and so on. The experimental utopians (as opposed to those who simply wrote utopian fiction) were not much different. While they spoke of abstract virtues such as Equality and Peace and Brotherhood, the distinctive appeal of their visions was in the details.

As it happened, few of the nineteenth-century utopian colonies looked anything like what their citizens had hoped for. They set out to raise granite palaces and feast on peach cobbler; they often ended up with drafty shacks, hard labor, and cold beans. Yet even when life within utopia looked just as shabby as life in that place they invariably called "the World," it *felt* extremely different. Within the communal utopias, when things were going well and the sun was shining, the most quotidian tasks were imbued with a sense of high purpose and historical consequence.

In 1844, on a summer afternoon at the Trumbull Phalanx, a Fourierist community in the wilds of eastern Ohio, a young Oberlin grad named Nathan Meeker took stock of his new home:

> Seating myself in the venerable orchard, with the temporary dwellings on the opposite side, the joiners at their benches in their open shops under the green boughs, and hearing on every side the sound of industry, the roll of wheels in the mills, and merry voices, I could not help exclaiming mentally: Indeed my eyes see men making haste to free the slave of all names, nations and tongues, and my ears hear them driving, thick and fast, nails into the coffin of despotism. I can but look on the establishment of this phalanx as a step of as much importance as any which secured our political independence; and much greater than that which gained the Magna Charta, the foundation of English liberty.

Looking upon the most ordinary scene of village life—a dusty orchard, a gristmill, men swinging hammers—Nathan Meeker saw the earth shifting on its axis. His impression may be hyperbolic, but it captures the daily experience of many utopians: a sense of actively transforming the world, of living on the cusp of an incandescent future.

The spirit of improvisation that prevailed within these communities charged life with extraordinary creativity. The utopians were in the business of reinventing society from the ground up, and they left no flaw or inconvenience unturned. Along with a flurry of radical social institutions, they produced dozens of new inventions: the flat broom, the lazy Susan, the clothespin, a new mop ringer, a hernia truss, motorized washing machines, a new mousetrap, vacuum-sealed cans, the circular saw, cut nails, a superior animal trap, a cheese press, a corn cutter, a pea sheller, an elastic women's sneaker, and new types of barns and houses. Almost every community designed some new type of costume, usually one that liberated female colonists from the suffocating garb of the Victorian era. Whatever truth there is in the axiom that communism suppresses innovation, the long list of marketable inventions to come out of the communistic utopian colonies offers a strong counterpoint.

Along with this invigorating sense of creativity, the citizens of the small utopias tended to have much more fun than the people living beyond their fences. Except for the Shakers, who felt theologically compelled toward tranquillity outside of their raucous prayer meetings, most of these communities kept up a dizzying schedule of contra dances, lectures, card games, séances, philosophical debates, cotillions, history lectures, picnics, stargazing expeditions, concerts, plays, tableaux vivants, boating trips, berry-picking outings, ice-skating parties, quilting bees, fishing trips, baseball games, oyster suppers, and croquet tournaments.

All of this took place at a time when rural Americans often went months without seeing a nonrelation. When the British journalist Frances Trollope (mother of novelist Anthony) came upon a rural western homestead in 1832, the woman working the stove told her, "I expect the sun will rise and set a hundred times before I shall see another human that does not belong to the family." By contrast, the utopians sat down to supper each afternoon with more than a hundred people. And while most Americans, even in big cities, seldom conversed with people outside of their class or denomination, the utopians lived intimately and in (theoretical) equality with people of every class and creed, although not every race. African Americans were mostly absent from these communities. This jumble of experience and opinion produced predictable tensions, but it also bred intellectual excitement and an enduring liberalism.

When the end inevitably came, some utopians returned to the World with a sense of relief, exhausted by the thousand small frustrations of clumsily enforced equality. Others were sick with disappointment. For a great many, their years spent living "in association," as they said, would be remembered as the highlight of their lives: a merry springtide of intellectual ferment, pleasure, and hope. For many, the end came like a casting out. After the Brook Farm Phalanx disbanded, one young communard wondered how, having known such intimacy and freedom, she could possibly face the "chilling cordiality of the world" or "feel contented again with the life of isolated houses, and the conventions of civilization."

An Age of Reason in a Patty-Pan

Today, thinking grandly about the future is regarded as a sin in and of itself. Calling a proposal "utopian" is among the more routine slurs on Capitol Hill. The supposed end of history—with the laurels for "final form of human government" going to Western liberal democracy—has been trumpeted for at least three decades. The prevailing view on both the left and the right is that the current state of affairs, while far from ideal, is better than the hazards inherent in trying to make things too much better. Not long before his death, the historian Tony Judt wrote that the task of today's intellectuals and political philosophers "is not to imagine better worlds but rather to think how to prevent worse ones." At best, American politics, in both rhetoric and practice, is concerned with finding the least bad version of the status quo—the prevailing as-

sumption being that what we have is well enough and well enough
ought to be left alone. Tocqueville saw this coming in 1835: "I cannot
overcome my fear that men may come to the point of looking upon
every new theory as a danger, every innovation as a vexing disturbance,
and every sign of social progress as a first step toward revolution."

Literature is a sensitive indicator of utopian sentiment. The shift in
attitude from the 1840s to today can be tracked in the library. Influential utopian novels of the kind written by Thomas More, Francis Bacon,
Étienne Cabet, or Edward Bellamy are seldom read, let alone written,
anymore, yet we require fifteen-year-olds to spend their holidays under-
lining paperbacks of *Brave New World* and *1984,* chilling visions of utopia run amuck. Dystopian blockbusters dominate the summer box
office. When utopia is not depicted as soul crushing, it is farce. Laurel
and Hardy's late, second-rate film *Utopia* (1951) nails the modern view
of utopia as fool's errand.* When the fat man and the thin man set out
to build paradise on a remote island, their naive fantasy is overrun with
slapstick venality. (Their island, the world discovers, sits atop a uranium
mother lode.) The cumulative moral is precise: Anyone nuts enough to
try building heaven on earth is bound for a hell of his own making.

One reason that history does not look kindly upon the utopians of
the nineteenth century is that they trafficked in extreme, absolutist visions of the future. Today, we have ample reason to recoil from such
visions. Many of the darkest episodes of the twentieth century—the
Thousand-Year Reich, Soviet gulags, the Khmer killing fields—were
born of utopian and millenarian ideologies. Regardless of the details,
we now flinch at the notion that there is one specific way in which the
world *ought* to be arranged. This reflex is well justified. Again and again,
collectively held visions of paradise have been used to justify systems of
terror and repression.†

---

* Also released as *Atoll K.*

† In 1994, Isaiah Berlin wrote: "There are men who will kill and maim with a tran-
quil conscience under the influence of the words and writings of some of those who
are certain that they know perfection can be reached. . . . And in the end the passionate idealists forget the omelette, and just go on breaking eggs."

Surprisingly, the American utopians of the nineteenth century and the European visionaries who inspired them shared our post-twentieth-century fears about the hazards of revolutionary social change. Owen, Cabet, and Fourier were all intimately aware of the darkest and most utopian episodes of the French Revolution. While their Jacobin comrades descended into paranoid, self-consuming terror, the communal utopians tried to take a different road to a similar, although not identical, paradise. They hoped that discrete experimental communities would demonstrate—to worker, boss, and baron—the obvious superiority of an egalitarian society. For their faith in the basic decency of the rich and powerful, the utopians were derided by the next generation of radicals as terminally bourgeois. Rather than exerting influence incrementally through politics and propaganda, or instantly through insurrection, the utopians hoped to construct the perfect society in miniature and then lead by example—to pull, rather than push, the world toward perfection.

Although it surely did not feel this way to them, theirs was a relatively low-stakes method of reform. If the scheme fails, the corrupt old world will always be right where you left it, just outside the gates. For the utopian vision to spread beyond the seminal prototype, it must prove itself. As Albert Brisbane, the leading American Fourierist, put it, the new order will take hold only "when practice has shown its superiority over the present system." In utopia, size makes all the difference. When Brook Farm collectivized agriculture and sent the intellectuals out to mow wheat, the results were goofy and edifying. When Mao Tse-tung tried the same trick, forty million starved.

Because of their small scale and grand ambitions, these communities offer an unusually clear window onto the practical working out of various social theories. Every community, utopian or not, is composed of notions about how people ought to live together. The state, Hegel wrote, is the ethical idea made actual. But on the scale of nations and empires, those actualized ideas are submerged in an obscuring bath of time and happenstance. A political notion—say, democracy—is animated within

the history of a democratic state, but only under the influence of countless personalities and externalities over the course of generations. By
contrast, utopias, both literary and experimental, tend to be born fully
formed from the mind of one individual. Fourier plotted every detail of
his perfect society—what time everyone would eat, how many people
would work in the pear orchard, how they would elect their foremen—
before he recruited a single follower. Within utopian communities, social and ethical ideas are put into play in a very narrow span of time
and space. Tracking the miniature revolutions that repeatedly sundered
New Harmony or the various Icarian villages is like watching several
centuries of modern history—the glacial advance and retreat of big
ideas about power, liberty, and community—transpire inside a beaker.
Emerson rightly called Brook Farm "a French Revolution in small, an
Age of Reason in a patty-pan."

The brief histories of these miniature societies reveal, with remarkable clarity, how their citizens approached a set of timeless questions.
Must the family be the base unit of civilization? How does diversity af-
fect a highly socialized society? Can citizens really be transformed by
the institutions within which they live? Is monogamy required for a
stable, prosperous society? Is private property? How much must theory
bend in the face of circumstance? How does spiritual authority interact
with political authority? Does social progress flow from the initiative of
self-advancing individuals or from broad, collectivist reforms? Is competition the ideal motor of innovation and prosperity? Can social solidarity be stimulated or must it arise spontaneously? Hovering above all
of these questions is the overarching dialectic that defines civil society:
the back-and-forth between individual liberty and mutual aid, between
the freedom to do as you please and the freedom from being cold, hungry, and alone.

The ideas that undergirded these communities, like the ideas enshrined
in our founding documents, were born out of the European Enlightenment. While the utopians' aspirations can seem alarmingly foreign,
their basic outlook was hyper-American—American, but more so (in

terms of ideals, if seldom reality). Americans cherish freedom of conscience; where better to nurture new heresies? America is profoundly egalitarian; where better to abolish property? Americans cherish liberalism; where better to emancipate women? America is a land of new beginnings; where better to kick off the millennium?

The lunatic optimism and creativity of our utopian predecessors can be infectious. They took no social institution for granted. With bearings fixed toward a meridian of joy and perfection, everything old and familiar—monogamy, property, hierarchy, family—went overboard. Mistakenly sensing that the world was on the brink of total transfiguration, they built their tiny societies according to a single criterion: their own shining vision of the future.

It is almost impossible not to mock the extravagant hopes of the nineteenth-century utopians. Yet it is difficult to linger amid the ruins of those hopes without sensing a deficit in our own time, a way in which their story mocks us. In the company of these strange, familiar Americans, we might revive their essential question: What sort of a future do we want?

THE SHAKERS

American Zion

And was Jerusalem builded here,
Among these dark Satanic Mills?
—WILLIAM BLAKE

Cottonopolis

Ann Lee was born four decades before the Dark Day, on Leap Day 1736. She was the second of eight children born to a Manchester blacksmith named John Lees and a woman whose name is lost to history. They lived in a small apartment on Toad Lane, a narrow street of smithies and alehouses.

In the mid-1700s, Manchester was ground zero for the nascent Industrial Revolution. When Lee was little, the blocks of the city were interspersed with small farm plots. Shiploads of cheap, slave-picked American cotton and a handful of technical innovations transformed the city. By the time Lee was a young woman, Manchester had begun to fill with unskilled workers from the countryside looking for work in the new mills. The invention of the spinning jenny, a machine that allowed one person to operate many yarn spindles at once, revolutionized the production of thread. Spinning, which had formerly been done by independent artisans or in the evenings by farmers' wives, became a profitable full-time trade. The jennies spun a surplus of thread, accelerating advances in weaving technology. Groups of wealthy landowners built large mills where water- and steam-driven looms churned out inexpensive cloth. Artisan weavers and spinners could not compete. Many sold their small plots of ancestral land and joined the exodus into the city. Peasants who had previously fed themselves from their own meager acreage and often didn't eat much at all began to live off factory wages.

Little is known of Lee's early life. She never went to school. When she was eight, she began to work on a loom. The hagiography written by her followers after her death offers a portrait of their prophet as a severe young woman. The plump little girl relished hard work, the official record reports, and was "never addicted to play as other children." From an early age she "was impressed with a sense of the great depravity of human nature, and of the odiousness of sin." In the cramped apartment that Lee shared with her seven siblings, her parents' sex life was probably on full display. It was certainly within earshot. Repulsed by the "indecent nature of sexual coition," Lee chastised her mother for submitting to her father's lust. This insolence earned her regular whippings. After Ann left the textile workshop, she worked as a velvet cutter. For a time she prepared fur for hats. Later she served as an assistant in a lunatic asylum.

Religion was one of the few things that was not in short supply on Toad Lane. By the time Lee was twenty-three, she and other members of her family had joined a prayer group led by Jane and James Wardley, a pair of Quaker tailors who lived in Bolton, a few miles north of Manchester. The Wardleys believed that God spoke directly to them and that the Second Coming of Christ was imminent. Like other religious dissenters of their day, they denounced the official Anglican Church as the work of the Antichrist. The group that met in the Wardleys' home felt the Holy Ghost in their midst and acted accordingly. Disturbed by their spastic singing and dancing, their neighbors called them jumpers, shiverers, or shaking Quakers.

Much of what the Wardleys preached derived from a group of French mystics who had settled in England at the end of the seventeenth century. In 1685, Louis XIV revoked the Edict of Nantes under pressure from the Vatican and his devoutly Catholic second wife. For a century, the edict had protected the rights of Huguenot Protestants to worship openly throughout most of France, though never in Paris. In response to their sudden loss of liberty, many Huguenots immigrated to England, Prussia, Holland, and North America. Others remained in France and waged a violent insurrection, burning churches and killing priests. They became known as Camisards for the light linen shirts (*camisa*) they wore to identify one another on night raids. Some Camisards were burned at the stake. Others were stretched on the wheel. Among those exiled to England, many settled in Manchester. The French Prophets, as they came to be known, danced wildly, spoke in tongues, wrestled with invisible devils, spoke of an imminent millennium, and specially prized the prophetic gifts of women.

By the time Ann Lee was worshipping with the Wardleys, the notion that the end of the world was imminent had special force in Manchester. The conditions in what William Blake would soon call Britain's "dark Satanic Mills" were indeed hellish. The workers' precincts were a knotted tangle of covered passages and narrow, winding alleys. Fresh water and plumbing were almost nonexistent. Slimy, stagnant creeks bubbled with miasmatic gases. The poorest workers went barefoot through alleys that dead-ended at muddy pools of urine and shit.

This gray, life-refusing landscape would have a powerful influence on modern utopian and socialist thought. A decade after Mother Ann and her Shaking Quakers left Manchester to build a new, perfected society in North America, Robert Owen, the founder of Indiana's New Harmony community, came to town. Owen was born poor, but he ended up on the winning end of the city's brutal economic equation.

Even so, his sympathies remained with workers like Ann Lee. His time in the mills inspired dreams of a secular paradise in which working people would enjoy all the comforts and dignity of the wellborn. A generation after Owen left, the mills of Manchester inspired and bankrolled the writings of Marx and Engels.

Manchester's factory economy, which took off when Lee was a young woman, left people who had formerly lived according to little more than the rain and the soil at the whim of a powerful new force: the global market. The constant presence of excess workers in the city was necessary for those rare times when cloth production peaked. When demand slackened, the looms slowed. Thousands of men, women, and children became instantly superfluous. Since they did not own (or hold tenancy upon) any land, they could not even raise the meager subsistence that their parents had. This situation—a permanently impoverished labor surplus—drove wages ever downward, creating huge fortunes for a small group of mill owners while ushering workers into lives of squalid confusion. Industrial accidents—crushed legs, mangled fingers, broken arms—were commonplace. In the damp slums, epidemics came and went like weather.

Many reformers assumed that the new competitive industrialism would not last long. How could something so inhuman survive? As one commentator later wrote of Marx, the utopian reformers in Manchester mistook "the birthpains of capitalism for its death throes." The religiously minded fell back on the eternal conviction that justice, in one form or another, was coming. Wrongs will be made right; the least will come first; Babylon will fall.

Second Coming

> And there appeared a great wonder in Heaven; a woman
> clothed with the sun, and the moon under her feet, and
> upon her head a crown of twelve stars.
>
> —REVELATION 12:1

In January 1762, when Ann Lee was twenty-six and had been worshipping with Jane and James Wardley for three years, she married a Manchester blacksmith named Abraham Standerin. Given Lee's distaste for sexual coition, the match was probably made by her parents. Abraham might have been her father's apprentice. Apparently he lacked his wife's intense piety. Official Shaker history (a highly biased source) recalls him as a randy lout with a strong thirst for ale. Once married, Lee was constantly pregnant. She carried four children to term, but all of them died in infancy or early childhood. The fourth delivery was particularly painful. The baby, named Elizabeth, was extracted with forceps. She lived longer than any of her siblings, dying at age six. The trauma of these serial deaths convinced Lee that God was punishing her for some grave sin.* She became terrified of Abraham's advances, avoiding their marriage bed "as if it were made of embers."

The early Shakers did not make any special effort to record their activities or beliefs. Lee, like most of the others, was illiterate.† The most reliable record of the groups' comings and goings in Manchester is their extensive rap sheet. Seeing themselves in heroic opposition to a corrupt Anglican establishment, the Wardley group went out looking for conflicts with the local authorities. On July 14, 1772, the Manchester constable noted that he had spent five shillings on beer for the twenty-four men who helped apprehend Shakers who were causing a "disturbance."‡ Lee seems to have been particularly gung ho. A week after the mid-July "disturbance," a shilling was paid to the jurors' bailiff for the arrest of her and her father. Three months later, a certain "widow Shepley" was compensated two shillings for damage done to her ironwork during the (presumably violent) arrest of several Shakers. Barging into churches

---

* Killing babies as a divine means of communicating with adults is a common enough theme in the Old Testament (see Job).

† The only extant handwriting from a woman who famously crusaded against matrimony is the single X that she inked onto her marriage certificate.

‡ Several police reports related to the Shakers include a line-item expense for beer. Writing in 1892, one Manchester journalist wryly admired this "ingenious system for combining the secular consumption of ale with the sacred joy of harrying the sturdy protestants."

and haranguing the assembled worshippers was evidently a favorite Sunday outing for the Shakers. In May 1773, six shillings were spent to provide meat and drink for Lee after she was jailed "for disturbing the congregation in the old Church."

On one occasion, after being locked up for "disturbing the Sabbath," Lee had a vision. Sitting in her cell, she saw Jesus standing directly in front of her. He showed her "the most astonishing visions and divine manifestations . . . in so clear and striking a manner that the whole spiritual world seemed displayed before her." She was able to look into the Garden of Eden at the very moment of the Fall. The true cause of Adam and Eve's expulsion from Paradise suddenly became obvious. It had nothing to do with eating fruit from the Tree of Knowledge of Good and Evil. The true "root and foundation of human depravity," Lee saw, was sex. Adam and Eve had misinterpreted the commandment to be fruitful. God wanted them to multiply in a spiritual sense, not to gratify Adam's lust. By forsaking their angelic natures and entering into the ranks of "natural generation," the first humans exchanged God's intimacy for a cursed, animal existence.

Lee later argued that the true nature of the original sin can be inferred from God's punishment. For the daughters of Eve, He made childbirth a painful and dangerous ordeal: "Unto the woman he said, I will greatly multiply thy sorrow and thy conception: in sorrow thou shalt bring forth children." It was a curse that must have resonated powerfully with Lee. Adam's sentence was equally familiar to the denizens of Toad Lane: "In the sweat of thy face shalt thou eat bread, till thou return unto the ground." To Lee and her confederates, these twin punishments summed up most of what they knew of life—hard labor, twice over. And it was not because of Eve's disobedience. It was because of Adam's lust.

Decades after Ann's vision, Shaker theologians found even more scriptural support for her interpretation of the Fall. They pointed out that Adam and Eve's immediate response to their sin was to cover their genitals with leaves, thus indicating "the principal seat of human depravity." If sex wasn't the sin, "why did not the shame fall upon the hand that took the fruit, and the mouth that ate it?" Those same theologians also noted that there was something awfully familiar about the physical form that Satan took in the Garden. "It may easily be determined," wrote one circumspect Shaker, "where it is that the head of the serpent lieth."

In the afterglow of her vision, Lee concluded that the only way to restore man's intimacy with God was to cease participating in "natural generation, or in any of the gratifications of lust."

Released from jail, Lee rushed to a meeting of the Wardley group. As she recounted her revelation, the others were struck by a powerful change in her—a new and potent charisma. They "saw at once that the candle of the Lord was in her hand." The force of her testimony was so strong that Lee, then in her midthirties, immediately assumed a position of leadership within the group. She adopted the title "Mother," previously reserved for Jane Wardley. "From this time she was received and acknowledged as the first visible leader of the church of God upon earth."

In the moment that Lee understood the true nature of sin, she was transformed from an ordinary woman into a "vessel to revive and bring to light His perfect law of righteousness for the direction and salvation of all souls." The Shakers gradually came to regard Lee's vision as the opening trump of the long-prophesied millennium: "Here commenced the real manifestation of Christ's second appearance." To them, Mother Ann Lee was not just a prophet or a seer of visions. In that damp prison cell, she became a medium for the Second Coming of Christ.

A Tree Like a Burning Torch

By the early 1770s, there were about thirty Shakers living in Manchester. Under Lee's leadership, they all adopted strict celibacy. They also became more brash in their declarations of the dawning millennium. As a result, they suffered rougher persecution. In the Shaker version of events (the only record that survives), the purehearted believers are repeatedly aided by miracles as they elude mobs of Anglican thugs. When a gang tried to stone Lee, their rocks fell short. When a man departed for London carrying an anti-Shaker petition to King George, he fell dead from his horse.

The Shakers began to move around at night to avoid trouble. One Saturday evening, while walking twenty miles to a prayer meeting, a group of them stopped to rest and eat. By the side of the road, a young Shaker named James Whittaker had a vision of his own. "While I was sitting there," he wrote, "I saw a vision of America; and I saw a large tree, and every leaf thereof shone with such brightness as made it appear like a burning torch, representing the church of Christ, which will yet be established in [that] land." The tree, the group decided, represented a flourishing Shaker society in the colonies. "God had a chosen people in America," Whittaker claimed. It was the "favored land prepared for the building up of Christ's Kingdom." Whittaker's vision was taken as a divine promise that the Shakers' "millennial church" would be established in North America. They must also have understood that they would enjoy greater freedom of conscience in the colonies.

On May 10, 1774, Lee and eight of her confederates, including her brother William, her niece Nancy, and James Whittaker, boarded the *Snow Mariah,* a square-rigged packet sailing out of Liverpool for New York. Lee's husband, Abraham, came along, too, despite his lack of faith. The Wardleys and Lee's father, along with perhaps fifty other Shakers, remained behind in Great Britain. The crossing took three months. The *Snow Mariah*'s captain, a man named Smith, despised the Shakers' loud, arrhythmic singing and herky-jerky dancing. He threatened to throw them overboard, but they kept at it. When, according to Shaker history, a rough sea knocked a board loose from the ship's hull, Captain Smith announced that they were all doomed. Lee calmly assured him that God would protect his one true church. A moment later, a heavy wave hammered the loose plank back into place.[*]

When the *Snow Mariah* docked in New York Harbor on August 6, the pilgrims split up to find work. William Lee, James Whittaker, and a relatively affluent Shaker named John Hocknell sailed north up the Hudson River to look for cheap land. Ann and Abraham stayed in the city. He found work as a smith. She was hired as a laundress in a home on Queen Street (now Pearl Street). When Abraham fell ill, Lee quit her job to nurse him. Once recovered, he refused to return to work and began spending his days carousing "with the wicked at public houses." One evening he brought home a "lewd woman" and threatened to marry her if Ann did not resume her conjugal duties. Lee said she'd rather die. Abraham left.[†]

Lee was alone in New York City, unemployed, penniless, and living in a small, cold room. A single line from the Shaker chronicle conveys her situation: "She sat down upon the stone, without any fire, sipped her vinegar, and wept." (Why she kept rocks for furniture and vinegar for drink is not clear.)

The following year, Lee moved upstate and the eight Shakers reunited near Albany, on two hundred acres of land in Niskeyuna that Whittaker and Hocknell had leased from Stephen Van Rensselaer, lord of the manor of Rensselaerswyck. They planted corn and wheat, cleared a small section of forest, and raised a two-story log home. The women slept on the ground floor, the men upstairs. Over the next four years, as the colony around them descended into rebellion, the Shakers improved their meager plot and kept to themselves. The only growth in their ranks came from a handful of believers who emigrated from Manchester and a single American-born convert. Learning the skills of frontier living as they went, they scraped a thin subsistence from their farm

---

[*] A slightly more plausible account of this incident reports that the Shakers manned the bilge pumps with "miraculous" strength.

[†] It is difficult to gauge the truth of this little morality play. What is certain is that when the Shakers reconvened in Niskeyuna, Abraham was no longer among them.

and awaited the moment when Mother Ann would open her gospel and commence building the millennial church.

Bedlam

In the spring of 1780, after the skies turned black and the moon went red, pilgrims began coming up the Niskeyuna trail in droves to hear the gospel of Christ's Second Appearing. Lee had seen their arrival in a vision, and the Shakers had been stockpiling food. At night, the cabin floor was covered with sleeping bodies. More people camped outside.

It is impossible to pin down a clear-cut Shaker theology, especially in the early years when the faith was unwritten. Even once Lee's successors began to set their beliefs down on paper, Shakers from any two decades might not agree precisely on all of their doctrines. Generally, they believed that Adam and Eve, like all subsequent humans, combined a bodily animal nature with an immaterial soul. By succumbing to Adam's lust, they allowed the former to dominate. Contrary to modern orthodoxy, the Shakers claimed that Jesus of Nazareth was a mortal man who had been imbued with the "Christ spirit" at the time of his baptism. Since they opposed "natural generation," they saw it as significant that Christ had been born of a virgin and died without having sex.

The people gathered in Niskeyuna believed that the Second Advent foretold in scripture—an event anticipated by so many of their contemporaries—would not come with the appearance of the messiah or a sudden rapture of souls. The millennium would take the form of the reappearance of the "Christ spirit" and the birth of the millennial church. The Shakers eventually called themselves the United Society of Believers in Christ's Second *Appearing*, not Christ's Second *Appearance*.*

---

* The Shakers did not begin calling themselves the United Society of Believers in Christ's Second Appearing until the 1820s.

The millennium would be a process: the gradual perfection of human society.

According to the Bible, the men and women of the earliest Christian community, the so-called Apostolic Church, experienced certain supernatural "gifts"—they could heal the sick, communicate directly with God, and experience bodily possession by the Holy Ghost. The Shakers, who saw themselves as the second and final iteration of this early church, believed that they had similar gifts. Their sensitivity to the Holy Ghost was manifested in their eponymous activity: shaking.

In their cabin in Niskeyuna, the British Shakers taught their American converts that the millennium had commenced in 1770, when the "Christ spirit" entered Mother Ann and, to a lesser extent, the group of "witnesses" who were gathered around her. Among the Manchester Shakers, Lee was seen as the lead prophet among a group of similarly inspired men and women. The heavenly "gift" was in all of them. As the embodiment of the Second Coming of the "Christ spirit," Lee was not considered a deity, although later Shakers sometimes spoke of her as if she were. She was a human with a uniquely powerful capacity for revelation. She could take confession, forgive sins, and "search the heart" of her followers. Even after her death, Lee remained the spiritual pillar of the sect. Later generations of Shakers felt her presence actively influencing their lives from the beyond.

In the years immediately following the Dark Day, the daily existence of the believers bore little resemblance to the modern image of the Shakers. This was not a quiet community of old women making ladder-back chairs and singing sweetly about "simple gifts." The converts who gathered at Niskeyuna spared little thought for their material conditions. They were determined to "come out of the World," to separate themselves from the daily rhythms of life in the colonies and the messy uprising coming to life around them. In the green hill country north of Albany, they lived in the fever and thrill of daily revelation. Their worship was constant but contained no liturgy. Tradition was anathema;

spontaneity was the hallmark of spiritual authenticity. No expression was too strange. They danced, shook, and giggled. They made animal noises; they shrieked; they rolled about in the dirt and stamped their feet. Their neighbors claimed that at night the Shakers stripped naked and ran through the dark. The Holy Spirit moved among them. Their bizarro carryings-on certified it.

One of the first accounts of an American Shaker meeting was recorded one week after the Dark Day by Valentine Rathbun, a Baptist minister and one of the sect's earliest converts. When Rathbun arrived at Niskeyuna, there were only twelve people on the property. He was welcomed, fed, and invited to watch the group worship. They began by sitting on the floor, singing a wordless tune, and violently shaking their heads. The melody and shaking intensified until, as Rathbun describes it, all hell broke loose. The meeting, which sounds more like an Acid Test than an eighteenth-century prayer service, unraveled into complete "bedlam."

> In the best part of their worship every one acts for himself . . . one will stand with his arms extended, acting over odd postures . . . another will be dancing, and sometimes hopping on one leg about the floor; another will fall to turning round, so swift, that if it be a woman, her clothes will be so filled with wind, as though they were kept out by a hoop . . . some sitting by, smoking their pipes; some groaning most dismally; some trembling extremely. . . . Then all break off, and have a spell of smoking, and sometimes great fits of laughter. . . . They have several such exercises in a day.

Although there is no mention of nude dancing in the Shakers' own reports, early apostates recall the practice with great consistency. Eunice Stanton, who followed her husband into "Zion" before leaving in disgust, contributed to a collection of anti-Shaker writings. "Their religion," she wrote, "consisted in confessing sin to the leaders, dancing and whirling, speaking in their unknown tongues, as they called it, stripping and dancing naked together, men and women." Others claimed that Lee's spiritual ecstasy was fueled by a mixture of dark rum and darkly repressed sexuality. "I have seen the Mother at Niskeuna, in the State of New York, in times of her intoxication, come into a room where many were gathered for a meeting and were, by her own orders, stript naked; I have seen her slap the men, rub her hands on all parts of their bodies, press the men to her bosom and make them suck a dry breast all this time she would be humming and making an enchanting noise."

The Grand Actress

In a time of intense millenarian expectation, these outlandish displays, so alarming to straight-backed New England Calvinism, struck a chord. Revolutionary New England, it turned out, was a very good place to start a new religion, and the sect grew briskly.* Along with the Shakers' sudden popularity came unwanted attention. Valentine Rathbun, the convert who documented the early prayer meeting, was an ardent patriot who came to resent the Society's stubborn pacifism. He left the sect to become a full-time Shaker baiter, whipping up hostility by claiming that the Shakers destroyed families and that they called all other Christians "boogers, devils and Sodomites." Neither claim was totally untrue. Rathbun published a pamphlet titled *Discovery of the Wicked Machinations of the Principal Enemies of America,* which, like *The Protocols of the Elders of Zion,* claimed to reveal a secret, far-reaching conspiracy in which the Shakers endeavored to strangle the newborn American Republic in the cradle. The pamphlet even includes a fictional dialogue in which the dastardly King George celebrates Mother Ann's ability to prey upon "the foolish and superstitious passions of the most ignorant of the Americans."

---

* The village of Niskeyuna, just west of the Hudson River on the eastern edge of New York, is not technically in New England, but the distinction was more or less irrelevant. Many of the first converts came from across the Massachusetts line.

In a time of aggressive, insecure nationalism, a group of recently emigrated Brits, led by a woman and denouncing any involvement in the war, raised more than a few red flags. In early July 1780, just a month and a half after the Dark Day, a newly minted Shaker named David Darrow tried to herd a flock of sheep from his farm in New Lebanon to Niskeyuna as an offering to the nascent community. A group of self-appointed patriots, suspecting that Darrow intended to convey the sheep to the nearby frontier, where hungry British soldiers were camped, seized the livestock and brought Darrow before the local magistrate. When the judge pressed him to swear allegiance to the cause of independence, Darrow refused, claiming that his new faith barred him from fighting or taking oaths. He was sent to prison.

Throughout the Revolution, the treatment of those loyal to the crown was brutal. Private mail was scoured for unpatriotic sentiments, and suspected royalists were tarred with scalding pitch. Loyalty oaths were administered door-to-door. Those who refused to sign might have their names printed up in the town square. In the region around Albany, the state of New York established a commission "for detecting and defeating conspiracies," a sort of Revolutionary War–era House Un-American Activities Committee. Three weeks after Darrow and his sheep were detained, the commission issued a writ for the arrest of the leading Shakers. "Frequent complaints have been made by sundry of the well affected inhabitants of this County," the warrant read, "that John Partherton, William Lees, and Ann [Lee] Standerren, by their conduct and conversation disturb the publick peace." In a nicely Orwellian phrase, the commission charged that the Shakers were "daily dissuading the friends to the American cause from taking up Arms in defense of their Liberties." Within three days, Jacob Kidney, an officer of the court, arrested the three Shaker leaders along with several others who happened to be with them.

The men were locked up in Albany's Old Fort. Mother Ann created such a fuss that she and a Shaker sister named Mary Parrington were transferred downriver to a jail in Poughkeepsie. The state's plan was to deliver Lee to British-controlled New York City, where the "grand actress," as she was called in court, would become the king's problem. Given their experiences in Manchester, the Shakers felt relatively at home in prison. Their evangelism continued uninterrupted. They even converted a few royalist inmates.

The men were released after four months. A month later, in December 1780, thanks to the intercession of Governor George Clinton, William Lee was finally allowed to pay his sister's bail. Mother Ann was set free with a stern warning not to do or say anything "inconsistent with the peace and safety of this and these United States."

Now certified traitors, the Shakers were unchastened. That spring, when the weather warmed and the roads dried, Mother Ann, William Lee, and James Whittaker left Niskeyuna on a missionary expedition throughout New England. For the next two and a half years they were constantly on the move, staying briefly in almost forty settlements throughout Massachusetts, Connecticut, and eastern New York. Traveling by foot along the roads and Indian trails that laced through the woods of New England, they went from village to village, spreading the good news of Christ's Second Appearing and trawling for what Lee called "gospel fish."

When the trio of missionaries (sometimes joined by others) reached bigger villages, they would set up a small revival. Even during the war, there wasn't much going on in these towns. The curious, the hostile, and the bored could be counted on to turn out for a bit of hellfire from a strong-voiced evangelist. The outrageous spectacle of a woman speaking publicly about salvation (or anything) helped gather a crowd.

The missionaries' usual approach was for James Whittaker to stand in the thoroughfare, exhorting passersby to come hear the new gospel. Whittaker, who later succeeded Lee at the head of the Society, was a handsome, fair-skinned man with dark eyes and black hair. His mother had been a member of the Wardley group, and he was the first man to grow up entirely in the Shaker faith. He was deeply devoted to Mother Ann. During one of her longer stints in the Manchester jail, he supposedly kept her alive by pouring milk and wine through the stem of a pipe inserted through the keyhole of her cell. In a style and vocabulary that would have been familiar throughout Puritan New England—the hectoring, semicrazed evangelism that was the legacy of Jonathan Edwards, the defining voice of the Great Awakening—Whittaker unfolded the peculiar notion that the millennium had begun and that the time to forsake sin was now.

When a small group of potential converts was gathered, Mother Ann took over. Unlike Whittaker's forceful street preaching, Lee's quiet charisma—her uncanny ability to elicit deep, emotional confessions from total strangers—worked best in private interviews. The conversions she inspired were occasionally so sudden that they seemed physical. Some described a feeling of being dowsed in cold water. Others likened her power to the "operations of an electerising machine." Lee's particular genius, her power to "search every heart," was an intuitive knowledge of people's needs. She tailored her pitch to the sinner— sometimes humming sweetly, sometimes scolding harshly, sometimes stroking an arm.

When Mother Ann and the other missionaries arrived in Harvard, Massachusetts, at the end of June 1781, the town was already in a state of spiritual upheaval. A contingent of Baptists was trying to break off from the township to incorporate its own village, and a small millenarian sect had set up shop in a large house at one end of the main street.[*] The sect, which might more properly be called a cult, had been founded by a pipe fitter turned New Light preacher named Shadrack Ireland who had died three years before the Shakers' arrival. Like Mother Ann, Ireland preached celibacy. Unlike Lee, he had abandoned a wife and

---

[*] Harvard remained a magnet for millenarian and utopian innovation. In 1843, at the peak of the nineteenth-century communitarian boom, the transcendentalist Bronson Alcott and the English reformer Charles Lane founded the short-lived vegan commune of Fruitlands in the town. That same year, a large contingent of Millerites, followers of William Miller, a New York farmer who predicted that the Second Coming would be in 1843, awaited ascension to heaven on a hill outside of the town.

child to share his bed with a series of devoted "spiritual wives." Ireland prophesied an imminent millennium and claimed he was perfect (freed from sin) and immortal. His home in Harvard, known as the Square House, was equipped with secret escape hatches and a hidden staircase that led to a lookout tower in which the paranoid mystic spent much of his time watching for the arrival of either Christ or the militia. After he died in 1778, Ireland's followers placed his corpse inside a wooden casket and bricked it into a corner of the cellar. They waited ten months for his resurrection before giving up and burying the pungent box in a cornfield in the middle of the night.

When the Shakers arrived in town, a group of Ireland's followers was still living communally in the Square House. A handful of them had traveled to Niskeyuna after the Dark Day and expressed interest in hearing more of the Shaker gospel. They were an eccentric bunch. One declared himself the Lord and went around in a brimless cap embroidered *GOD*. Much of what Lee preached—celibacy, communalism, the dawning millennium—was familiar to Ireland's flock. She converted a few of them, purchased the Square House, and established it as her base of operations from which to evangelize the surrounding towns.

Word of Lee's presence in Harvard spread, drawing hundreds of seekers to the town. Most of them were respectable artisan-class Yankees. Some were militiamen or soldiers in the Continental army. Inside the Square House, the Shakers schooled potential converts in their rowdy style of worship. They danced and sang around the clock, making as much noise as humanly possible. Shaker carpenters reinforced the floors of the Square House with heavy timbers so that it could withstand the believers' violent stomping and leaping. The startled citizens of Harvard claimed that the Shakers' "hooting and tooting" could be heard two miles away.

Since the days of Jane and James Wardley, the Shakers had required new converts to offer a full confession to a spiritual "elder." The experience of enumerating all of one's past sins in detail, lingering especially on carnal indiscretions, helped draw a bright line between the corrupt life in the World and the new, purified existence within "gospel order."

To the Shakers' antagonists, this practice, combined with their belief in celibacy, carried a disturbing whiff of the church in Rome. At a time and place when it was common to equate the pope with the Antichrist, this imagined connection to Catholicism was almost as damning as the believers' refusal to fight.

Not long after the Shakers' arrival in Harvard, people in the town began demanding their expulsion. Angry crowds gathered outside the Square House, threatening violence. It was a drama that was enacted almost everywhere the missionaries stayed for more than a few days. Mobs, inevitably fronted by a coalition of local clerics and cider-soaked militiamen, accused Lee of heresy, witchcraft, treason, and luring wives and mothers from their husbands and children. The most inflammatory accusation, especially given Harvard's proximity to Boston, the moral nerve center of the Revolution, was that the believers were intentionally subverting the long, exhausting war effort. The idea of a woman leading anything besides a schoolroom was so foreign that some people claimed Mother Ann must be a man in drag. And to the residents of war-addled New England, there was only one reason for a man to dress as a woman: he was a spy. On more than one occasion, thugs broke up prayer meetings, bloodying the lead members and driving off their initiates. Mother Ann may have been sexually abused under the pretense of finding out "whether she was a woman or not."

While the Shakers probably did dissuade some men from joining the rebellion, they had no special loyalty to Great Britain. When, in October 1781, Lee learned that Cornwallis had surrendered at Yorktown, she knelt and offered a prayer of thanks. The Shakers struggled to remain aloof from the Revolution, but they believed that the fate of the United States was somehow entwined with the coming perfection of society. James Whittaker's roadside vision of a burning tree—a vast millennial church to be built in the New World—had never faded from view. Lee preached that the Revolution was a work of God, intended "to open the way for the Gospel."

———

During the summer of 1781, a rumor spread through Harvard that the Shakers were stockpiling food inside the Square House. Hoarding was a serious wartime offense, particularly in the eyes of the underfed mobs who dispensed patriotic justice with pitch and horsewhips. Someone also claimed to have seen Shaker men carrying a chest of guns into the house. In August, the local militia came to search the property. The Shakers let them in, but the soldiers failed to find any weapons or evidence of hoarding.

That winter, the lead Shakers traveled from Harvard to the home of a new convert in Petersham, Massachusetts. As a heavy snow fell, the house filled with initiates and curious locals. In the early evening, as James Whittaker read aloud from the Bible, someone in the crowd shouted, "Knock out the lights." The room went dark and three men in blackface grabbed Lee by the waist. They tried to drag her outside, but a group of Shaker sisters grabbed her by the arms. After a violent tug-of-war, the men ran off.

Later that night, when everyone but the Shaker elders and their host had left, thirty men charged into the house. They moved from room to room searching for Lee, beating the men as they went. They found Mother Ann in an upstairs bedroom and pulled her feet first down the stairs, sending her dress over her waist. Outside in the snow, they loaded her onto a sleigh and drove three miles to a local tavern. Lee's brother William was badly injured, but he gave chase on foot. By the time he reached the tavern, the mob had cooled off. The tavern keeper, under pressure from his wife, offered a free round if the men would let Mother Ann go. When Lee promised not to bring charges, they allowed her to leave with her brother.

Back in Harvard that summer, on August 18, 1782, the Shakers welcomed converts from throughout Massachusetts to the Square House for a large jamboree. As they danced and sang, creating their usual ruckus, local militiamen gathered outside. By dusk, almost four hundred men had congregated in the street. They demanded that "the

Elect Lady" be sent out. Lee, however, was not there. The mob, which by now had been sent away from the Square House empty-handed too many times, refused to disperse. The confrontation devolved into a siege.

A leader of the mob announced that those converts who were from Harvard could return to their homes, but the "distant Shakers" had to leave town immediately. Seeing no other option, the believers formed themselves into a procession. The local Shakers refused to part with their out-of-town brothers and sisters. The entire group was marched seven miles to the edge of town. Men on horseback whipped them as they went. One Shaker later recalled that the forced march out of Harvard was "one continued scene of cruelty and abuse; whipping with horsewhips, pounding, beating, and bruising with clubs, collaring and pushing off from bridges into the water and mud . . . and every kind of abuse they could invent without taking lives."

Heaven Is a Place Where
Nothing Ever Happens

> We shall have one meeting together which will never
> break up.
>
> —JAMES WHITTAKER

The special appeal of the Shaker gospel was that it offered a total, all-consuming life of the spirit. While Mother Ann proclaimed the gospel of Christ's Second Appearing, other revivalists—Universalists, New Lights, Freewill Baptists—rode the same trails, offering their own novel visions of salvation to the traditionally Calvinist population of New England. For a weekend, or a month, or even a full season, these traveling evangelists would set up in a tent or barn or open field and lead raucous prayer meetings. Since the evangelists were eager to save as many souls as possible, they tended to focus on the quantity, rather than the durability, of their conversions. When they packed up and moved on to the next town, local enthusiasm inevitably cooled. People who had been reborn in the emotional flurry of communal excitement slid back into the normal rhythms of life. Even when a revival created sufficient local enthusiasm to build a church and establish a permanent congregation, there were still six long days between any two Sabbaths. By contrast, the community that was forming at Niskeyuna and Harvard and in the homes of a few other scattered believers throughout New England left no space for secular life. The converts lived, worked, and worshipped under one roof. James Whittaker said that he wanted Shaker life to be a "permanent revival."

Joining this endless revival meant giving up the trappings of "worldly" existence, most notably marriage and family. The Shakers not only denounced carnality, they viewed the nuclear household as an impediment to the new millennial dispensation: a citadel of old thinking and anticommunal loyalties. A short hymn expresses the Shaker view starkly: "Of all the relations that ever I see / My old fleshly kindred are furthest from me / So bad and so ugly, so hateful they feel / To see them and hate them increases my zeal / O how ugly they look! / How ugly they look! / How nasty they feel!" This strong prejudice against the biological family unit was shared by almost all nineteenth-century utopians.

Not surprisingly, many of the Shakers' loudest critics had family members living "within gospel order." The sect's feminism made matters worse. Since every effort to promote the rights of women is eventually cast as an assault on the family, the Shakers' attempt at gender equality was regarded as a direct attack upon the Christian household.

To replace their "old fleshly kindred," the Shakers invented a new type of home. As they traveled through New England, the missionaries instructed converts within each region to gather onto a single property, usually the farm of some new Shaker. Believers would sell whatever land they owned and bring their livestock, their linens, their tools, and their savings onto the newly formed collective. If an entire family took up the gospel at once, they would cease to live as a family, entering Zion as individuals. An experienced Shaker would then be sent to live with them. To enter the Shaker order was to shed many of the most ancient and universal human customs. Like the secular utopians they would soon inspire, the Shakers actively and consciously redesigned the entire architecture of social relations to reflect their vision of the millennium.

On September 4, 1783, the day after John Adams, Benjamin Franklin, and John Jay signed the Treaty of Paris, formally ending the war with Great Britain, Lee and her companions returned to Niskeyuna. Their turbulent two-year odyssey through New England had yielded at least a thousand converts.

Over the next two decades, the various farms on which those converts had begun to gather would become the nucleus of the Shaker Zion, a network of eighteen large, prosperous villages. The believers gradually came to conceive of their fledgling community as a favored nation within, but walled off from, the corruption of "Babylon." In the same way that "Israel" refers simultaneously to a piece of land and a group of people, wherever they may be, the Shakers used "Zion" to describe their physical network of villages and the unified body of believers. The scriptural dichotomy of Zion and Babylon—good and evil made manifest as cities—has been picked up by a wide array of separatists. Even the secular utopians of the nineteenth century spoke of building a communistic Zion within the belly of America's "industrial Babylon."

At the end of the Revolution, the Shaker Zion was still makeshift. The believers living on each communal farm began working the land, cooking, and keeping house collectively. Without articulating a plan—that came later—they began practicing an ad hoc sort of communism, pooling their wealth, raising their children cooperatively, and placing their possessions into a common stock.

Lee returned to Niskeyuna looking thin and frail. Life on the road, to say nothing of the beatings she suffered, had taken a heavy toll. She was only forty-seven, but years of poverty and fasting had wasted her once robust body. Her skin was covered in a downy fuzz, a symptom of malnutrition.

In her weakened state, Mother Ann continued to preach the values that would define the United Society in the next century. Speaking to her rapt followers at Niskeyuna, she equated cleanliness and chastity with saintliness. The Zion she conjured in their minds was the precise opposite of the world in which she was born. Toad Lane's cramped, fetid squalor inspired a passion for uniformity, tidiness, restraint, and a well-scoured home. Order, the defining Shaker virtue, was a reaction to disorder. Lee's message was stern: "Good spirits will not live where there is dirt." And: "There are no slovens or sluts in Heaven."

William Lee had been his sister's first convert. He was a brawny, good-looking man. Like his father, he worked as a blacksmith. Before joining the Wardley prayer circle, he had served in the Oxford Blues, a mounted regiment of the Royal Guard. But during the forced march out of Harvard, he had been badly beaten with a stick, and eleven months after returning with Ann to Niskeyuna, he died. It is not clear what killed him, only that "he [gave] up his life in sufferings."

Seven weeks later, on September 8, 1784, Lee sat up in the middle of the night to announce that she could see William descending in a golden chariot. He had come, she said, to collect her. Then she died, "without a struggle or a groan."

The *Albany Gazette* carried the news: "Departed this life, at Nisquenia, Mrs. Lee, known by the appellation of the *Elect Lady* or *Mother of Zion,* and the head of that people called Shakers." Mother Ann had never claimed immortality, but many of her followers had expected her to lead them into the millennial paradise. While Lee's death caused some converts to leave the faith, it did little to slow the spread of her gospel. Her successors never matched Mother Ann's otherworldly charisma, but they more than compensated with organizational acumen and an unwavering vision of the American Zion.

James Whittaker, Lee's constant companion since he had fed her through the stem of his pipe, was her anointed successor. Soon after

Mother Ann's death, he took to the road, actively coaxing the converts
Lee had won into collective homes. As head of the church, the thirty-
four-year-old Whittaker emphasized an ascetic, separatist vision of
Shakerism. Unlike many of the other early Shakers, he could read and
write. Whittaker tightened and formalized restrictions on acceptable
Shaker conduct and initiated a decisive break from the World. He was
particularly energetic in his denunciations of sex, enjoining converts to
become "eunuchs for the Kingdom of Heaven's sake."[*]

George Darrow, whose brother David had been arrested while herding sheep to Niskeyuna, owned a large farm on a series of steep hillsides
in the Berkshire foothills, near the village of New Lebanon, just west of
the New York–Massachusetts line. Unlike the homestead in Niskeyuna
thirty-five miles to the northwest, Darrow's farm was on the east side of
the Hudson River, making it more accessible to the new communal
homes being set up throughout Massachusetts and Connecticut. Whittaker decided to make Darrow's farm the headquarters of Zion, and
converts began collecting on the property. They pooled their money
and started buying up the surrounding farms. Whittaker called a moratorium on "preaching unto Babylon," turning the Society's energy inward and working to consolidate the remarkable gains of the previous
few years.

A year after Lee's death, on October 15, 1785, while the Berkshires
flamed with autumn color, the Shakers in New Lebanon celebrated the
completion of the United Society's first official meetinghouse. The large,
rectangular building was capped with a vaulted gambrel roof, eliminating the need for structural pillars and creating a wide-open interior space

---

[*] One of the more extravagant libels told about the Shakers was that all of their men
were actual, rather than spiritual, eunuchs. In 1840, at the White Water Shaker Village in Ohio, there was a legal battle in which non-Shakers claimed that two boys,
aged fourteen and nine, who had formerly lived within the community had been
"emasculated." In response to these accusations, a mob surrounded the community
and five Shaker elders were locked in the Cincinnati jail. The crisis ended when a
local physician inspected the boys and determined that they "labored under a natural
deformity and no privileges had ever been taken with them."

that was well suited to the dancing and shaking that formed the core of Shaker worship. The outside of the meetinghouse was painted bright white, making it stand out on a hilly landscape dotted with brown and red barns. The interior woodwork was painted a rich, dark blue. The only furnishings were movable, chocolate-colored benches.*

The most peculiar feature of the building was that it had two identical front doors set side by side, both painted dark green. One was for men, one for women. This architectural doubling became a hallmark of Shaker construction. In the front yard of many subsequent Shaker buildings, twin gates led to twin walkways, which led to twin doors, which opened onto twin staircases. Inside and out, everything was built with fanatical symmetry—a visual emblem of equality, separateness, and order. Oddly, while the United Society went to great lengths to symbolically separate "brothers" from "sisters," they never took the most obvious precaution: housing men and women separately. If monasteries and nunneries are built to protect their inhabitants from lust, Shaker buildings aspire to slay it altogether.

The meetinghouse was a sanctified space, a permanent, physical expression of the Sabbath. Except for nearly constant sweeping, no work was allowed within its four walls.† Neither was fidgeting, chattering, or thoughtless movements of any sort. As the village in New Lebanon grew into the spiritual and administrative capital of Shakerdom, the building's significance grew. Like the stone omphalos that formed the sacred navel of the Attic world, the meetinghouse formed the symbolic center of Zion, organizing the Shaker universe around itself.‡

---

* This precise color scheme was eventually mandated for all the subsequent Shaker meetinghouses. The Shakers' "Millennial Laws" further stipulated that "no buildings may be painted white, save meetinghouses."
† The pine floor, according to one visitor, "was as clean as a dining table."
‡ For the Shakers, the building was made sacred only by the activity conducted within it. When the community at New Lebanon swelled to more than five hundred, the Shakers built a much larger meetinghouse nearby and retrofitted their old temple as a seed warehouse.

Father and Mother

On July 20, 1787, three years to the day after the death of William Lee, James Whittaker died suddenly while visiting converts in Enfield, Connecticut. He was thirty-six. The title of "first elder" then fell to Joseph Meacham, the popular former New Light evangelist from New Lebanon who had led his flock to Niskeyuna in the wake of the Dark Day. Meacham was born in Connecticut, where his father had been converted in the church of Jonathan Edwards. Mother Ann had reportedly predicted his arrival at Niskeyuna, calling him "the wisest man that has been born of a woman for six hundred years." (It is not clear which fourteenth-century prodigy she had in mind as his predecessor.)

In the same sense that the Apostle Paul is sometimes identified as the founder of Christianity, Joseph Meacham can fairly be called the founder of Shakerism. Like Saint Paul, he gave intellectual and institutional coherence to the often elliptical sayings of his chosen messiah. Like Paul, he channeled the feverish energy of a mystical sect into something stable and coolheaded, buttressing a young faith with customs, institutions, and hierarchy. Without the administrative genius of Meacham, the United Society of Believers in Christ's Second Appearing might have faded away at the close of the eighteenth century.

A year after assuming leadership, Meacham made a surprising decision. He selected a twenty-eight-year-old Shaker sister named Lucy Wright to serve as his co-elder at New Lebanon, designating her "first in the female-line." Meacham remained first elder, but Wright became his partner in the practical and spiritual administration of the sect.

Tall and attractive, Wright came from a well-to-do family in the Berkshires. She had married a merchant named Elizur Goodrich when she was eighteen, and the newlyweds were born again at a revival in New Lebanon. Along with several other members of the Goodrich family, they followed a trail of confounding rumors into the woods of Niskeyuna. Mother Ann had made a special effort to convert Wright. "If you gain her," Lee told the other lead Shakers, "it will be equal to gaining a nation." Wright and Goodrich forswore "fleshly relations" and joined up. (Like many other previously married Shaker women, Wright went back to using her maiden name upon entering Zion.)

Wright's elevation to "first in the female-line" gave her more authority than any Shaker besides Joseph Meacham. Like the meetinghouse with its twin doors, the Society now had parallel lines of authority, one male and one female. This structure reflected the sect's evolving belief that the Godhead, like everything within creation, has both a male and a female aspect. These two aspects, different but equal, were often personified as Almighty God the Father and Holy Mother Wisdom. This dual nature is reflected in Christ's two earthly vessels: Jesus of Nazareth and Ann of Manchester.

Whether or not Meacham's decision to "elevate" Wright was inspired by such theological considerations or more mundane, administrative concerns, his outlook on gender equality was ahead of its time. When he had first arrived at Niskeyuna as a pilgrim, he had found it difficult to reconcile the sect's female leader with his Christian faith. After all, the New Testament is unequivocal about the subordinate role of women within society and the church. By the time he became first elder, his views had evolved. "The man cannot gather and build the church of Christ in this day without the woman nor the woman without the man," Meacham wrote. "A just equality is necessary."

The elevation of Lucy Wright was met with predictable complaints by some Shaker brothers. Submitting to the spiritual authority of an inspired female prophet (Mother Ann) is one thing; submitting to the temporal authority of a female administrator is a very different matter. Despite some early grumbling, the equality of the sexes in all matters— in theory, if not in practice—became a cornerstone of the United Society.* By the middle of the nineteenth century, at a time when almost no American women occupied positions of authority outside of the home,

---

* Despite their stated beliefs, individual Shakers were people of their time. Tensions over what some brothers called "petticoat government" periodically threatened the stability of the church.

Shaker "eldresses" administered an immense financial and religious organization.*

Meacham and Wright extended James Whittaker's moratorium on evangelism, focusing instead on gathering converts into "gospel order." Now under the leadership of two native-born Yankees, the Shakers began to evolve from a small band of despised separatists into a widely admired national religion.

Unto Every Man According as He Has Need

On Christmas Day 1787, the brothers and sisters in New Lebanon sat down at several long tables for a holiday meal. Before eating, they recited a pledge: "There can be no church in complete order, according to the law of Christ, without a joint interest and union, in which all the members have an equal right and privilege, according to their calling and needs, in things spiritual and temporal." For a decade, the believers had been sharing their food, their land, and their money out of a strong sense of solidarity and the necessities of rural separatism. The Christmas Day pledge formalized this collectivism. Every Shaker now held an equal "joint interest" in the total material wealth of the United Society.† Whatever was owned by one Shaker was owned by all Shakers. Labor and compensation were officially unhitched. Within a decade, this verbal covenant was set in writing for new members to sign.

Shaker communism may have begun as a practical matter, but, like Ann Lee's vision concerning celibacy, it was soon stamped with the im-

---

* During the twentieth century, the church's membership became overwhelmingly female. By 1936, 88 percent of Shakers were women.

† The Shakers were surprisingly savvy about fiscal and legal matters. Realizing that their policy of "joint interest" made them vulnerable to lawsuits from without, they refused all applicants until their debts had been paid. Despite this caution, the Society spent a lot of money settling financial claims.

primatur of holy writ and reinforced with scriptural citations. The Shakers found biblical precedent for their economic arrangements in the Acts of the Apostles, the book of the New Testament, first written in Greek, that describes the comings and goings of the earliest Christians during the years immediately following the execution of Jesus. This first-century community started small—just 120 Christ-following Jews, including the apostles and Jesus's mother, living together in Jerusalem. Following a mass conversion on the Jewish feast day known as Pentecost, the community swelled to about three thousand. While this group awaited their messiah's promised return—they seem to have expected him soon—their leaders, the small group of men who had traveled around with Jesus during his life, organized their temporal affairs in the manner in which they believed their God desired.

> And all that believed were together, and had all things common; And sold their possessions and goods, and parted them to all men, as every man had need. . . . And the multitude of them that believed were of one heart and of one soul: neither said any of them that ought of the things which he possessed was his own; but they had all things common. . . . Neither was there any among them that lacked: for as many as were possessors of lands or houses sold them, and brought the prices of the things that were sold, And laid them down at the apostles' feet: and distribution was made unto every man according as he had need.* (Acts 2:44, 45, 4:32, 34, and 35)

For the Shakers, this sketchy account of collectivism in the Middle East during the first century presented a clear mandate for how a Christian community ought to be arranged. Many of the people described in Acts had actually spent time with Jesus. Others among them, notably Paul, had supposedly been visited by Christ after his crucifixion. If any-

* Here, tucked deep within the King James Version, is the first draft of the famous Marxist slogan "From each according to his ability, to each according to his need!"

one would know how a Christian community ought to be organized, they would.

The Shakers were not alone in reading the book of Acts as a manual for Christian economics. Throughout the nineteenth century, American utopians, even those that were secular in their orientation, cited those five verses of scripture in support of what Oneida Community founder John Humphrey Noyes called "Bible Communism." Like the Shakers, Noyes claimed that Christianity not only sanctioned collective ownership, but demanded it. Étienne Cabet, the founder and leader of Icaria, took Bible-based communism to its furthest extreme. He claimed that communism and Christianity were not merely complementary, they were indistinguishable. For Cabet, the abolition of private property had been Christ's central doctrine: *"Le communisme, c'est le Christianisme."*

Acts may have been the spiritual inspiration, but it was the Shakers' extraordinary material success that made communism seem practically feasible for almost every American utopian society of the nineteenth century. Using a metaphor that evoked the Jacksonian-era debate over the legitimacy of paper currency, John Humphrey Noyes called the Shaker villages the "specie basis" backing up the "paper theories" of subsequent utopian socialists. A broad range of reformers, both secular and religious, looked upon the prosperous Shaker villages and took the economic viability of communism for granted. "It is very doubtful," Noyes wrote, "whether Owenism or Fourierism would have ever existed, or if they had, whether they would have ever moved the practical American nation, if the facts of Shakerism had not existed before them and gone along with them."

Across the Atlantic, the Shakers' effort to imitate the primitive church bolstered a more familiar strain of communism. In 1845, Friedrich Engels wrote: "The first people in America, and actually the world, to create a society on the basis of common property, were the so-called Shakers. . . . Their barns are always full of grain, their storerooms full of cloth, so that an English traveler who visited them said he could not understand why these people who owned an abundance of everything, still worked." For Engels, the prosperity of Zion was a succinct rebuke to the most persistent critique of collective ownership: that it could not produce or maintain abundance. While Engels's history is dubious— the Shakers were not the first communists in North America, let alone the world—his claim that they were demonstrates the United Society's influence on modern socialist thought.*

Rising Up to Paradise

And I John saw the holy city, new Jerusalem, coming down from God out of heaven, prepared as a bride adorned for her husband.

—REVELATION 21:2

The millennium, as it is described in the last book of the New Testament, is not only an era—the thousand-year reign of heaven on earth—it is also a place: the holy city of New Jerusalem, which God will lower down to earth at the end of history.† Convinced that the millennium had commenced unfolding at the time of Mother Ann's jailhouse vision of Eden, the Shakers got to work constructing their own New Jerusalem.

The white, gambrel-roofed meetinghouse in New Lebanon was designed by a Shaker builder named Moses Johnson. When it was completed in 1787, Joseph Meacham dispatched Brother Moses to the other fledgling communities with a mandate to replicate the building. Within seven years, identical meetinghouses had been built in ten communi-

---

* The first communistic colony founded in the New World was Plockhoy's Commonwealth, also known as Valley of the Swans, established on the Delaware River by Dutch Mennonites in 1663.
† According to the most literal interpretation of Revelation, New Jerusalem will be laid out as a perfect square (or maybe a cube), fifteen hundred miles on each side (or maybe all the way around). The city will be made of pure gold and surrounded by a jasper wall with gates of pearl.

ties. These structures, situated near the center of most villages, set the tone for a style of construction—austere, unusually large, obsessively symmetrical—that came to define the United Society in the minds of outsiders.

While meetinghouses were being built elsewhere, the believers in New Lebanon started work on an immense wooden dormitory in which to lodge the converts pouring in from around New England. The Great House, as they called it, had no accommodation for families. Bedrooms were designed to be shared by several people of the same sex. As familial bonds dissolved, child care became the obligation of the whole society. Separate dorms were built for children as well as for the elderly and infirmed. The elders in charge of each village lived in their own small dormitories. Decades later, the Shakers began building special homes for novice converts, allowing people to enter the difficult austerity of Zion by degrees.

The village in New Lebanon became the proving ground for the Lead Ministry's social innovations and the architectural prototype for the eighteen other villages that the United Society would build over the next three decades.* Father Joseph and Mother Lucy were understood to have inherited the inspired gifts of the first Shakers. Their directives, even those concerning the most trifling affairs—where to place a barn, what color to paint a bench—were handed down with the authority of revelation. As they built, Shaker carpenters and masons believed that they were working with heavenly blueprints.

By 1796, there were eleven Shaker communities: two in New York, four in Massachusetts, two in New Hampshire, two in Maine, and one in Connecticut. Along with meetinghouses and dormitories, each village had industrial-sized kitchens, bakeries, barns, and workshops for spinning, woodworking, and other light industries. At every turn, the Shakers encountered the economic advantages of their collectivism. Not only could they buy bulk materials on the cheap, they were able to

---

* Variations in climate, topography, and local resources and markets gave each settlement a distinct culture and appearance.

invest in expensive but cost-saving improvements that individual home-steaders could not afford. They could, for instance, build and operate their own sawmills and gristmills. Individual homesteaders, who seldom had sufficient grain, timber, or capital to justify such an investment, had to pay someone else to do their milling.

By collectivizing all of the labor of rural living, the Society also enjoyed the benefits of specialization and expertise. The typical Yankee homesteader was, by necessity, a jack of many trades and a master of none. He maintained his fences, doctored his sheep, plowed his fields, built his home, shoed his horse, butchered his meat, and marketed his surplus. His wife was milkmaid, cook, weaver, teacher, laundress, mid-wife, and gardener. If a Shaker had a particular knack for breaking horses or weaving or keeping accounts, he or she could devote the days to that skill without worrying about who was milking the cows.

Two years after the village at New Lebanon was founded, its farm was thriving. The Shakers found a particularly profitable niche selling vegetable seed, a business that allowed them to cash in on their growing reputation for piety and fair dealing. Standing inside of a dry goods shop, anyone could judge the quality of a plow blade or a keg of molas-ses, but good seed is indistinguishable from bad. The word *Shaker*, stamped neatly on an envelope, functioned like a brand in an era before brands, assuring customers that the sellers had their good name on the line. As the Shakers' reputation for quality and craftsmanship grew, they did a brisk business in herbal medicines, furniture, and produce. In New England it was proverbial that in a bushel of Shaker apples, the quality and size of the fruit at the bottom was the same as at the top.

Like almost all utopians of their era, the Shakers believed that a well-ordered environment would produce well-ordered citizens. A person riding a rural New England road could never mistake a Shaker village for a typical community. In most small settlements, growth was haphaz-ard. Each landowner laid out his farm according to the location of water, drainage, windbreaks, and good tillage. Many people built their houses as far from their neighbors as the limits of their property al-

lowed. By contrast, the Shakers planned their villages carefully, cluster-
ing buildings together for convenience and always striving for an
appearance of order and uniformity. The meetinghouse, the workshops,
and the main dwellings were usually arrayed along a straight central
thoroughfare. The Shakers often laid slab sidewalks on either side of
this road, a luxury familiar to city dwellers that was unknown in rural
communities, where wading through mud and dust was an unavoidable
fact of life. At the village in Canterbury, New Hampshire, there was a
brother named Micajah Tucker whose sole job was to quarry, dress, and
skid granite pavers into place with a team of mules. The Shakers' passion for tidiness justified this enormous expense. Their collectivized
labor made it possible.

Rather than adapt their settlements to the peculiarities of the landscape, the Shakers went to incredible lengths to bend topography to
their will, becoming expert at grading land, draining marshes, straight-
ening creeks, and forcing springs into underground pipes. Walls built
over uneven ground ran level at the top. This approach to landscaping
mirrored the sect's general sense of human nature—their belief that
sanctity is the suppression of wildness; that beauty is the triumph of the
right angle.

Inside, everything was spotless. Slightly tattered bonnets were thrown
away. Linens were always perfectly white. When a chair was not in use,
it was hung on one of the peg rails that ran around the walls of most
rooms, making way for one of the Shakers' defining pastimes: sweeping.* "Gentiles" who visited Zion found this fanatical tidiness striking.
"The plan, the life, the thought of Mount Lebanon are written in its
grassy streets," wrote one English visitor. "The granary is to a Shaker
what the Temple was to a Jew. . . . The paint is all fresh; the planks are
all bright; the windows are all clean. A white sheen is on everything; a
happy quiet reigns around." A Quaker who toured the village in Han-

---

* A common spiritual "exercise" was to mime the act of sweeping away "devils" with
invisible brooms.

cock, Massachusetts, marveled that the Shakers not only milled the timber for their workshops with great precision, they also cut their firewood to uniform lengths on the same water-driven blade. Thus cut, stove wood was "split and piled up as neat as a mason's work in a wall." Another visitor wrote that "the very dust in the road seemed pure."

A Shaker's entire village was her church. She tried to act accordingly. As a result, life within Zion not only had a distinctive look, it also had a distinctive pace. The believers labored constantly, but with a deliberate and placid slowness. They never took a day off, but according to many visitors, life within the villages conveyed a feeling of "Sabbath calm." Ann Lee and her successors preached that manual labor could be an expression of faith—an all-day prayer murmured with broom and rasp. "Put your hands to work and your heart to God," Lee is said to have told her followers. It is not a coincidence that the Shakers called less materially productive modes of worship—singing hymns, meditating, dancing—"laboring."

The Shakers believed that their tidy, highly planned villages were an earthly reflection of how things looked in heaven. In 1843, when the United Society was at its demographic peak, spirit visitations were an almost daily occurrence in most villages. Often these spirits were notable characters from scripture or great historical personages.* During one episode, a group of young Shakers at New Lebanon were visited by the spirit of "first father Adam." Communicating through a medium, Adam drew the youngsters a diagram of heaven. The result looks like a mandala, a highly geometric map of circles within squares within circles, symmetrical in the four cardinal directions. It shows a city bisected by a perfectly straight river that is flanked with golden sidewalks. The recipients of this vision claimed that this Euclidean paradise, clearly inspired by Revelation's account of New Jerusalem, hovered directly

---

* This era of rampant spiritualism was known as "Mother Ann's Work," because Lee, who by then had been dead for sixty years, was thought to be rallying her drowsing church.

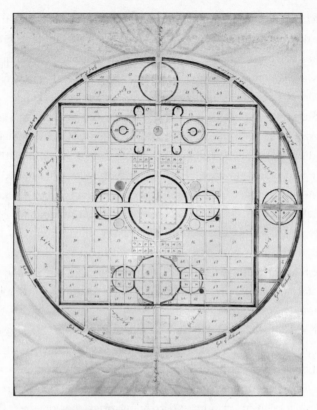

The Holy City, a "gift drawing" by sister
Polly Jane Reed, New Lebanon, 1843.

The Philadephia Museum of Art/Art Resource, N.Y.

above the actual village of New Lebanon. They believed that when the
millennium came into full flower, their earthly facsimile of heaven
would somehow expand and merge with the paradise above.

With heaven hovering over them, metaphysical conjecture and workaday concerns were inseparable. "Order is the creation of beauty," ad-
vises *The Youth's Guide to Zion*, a slim pamphlet printed for young believers
at Canterbury Village. "It is heaven's first law, and the protection of
souls. Keep all things in order, as keeping the law of heaven and keep

the order of Zion, that heaven may protect you." To the youth of Zion, this was not just a mystical aphorism, it was also a reminder to keep the woodpile neat. Order, in its multifaceted Shaker sense, was understood as a terrestrial reflection of how things are in heaven. And heaven looked an awful lot like a Shaker village: "The beauty and glory of the heavenly world," wrote Brother Calvin Green, is characterized by "its regular order, perfect symmetry of arrangement, proper proportions and mutual correspondent relation, and its beauteous colors of which the colors in the natural creation, and its harmonious order when unobstructed are an emanation and representation."

Everything the believers produced was to be made, as Joseph Meacham instructed, "plain and without superfluity." While the Shakers eschewed decoration, they did spend a great deal of time fussing over the way things looked. Theirs was not the incidental simplicity of the ascetic who can't be bothered with material trifles. The Shakers spared no expense to achieve their precise aesthetic visions. They worked with the finest materials and built everything to last. They were especially finicky about color, favoring bright, rich tones and often using the most expensive paints.*

It is somewhat trite to say, as the writer and monk Thomas Merton famously said, that the Shakers built each of their chairs as if an angel might sit in it, but their spiritual orientation, particularly their belief in a heavenly realm that is dimly reflected on earth, clearly shines through in their handiwork. Shaker crafts reflect a platonic impulse to unite the

---

* Scholars who study the United Society sometimes lament the public's fixation on Shaker design and crafts. Interest in Shaker design does tend to eclipse all other, more meaningful curiosity about the Society. Stephen J. Stein opens his brilliant and definitive history of the United Society by quoting an aged Shaker sister who told a *New Yorker* reporter: "I almost expect to be remembered, as a chair or a table." There is obvious irony in the spectacle of horn-rimmed design hounds bidding outrageous sums to acquire the washbasins of these long dead communists. However, Shaker artifacts can reveal deep truths about the disposition of the people who made them. What's more, many of the first outsiders to study the United Society in any detail, notably the historians Faith Andrews and Edward Deming Andrews, were drawn to the subject by a passion for Shaker crafts and ephemera.

messy, imperfect material world with a numinous sphere of eternal forms. Whether or not they expected an angel to have a seat—and there were plenty of reports of angels coming and going—the Shakers built their chairs to resemble, as closely as possible, the pure idea of chairness. Their stringent prohibitions against ornament and "superfluity" reveal an intuitive understanding that nothing is more mired in human affairs than decorative frippery; nothing says *temporal* like the fiddlehead scrollwork or pink-bottomed cherubs that constituted high design during the Shakers' heyday.*

The most obvious expression of the sects' ever-increasing fixation on order was their evolving method of worship. During their first, impoverished decade in the United States, individual Shakers demonstrated their union with the divine—their *possession*—through spontaneous, ecstatic noises and movements. They laughed, wept, and howled—yodeling animal nonsense into the night woods. Their bodies, bone tired from hard labor, were racked by "the jerks," swaying trances, and the dervishlike "whirling gift." Some mimed domestic tasks—sweeping and sowing, or picking and devouring spectral fruits. Others danced and chanted in crude imitation of Native Americans, Africans, and imaginary prehistoric races whose spirits supposedly possessed them. Shaker sisters spun until they collapsed, lifeless with the "fainting gift." Shaker brothers crowded together and leapt up and down, soaking their woolen coats with sweat and bloodying their heads on the low rafters.

Father Joseph, who reportedly had no "gift" for physical possession, gradually supplanted these chaotic, individualistic expressions with a set of standardized hymns and dances. New "laboring exercises" such as the circle dance and the square order shuffle had the elaborate cho-

---

* Decades of exposure to modernist design has made it easy to appreciate the sect's ethereal minimalism. That was not always the case. While touring a Shaker village in 1842, Charles Dickens offered this assessment of Shaker aesthetics: "We walked into a grim room where several grim hats were hanging on grim pegs, and the time was told grimly by a grim clock."

The "whirling gift."

Illustration from David R. Lamson, Two Year's Experience
Among the Shakers *(West Boylston, MA, 1848)*

reography and martial precision of a sexless cotillion. Ranks of believers—men on one side, women on the other—clapped, swayed, marched, turned, and stamped their feet in perfect unison. In the meetinghouse of Canterbury Village, copper tacks were embedded in the floorboards, Arthur Murray style, to help dancers keep track of the complex steps. This change in how the Shakers shook—from the Dionysian to the Apollonian or, approximately, from the spirit of Jerry Lee Lewis to the Electric Slide—reflected the Society's increasing preoccupation with order and communalism. Even their union with God was now expressed en masse.

For Meacham and the other lead Shakers, the orderly rhythms and appearance of life within a Shaker village not only sanctified the fellowship within, they broadcast the Society's blessings to the wider public. At a time when most homesteads were encircled by stone walls or rail fences, people inevitably judged their neighbors by the quality of their enclosures, not unlike the way suburbanites announce their values with the lushness of their turf. The walls and fences that hemmed in Zion— laid straighter and neater than anyone else's—proclaimed the orderly life they enclosed. Plant your rows straight, Meacham taught, that they may preach unto the World.

This silent, passive mode of evangelism was the only sort that interested Father Joseph. The decade of his leadership (1787–1796) was a busy time in the wider Republic. Independence had been won at a great cost. The financially strained and tenuously confederated states had turned their energy toward building the institutions required for an entirely new type of government. Rather than evangelizing to the preoccupied young nation, the Shakers let the orderly conditions of their life speak for them.

Meacham died at New Lebanon in August 1796. He was fifty-five. Under his leadership, the free-flowing mysticism of the early sect was channeled into a set of enduring customs and social institutions. From whole cloth, he created an elaborate, four-tiered hierarchy with which to govern the rapidly expanding millennial church. At the top was the Lead Ministry in New Lebanon, led by him and Lucy Wright. They received their authority from revelation and their spiritual union with Mother Ann. Meacham and Wright settled matters of Society-wide concern and dealt with questions coming in from the various villages. Should they allow a particular dance? Approve a new hymnal? Settle a certain lawsuit? Below the Lead Ministry, there were various categories of elders and eldresses, some of whom moved around within a particular region, conveying directives from New Lebanon and overseeing a cluster of villages known as a "bishopric." Within each particular village there was a group of elders, usually two men and two women, who dealt with matters relating to that specific community.

Each village was itself made up of several "families" that were overseen by two elders and two eldresses. By the time Meacham died, these families had become the basic unit of Shaker life. As the population of a village expanded, it would be subdivided into separate families, with no one family exceeding a hundred Shakers. Each family functioned as an independent economic unit. Its members ate together, ran their own businesses, kept common accounts, and received discipline from the same small group of elders. For the average Shaker, these "family elders" were the most relevant sources of daily authority.

At each of these four levels of authority—family, village, bishopric, and Lead Ministry—power was divided equally between men and women. At no level, except sometimes at the very top, was a single individual in charge. Elders and eldresses enjoyed certain privileges, but all Shakers lived in the same spare, dormitory-style rooms and ate the same simple (usually vegetarian) food. And everyone worked. Even Wright and Meacham, who had their hands full with administrative and theological matters, put in time at the loom or in the field.

The genius of this structure, and a major reason the Shakers thrived for so long, was that having found the ideal scale on which to practice their intense brand of communalism, they could stick with it. Their system of communities (families) within communities (villages) within a single community (the United Society) allowed the Shaker population to expand and contract without much disturbance to their social and economic order. If enthusiasm for the gospel increased or decreased in a particular region, the nearest village would simply add or subtract a family. Limiting these families to one hundred members allowed for a group that was large enough to be financially self-sustaining—they could raise most of their own food, operate several light industries, and reap substantial economies of scale—but small enough to foster social cohesion, mutual accountability, and spiritual intimacy. In a group of one hundred, everybody knows one another. It is easy to spot a shirker.

The ancient question of just how many people ought to live in the perfect society was a pressing concern for all of the nineteenth-century utopians. Aristotle wrote that mutual familiarity among citizens and the uniform dissemination of information were the main prerequisites of a healthy polity. The state, in his view, should be large enough to be self-sustaining but small enough so that everyone can make personally informed choices about whom to elect for positions of leadership. As a rule of thumb, he suggested that a state, by which he meant a city-state, ought to be no larger than a crowd that can be gathered within earshot of a single herald or "can well be taken in at one view."*

Jean-Jacques Rousseau's view was similar. He claimed that true democracy—the organic operation of popular sovereignty that he called "general will"—could function only on the scale of a small city. He likely had his birthplace of Geneva in mind, or maybe the island of Corsica. Robert Owen, who modeled his American utopia on an industrial factory town, hoped to initiate the "New Moral World" with a nucleus of five hundred and then slowly build up many separate colonies of five thousand people. This put him very close to Plato, who wrote that the ideal republic would have 5,040 citizens: a bureaucrat's dream figure, because it can be divided by so many other numbers, thus allowing for the formation of countless uniformly sized subgroups.†
Charles Fourier—a thinker defined by his numeric precision—believed that the ideal community should house exactly 1,620 people, twice the 810 personality types he had identified. He reasoned that by having one man and one woman of each type within every community, all of life's necessary work can be accomplished by someone constitutionally suited to his or her job.

Economically speaking, the ideal size of a cooperative community waxes and wanes with changes in technology. During the first few decades of the nineteenth century, the Shaker villages and other similarly sized utopian communities had a significant edge over "isolated" family farms. Along with building mills and buying other expensive machinery, the communitarians could manage large swaths of land for cash cropping, purchase raw materials in bulk, and market their produce and handicrafts on a large scale. As industrialization supplanted traditional

---

* Aristotle makes an allowance for the advance of communications technology. He says that if a polis can somehow employ the services of Stentor, the mythically strong-lunged herald of the *Iliad*, then it can expand a bit.
† Among other exciting mathematical properties, 5,040 has sixty divisors. It can be divided by every whole number from 1 to 12, except 11.

home industries, these financial advantages diminished. A group of twenty Shaker sisters making "fancy goods" could easily outcompete twenty farmer's wives stitching independently. Neither could compete with factory-made products.

Gaining a Nation

Meacham had made it clear that Lucy Wright would assume sole leadership after his death. When she took over, some Shakers were anxious about the return to female authority. Whatever their feelings about the duality of the Godhead, the believers were people of their time. The concept of female authority was still novel, if not offensive, to most Americans. A Shaker brother named Angell Mathewson was kicked out after declaring that "wimmin are fools & that men that are willin to have a woman to rule over them are fools also."

The apostasy of a few chauvinists had little effect. When Mother Lucy assumed the position of first elder in 1788, the United Society was large and stable. The federal census of 1800 counted 1,373 Shakers living in eleven villages throughout New York and New England. By then, Zion had also become a relatively comfortable place to live. The fields had been cleared of stone and the swamps drained. The mobs of drunken patriots had been replaced with gentiles eager to buy Shaker seed, flat brooms, and patent medicine. Hostility toward the sect continued, but the field of battle shifted mostly to the press and the courts. To enter Zion at the opening of the nineteenth century was to join a prosperous society that was, if not universally admired, at least tolerated.

At a time when state governments provided almost no services, life within "gospel order" offered a rare social safety net. Despite the hysterical protests of anti-Shaker activists, poor and unwed women frequently brought their infants to be raised by the Shakers. Countless orphans were fed, educated, and raised to adulthood within the Society. The guarantee of three squares and a warm bed also attracted many adults with dubious faith in the doctrine of Christ's Second Appearing. Within Zion, these lukewarm believers were known derisively as "winter Shakers" or "bread-and-butter Shakers."

Because foundlings and winter Shakers do not a millennial church make, Lucy Wright reopened the Shaker gospel at the start of the nineteenth century. Starting with the Dark Day, the Shakers always practiced a distinctly opportunistic form of evangelism, bringing their message to places where the public had already been excited by some other spiritual tremor. In 1802, word arrived at New Lebanon that a "marvelous light" had been seen above the home of a farmer named James Wicker in Pittsford, Vermont. People began to congregate on Wicker's farm, and a spontaneous revival sprang up. Mother Lucy dispatched a young elder from Schenectady named Benjamin Seth Youngs and a recent convert named Issachar Bates to investigate the scene. On the day they arrived, a large crowd had gathered outside of Wicker's farmhouse to hear the sermon of a circuit-riding Methodist. As luck would have it, the Methodist was sick. After waiting around for a while, the crowd asked the two Shakers to speak.

After they had delivered a long sermon about the arrival of Zion and the true road to spiritual perfection, a man in the crowd gripped Bates by the shoulders and said, "I want you to go with me and hear me confess my sins." Bates and Youngs took over a room in Wicker's home, and one by one, people from the crowd filed inside to make confession, the first step to entering Zion. By late afternoon, at least a dozen people had taken up the Shaker cross.

At the end of this emotional day of confession and conversion, a man rushed inside saying that something unusual was happening in the sky. Issachar Bates recalled the sight: "There was a bright road across the centre of the Horizon from east to west, about two rods wide, as it appeared, of a palish red, with a bright border on each side. O how soon we interpreted this sign: that this same light and power was going to reach those waiting souls in the west."

———

Later that same year, the elders at New Lebanon began hearing strange reports from the southwestern frontier. The stories strained credulity. In the valleys of Kentucky, Ohio, and Indiana, evangelists of every stripe— New Lights, Baptists, Methodists, Presbyterians—were preaching the Second Advent. In response, people were gathering by the thousands in the wilderness. They exhibited strange effects: writhing in the dirt, barking like dogs, tearing at their clothes, speaking in tongues. At a camp meeting in Cane Ridge, Kentucky, one minister kept count as three thousand sinners suffered "the falling exercise"—collapsing on the ground as if dead. The Holy Ghost was said to be among them. It was a modern Pentecost.

This was the Kentucky Revival, the first western stirring of what would become known as the Second Great Awakening. Shrugging off the constraining Calvinist dogma of predestination—the belief that every individual's salvation or damnation is determined and fixed before birth—the frontier revivalists preached that salvation was free for the taking. This powerful shift in theology, putting salvation in the hands of the sinner, unleashed a desperate, emotional faith—a rowdy land rush for acreage in the Kingdom of Heaven.*

The typical pattern of the revival was for an evangelist to spread word of a camp meeting, sometimes as far as a year in advance. In a forest clearing or large meadow, he would build a platform of unmilled logs, sometimes capped with a pitched roof. As people trickled in, a city of tents and tarp-covered buckboards spread out around the preacher's scaffold. With crowds in the thousands, one man's voice could not reach everyone. Other evangelists, preaching from stumps and tailgates with their hands cupped around their mouths, gathered their own crowds. At the height of a large meeting, six or seven preachers might be roaring away simultaneously, each offering slightly different paths to paradise, each painting slightly different visions of Hades. Enterprising frontiers-

---

* To many orthodox Congregationalists, the emotional displays in the West were, at best, unseemly. From Boston, capital of the old Puritan empire, the frontier was often seen as a spiritual wasteland—an unruly wilderness sparsely populated by savages, papist immigrants, and drunken adventurers.

men came with barrels of whiskey to sell by the cupful. They found few takers. Stronger stuff was going around.*

With their plain-speaking preachers, open-air churches, and rejection of traditional denominational authority, the camp meetings expressed a distinctly American scorn for elites. Children, in their innocence, were considered uniquely receptive to the workings of the Holy Ghost. In the summer of 1801, on the third day of a five-day meeting near Indian Creek, Kentucky, a boy of twelve clambered atop a high stump. With tears streaming, he sermonized so passionately about sin and salvation that the crowd felt certain God spoke through him. After over an hour of steady preaching, the child was hoisted above the crowd by two large men. Exhausted, he wiped the tears and sweat from his face with a handkerchief. Dropping the sopping rag to the ground, he wailed, "Thus, O sinner!, shall you drop into hell." The entire crowd collapsed.

An outpouring of ecstatic religiosity is one of the supposed signs of the end times.† So, in a distinctly circular bit of logic, the participants in the Kentucky Revival saw their fervor as confirmation of their own prophetic claims. The more people who showed up and the more violent their possession, the more the revival looked like "the living work of God," thus heightening their fervor, thus confirming their prophecy, thus bringing more people.

For the settlers in the West, people who often went weeks without seeing a nonrelation and months without seeing a stranger, the sheer scale of the gatherings created a powerful effect. "Before he began to speak, the preacher had already effected the release of his audience," wrote the critic and historian Gilbert Seldes. "He had set them free

---

* On the day of the Pentecost, according to Acts, bystanders mistook the hubbub of Holy Ghost possession for a raging wine party. In response, the Apostle Peter said it was too early in the day to be drunk: "It is *but* the third hour."

† "And it shall come to pass in the last days, saith God, I will pour out of my Spirit upon all flesh: and your sons and your daughters shall prophesy, and your young men shall see visions, and your old men shall dream dreams." (Acts 2:17)

from loneliness and the burdensome companionship of their own troubles. He had moved them bodily, had changed for a moment the orbit of their lives. The strange wind that had blown them together swayed the multitude like a field of grain. The preacher had only to put in the sickle and reap."

Turtle Creek

The elders at New Lebanon were keen to put their sickle in, too. In the frozen predawn blackness of January 1, 1805, Issachar Bates and Benjamin Seth Youngs, the two missionaries who had done so well in Vermont, departed New Lebanon. They were joined by John Meacham, the son of Father Joseph. Bates, a father of nine who had fought in the American Revolution, was the eldest of the three, but the most recent convert. He was probably sent west because, along with having "a testimony as hot as flames," he was an experienced fighter and brawny woodsman. By contrast, Benjamin Seth Youngs weighed less than a hundred pounds but had grown up entirely within the faith. As for Meacham, he had the increasingly rare distinction of having personally known Mother Ann.

The three men traveled on foot, their few possessions loaded onto a single horse. Seeking the headwaters of the new spiritual currents, they walked south and west across New York, Pennsylvania, Maryland, Virginia, and Tennessee. By March, having traveled more than a thousand miles in three months, they arrived in Kentucky. They were dressed in brown overalls, blue vests, gray coats, and white fur hats. Despite their long, difficult journey, they had kept themselves remarkably neat. In the town of Paint Lick, they addressed a revival of New Lights without much effect. From there they went to Cane Ridge, a wooded promontory near the town of Paris that had been the sight of the largest camp meetings. Turning north, they walked into Ohio.

Among their few belongings was an epistle written by the elders in

New Lebanon. It was a broad appeal to an unknown audience. The document explained that for almost two thousand years the earth has been under the sway of the Antichrist. "Since the falling away of the Apostolic order" a few decades after Jesus's death, Christianity has been "under a sackcloth and darkness." At long last, the prophesied millennium has finally begun. The spiritual "gifts" manifested during Christ's first sojourn on earth have been restored to a group of "witnesses" in New York. These modern apostles can "testify to all people that Christ hath made his second appearing here on earth." The path into the millennium has been revealed in all of its simplicity: Stop having sex. It is "impossible for those who live in the works of natural generation, copulating in the works of the flesh, to travel in the great work of regeneration and the new birth." Except for an oblique reference to the "first pillar" of the new dispensation, the epistle sent west from New Lebanon did not mention Mother Ann or any other woman.[*]

On March 22, the three missionaries arrived at the Ohio village of Turtle Creek, where they met Richard McNemar, a Presbyterian minister turned New Light revivalist. McNemar was impressed by the three visitors' reserved manners and tidy appearance. When they asked to address his congregation, he happily turned over his pulpit.[†]

The next Sunday, Bates and Youngs offered the breakaway Presbyterians of Turtle Creek their usual pitch: The millennium has already begun; spiritual perfection is free for the taking. "The power of God, revealed in this day, does enable souls to cease from sin; and we have received that power; we have actually left off committing sin." According to the Shakers, the doctrine of inherent depravity—the permanent taint of original sin—is "one of the most destructive errors that ever proceeded from the powers of darkness." To regain the innocence of

---

[*] It would be two decades before the Shakers started openly and directly referring to Ann as the "second appearing" of Christ in their public evangelism.
[†] Like the famously clean-cut Mormon missionaries, the Shakers understood that the bearing and appearance of their representatives was almost as significant as the gospel they proffered.

Paradise, one must come out of society and "take up a full cross against the world, the flesh, and all evil."

Malcolm Worley, a wealthy local farmer known for his fickle spiritual enthusiasms, was deeply impressed by the Shakers' sermon. He put them up in his house and quickly became their first convert in the West. Worley's confession was soon followed by the conversion of his entire family and a former slave named Anna Middleton.

From Worley's home, the three Shakers moved into the log cabin of Richard McNemar. Although he was an avid revivalist, McNemar was also a trained theologian, literate in Greek, Latin, and Hebrew. After talking at length with the missionaries, he wrote: "For upwards of 15 years my soul has been on the wheel, forming into union with professed followers of the Lamb, but never did I find my mate, until I found the spirit of New Lebanon. Now I can say with the prophet, 'This is my God, I have waited for him!'"*

McNemar's conversion, like that of Joseph Meacham, was a turning point for the Society. Much of his flock and several of his schismatic Presbyterian colleagues followed him into "the spirit of New Lebanon." For frontier revivalists, the appeal of the United Society was the same as it had been in Niskeyuna in the weeks after the Dark Day. They had been whipped into a frenzy of millenarian anticipation by the camp meetings, but their world remained stubbornly unchanged. The missionaries' stories of the life within the tidy villages of Zion—their recollections no doubt sweetened by homesickness—promised something immediate and concrete: a tangible sacrifice and a transformed existence. New Jerusalem is coming, shouted the revivalists. It is already here, came the Shaker response. "We have news of a Zion," McNemar

---

* According to one account (not McNemar's own), the Shakers had cured his young son of a peculiar malady. After almost being killed by a large black snake, the boy periodically suffered screaming fits that could be stopped only by the firm embrace of his mother or father. His last attack supposedly occurred during the Shakers' first meeting in the McNemar home. A third account of McNemar's conversion claims that he saw the arm of a woman rise from the ground and beckon him to follow.

wrote from Ohio, "and what if her foundations are already laid. May it be that God has sent down the new Jerusalem for the refuge of souls, before he began to tear down the old buildings?"

By the end of May 1805, an informal community—"united in one common worship"—was gathered together in Malcolm Worley's house. In midsummer, three more male elders arrived from New York. Among them was David Darrow, the farmer who had been arrested while driving sheep to Niskeyuna during the Revolution. He had been selected by Lucy Wright to serve as first elder in the West. To the western Shakers, Darrow was known as Father David, a spiritual "parent" on a par with Mother Lucy. The six elders from New Lebanon were soon joined by a contingent of eldresses, including Ruth Farrington, who as a teenager had participated in the New Light stir in New Lebanon. Working alongside Darrow, she became first eldress in the West.

The seasoned Shakers sent from the East lived among the new converts, organizing missionary outings and coaching the initiates in the routines of life within gospel order. They taught the westerners how to dance the square order shuffle, how to tie a Shaker bonnet, what to eat, and how to organize collective farms and industries.

The land around Turtle Creek was well forested, fertile, and almost totally clear of stone. At $3.00 an acre, it was also incredibly cheap. By merging the property owned by Worley and McNemar and purchasing more land nearby, the Shakers formed a new community, a western replica of the eastern villages. Within a year, there were 220 adult converts living collectively in the West. Over the next six years, the Shakers at Turtle Creek built a meetinghouse, a sawmill, and several large dwellings. The village became the staging ground for the United Society's ongoing evangelism up and down the scorched revival circuit of the Ohio River valley.

The Shaker experience on the frontier echoed their early history in New England. Along with a rapid intake of souls, they encountered violent persecution from drunken rowdies and the families of converts. People threw rocks through their windows, torched their barns, and knocked over their fences. Shaker cattle were stolen or set free. Their horses were branded and had their ears cropped. At camp meetings, Shaker preachers were shouted down and cursed as devils. Equality of the sexes and celibacy remained the main sources of ire, but darker slanders circulated, too. Alarmed by the notion of coed homes full of unmarried adults, some claimed that the Shakers murdered the newborn "fruits of their unlawful embraces."

All of this abuse came on top of the usual tribulations of frontier life: malaria, malnutrition, raids by freshly displaced Native Americans, and the brutal labor required to break ground in the virgin wilderness.* As it had in the East, the Shakers' collectivism eased these trials, giving them many practical advantages over other frontier homesteaders. Before long, the neighbors who denounced the believers as devils were buying their products and paying to use their mills.

Millennial Laws

Lucy Wright died at Niskeyuna (by then referred to by the old Dutch name Watervliet) on the afternoon of February 7, 1821. She was sixty-one. She had led the United Society through a quarter century of remarkable expansion. After her death, no other Shaker would ever be designated Mother or Father. The thousand-mile journey into the (old) Southwest that she commissioned in 1805 had succeeded beyond every expectation. Within a decade of the three missionaries' arrival in Ohio, there were five Shaker communities in the region. A decade later, at the time of Wright's death, half of the four thousand active Shakers lived in the West, in a total of seven communities—four in Ohio, two in Kentucky, and one in Indiana. The community founded on Malcolm Worley's farm in Turtle Creek came to be known as Union Village.† It

---

* An 1807 Shaker mission to Native Americans in western Ohio yielded no converts.
† The Ohio villages, in order of their founding, were Union Village, Watervliet, North Union, and White Water. The Kentucky villages were Pleasant Hill and South Union Village. The village in Indiana was known as West Union Village.

functioned as a sort of New Lebanon West, housing the lead western ministry and supporting the communities around it with money and instruction in the Society's increasingly complex regulations and customs.

Even as Zion sprawled from Maine to Indiana, Mother Lucy resisted formally codifying Shaker beliefs. The expansion of the sect required a certain amount of written theology, but Wright kept it to a minimum, sensing the hazards of fixing their vital, changing gospel on paper. When a draft of Shaker regulations came across her desk, she forbade its publication.

After Wright's death, leadership of the Society passed to a group of four elders, two men and two women. Within six months they authorized the publication and distribution of the Millennial Laws, a list of 125 rules governing every aspect of life in Zion. When two Shakers walk together, the Millennial Laws instruct, they must walk in step. When walking indoors, they should be as quiet as possible. When entering a meetinghouse, they should tiptoe. Shakers "should not slip their feet on the carpet or floor, but lift them up and set them down plumb." In fact, there should not be any rugs at all; devils hide in rugs. Shakers should not play with cats. No pets allowed, period. There should be only one rocking chair per room, unless it is a room for the elderly. (Two youths rocking simultaneously might awaken carnality.) There should be no intermingling of plants in the garden. No gathering of nuts to give as gifts. When praying, a Shaker should fold the right thumb over the left, never the left over the right. No vulgarity, including, but not limited to, the phrases "My stars!" "My gracious!" or "Good heavens!" Suppertime presented a particularly daunting thicket of regulations: "When you take a piece of bread, take a whole piece." "When you cut meat, cut it square." When you are finished eating, "cross your knife & fork on your plate with the edge towards you."

Looked upon from the bird's-eye view of history, the native ordinances of any separatist enclave tend to reveal the aggregated compulsions and phobias of the community's leader(s). The countless trifling regulations that gave Shaker life its distinctive texture can certainly be understood as a collection of the lead elders' personal crotchets, writ large upon all of Shakerdom. Most significant, Shaker celibacy, the doctrine that propelled Ann Lee to the head of the Wardley prayer group and distinguished the United Society from countless other millenarian sects, was founded upon the rock of one woman's seriously justified terror of childbirth.

By encircling daily life with countless small prohibitions, the Shakers tried to suppress impulse to the vanishing point, to transform themselves from animals to saints. When you cut your food into squares, dinner ceases to be a gratification of appetite and becomes an exercise in geometry. Just as important, the sect's ever-multiplying regulations gave Zion its own idiosyncratic rhythms, separating the believers as much as possible from their former lives in the World.

As the nineteenth century progressed, the chaste Shakers birthed more and more regulations. Naturally, the rules concerning sexuality were the most stringent. Some are laughably obvious: When a sister mends a brother's trousers, he must take them off first. Others are subtler, suggesting the extent to which a celibate coed village might sometimes have felt like an erotic powder keg. Men and women should not pass on the stairs. Men's clothes should never be hung beside women's clothes. No watching animals have sex.* There is an occasional whiff of sadism to Shaker discipline. One ex-Shaker recalled how three young women at Watervliet were caught "attending to the amour of two flies in the window." Hannah Matterson, the eldress who caught them, told the girls that "for thus gratifying their carnal inclinations, and as a mortification to the same, they must strip themselves naked and take whips . . . and whip themselves, and then whip each other." When the girls were finished whipping one another, they had to dunk themselves

---

* This particular rule must have been difficult to obey on a farm. During Mother Ann's ministry, a boy in Massachusetts took up the Shaker cross after admitting to having had sex with several farm animals. His confession to Ann apparently put an end to a spate of disease among the local livestock. "If you commit sin with beasts," Mother Ann taught, "your souls will be transformed into the shape of beasts."

in a cold brook. Two male elders apparently supervised this scene with approval.

Bow and Be Free

By the middle of the 1820s, less than half a century after the Dark Day, the Shakers had built nineteen villages in eight states.[*] When they counted themselves in 1823, there were four thousand resident believers.[†] That same year, the *Summary View of the Millennial Church*, an official account of the Shakers' beliefs and history, was distributed by the church. Stephen J. Stein, the leading contemporary historian of the United Society, writes that the publication of the *Summary View* "signals the completion of the establishment of the Shakers as a society." Their story, their theology, and their folkways were more or less fixed.

Two years later, on thirteen hundred acres of rich farmland along Sodus Bay, a natural harbor on Lake Ontario in western New York, the Shakers established their last successful colony.[‡] Equidistant from Union Village and New Lebanon, Sodus Bay Village represented a geographic bridge between the sometimes divergent worlds of eastern and western Shakerdom.

The population of Zion continued to expand for another two decades, peaking at the end of the 1850s at somewhere around six thousand believers, before beginning a long, gradual contraction that lasted

---

[*] The seven western villages are listed above. The twelve eastern villages were Watervliet, New Lebanon, and Sodus Bay in New York; Hancock, Harvard, Tyringham, and Shirley in Massachusetts; Enfield in Connecticut; Canterbury and a second Enfield in New Hampshire; and the villages of Alfred and Sabbathday Lake in Maine. At the end of the nineteenth century, there were two short-lived efforts to establish Shaker villages in the South, one at Narcoossee in central Florida, where the believers raised and sold pineapples, and one at White Oak in southern Georgia.

[†] That number is almost certainly high. Shaker demographics are famously difficult to pin down.

[‡] There were a few subsequent efforts to start communities elsewhere, including in the South, but none of them lasted more than a few years.

into the middle of the twentieth century, when the Shakers all but vanished. Today, a tiny, noble remnant—two sisters and one brother—keeps the flame at Sabbathday Lake Village in southern Maine.

With the distribution of the *Summary View* and the establishment of Sodus Bay Village, the Shakers' social structures and physical domain were set. The United Society had not yet reached the peak of its influence or size, but it had become what it was to remain. In the coming decades, despite a period of energetic revival and spiritualism that began in the late 1830s, the emphasis of Shaker doctrine shifted gradually from millenarian prophecy toward an array of distinctive social doctrines, most notably communism, pacifism, and the equality of the sexes.

The Shakers' aversion to the world as they found it and their exuberant millenarian hopes combined to liberate them from any regard for the established forms of human association. Within their villages, they built an entirely new kind of society, one founded upon total equality, spiritual transcendence, and a utopian faith in the perfectibility of life on earth. "We are the people who turned the world upside down," Ann Lee liked to say.

Ultimately, life within Zion was less about what the Shakers did than about what they didn't do—namely, just about everything that might be called "worldly." To them, this state of total abstention—what they called being "simple"—added up to a doctrine of radical freedom: freedom from appetite, from nature, from impulse, and, perhaps most important, from the conventions of the World. By scorching out the lusty, scuffling habits of Babylon, the Shakers hoped to perfect and liberate their souls and their community. Their best-known song celebrates this remarkable paradox: "I will bow and be simple. / I will bow and be free."

NEW HARMONY

———

The Great Infidel Experiment

The change has come upon the world like a thief in
the night!

—ROBERT OWEN

A Visitor at Watervliet

A little before noon on November 11, 1824, just a few months before
the establishment of the Shaker village in Sodus Bay, a light carriage
came bouncing up the Albany Post Road toward Watervliet (formerly
Niskeyuna). It had been forty-four years since the Dark Day, when Joseph Meacham followed a trail of anxious hearsay into the woods north
of Albany. Now, on a bright fall day, another seeker traveled the same
route. Navigating the rough road, alternately sandy and muddy, the carriage wended through hilly country dotted with small farms and large
stands of oak and elm, shining red and orange with autumn color.

Seven miles out of Albany, the carriage turned off the main road
through a white gate hung between granite posts. Robert Owen, a
Welsh textile magnate and one of the most famous men in Europe,

stepped down and stretched his legs. With him were his son William and his friend Captain Donald MacDonald. Elder Seth Wells greeted the three men, doffing his straw hat and offering glasses of mead.

The sodden woodlot that had been home to Ann Lee was now one of eighteen pristine Shaker villages. The brothers and sisters at Watervliet had drained the swamp, straightened the creek, and cleared the surrounding timber. They had put their original pastureland to good use and rented a thousand acres more. Near the site of their old log cabin, they had built immense brick dormitories, workshops, a dairy, and a white meetinghouse. When Owen arrived, three years after the death of Mother Lucy Wright, all was thrumming with activity and fresh with whitewash.

Two hundred and fifty believers were living in the village. The men were dressed in brown frock coats, baggy pants, and broad-brimmed straw hats. The women wore long brown gowns, white neckerchiefs, and boxy visored bonnets that gave them a bowed, reverent aspect. Led about by Elder Wells, Robert Owen spent the afternoon touring the farm, the dwellings, and the spotless workshops. He was full of compliments, praising the Shakers' clever contrivances, their ingenious architecture, the straightness of their rows.

Owen was fifty-three, handsome in the soft, rosy-cheeked manner of a kindly patriarch. He wore small spectacles on the tip of his long, slim nose and took in the world with the dilated, calculating eyes of a full-time reformer. He was not tall, but he moved with an upright, energetic carriage.

The Shakers were used to visitors, and since Owen arrived at Watervliet bearing a letter of introduction from Governor DeWitt Clinton, they had some sense of his importance in the eyes of the World. They probably did not know that his arrival in the United States just seven days earlier, after a five-week passage from Liverpool, had been reported in most of the New York papers or that even before he landed, several "Owenite" groups had been convened to discuss his theories. Owen had spent his first few days in the United States being feted by the worthies of Manhattan society. But after only a week on dry land, he boarded a northbound Hudson River steamer, intent on seeing the Shakers.

In Albany, he and his son William were hosted by Governor Clinton. In addition to formally introducing Owen to the Shakers, Clinton wrote generous letters of introduction to General Andrew Jackson and former president Thomas Jefferson. Owen would meet them both in the coming months, along with President James Monroe and President-elect John Quincy Adams.

Owen had come to the United States at a propitious moment. Four years earlier, Monroe had won reelection by an unprecedented landslide, receiving every electoral vote but one. It was the so-called Era of Good Feelings. A strong sense of national unity and isolationism prevailed. It had been half a century since the Revolution, and the world's great experiment in popular rule, like the Shaker Zion planted within it, seemed to be stabilizing.

Three months before Owen's arrival, Americans had celebrated themselves by celebrating the return to the United States of the Marquis de Lafayette, the French general and Revolutionary War hero. Lafayette's service in both the American War of Independence and the French Revolution had made him a living icon of republicanism. When he sailed into New York Harbor, his ship was met by an immense flotilla of steamboats and a cheering crowd of fifty thousand.

Lafayette's arrival in New York marked the start of a rolling, nationwide jubilee that culminated two years later, on July 4, 1826, the fiftieth anniversary of the Declaration of Independence. Americans, in their struggle for self-determination, had accomplished what many observers thought impossible. The old Frenchman walked among them as a living reminder of that fact.*

---

* Lafayette, the last living general of the American Revolution, toured all twenty-four states. Most named cities in his honor. In small towns across the country, including

On New Year's Day 1824, Lafayette was in Washington to be honored by the Congress and the president. Henry Clay offered a toast: "To the great apostle of liberty." The apostle raised his glass with a counter-toast: "To the perpetual union of the United States. . . . One day," he said, "it will save the world."

Robert Owen's reception three months later was less grand, but he also believed that global salvation would commence in the United States. He had come to North America to initiate what he called "the New Moral World"—a new type of society founded upon total equality, brotherly love, and reason. More specifically, he had come to buy a town in Indiana.

Owen's intentions were as vague as they were ambitious. He had a well-earned reputation as a brilliant organizer of people and machines, but he was given to soaring leaps of enthusiasm. His homegrown philosophy, more a religion than a science, epitomizes the brand of utopianism that flourished during the first half of the nineteenth century. The New Moral World was a secular New Jerusalem, a rationalist's answer to the millenarian fervor that was already sweeping the United States. Owen believed that technology, new social structures, and mass education would soon create a perfected human society. "What ideas individuals may attach to the term 'Millennium' I know not," he told a group of Scottish millworkers in 1816, "but I know that society may be formed so as to exist without crime, without poverty, with health greatly improved . . . and with intelligence and happiness increased a hundredfold: and no obstacle whatsoever intervenes at this moment except ignorance to prevent such a state of society from becoming universal." In other words, paradise is possible right now; only shoddy thinking and old habits stand in the way.

The plan was simple. Owen would build one perfect community as

---

Harvard Shaker Village, he was greeted by musical performances, parades, and gatherings of Revolutionary War veterans. As a gesture of gratitude, Congress gave Lafayette $200,000 and a substantial chunk of Florida.

a showcase for his revolutionary ideas. This prototype of the so-called New Moral World would then inspire rapid and endless duplication. Everyone would rush to overturn the old, irrational order.[*] Once the new system became universal, the globe and its inhabitants would be perfected. Voilà, utopia.

When Owen arrived at Watervliet in 1824, he had already been studying the Shakers from across the Atlantic for at least five years. Starting in 1818, when he printed a pamphlet on the wonders of Shaker communism and the beauty of Shaker villages by a Quaker named W. S. Warder, Owen's various newspapers—he was a prolific publisher—printed laudatory accounts of Shaker life and industry. While Owen opposed all religion, he believed that the Shakers, with their highly planned villages, total lack of private property, and ability to "neutralize family loyalties," were on the right track. Like Engels, he saw the United Society as an object lesson in the benefits and viability of "the principle of combined labor and expenditure." He regarded the United Society's material success as a "conclusive argument against the system everywhere existing among the bulk of mankind."[†]

Secular socialists such as Owen and Engels did not regard the fact that the Shakers were a celibate order dedicated to mystical principles—what Owen dismissed as "their idle peculiarities, foolish prejudices, and disgusting prohibitions"—as particularly relevant to their great economic success. On the contrary, the United Society's secular admirers took the sect's spiritual eccentricities as further evidence of the viability of communism. If *they* can do it, Engels wrote, "how much sooner must it be feasible for others who are free from such insanities?" Horace

---

[*] Arthur Bestor, the most influential historian of American utopianism, named this theory of reform "communitarianism." Owen and his fellow communitarians were united, Bestor wrote, by "the idea of employing the small experimental community as a lever to exert upon society the force necessary to produce reform and change."

[†] The word *socialism* was first put into wide circulation by the followers of Owen. Engels wrote that he and Marx were obliged to describe their scheme as "communism" because in 1847, when they wrote their manifesto, the word *socialism* was so thoroughly associated with Owenism.

Greeley, editor of the *New-York Tribune* and the most influential American journalist of his day, expressed the same point more generously: "Let us, then, profit by the lessons which these enthusiasts read us, while disregarding their unpardonable errors. Let us remember that they have solved for us the problem of the possibility, the practicality, of a social condition from which the twin curses, pauperism and servitude, shall be utterly banished. They have shown how pleasant may be the labours, how abundant the comforts, of a community wherein no man aspires to be lord over his brethren—no man grasps for himself, but each is animated by a spirit of devotion to the common good."* Faced with the comfort and beauty of a Shaker village, Greeley wondered how anyone could "refrain from thinking lightly of that blind dogmatism which asserts the impossibility of inducing men to labour except for their own selfish gratification, and affirms the necessity of the stimulus of personal acquisition to save mankind from sinking back into the darkness and destitution of barbarism."

Then, as now, the principal economic case against communism was that it suppresses productivity and innovation by diminishing competition, thrift, and personal incentive. John Stuart Mill laid out the counterargument as it was understood by Owen: "The objection [to communism] supposes that honest and efficient labor is only to be had from those who are themselves individually to reap the benefits of their own exertions. But how small a part of all the labor performed in England, from the lowest paid to the highest, is done by persons working for their own benefit." Like Mill, Owen saw that industrialism had made this problem of workers laboring almost entirely for someone else's benefit even more acute. "A factory operative has less personal interest in his work than a member of a Communist association, since he is not, like him, working for a partnership of which he is himself a member. . . . And though the 'master's eye,' when the master is vigilant and intelligent, is of proverbial value, it must be remembered that in a

---

* To Greeley, the Shakers' most unpardonable error was celibacy, which he thought rendered them an "unaspiring and unpoetical people."

Socialist farm or manufactory, each laborer would be under the eye, not of one master, but of the whole community."

Touring Watervliet on that cold, sunny afternoon, Owen saw physical proof for this line of reasoning in the Shakers' tidy whip-making shop, their state-of-the-art blacksmithing facilities, their fine merino sheep, and their plump dairy cows. Most of all, like so many visitors to Zion, he saw it in the crisp whiteness of the Shakers' linens and the countless small ways in which everything was "uncommonly neat and clean."

After a thorough tour of the village, Owen and his two companions sat down for a midday supper with a whaler visiting from Massachusetts.* The Shakers seldom dined with visitors, but they laid out a huge Yankee spread: fresh pork, boiled beef, potatoes, apple pie, bread, cheese, turnips, and mashed squash. All of it washed down with fresh cider.

Before Owen left Watervliet, he explained to the Shakers that he had come to the United States to establish a community similar to their own. The Shakers asked who would live there; would it be a society "of Quakers? or Jews? or what?" Owen, no doubt glad for the question, proudly explained that everyone would be welcome. His hosts, too polite to object, shook their heads.

Around four in the afternoon, the three visitors climbed back into their carriage to return to Albany. On the way back, at a scenic spot overlooking the city and the Hudson River, they came across a pair of handsome young Shaker brothers driving two carts back toward Watervliet. When Owen told them how impressed he was by what he had seen of their village, the Shakers suggested that he join. Owen responded that he was founding an even better community. Soon, he said, they would want to join up with him.

Would this community forbid marriage? one brother asked.

It would not, Owen replied.

* A man raised in the "crazy society of Neskyeuna Shakers" makes a memorable appearance in *Moby-Dick*, where he claims to be the archangel Gabriel and prophesies that killing the white whale will bring doom.

"Then," the Shaker said, "there will be continual quarrels."

As Owen's carriage made its way back into Albany, a light dusting of snow began to fall. In his diary, William Owen wrote, "I do not know when I have spent a day so agreeably before. Even this sample made us all in love with a community."

Determined Man

Robert Owen spent his long life in the service of a single idea. "The character of man," he wrote again and again, "is, without a single exception, always formed for him." To reach this conclusion—that man is a wholly determined product of his environment—Owen seems to have overlooked the data closest at hand: his own improbable biography. The bare facts of his life describe a Horatio Alger ascent from hardscrabble roots to incredible wealth and influence.

He was born in Newtown, Wales, in 1771, the year after Ann Lee's jailhouse vision in Manchester. He was the sixth child of a saddle maker. At ten, Owen left home to join an older brother who was working in London. From there, he went to Stamford, in Lincolnshire, to apprentice with a wholesaler and linen draper named McGuffog. Owen spent his nonworking hours in the draper's large private library, skimming the confident literature of the English and Scottish Enlightenment and diligently transcribing the sayings of Seneca into his diary. Amid the draper's volumes, the precocious self-improver thrilled at the power of big questions with lucid answers.

McGuffog was a Presbyterian. Mrs. McGuffog was Episcopalian. On Sundays, their earnest young charge was compelled to attend one service in the morning and another in the evening. This double dose of religion backfired. Presented with two subtly divergent methods of worship, Owen determined to find the one true church, but during his evening researches in the library, something else happened. "Before my investigations were concluded," he recalled, "I was satisfied that religions, one and all, had emanated from the same source, and their varieties from the same false imaginations of our early ancestors."

As an adult, Owen fancied himself a revolutionary philosopher. In fact, he never became a particularly incisive thinker. What he lacked in acuity, however, he made up for with a visceral, unremitting sensitivity to human suffering. Having given up on Christianity, he wrote, his "religious feelings were immediately replaced by the spirit of universal charity—not for a sect or a party, or for a country or a colour—but for the human race." This universalism became Owen's religion. Like many universalists, he tended to see social problems in soft focus, thinking more about the People than people.

Owen's commitment to strict determinism (his so-called theory of character formation) barred him from taking any credit for his ideas or his considerable material accomplishments. He was, according to his own theory, nothing more than the hapless by-product of externally determined circumstances. He attributed the singularity of his vision and success to a series of happy accidents. He was exceptional only because his life was "more varied, extended and singular, than perhaps has ever fallen to the lot of any one man."

Owen's autobiography, which feels even more reverse-engineered than most autobiographies, narrates how even the most mundane experiences led him, domino-like, to his world-saving insights and fabulous wealth. At age five, he was so eager to be the first boy at school that he bolted a hot bowl of flummery, badly scorching his stomach. The shock caused him to faint and left him with a sensitive gut for the rest of his life. His tender stomach caused him to favor simple foods and to closely watch what he ate. The practice of watching what he ate caused him to cultivate a "habit of close observation and of continual reflection." This habit caused him to perceive the world around him with unusual clarity. This heightened perception led to his success in business and his keen insight into social problems. So the scalding breakfast *caused* Owen's immense fortune and his world-shaking insight into social problems. Of course, there is a shorter causal chain linking the breakfast to the success. A five-year-old who is frantic to be first at school might be bound for some measure of distinction.

In 1788, when Owen was seventeen, he moved to Manchester seeking work as a wholesaler. It had been a decade since Ann Lee and her Shaking Quakers had quit the Cottonopolis. Conditions had gone from bad to worse. In the final three decades of the eighteenth century, workers poured in from the countryside, more than tripling the city's population, from twenty-seven thousand in 1771 to ninety-five thousand in 1801. Because everyone was from somewhere else, there was little sense of community. Social stratification was glaring. The rapidly expanding city was being laid out so that wealthy Mancunians could travel from home to church to mill without ever glimpsing the neighborhoods in which their employees lived. Homes in the wealthier districts faced outward toward the fresh country air. In the slums, the smell of putrefaction from tanneries and bone mills was constant.

Even for the steadily employed, food was scarce and of the lowest quality. Moldy bread and rancid meat were the norm. Pigs wandered the streets, rooting offal. When they dropped dead, they were dragged off by unscrupulous butchers and sold as fresh. Butter sellers would spread a thin layer of sweet butter over lumps of heavily salted rancid butter. Flour was cut with gypsum and chalk, cocoa and coffee with fine dirt. Bitter gin and "Port wine" (red-tinted liquor) constituted life's few luxuries. Laudanum, sold as patent medicine, was the preferred narcotic of colicky babies and their mothers.

To Owen and, a few years later, Marx and Engels, Manchester presented a spectacle of competition and technology run amuck. When Engels was twenty-two, his father sent him to Great Britain to manage the family thread business, hoping to put some miles between his son and the coffeehouse radicals he had been spending his days with. In Manchester, the prosperous young German brimmed with empathy for the British underclass. He spent his days wandering the same neighborhoods in which Ann Lee had grown up. It was there that he wrote his first book, *The Condition of the Working-Class in England in 1844*, which catalogs the grinding misery of Manchester's millworkers.

The new textile machines churned out unprecedented profits and material abundance, but they did so by eroding traditional economies, squeezing out the artisan class, and forcing almost everyone into the factories. The most distressing fact was that this wasteland sat at the heart of the world's richest nation. By all accounts, Manchester represented the leading edge of the new paradigm. "From this foul drain the greatest stream of human industry flows out to fertilize the whole world," Tocqueville wrote of the city in 1835. "From this filthy sewer pure gold flows. Here humanity attains its most complete development and its most brutish, here civilization works its miracles and civilized man is turned almost into a savage." This dark preview of the shape of things to come pressed hard upon the utopian imagination. The dream of an egalitarian, semi-industrialized heaven on earth that defined the golden age of American utopianism was a direct reaction to the great Cottonopolis, a place that Engels called "Hell upon Earth."

Paradoxically, the new machines and the factory system, which was itself a sort of new machine, inspired horror and hope in almost equal measure. Loom-smashing radicals such as the Luddites may have seen technology as the main cause of social distress, but Owen and Engels imagined a future in which the industrial miracle would serve the common weal, in which working hours would be dramatically cut and abundance secured for all. They reasoned that productivity could not rise endlessly. If one man could produce as much as twenty men had a decade earlier, surely everyone would soon work much less and have more.[*]

For all of its horrors, Manchester was a boomtown. Owen, who had a gift for seeing the full potential of the new machines, thrived. He moved quickly from job to job, each time ascending a rung up the industrial ladder. The same mechanistic thinking that hindered his social

---

[*] To the fathers of Marxism, Manchester also offered a very specific form of hope. It was not merely a wasteland of greed, it was also the birthplace of the one thing that could save the world: the industrial proletariat.

theories—an oversimple if-A-then-B mode of reasoning that skimmed
over the vagaries of human life—made him very good at organizing the
flow of labor and machinery on a factory floor.*

By 1791, at the age of nineteen, Owen was a partner in a mill with
five spinning jennies. It was a very good time to be in the spinning business. A pound of raw cotton that cost $1.25 could be spun into $50
worth of yarn. Owen may have been the first operator to see the profit-
ability of the silky, long-fibered cotton grown on the Sea Islands off the
coast of Georgia and South Carolina. The cotton, which was less white
than the top strains, was priced low, but its long fibers made it ideal fod-
der for the new machines.

As Owen began to make money, he passed his leisure time at meetings of the Manchester Philosophy Society, discussing the latest progressive ideas with local businessmen and visiting eminences such as
Samuel Taylor Coleridge. He began to wonder why so much money
and effort was spent on the upkeep of Manchester's "dead machinery"
while so little thought was given to the maintenance of its "living machinery."

New Lanark

In 1799, Owen corralled a group of partners into helping him buy, for
£300,000, an immense textile mill in New Lanark, Scotland. The New
Lanark mill was owned and operated by an industrialist named David
Dale, whose daughter Caroline had caught Owen's eye. It is not clear
whether it was the factory or the daughter that first attracted Owen. He
was shy around women. Perhaps buying a mill was the easiest come-on
he could think of. Either way, his bid to buy New Lanark transformed
Owen—a prodigy, but also an upstart with unsettling ideas about
God—into a worthy suitor. The deal was set and the marriage made.

---

* In 1819, a British parliamentarian said that under Mr. Owen's authority, "society
would become one vast spinning-jenny."

New Lanark represented an earlier phase of the Industrial Revolution than what was happening in Manchester. The turbines inside Dale's mill were spun by the thundering falls of the river Clyde. Before the widespread reliance on steam-driven machinery, the location of large manufactories was determined by proximity to strong, steady waterpower. As a result, many industrial enterprises were located far from traditional population centers. In these isolated company towns, everything from the homes in which workers slept, to the churches where they prayed, to the stores where they shopped, was owned by the boss. These remote industrial kingdoms created a natural opening for what we would now call social engineering.*

Within a year of co-purchasing New Lanark, Owen was installed as its manager. David Dale, a pious man who served as a lay preacher to his workers, had been widely regarded as an enlightened employer. Even so, Owen found the mill's fifteen hundred employees in desperate shape. The workers, he recalled, were "indolent, dirty, imbecile, and demoralized." Because the mill was remote and the wages low, it was difficult to find employees other than people whom Owen described as "destitute of friends, employment, and character." Crowded into granite four-story homes, they "lived in idleness, in poverty, in almost every kind of crime; consequently, in debt, out of health, and in misery."†

For the next twenty-four years, Owen ran New Lanark like his own private social laboratory, making himself responsible for the moral, intellectual, and physical health of his employees. He put an end to the practice of employing orphans leased to the mill by the parish poorhouses. The company store began to sell coal and food at cost. Owen established a workers' savings bank, a free medical clinic, a network of

---

* When the importance of waterpower declined, this model persisted in places where a specific resource anchored an industry, such as Pennsylvania coal towns, Rocky Mountain silver mines, or Fordlandia, Henry Ford's Amazonian rubber plantation.

† One contemporaneous biographer of Owen, dismayed at every turn by his subject's "paganism," insisted that Owen must have exaggerated the circumstances of pious David Dale's employees. "Having conceived himself to be Hercules, it was natural that [Owen's] exuberant fancy should find an Augean stable to test his powers."

community gardens, and an insurance fund for the sick and injured. Although the mill consistently earned a profit, Owen's efforts were resisted at every turn by his investors. He was repeatedly forced to seek new partners. Eventually he found a group of backers, many of them Quakers, who gave him a free hand.

Owen related to his employees, some of whom were older than him, like a stern father. To curtail what he regarded as the "monstrous vices" of the British working class, he policed every aspect of their lives. He established strict curfews and levied fines for public drunkenness and extramarital pregnancy. At every workstation in the mill, he installed a rotating three-inch block of wood known as a "silent monitor." The monitor was painted a different color on each side—yellow, white, blue, and black. Every day, a foreman would walk the mill floor, turning the blocks to indicate the quality of each worker's conduct and output. Each day's color was then recorded in a "book of character." Although there were no specific consequences attached to the colors, anyone with a block showing black could expect a disappointed gaze when Mr. Owen made his daily rounds.* Like Ann Lee, Owen was fixated on order and tidiness. He installed modern plumbing in the workers' apartments and hired a team of full-time sanitary agents. The millworkers came to dread the intrusions of these so-called bug inspectors.

In 1807, Thomas Jefferson embargoed trade with France and the United Kingdom to protest the abuse of American merchant ships during the Napoleonic Wars. The British textile trade, which ran partly on American cotton and American customers, was badly hobbled. When mills throughout the nation fell silent, Owen continued to pay full

---

* Like a miniature version of Jeremy Bentham's Panopticon, Owen's "silent monitor" secured discipline with a vague but constant specter of observation. Bentham and Owen were friends, and in 1812, when Owen sought reform-minded investors to help him secure a controlling stake in New Lanark, the great utilitarian philosopher was among the first to lend his cash and his prestige. In his writings, Owen sometimes uses Bentham's definition of moral conduct as that which secures the "happiness of the greatest number."

wages. For four months, the workers at New Lanark did little but sweep and oil machinery. Along with Owen's other reforms, this decision made him very popular with his employees. When he returned to New Lanark after a trip to London to find philanthropically minded partners, he was greeted by a cheering crowd of workers. They unhitched his horses and pulled his carriage through the town themselves.

Owen's experiences at New Lanark led him to conclude that all of the ills of the world—vice, crime, poverty, sickness—are by-products of a poorly arranged society. He believed that individuals are inherently good and that society corrupts them in ways that are beyond their control. This view of things ran counter to the reigning Protestant view that humans are tainted by sin when they drink their first breath and that they have the freedom to *choose* virtue or vice.

Owen's sense of human nature and his theories about how to change it rested upon the most basic conclusions of Enlightenment philosophy. From Rousseau he took the idea that man is born good and that it is society that corrupts us. In Rousseau's imagined state of nature, prehistoric man did not quarrel with his colleagues because he did not crave property beyond his basic needs.* This kindly, upright ape had self-interest, but it was tempered by an inborn reluctance to cause suffering. From John Locke, Owen took (and greatly oversimplified) the notion that the human mind is a "white sheet" upon which sensory experience inscribes our knowledge, ideas, and character. From René Descartes, Owen took the idea that human nature can be perfected through intensive education.

For Owen, a highly disciplined autodidact with meager appetites, a belief in the total plasticity of human nature came naturally. At his most optimistic, he claimed that the reorganization of the existing social order would stimulate the mental and physical perfection of the species, creating "men and women of a new race, physically, intellectu-

---

* This account was Rousseau's reply to Thomas Hobbes's description of the presocial world as a tooth-and-claw "estate of war."

ally and morally; beings far superior to any yet known to have lived upon the earth."

The thing that made Owen a utopian, rather than just an ambitious reformer, was that he took these foundational modern ideas—that man is not inherently corrupt, that character is formed from without, and that we can control how that happens—and concluded that the right sorts of institutions can mold individuals, and thus society, in whichever way we desire.

In 1816, to begin the work of molding his fifteen hundred employees into ideal citizens, Owen opened the Institute for the Formation of Character in a large two-story building in New Lanark. The institute offered a comprehensive, nonreligious education for the children of his employees and character-shaping daycare for children as young as two. In an era when kids were generally regarded as short, depraved adults, Owen's institute was founded upon the assumption that children are "without exception, passive and wonderfully contrived compounds; which . . . may be formed collectively to have any human character . . . [and] may be ultimately molded into the very image of rational wishes and desires."*

The institute's surprisingly modern pedagogy eschewed rote learning, Bible study, and corporal punishment. Despite Owen's self-proclaimed passion for reading, he thought it was pointless for young kids to be "annoyed with books." Instead, he advocated "steady kindness," dancing, singing, and educational drawings (large posters of animals, continents, and so on). In the evenings, the institute's classrooms were turned over to New Lanark's adult population for night classes. At a time when millworkers were treated like disposable machine parts, Owen's scheme to educate his employees and their children was considered radical.

---

* Owen's theory of "character formation" rests upon the Socratic assumption that *knowing* what is right is identical to *doing* what is right. In other words, vice is just a species of misunderstanding.

The Most Popular Man in Europe

After a few years under Owen's management, the health and content-ment of New Lanark's workers became self-evident. Reports of Owen's progress were so compelling that the mill became one of the most vis-ited tourist destinations in Europe—a showcase for the new, humane version of industrialism. Between 1815 and 1825, more than twenty thousand visitors signed the New Lanark guestbook. One American guest reported that there "is not, I apprehend, to be found in any part of the world, a manufacturing community in which so much order, good government, tranquility, and rational happiness prevail."

Owen, already rich, became famous. In the press he was "Mr. Owen the Philanthropist" or "the Benevolent Mr. Owen." He made powerful friends such as the Duke of Kent, father of Queen Victoria. Grand Duke Nicholas of Russia, soon to be czar, proposed moving two million Englishmen to Russia under Owen's authority, as a way to relieve over-population in the United Kingdom. Engels called Owen "the most popular man in Europe."

Casting his sights beyond the Clyde, Owen used his newfound celeb-rity to back progressive legislation in Parliament. In 1815, he drafted a bill for the "Preservation of the Health and Morals of Apprentices . . . in Cotton and other Mills." The bill had three central provisions: chil-dren under ten should be prohibited from working in mills; workers under eighteen should not work more than twelve hours a day; and young millworkers should receive a half hour of schooling each day.

Owen went to Parliament expecting an enthusiastic response. Instead, the committee assigned to review the bill met him with startling hostility. "The employments of these Children in Cotton Mills is not sedentary," one of the bill's opponents insisted; "it is neither laborious, nor such as tends to cramp their limbs, to distort their bodies, or to injure their health. Generally speaking those who are introduced young are the most orderly, as might be expected from early habits of industry, attention, regular-ity, cleanliness, and subordination." A coalition of mill owners lobbied against the bill. In familiar language, they decried the proposed intrusion of big government into their industry. "Legislative interference betwixt the free labourer and his employer," they insisted, "is a violent, highly dangerous, and unconstitutional innovation." If children work fewer than twelve hours a day, some critics pointed out, their families will end up on the dole ("parochial relief"). As for the outlandish notion of providing young workers with thirty minutes of reading and arithmetic lessons each day, they claimed that "the unnatural mixture of education with work proposed by [Owen's] Bill, would not only be expensive and vexatious to the employer, but impracticable in execution." Owen's proposed reforms would merely deprive the "heads of families of their natural control over their children" and "reduce the productive labour of the Country." In short, the bill was an unpatriotic, antifamily job killer that would erode the morals of the working class by "throwing them idle and disorderly on the community too early in the evenings."

After four years in committee, the bill passed into law. By then, its key provisions had been gutted and it had been declawed of any enforceability. For a man accustomed to enacting sweeping reforms by fiat, the experience was acutely frustrating. In his own mind, Owen's schemes blazed with self-evident perfection. As Emerson later observed, he "had not the least doubt that he had hit on a right and perfect socialism, or that all mankind would adopt it." Resistance baffled him. All opposition was filed under "Honest Misunderstanding." "As soon as they understand the plan," went Owen's standard response, "they will be eager to adopt it." Not until much later in his life did it occur to Owen that the rich and powerful understood his ideas just fine; they simply liked things the way they were.

In June 1815, the Prussian army and the Duke of Wellington's Anglo-Allied forces defeated the imperial French army on a field near the Belgian village of Waterloo. In the United Kingdom, the end of the Napoleonic Wars caused an economic crisis. The long conflict had stimulated production, raised prices, and spurred mechanization. When the fighting stopped, demand fell sharply. An army of crippled veterans returned to the job market, only to discover that some of their former occupations were performed by machines. Galled by the conspicuous wealth of the ruling class, hungry Britons rioted. Unemployed artisans smashed looms and burned mills. The conservative Tory government failed to grasp the severity of the crisis and clung to the old notion that "poor relief" should be conducted, as it always had been, on a patchwork basis by local parishes and the spontaneous generosity of the landed gentry.

In March 1817, while Owen's child labor bill languished in a legislative backwater, he was invited to the House of Commons to speak about a proposal he had written for building small, self-sustaining "villages of unity and cooperation" to house and employ the indigent. Owen's plan had initially been submitted to a meeting of prominent citizens summoned by the archbishop of Canterbury to address the rising tide of unemployment. The archbishop's group, not knowing what to make of Owen's plan, shunted it to a parliamentary committee on poor relief.

When Owen sat down to testify on behalf of his proposal, the forty members of the committee conferred among themselves. After a few minutes, they asked Owen to wait outside. As the only witness scheduled for the day, Owen knew that they were debating whether or not to even let him speak. It is easy to picture him waiting in that wood-paneled anteroom—the earnest, self-made industrialist, clutching a thick roll of diagrams and charts. (Owen adored diagrams and charts.) Several hours ticked by. His patience began to slip. When the session ended, the committee asked Owen to return the following day. He came back but was once again kept waiting for hours. Eventually someone stepped out to tell him that on second thought, the committee had no need of his testimony.

The snub sent Owen into a flurry of activity. He resolved to bring his plan directly to the public. In the coming months, he loosed a torrent of propaganda—pamphlets, posters, editorials, lectures—on the British public, giving birth to the social movement that came to bear his name.*

---

* Owen's brief, miserable tangle with politics is a common experience for utopian reformers. The gulf separating idealism from the slow, corrupt business of legislation offends and then spurs the utopian imagination.

Owen gave long, passionate speeches to large gatherings of workers. When newspapers printed transcripts, he bought thousands of copies and mailed them to every imaginable person of influence. On one occasion, "all the mail-coaches in the kingdom" were delayed twenty minutes so that clerks in London could sort the pamphlets Owen had posted.

Having commenced his new career as a reformer and propagandist, Owen realized the power of his own biography. The story of his ascent in business, offered as a preamble to his ambitious proposals, convinced readers that he was not some dreamy aristocrat or theory-drunk Jacobin. Rather, he was what people then called "a man of affairs." Until the very end of his life, even after he had begun chatting regularly with the ghosts of Benjamin Franklin and Lord Byron, Owen's supporters pointed to his tenure as the profitable manager of Britain's largest mill as certification of his competence. Like a decorated veteran turned peacenik, Owen found that his triumphs on the front lines of the Industrial Revolution gave moral and intellectual heft to his increasingly radical critique of capitalism.

In August 1817, in front of several thousand people at a much hyped meeting at the City of London Tavern, Owen explained his belief that the world will never improve as long as human relations are founded upon old, irrational ideas. A total "mental revolution" was required. Competition must be replaced by cooperation, and superstition must give way to reason. Owen then said something that instantly polarized the crowd. The chief obstacle between the human race and perfect happiness, he claimed, is "the fundamental notion of every religion that has hitherto been taught to man!"

By the fall, just five months after he'd been sent away from Parliament, Owen had spent £4,000 on his media blitz. Robert Owen— philanthropist and infidel—had become a household name. The parliamentary flunkies who kept him waiting for those two days in March 1817 probably deserve an honorable mention in the annals of socialism.

The Leopard Lies Down
with the Kid

Owen's prose sometimes gives the impression of a man whipping himself into a frenzy. The more he spoke and wrote during the summer of 1817, the more expansive his vision became. What had begun in the early spring as an ambitious scheme for "poor relief" had developed, by the fall, into a full-blown program for "the emancipation of mankind."

On September 6, less than a month after the City of London Tavern rally at which Owen declared his opposition to "every religion," he published a long letter in the London papers that almost seems to document the birth of a utopian in real time. The letter begins with a proposal to gather groups of five hundred poor people into "villages of cooperation" centered upon enormous apartment complexes that Owen calls "parallelograms." The people living within these parallelograms will support themselves by farming cooperatively and running some sort of manufacturing enterprise.

Gazing happily upon this scheme, Owen then decides that no rational person, no matter how plush their present circumstances, would choose to live "among the folly, insincerity, and counteraction of society as it is now constituted," when a more cooperative, productive, pleasant, and easy life was on display inside the new villages.* So, he concludes: "The change from the OLD system to the NEW must be universal." Everyone in the world, rich and poor, must gather into carefully organized cooperative colonies. The idea, having been spoken aloud, assumed the weight of historical necessity. "To resist the introduction of this plan, in any part of the world," Owen wrote, "will now

---

* Addressing himself directly to wealthy skeptics, Owen later wrote: "You may shut yourselves up in your parks as usual; but when you peep over the walls, you will find us all so happy in our villages of co-operation, that you will of your own accord throw away privileges that only interfere with your own happiness."

be as vain and useless, as for man by his puny efforts to endeavor to preclude from the earth the vivifying rays of the sun."

The good news was that this total reorganization of all human life on earth would be accomplished without spilling a single drop of blood. Unlike the gory revolution in France, the memory of which still hung over Europe in 1817, Owen's proposed revolution would not only be bloodless, it would be polite. The transition into the New Moral World will come, he wrote, "without inconvenience" or "hurt the feeling of a single individual."

Marx and Engels would later admit a significant debt to Owen's insights—"Every social movement, every real advance in England on behalf of the workers links itself on to the name of Robert Owen," Engels claimed—but they found this vision of a peaceful, voluntary, irresistible revolution absurd. Engels, who worked as a reporter for Owen's reformist newspaper, called his erstwhile publisher "one of the few born leaders of men," but he added, with harsh accuracy, that Owen was "a man of almost sublime, childlike simplicity of character." The hazy endgame of the Marxist program—the abundant, poststate, postscarcity communism in which we will hunt grouse in the morning, fish trout in the afternoon, tend cattle in the evening, and criticize opera after dinner—may seem utopian, but the means of getting there—insurrection followed by the dictatorship of the proletariat—are undeniably gritty.

Owen, by contrast, was so certain that he had discovered the glide path to a utopia that he mostly worried over the speed with which the change would occur. "The only real practical difficulty," he wrote, "will be to restrain men from rushing too precipitously" into the New Moral World.

Owen claimed that the evolution of his own thinking represented a tangible leap forward in history. "In the day and hour when I disclaimed all connection with the errors and prejudices of the old system—a day to be remembered with joy and gladness henceforth throughout all future ages—the Dominion of FAITH ceased; its reign of terror, of disunion, of separation, and of irrationality was broken to pieces like a potter's vessel.'"* Under the bright light of material equality and rational education, old distinctions of faith and class would wither. "Ere long there shall be but one action, one language, and one people."

Oddly, at the peak of Owen's diatribe against the Dominion of FAITH, his prose slips into the ancient, ecclesiastical phrasing of millenarian prophecy. As his enthusiasm swells, his syntax shifts. "Even now, the time is near at hand when swords shall be turned into ploughshares, and spears into pruning hooks." The neat charts and powdered-wig prose of the British rationalist give way to the vivid allegories of the pulpit. "Then shall the wolf dwell with the lamb; and the leopard shall lie down with the kid; and the calf and the young lion, and fatling together, and a little child shall lead them."

In the penultimate paragraphs of Owen's September letter, King James's *th* suffix begins to sprout like a tail from unsuspecting verbs. "TRUTH," Owen declares, repurposing snatches of Corinthians, "envieth not, vaunteth not itself . . . thinketh no evil; rejoiceth not in iniquity. . . . The marvelous change which all the armies of the earth could not effect through all the ages that have passed has been accomplished by the invincible and irresistible power of TRUTH alone." Capital letters roll down like waters and metaphor like a mighty stream.

The tendency to prematurely declare victory is endemic to utopian tracts. The vision gleams so brightly that the nuts and bolts of actually constructing the new society appear negligible. The insight—"TRUTH alone"—is the real accomplishment. Rebuilding civilization: a trifling afterthought.

Owen concludes in an all-caps trump of jubilee: "THE WORLD APPROVES—AND NONE CAN RESIST. THUS, IN THE FULL-

* This letter includes a postscript in which Owen claims that "no intelligent mind will for a moment suppose from what I have said, that I am an enemy to all religion." Maybe so, but his assault on "existing creeds or faiths, which have deluged the world with blood and rendered it a curse and desolation," is jarringly full-throated for the conservative 1810s. In Owen's blunt characterization, religion is a three-way conspiracy between ignorance, superstition, and hypocrisy. In the decades to come, as Owen debated prominent churchmen with ever-increasing gusto and indelicacy, his flair for blasphemy gradually overshadowed all of his other ideas.

NESS OF TIME, ERE ITS COMMENCEMENT WAS WELL KNOWN, IS THE GREAT WORK ACCOMPLISHED. THE CHANGE HAS COME UPON THE WORLD LIKE A THIEF IN THE NIGHT! NO MAN KNOWS WHENCE IT COMETH, NOR WHITHER IT GOETH!"

While proclaiming this gospel to working people through lectures and leaflets, Owen also lobbied the European power elite. He figured that converting a few heads of state to his theory would be the easiest way to establish the first parallelogram and commence the New Moral World. Owen had a gift for winning the confidence of powerful men.* "Not only men of his own class, but statesmen and princes listened to him approvingly," Engels wrote. Despite the stridency of Owen's harangues about the idiocy of religion and capitalism, he was a charming conversationalist. Emerson, hardly a fan of Owen's ideas, called him "the most amiable, sanguine, and candid of men."

At the 1818 Congress of Aix-la-Chapelle, a gathering of European bigwigs organized to coordinate policy toward the newly dismantled French Empire, Owen moved easily among the crowd, pressing his pamphlets into the palms of aristocrats, statesmen, monarchs, and industrialists.† Only the Russian emperor refused the proffered materials. The czar's ornate costume, Owen recalled, "fitted so tightly to his person, that, having no pockets, he had no place in which he could put so large a packet." (More than any of the other statesmen at the congress, the czar and his family might have benefited from a preview of coming revolutionary attractions.) Owen convinced John Quincy Adams, then serving as ambassador to the United Kingdom, to bring a bundle of pamphlets to President Monroe, the members of his cabinet, and the

---

* He had an even greater gift for *thinking* that he had won their confidence, often mistaking courtesy for agreement. After a thoughtful but fleeting exchange with Jefferson, Owen described the former president as a "friend and warm disciple."

† In an era when information and reputations traveled slowly, personal letters of introduction were precious currency. Owen seldom left a meeting with one important person without securing an introduction to another, more important character.

governors of every state. Owen even sent a bound copy of his writings to Napoleon, then incarcerated on Saint Helena. Owen claimed that, having read about the New Moral World, the jailed emperor vowed that if he were reinstated upon the French throne, he would "do as much for peace as he had previously done in war."

Amazingly, Owen's radical declarations did not cost him all of his powerful friends. When his book *A New View of Society* came out, the critic William Hazlitt marveled at its positive reception in the mainstream press. "Mr. Owen is the first philosopher we ever heard of," Hazlitt wrote in his review of the book, "who recommended himself to the great by telling them disagreeable truths." Hazlitt did not find much to admire in Owen's theories, but he was delighted by the topsy-turvy notion that the poor might not be inherently depraved and the rich might not be inherently virtuous. "Lord Wellington," the critic extrapolated, "might have entered houses, instead of entering kingdoms, by force; the Lord-Chancellor might have been a Jew-broker . . . [and] the Queen (God bless her) might have been an old washer-woman, taking her snuff and gin among her gossips."

Perhaps, the bracingly cynical Hazlitt suggested, the New Moral World is simply too far-fetched to scare anyone. Maybe the powers that be even regard Owen's theory as useful distraction from less decorous brands of revolution. Hazlitt predicted that if the New Moral World were actually to take root, Owen would promptly be "marked as a Jacobin, a leveler, an incendiary."

When at last Owen's genteel respectability began to evaporate, it had less to do with his leveling economics than his unremitting attacks on "priestcraft."

A Place Prepared

In August 1824, a man named Richard Flower turned up in New Lanark with a proposition for Owen. Flower, who lived in a colony of British-born farmers in Illinois, had been sent to Scotland by his neighbor, a sixty-seven-year-old German mystic named George Rapp. Rapp was the leader and prophet of the Harmony Society, a millenarian sect of Germans living in the wilderness of southern Indiana, just across the Wabash River from Richard Flower's community in Illinois.

In 1791, Rapp, a Pietist weaver from the German town of Iptingen, declared himself a prophet of God and announced that the Second Coming was imminent. Like Ann Lee, he preached a return to the communism of the primitive Christian Church and, eventually, celibacy. By the turn of the century, twenty thousand German peasants had pledged faith in his prophecy.

Rapp, a charismatic preacher with a long white beard, interpreted the Napoleonic Wars as evidence of the approaching end times. He claimed that his church, the Harmony Society, represented "the woman clothed with the sun" mentioned in Revelation who "fled into the wilderness, where she hath a place prepared of God." Rapp decided that North America, beyond the reach of the corrupt churches of Europe and the Lutheran establishment that had imprisoned him, was that prophesied wilderness—a vast green antechamber to the reign of heaven on earth.

Between 1803 and 1805, five hundred Rappites settled in the woods north of Pittsburgh. They pooled their wealth, adopted a simple woolen costume, and stopped having sex. Unlike the Shakers, the Rappites did not proselytize to their fellow Americans. Their reluctance to speak English or admit non-Germans helped insulate them from the nation taking shape around them.

In 1814, the Harmony Society abandoned its Pennsylvania colony. Father Rapp led his followers to the western frontier, where they bought thirty thousand acres alongside the Wabash River in Indiana. There they began to build a new settlement. They called it Harmonie. Eight hundred Rappites were soon living in the settlement. Their industries thrived, and they shipped lard, whiskey, fur hats, wool broadcloth, and flour downriver to sell in New Orleans.

Nearly a decade later, in the early 1820s, Father Rapp had a revelation instructing him to move the entire community back to Pennsylvania. One reason for the move may have been that the community was too far from the markets in which the Rappites sold their popular products. Rapp may also have sensed that periodically uprooting his followers would keep them together.

Having decided to move back east, Rapp commissioned Richard Flower to find a buyer for the Indiana village. Flower went directly to New Lanark.

His timing was perfect. Seven years had passed since Owen announced the dawning of the secular millennium. Although the world remained unperfected, the intervening years had done little to dampen his enthusiasm. At the same time, Owen had begun to feel the limitations of his Scottish social laboratory. Despite New Lanark's patina of progressive reform, the mill's twenty-five hundred workers—however well educated and well housed—were still engaged in a capitalist enterprise. It was hardly the right place to eradicate the "old competitive system." Owen had also wearied of continually persuading his investors to sign off on his reforms. Even some of the philanthropic Quakers who supported him had withdrawn their funds because Owen refused to offer any sort of religious instruction and because he encouraged dancing in his school. With $250,000 burning a hole in his waistcoat, Owen wanted what any utopian wants: a staging ground equal to his vision.

He was already well aware of the Harmony Society and their settlement in Indiana. Several of his newsletters and pamphlets mentioned the sect alongside the Shakers as living evidence of communism's capacity to produce abundance. Owen had even written to Father Rapp requesting details about the community's economic arrangements.

Flower offered Owen a bargain. For $150,000, he could buy the entire village of Harmonie, including twenty thousand acres of farmland, a herd of cattle, a flock of sheep, an orchard, a brewery, a dye works, a vineyard, a ropewalk, assorted farm equipment, and nearly two hundred buildings, including several large dormitories and two churches. Owen knew he could never come close to building a parallelogram for that price in the United Kingdom.

For Owen, as for other European utopians, the North American continent was more of an idea than a physical location—simultaneously a garden of primitive innocence and the land of the future. He believed it was destined to be "the cradle of the future liberty of the human race." Despite his hostility to organized religion, Owen sensed the hand of providence in Flower's proposal. "Here it is," he wrote,

> . . . in the heart of the United States and almost in the centre of its unequalled internal navigation, that Power which directs and governs the universe and every action of man, has arranged . . . to permit me to commence a new empire of peace and good will to men, founded on other principles and leading to other prac-tices than those of present or past, and which principles, in due season, and in the allotted time, will lead to that state of virtue, intelligence, enjoyment, and happiness which has been foretold by the sages of past. . . .

Fired up, Owen made haste. In September 1824, a month after meeting Flower, he and William sailed west from Liverpool. After five weeks at sea and one week in New York City, they were touring Water-vliet. Less than a month after that, Owen and William arrived by steam-boat at Harmonie, where they were hosted by Frederick Rapp, Father Rapp's adopted son and right hand.

Glad Tidings

The second day of 1825 was cold and clear in southern Indiana. Rob-ert and William Owen spent the morning listening to Frederick Rapp preach the coming millennium to those Rappites who had not yet de-parted for Pennsylvania. Afterward, father and son strolled along the Wabash. The river—quick, wide, and muddy—hugged the western edge of Harmonie. Sandy bluffs rose steeply from the water, leveling off onto the prairie, where thick stands of oak, walnut, sassafras, and beech stood leafless amid the rolling grassland.

From the top of a low, conical hill, Owen and his son surveyed the village. It was laid out in a neat grid of log shacks, two-story frame houses, mills, and large apartment buildings made of brick. In the center of town was the mansion in which Father Rapp had lived. There were also two large churches, one white clapboard, the other a redbrick, cross-shaped building, the design for which had come to Father Rapp in a dream. In between the homes were gardens, chicken coops, and workshops for the production of hats, shoes, pottery, bricks, and textiles. The Rappites had planted orchards of apple, cherry, peach, and pear. On the gentle slopes beyond the village they had planted wine grapes, with vines brought from South Africa. Rapp's followers seldom drank, but they had also built a brewery and a distillery to produce beer and whiskey for sale. Near the center of the village was a hedge maze of beech shrubs radiating outward from a small, rustic meditation hut—a symbol of the soul's winding journey toward salvation.

Looking down upon all of this, Owen saw the faint outline of the paradise he was about to build. "We contemplated with pleasure," William wrote in his diary that evening, "the prospect of seeing a large number of friends and associates winding around [the base of the hill], accompanied by bands of music, and raising their voices in joyful shouts or in melodious strains."

The next morning, Owen sat down with Frederick Rapp and signed the deed for the village of Harmonie. That same day he left, boarding a keelboat for the East. William stayed behind to hash out the details of the purchase.

In Pittsburgh and Philadelphia, Owen addressed large public meetings, triumphantly declaring the inauguration of the New Moral World in a place he now called New Harmony. No arrangements had been made to admit members, but Owen issued a blanket invitation to "the industrious and well disposed of all nations." He did not mention how people ought to measure their own industry or disposition.

Owen should have been the perfect man to lead the charge into utopia. For a quarter century his mill had churned out top-quality cloth, steady profits, exemplary employees, and well-schooled youngsters. By all accounts, he was a man who could make the trains run on time. His tenure in New Lanark had also made him very rich. Among the utopian visionaries of the nineteenth century, only Owen could personally bankroll the construction and early operations of his colony. Yet, while he had spent almost a decade writing about parallelograms and "villages of cooperation," Owen still hadn't hammered out the details for how his community would actually operate. Utopians are typically faulted for excessive specificity—for planning every detail without regard for the shifting contingency of all human endeavors. Owen had the opposite problem. The New Moral World was to be built upon a sturdy foundation of capital-letter virtues—Reason, Cooperation, Education, Equality—but it lacked any actual blueprints. When Owen flung open the gates of his utopia in 1824, many basic questions had not been asked, let alone answered. What exactly would be the relationship between the founder's bank account and the community? Was Owen to be a landlord or a benefactor? Would people pay to join? Would there be work requirements? Free housing? Would members put their property into common stock? Would they earn a salary for their work? Most important, what would be the criteria for admission? Who would the New Harmonites be?

A month after buying the village, Owen arrived in Washington, D.C., with an ambitious agenda: to convert the federal government of the United States to socialism. The capital gave him a grand welcome. President-elect John Quincy Adams hosted Owen for dinner. Outgoing president James Monroe introduced him to his cabinet and offered letters of introduction to Jefferson and Madison, both of whom Owen would soon visit at their respective homes. At a meeting at the Dennison Hotel, Owen explained his theory of character formation and cooperative living to a gathering of Choctaw and Chickasaw chiefs.

To satisfy local curiosity, Speaker of the House Henry Clay arranged for Owen to address members of the government in the Capitol Building's Hall of Representatives. It was a major event. On the evening of February 25, Owen spoke for three hours to an audience that included President Monroe, his cabinet, President-elect Adams, and members of the House of Representatives, the Senate, and the Supreme Court. Ten days later, Owen gave a second speech in the same place to most of the same people. Adams, who was inaugurated between the two speeches, returned to the Capitol on his third day in office for Owen's second address. Even outgoing president James Monroe came for both speeches.

Combined, these speeches offer a complete articulation of what Owen hoped to accomplish in the United States. He began with typical immodesty, informing his audience that his arrival in their country represented a turning point for the fifty-year-old Republic and the human race in general. "Changes [are] at hand greater than all the changes which have hitherto occurred in the affairs of mankind."

He explained that he had come to the United States to eradicate every social evil. He would accomplish this great work by gathering Americans into "communities of cooperation." The United States, Owen claimed, was the ideal starting place for the new social system because the Republic's youth protected its people and institutions from the inertia and moral rot infecting old Europe. Owen explained that genuine progress will remain impossible as long as the profit motive— "the degrading and pernicious practice of buying cheap and selling dear"—remains at the core of social relations. He held up the prosperity of the Shaker Zion as local evidence for the "the gigantic superiority of union over division, for the creation of wealth."

Owen explained his belief that the United States had won its "political liberty" but had not yet secured its "mental liberty." By following his lead, the government of the United States can "give and secure liberty, affluence, and happiness, to America and to the world." Owen invited the assembled lawmakers to "manfully and promptly step forward, and place themselves in the gap between the present and the future, and from this Capitol . . . say to the world, 'Now shall the government of force, and fraud, and disunion cease, and henceforth, truth, and sincerity, and charity, and kindness, and union, shall take their place, and superstition, and prejudice shall no longer have domin- ion here.'"

The approaching anniversary of the Revolution and the changing of the guard in the White House that took place between Owen's two speeches lent some credence to this impression of a turn toward the future. James Monroe left office as the final Founder to serve as presi- dent. The ascent of Adams, son of the Republic's second president (and the first president inaugurated in pants rather than breeches), repre- sented the start of a new, future-facing age.

Overestimating the liberality of his audience, Owen threw a few sharp jabs at the "unmeaning phrases, forms, and ceremonies" of reli- gion, which have divvied up the brotherhood of man and made the world "a chaotic scene of confusion, disorder, and misery."*

Despite this impiety, Owen's remarks were met with enthusiasm. Full transcripts of both lectures were printed in the *National Intelligencer,* and prominent papers carried favorable reviews. The two speeches probably represent the first and last time that multiple American presi- dents, members of their cabinets, senators, congressmen, and justices of the Supreme Court sat together to learn about the folly of revealed religion and the wonders of communism. The fact that Owen's ideas were given a civil hearing suggests that in 1825, American capitalism had not yet secured its position as a sacrosanct national ideology. His ideas might have struck many legislatures as foolish, but nobody screamed heresy.

One reason Owen continuously got away with such inflammatory statements was that his affable manner of speaking contrasted starkly with the substance of what he said. After hearing him lecture in Cincin- nati, Frances Trollope noted how his disposition took the edge off his heresies: "The gentle tone of his voice; his mild, sometimes playful, but

---

* To preempt charges of blasphemy, Owen made the peculiar claim that his ideas constituted a "rational religion" and were thus protected by the First Amendment, as if only religious ideas were constitutionally protected or conservative umbrage re- quired legal sanction.

never ironical manner; the absence of every vehement or harsh expression; the affectionate interest expressed for 'the whole human family,' the air of candor with which he expressed his wish to be convinced he was wrong, if he indeed were so—his kind smile—the mild expression of his eyes—in short, his whole manner, disarmed zeal, and produced a degree of tolerance that those who did not hear him would hardly believe possible."

New Jerusalem

During Owen's second speech in the Capitol, he unveiled a large architectural rendering of the enormous "parallelogram" he intended to build in Indiana. The drawing, done by English architect Thomas Stedman Whitwell, depicts a building the size of a small town, laid out as an open rectangle, with accommodations for twenty thousand people. Owen explained that each of the four sides would be a thousand feet long and three stories high and would contain "every domestic arrange-

The parallelogram: Robert Owen's man-made New Jerusalem, drawn by architect Thomas Stedman Whitwell, 1825.

Library of Congress Prints and Photographs Division (LC-USZ62-55096)

ment that can be required for 5,000 people": chapels, laboratories, lecture halls, and ballrooms. The first two floors of the parallelogram would be made up of apartments for married couples. The top floor would house singles and children over the age of two. Inside of the immense quadrangle formed by this apartment complex, there would be four freestanding buildings, each containing dining rooms, laundries, and breweries for the people living on each of the parallelogram's four sides. Those inner buildings would also contain schools in which public education from infancy through university would be provided for free. This entire structure—"the future habitation of the human race"—would be designed and built by "men of great science and practical experience."

Owen announced that he would build the first parallelogram in Indiana, near the village he had just purchased. When it was finished, he would build others, with each one situated on a rural estate of two thousand acres or more. By placing these structures in the hinterland, Owen intended to combine the best of town and country, agriculture and industry. The citizens of each parallelogram will grow their own food and manufacture their own goods in state-of-the-art factories. The surrounding land will be "cultivated like a garden, and laid out as a pleasure grounds." By living together in a single building, working people will enjoy the "scientific domestic arrangements" typically reserved for the rich: hot and cold running water, central heating, gaslights, industrial kitchens, and high-tech laundries. In an era mad for mechanization, Owen described this engineer-built New Jerusalem as "a new machine for performing, in a superior manner, all the purposes of human life." His conception of the millennium as the endless reduplication of a single prototype utopia further reflects the logic of industrial manufacturing.*

---

* Late in 1825, Owen brought a six-foot-square model of a parallelogram from the United Kingdom. President Adams, whose millenarian outlook bore a passing, if much diluted, resemblance to Owen's, displayed it for the public in the White House.

Horn of Plenty

While Owen traveled through the East proclaiming the dawning millennium, New Harmony was left to the care of twenty-three-year-old
William Owen. The old Rappite village was soon inundated with people answering Owen's broad summons. Freethinkers, atheists, and committed socialists came with their arms full of Owenite literature. So did
families of frontier Methodists and young, single laborers expecting to
find salaried work. (What other kind of work was there on someone
else's land?) Some of those who came were passionately determined to
help build the new egalitarian world. Others were hoping for an inexpensive summer lark. Like the "bread-and-butter Shakers" who drifted
in and out of the United Society, hard-up westerners came to New
Harmony seeking refuge from an uncertain economy. By the time
Owen returned to the community in April, four months after his departure, eight hundred people were waiting for him.

By then, some collective labor was already under way. A group of
hatters had found one another and begun making hats. Seventeen men
were at work in the boot and shoe shop. The chandlery was producing
plenty of candles. At the ropewalk running through the village orchard,
rope was being twisted from the community's own hemp and flax. In
the apothecary shop, an Owenite physician was dispensing free health
care with supplies paid for by Owen. And since eight hundred people
must eat, cooks, bakers, and butchers were busy preparing huge communal meals.

Packed though it was, New Harmony lacked the skilled artisans and
farmers required to truly get its workshops and farm under way. Urban
intellectuals were drawn by Owen's idealism and the possibility of asserting, for all the world to see, the capacity to create a more cooperative social order. Unskilled laborers, many of whom shared this
aspiration, were drawn by the promise of shelter and board. Artisans
and mechanics, however, the people most needed to get the communi-

ty's moneymaking enterprises running, had the least incentive to join. While their talents and tools could earn them a moderate living elsewhere, they lacked the financial security to leave home on an idealistic adventure. Owen returned to find the Rappite-built mills silent and the pottery shed empty. While the colony was underwritten by the finest textile operation in the United Kingdom, its extensive spinning, weaving, and dyeing works were gathering dust.

A shortage of housing quickly became the community's chief complaint. In its first incarnation, Harmonie had housed nearly one thousand Rappites. By the first spring of Owen's experiment, the village was on track to exceed that number. Rather than laying foundations for the parallelogram, carpenters and masons got busy retrofitting attics and disused log cabins into livable apartments.

Of course, as far as Owen was concerned, those structures were temporary. He had already picked out a nice flat plot for the parallelogram a few miles from the center of the village, on a high, grassy bluff overlooking the Wabash. A team of men was already firing bricks for the grand building.

Owen was remarkably sanguine about the amount of labor that would be required to build one of the world's largest structures. He believed that productivity would increase exponentially once labor relations were properly organized and technology was yoked to the common weal. Although the New Moral World was conceived in opposition to the inhuman conditions of early industrialization, Owen was hopeful about the role that mechanization would play in the coming utopia. "Mechanism and Science," he announced, "will be extensively introduced to execute all the work that is over-laborious, disagreeable, or in any way injurious to human nature." In the Owenite millennium, swords are as likely to be beaten into pistons as plowshares.[*]

---

[*] In 1855, Owen's hopes for a mechanically induced millennium reached even greater heights. At a convention in London devoted to "The Millennial State of Life on Earth and the Means of Speedily Attaining It," he unveiled a painting of a hypothetical "war machine" called the Devastator. It was a six-wheeled, steam-driven armored vehicle with scythes protruding from its sides and a circular battery of

Until then, Owen's plan to increase productivity was simple: collec-tivize everything. Like other utopians of his day, he regarded moral and economic calculations as inextricable. He believed that economic competition—the chaotic scrimmage of each against all—wastes not only energy and raw materials, but the humanity of the contestants. Virtuous (that is, cooperative) labor will necessarily be productive labor. Plus, with everyone working—no more idle rich soaking up the wealth generated by the laboring class—each individual's load will be substan-tially lightened. "When the new arrangements shall be regularly orga-nized and completed," Owen predicted, "a few hours daily of healthy and desirable employment, chiefly applied to direct modern mechani-cal and other scientific improvements, will be amply sufficient to create a full supply, at all times, of the best of everything for everyone, and then all things will be valued according to their intrinsic worth, will be used beneficially, and nothing wasted and abused."

While the Shakers looked to the primitive Christian Church as an exemplar of practical communism, secular utopians such as Owen found a model closer to home—namely, in the home. Economically speaking, the average rural family functions very much like a small com-munistic commonwealth. The various members pool their labor and hold their wealth in common. Rather than competing among them-selves for resources, they endeavor to advance their interests as a unit. By divvying up life's essential functions—enacting what, on a larger scale, would be called "a planned economy"—the average family achieves far more than its members could independently. If each family member tended her own garden, kept her own milk cow, earned her own cash, and built her own shelter, life would be very difficult and the quality of each member's material conditions would diminish consider-ably. Making a stew to feed five people is vastly more efficient, in terms

---

rapid-firing cannons. Like early boosters of the atom bomb, Owen hoped the Dev-astator would be so awesomely destructive that it would make combat futile and thus "compel war to cease." Without apparent irony, he dubbed this rolling death wagon "the universal peace maker." The British War Department rejected the design.

of labor, ingredients, and hours, than five people preparing five separate meals.

Like other nineteenth-century utopians, Owen believed that the effects of this wondrous horn of plenty called collectivism would be amplified as it was scaled upward. Making stew for five hundred requires more labor than making stew for five, but nowhere near one hundred times more. By applying this logic to every department of human exertion—laundry, child rearing, planting, building, teaching, butchering, cooking—the utopians hoped to increase productivity and quality until life became exponentially easier, richer, and more comfortable. Some communitarians even feared that collectivism would send productivity too high, corrupting people with abundance and idleness. "So soon as we have over-supplied all our wants and all the wants of our neighbors, we shall begin to starve," worried Owen's eldest son, Robert Dale Owen, "not from famine or failure of crops, or loss of property; no, only because we have too much of everything."

During the spring of 1825, the growing stack of bricks for the parallelogram and the absence of much order in the village gave the community a provisional feeling. As long as the thousand-odd colonists believed that the *real* New Harmony would commence soon, they worked with genial enthusiasm. At least on good days, they took pleasure and sustenance from the belief that their collectivized labor, and therefore their lives, had, as Owen frequently reminded them, great historical importance. They were building an entirely new type of society. And they were doing it together. Like the revolutionary generation before them, the New Harmonites were not merely living in the world, they were remaking it. They performed the same chores as their pioneer neighbors—chopping wood, mending fences, clearing stone—but in doing so, they were also laying siege to the corrupt old order. Mundane tasks became infused with a poetic significance. Washing linens in steaming tin vats is hot, heavy work. Washing those same linens as a means of changing the course of human history and doing so alongside your sisters in the struggle for global regeneration makes for a lighter load. At times, this sense of high purpose was the chief consolation in their difficult life on the frontier.

Even Robert Owen knew that human nature could not be transformed overnight. Sticking to the plan he had formulated in 1817, he announced that some type of intermediate society was required to soften the transition from the old, competitive world into the new, cooperative one. Not long after he returned from the East, Owen presented the community with a constitution for what he called "the Preliminary Society." "The Society is instituted generally," it read, "to promote the happiness of the world and to prepare [the members] to become associated in Independent Communities, having common property."

While the New Harmonites prepared themselves for thoroughgoing communism, they earned their room and board by working on the farm or in various collective enterprises. Whatever they ate at the tavern or took from the community store was debited from personal accounts, which they replenished with cash or with their labor. (Of course, this meant that wealthier communards could exempt themselves from doing manual work.) To get the ball rolling, everyone in the community was given $80 of credit at the store, doled out in weekly installments like an allowance. While some cash circulated within the Preliminary Society, its use was meant to be limited. There was no rent, but everyone had to supply their own furniture, linens, and tools. That, at least, was the theory. In actuality, the bookkeeping was a mess, with debits rapidly outpacing credits and Owen covering the balance from his own pocket.

In June, four weeks after signing the constitution for the Preliminary Society, Owen once again left, traveling east to New York and then sailing to the United Kingdom. Because he intended to spend the foreseeable future at New Harmony, he needed to tie up loose ends in New Lanark and arrange for the passage of the rest of his family to the United States. As it turned out, pious, wellborn Caroline Dale Owen had no interest in leaving her comfortable home in Scotland for a radical atheistic colony in the American wilderness. All four of her sons and one of her three daughters eventually followed their father to Indiana, where each went on to illustrious careers as scientists, reformers, and politicians. Caroline and her other two daughters remained in the United Kingdom. Within seven years, all three women died.

While his father was away, William and a small committee of advisers—appointed by Owen and ratified by a general vote of the community—were left in charge. Deprived of badly needed leadership, the community slipped into disarray. During the spring and summer of 1825, when the citizens of New Harmony ought to have been busy planting, they spent their time sorting out who would sleep where. (They did manage to put in a field of barley, securing beer for the coming winter.) Some of the Rappites' well-fertilized fields went to seed. Fences fell into disrepair. The German citizens of Harmonie had sold their surplus produce to settlers up and down the Wabash. The New Harmonites were forced to buy potatoes, turnips, and cabbages from their neighbors.

The constitution of the Preliminary Society had neglected the most preliminary question of all: Who could join? While the colonists struggled to weld themselves into a community, Owen continued to declare the imminent secular millennium to anyone who would listen. Practically everyone who turned up was granted membership.

This open door policy had one exception: African Americans. In general, the communal utopians of the nineteenth century held significantly more advanced views on race than their white countrymen. Many of them, including Owen and his closest collaborators, campaigned vigorously for an end to slavery.* Yet despite the rhetoric of its

---

* Soon after his triumphal trip to Washington, Owen predicted that by 1827, his system would "extend to the blacks & the Indians who by singular circumstances have been prepared in a peculiar manner for the change which I propose." It is not clear which "singular circumstances" Owen was referring to. Perhaps he meant their familiarity with hard, uncompensated labor and their exclusion from the corrupting forces of American commerce.

founders, New Harmony's first constitution stated that "persons of all ages and descriptions, exclusive of persons of color, may become members of the Preliminary Society." This hypocrisy plainly reveals the bone-deep white supremacy of even the most progressive, antislavery white reformers of the 1820s. For all their talk about the brotherhood of man, most of the citizens of New Harmony did not want to live on equal footing with black people. Nor were they willing to endure the public outrage that an integrated, egalitarian colony would invite. Tellingly, they did not feel compelled to offer any sort of rationalization.

Another, less obvious reason why many nineteenth-century utopians failed to take up the cause of racial justice with more vigor lies in the nature of utopian thinking itself. Many of the communal utopians regarded slavery and racial prejudice, like practically every other social ill, as symptoms of a more fundamental corruption. Some utopian socialists even made the preposterous claim that "wage slavery" in the industrial North was as bad as chattel slavery in the agricultural South. At least slaves, they argued, were fed and clothed.* Rather than root out society's evils one by one, the utopians aimed for a complete overhaul. This is partly what distinguished them from even the most ambitious, non-utopian social reformers of their day. The utopians looked upon every major progressive cause of the century—the fight to end slavery, women's rights, public education, temperance, the peace movement—as palliatives, when what was needed was a cure. The constitution of Mas-

---

* To the shame (presumably) of the communal utopians, George Fitzhugh, a prominent pro-slavery "sociologist" and pseudosocialist from Virginia, quoted Owen and Fourier in his defense of the South's "peculiar institution." Fitzhugh repurposed the utopians' wide-ranging critique of capitalism to argue that the industrial North was in no position to judge the slave states. Fitzhugh claimed that the utopians had gone halfway toward a great truth. Having seen the advance of free market industrialism in western Europe, they understood that the most desirable social system would be one in which intelligent planners controlled economic and social arrangements. Fitzhugh claimed that once the utopians shook off their absurd attachment to ideas of liberty and equality, they would see the glories of the Christian, slave-powered economy, a model that he saw endorsed in the Old Testament.

sachusetts's Brook Farm Phalanx clearly addressed itself to the white abolitionist milieu out of which many of its members came when it stated: "We propose a radical and universal reform rather than to redress any particular wrong, or to remove the sufferings of any single class of human being."

A Boatload of Knowledge

Because Owen believed that technology and education would trigger the New Moral World, he intended to make New Harmony a global capital of scientific research and pedagogical innovation. In November 1825, on his way back to Indiana from New Lanark, he stopped in Philadelphia with that goal foremost in his mind. By then, he had been gone from his community for seven months. During that time, William had repeatedly urged his father to recruit tradesmen to help jump-start the community's industries. Aside from placing a single notice in the Pennsylvania papers advertising for "work people," Owen made no apparent effort to hire artisans or mechanics. Instead, inspired by Francis Bacon's *New Atlantis* (1624), a fictional utopia in which all civic life revolves around a research institute called Saloman's House, he set about recruiting a cadre of artists, educators, and scientists.*

By the time Owen arrived in Philadelphia, his ideas had already circulated widely among that city's intelligentsia. In an era when universities were chiefly theological in orientation, scientific research ("natural philosophy") was conducted mostly in the evenings by gentlemen with butterfly nets and hand-cranked electrostatic machines. Owen's vision of an egalitarian society devoted to scientific inquiry and public, nonparochial education presented an enticing prospect. With surprising ease, Owen rounded up a group of illustrious scientists and educa-

---

* A lithograph Owen printed of his projected parallelogram was captioned "Design of a Community of 2,000 Persons, founded upon the principle, commended by Plato, Lord Bacon, Sir T. More, & R. Owen."

tors who were willing to leave the redbrick comfort of Philadelphia for
the excitement and uncertainty of a muddy frontier settlement.

Exercising his strong instinct for ballyhoo, Owen conveyed the members of this newly acquired brain trust to Pittsburgh, where he loaded
them all onto a specially built, eighty-five-foot keelboat called the *Philanthropist*. Flying a long, thin banner emblazoned with the word *Harmony*, the intellectuals set off down the Ohio River. Owen and the press
called the voyage "the Boatload of Knowledge."

Along with a heavy cargo of books, specimens, and laboratory
equipment, about forty people sailed aboard the *Philanthropist*. Besides
Owen, who disembarked halfway to attend to some business, the most
well-known passenger was William Maclure, a large, redheaded Scots-
man who had earned a fortune as a merchant before moving to the
United States to devote his life to science and educational reform. In
1809, Maclure drew the first geologic survey of the United States. He
was the first president of the American Geological Society and is usually credited as being the father of American geology. When he departed for Indiana, he was also serving as president of the Academy of
Natural Sciences of Philadelphia. It was largely because of his enthusiasm for Owen's ideas that so many other gifted scientists went to New
Harmony.

Like Owen, Maclure took a radical view of American democracy.
He believed that the promise of 1776—genuine, practical liberty—
could be fulfilled only in a society of material equality. Also like Owen,
he regarded secular, mass education as the shortest route to such a society. Along with lending his considerable contacts and reputation to New
Harmony, Maclure pitched in $150,000, a sum sufficient to effectively
make him Owen's partner in ownership of the community. He agreed
to take charge of establishing the New Harmony school.

Other members of the Boatload of Knowledge included Thomas
Say, the first great American entomologist; the French naturalist Charles
Alexandre Lesueur; Robert Dale Owen, Owen's eldest son; a Dutch
geologist; a prominent Swiss educator; a chemist; an ichthyologist; and
various other notable scientists, professors, and artists. In the assessment

of one historian, the southwesterly voyage of the *Philanthropist* was "one of the significant intellectual migrations in history."* The fact that so many well-regarded thinkers followed Owen into the wilderness indicates the high hopes that many intelligent people had for the experiment on the Wabash.

Drifting down the Ohio River, the boat functioned as a floating whistle-stop tour, docking in small towns to drum up enthusiasm for New Harmony. Some people were so impressed that they decided to join the community on the spot. A judge in one Pennsylvania river town sent his ten-year-old son aboard so that the boy could be educated at New Harmony.

Near the town of Beaver, Pennsylvania, the *Philanthropist* was driven ashore by ice. For a full month, the boat was held in place by the frozen river. For some of the passengers, the isolation and unremitting cold were unbearable. A few of the women wept openly at meals. Twenty-four-year-old Robert Dale Owen was thrilled by his first encounter with the American frontier. He spent the month ranging over the countryside, learning to handle a rifle, ice-skating, and setting fire to dead trees. The well-heeled, European-born passengers were excited to encounter genuine American backwoodsmen. For their part, the woodsmen were scandalized to see people hunt on the Sabbath.† The scientists spent the icebound month shooting and stuffing woodpeckers, partridges, doves, and squirrels for the natural history museum they intended to build at New Harmony. In the evenings, they huddled around the stove, playing

---

* Accounts of who exactly sailed aboard the *Philanthropist* vary widely. Much of the confusion stems from the fact that several people disembarked or embarked during the journey. The passenger manifest has tended to swell over the years: "If everybody alleged to have traveled on the boat actually went aboard," one historian noted, "it would have sunk at its moorings in Pittsburgh."

† How people spent their Sundays was a big deal at the time. Some American towns strung chains across their streets to prevent traffic on the Sabbath. Sunday newspapers were often illegal. And a popular novel that depicted a family sailing on a Sunday (even after they had gone to church) was withdrawn amid public outcry. Sabbath breaking would become a major source of friction within some of the more religiously diverse utopian colonies.

whist, discussing what type of costume they should adopt for their new utopian society, and reading aloud from books of French socialist theory.

After a stretch of mild days, the crew cut through enough ice to pole out into open water. On January 24, 1826, the Boatload of Knowledge finally docked at New Harmony. Owen, who had traveled most of the way back to New Harmony overland, beat the *Philanthropist* by a week.

The Community of Equality

With their benefactor and his brainy retinue finally on the scene, the one thousand citizens of New Harmony expected their enterprise to gain some momentum. The day after the *Philanthropist* docked, Owen announced that the community was ready to depart the constitution of the Preliminary Society, in which "a certain degree of pecuniary inequality" had been tolerated, and venture boldly into the high meadows of full-blown communism. Owen had initially predicted that this transition would take three years. Now it was happening in less than one. A constitutional convention sprang to life, and a committee of seven men was elected to draft the new document. Debates were held, amendments made, and a vote called. At the start of February, "the Constitution of the Community of Equality" was unanimously ratified by a vote of the whole community. The sketchy, unbalanced ledgers of the Preliminary Society were closed up and put away.

The Constitution of the Community of Equality was intentionally silent on most specifics; rules and regulations were going to be developed democratically over time. The community's chief purpose, the document stated, was happiness. "Equality of rights, uninfluenced by sex or condition, in all adults," was guaranteed, as were "equality of duties" and "freedom of speech and action." Community of property was now the official rule. Every New Harmonite over twenty-one had an equal vote in all matters and an equal share in the land and its produce. The fact that women now had the same political and economic rights as men was no small matter.

The Community of Equality was officially divided into six departments of labor: education, manufacturing, agriculture, commerce, domestic operations, and "general economy." Workers within each department would elect their own superintendent, and the six superintendents would form an executive council that oversaw all day-to-day operations. With the ratification of the new constitution, the colonists finally established a procedure for admissions. Consent by a simple majority was required to admit a new member. A two-thirds majority was needed to throw someone out. Everyone already living within the densely populated colony was grandfathered in.

New Harmony wasn't just crowded; it was probably the most diverse small town in the United States, except, of course, racially. A notice in the *New Harmony Gazette* from October 1825 reported that the community had members from every country in northern Europe and every state except Florida and Louisiana. In most frontier settlements, civic and intellectual life amounted to little more than a few hours of hellfire on Sundays, the occasional snake-oil show, and a week-old newspaper shared over the local cracker barrel. At New Harmony, every free moment was taken up with social and intellectual diversions. Every Tuesday, there was a community dance in the old Rappite chapel, which had been renamed the Hall of New Harmony. A ring of benches in the middle of the large room demarcated a special dance floor for children. The colonists even invented a few original dance styles, including one called "the New Social System." On Thursday evenings, one of several bands would typically play. Josiah Warren, an accomplished bandleader who went on to become the first prominent American anarchist, conducted the large, brass-heavy New Harmony Orchestra. A group of experienced actors staged frequent plays and recitations. Shakespeare and Byron were special favorites.

The colonists were hardly the oversexed bacchants their critics made them out to be, but the community's diverse population, pervasive sense of social experimentation, and busy social calendar lent New Harmony a general air of maypole jollity. At a time when interactions between unmarried men and women were tightly restricted, the young singles of New Harmony enjoyed a thrilling liberty. They called one another by their first names and chatted casually at dances with people from every socioeconomic background. In the evenings, young people strolled the gardens in pairs. One visitor recalled a moonlit "aquatic party" during which young men and women rowed dinghies through flooded meadows by torchlight. Robert Dale Owen recalled, "There was something especially taking, in the absolute freedom from trammels, alike in expression of opinion, in dress, and in social converse."

Intellectual life was just as busy. Along with the impressive roster of scientists and teachers who had come aboard the *Philanthropist*, New Harmony attracted a steady stream of journalists, social theorists, spiritualists, preachers, and health foodists. Lectures and debates were offered on every imaginable subject. Under the editorship of William Owen, the *New Harmony Gazette* reported on the life of the community and the progress of various progressive causes out in the World. On Sunday mornings, in lieu of church, Robert Owen held forth in the Hall of New Harmony on everything from European history, to advances in steam technology, to the importance of education.

The Priestess of Beelzebub

During these Sunday talks, Owen kept the colonists informed about the spread of the New Moral World beyond their village. His vision of a man-made millennium hinged upon the assumption that a single working model of the new social system—New Harmony—would create "a general desire throughout society to establish others, and that they will rapidly multiply." Paraphrasing Jesus's parable about the Kingdom of Heaven being a mustard seed, Owen predicted that the utopia they were planting by the Wabash would spread "from Community to Community, from State to State, and from Continent to Continent, until this

system and these TRUTHS shall overshadow the whole earth,—
shedding fragrance and abundance, intelligence and happiness, upon
all the sons of men."

For a brief time, that is exactly what seemed to be happening. While
New Harmony took its first, stumbling steps, replicas sprang up elsewhere. During 1825 and 1826, a total of ten Owenite communes were
founded in the United States. Four of them, including New Harmony
and its small nearby satellites, were in Indiana; two were in Ohio; two
were in New York; and there was one each in Tennessee and in Pennsylvania.* Unlike New Harmony, most of these offshoots were small,
underfunded efforts with little direct connection to Owen himself.

The most notable spin-off was established near Memphis in 1825 by
the Scottish feminist and writer Frances Wright. In her twenties, Wright
toured the United States and fell in love with the country. Traveling the
muddy West, she saw nothing less than the birth of a "young Rome."
Back in Europe, she wrote *Views of Society and Manners in America*, a bestselling celebration of the egalitarian virtues of the American Republic.†

In 1824, Wright returned to the United States in the entourage of
General Lafayette during his jubilee tour. She and Lafayette were so
close that they were rumored to be lovers, despite the fact that he was
four decades her senior.‡ Lafayette gave Wright entrée to the best homes
in the United States. She stayed with the Jeffersons at Monticello and
the Madisons in Montpelier. Her interest in communalism led her to
several Shaker villages and the Rappite community in Pennsylvania.

---

* A decade after the collapse of New Harmony, during the communitarian boom of
the 1840s, a second wave of enthusiasm for Owen's ideas gave birth to another nine
loosely Owenite communities in Pennsylvania, Ohio, Indiana, and Wisconsin.
† Wright's breathless passion for all things American—James Fenimore Cooper
called her book "nauseous flattery"—reads as an implicit critique of the fusty, caste-
bound British society in which she was raised.
‡ Annoyed by such rumors, Wright, an orphan, asked Lafayette to adopt her. His
family objected. Rumors of her sleeping with many of the men she worked with,
along with frequent allusions to her "mannish" disposition, clearly stemmed from the
sheer anachronism of a woman moving unaccompanied through the world of men.
Wright's harshest critics on this score were usually women. She charmed Jefferson,
but the ladies of Monticello could not abide her bold manners.

After hearing Owen's speech in Washington, she stepped off the Lafayette caravan to lend her considerable energies to the utopia taking shape by the Wabash.

Wright's sense of the United States as a world-saving beacon of freedom and equality translated into a bitter hatred for slavery. At New Harmony, she struck upon the idea of using Owen's communitarian scheme as a mechanism of emancipation. She bought six hundred acres of virgin woodland on Tennessee's Wolf River, a densely timbered, malarial region recommended to her by Andrew Jackson. (General Jackson had just "cleared" the region of its indigenous residents.) Wright called the place Nashoba, after the Chickasaw word for "wolf."

Nashoba was intended to function as a self-sustaining freedom machine. The colony would purchase slaves, educate them, have them work on a collectivized farm to raise funds to buy more slaves, and then free them. By educating black and white children together, Wright intended to prove their innate equality—an antislavery application of the Owenite axiom that environment determines character.

At Nashoba, women were meant to be equal to men; religion was sparse; white and black children were schooled side by side; and a liberal sexuality was embraced. In a letter to her friend the novelist Mary Shelley, Wright explained that the community was "an establishment where affection shall form the only marriage, kind feeling and kind action the only religion, respect for the feeling and liberties of others the only restraint, and union of interest the bond of peace and security."

In actuality, the Nashoba Community was a disaster. Labor was badly disorganized and the land was unyielding. Crops failed and illness was widespread. Like Owen, Wright was often absent from a community in need of strong leadership. In the spring of 1827, after suffering a nearly deadly bout of malaria, she returned to Europe to recuperate. During her absence, a feckless medical student named James Richardson was left in charge. Wright returned in 1828 with Frances Trollope, a woman whose published impressions of the "American character" were as grim as Wright's were rosy. The two women found the community in total disarray. Richardson had conducted a love affair with a former slave named Mam'selle Josephine and recorded the details in the community journal. When the journal was published, a predictable uproar ensued. With Nashoba falling apart and beset by scandal, Wright returned to New Harmony to help William Owen edit the *New Harmony Gazette*, which for a time was called the *New Harmony and Nashoba Gazette*. (Incidentally, this made her the first female newspaper editor in the United States.)

In Wright's continued absence, Nashoba was not much better than any other poor southern plantation, with the black colonists more or less forced to labor by their white "benefactors." Wright gave up on the community and deeded the property to a group of trustees that included Owen, an atheist "preacher" named Robert Jennings, the geologist William Maclure, Robert Dale Owen, a former Shaker named Richesson Whitby, and General Lafayette. Wright eventually paid for a contingent of Nashoba's African American residents to move to free Haiti. She also set aside a large financial bequest as "a perpetual trust for the benefit of the negro race." The money was spent mostly on the operation of a school for the children still living on the site of the commune.

During its brief existence (1825–1828), the Nashoba Community embraced every single American bugaboo of the day: communism, atheism, feminism, abolitionism, free love, divorce, and interracial sex. The women were even reported to wear pants. Wright's talent for inflaming conservative sensibilities was remarkable. More than anything she said or wrote, however, it was her gender that sent her antagonists raving. In the assessment of one fairly typical critic, she had "unsexed herself and become so intoxicated with vanity, as enthusiastically to preach up a 'reformation' in favor of promiscuous intercourse of sexes and colours, the downfall of all religion, and the removal of all restraints imposed by virtue and morality!" The press called her "the priestess of Beelzebub." For a time, antebellum conservatives used "Fanny Wrightism" as a handy synecdoche for all things progressive and loathsome.

Ere Long

Meanwhile at New Harmony, the Community of Equality ran aground. Just two weeks after the colonists established full communism and full adult suffrage, they began to waver. Once the fanfare surrounding Owen's return and the drafting of the Constitution of the Community of Equality subsided, people noticed a fact that had been there all along: the community was losing money. New Harmony had operated for a year without settling on a single system for tracking debits and credits. The colonists were stuck in an untenable middle position between full communism, in which labor and compensation were fully disconnected, and a system of joint-stock ownership and profit sharing. Instead of producing the abundance they had anticipated, the community was hemorrhaging cash, most of it Owen's.

They gathered to discuss the situation and decided that Owen should retake the reins, at least until the bookkeeping could be sorted out. A resolution overturning the brand-new constitution was passed. Owen and a committee of his choosing assumed responsibility for the practical administration of the community. The economic effect of this shake-up was that Owen and his fortune were officially on the hook for everything. "He would be responsible," the new resolution stated, "for the loss if any, and to keep the gain if any." Even the most hopeful communards must have begun to doubt whether New Harmony would produce a gain anytime soon.

Even as Owen's savings rapidly drained into the community, skeptics among the rank and file began to wonder if they were being conned. Lots of labor was happening, but nobody was getting paid. The most cynical colonists suspected that the whole enterprise was a scam, set up by "aspiring aristocratical spirits" to dupe hardworking idealists out of their labor. To some, the fact that New Harmony attempted any sort of bookkeeping evidenced Owen's hypocrisy. If the plan was to abolish private property, why keep track of who owed what? Why didn't Owen just turn over all of his property?

Paul Brown, a footloose young communist from the East, heckled Owen in the Hall of New Harmony and groused about the constant concerts and balls—pastimes that, in Brown's estimation, wasted expensive candles and bred an "aversion to serious duties." Even though Owen lived modestly above the New Harmony tavern while subsidizing the food and shelter of one thousand, Brown accused the community's founder of drinking more than his share of coffee. Brown, a living parody of sullen radicalism, later wrote that life within the community had been "unbearable" for him because of the constant noise of children's laughter.

If nothing else, the fact that a firebrand such as Paul Brown was granted space in which to deliver his harangues—both in the main hall and in the pages of the community paper—certifies the genuine freedom of expression that prevailed within the community. The *Gazette*, which was published by Owen and edited by his son, printed thirty of Brown's editorials.

Paul Brown's was one of the louder, more divisive voices amid what Owen proudly called the "Babel-like confusion" of New Harmony. Owen was convinced that distinctions of class and denomination would eventually dissolve in the face of equality and abundance. "Ere long," he had prophesied in 1817, "there shall be but one action, one language, and one people." Instead, under the pressure of an uncertain future, the overcrowded colony's mix of radicals, scientists, affluent urbanites, and pious western farmers began to splinter along predictable lines.

In April 1826, Prince Bernhard of Saxe-Weimar Eisenach came to New Harmony. Unlike most visitors, the celebrated hero of Waterloo had no particular enthusiasm for the community's utopian ambitions, believing that collectivism inevitably attracted "lazy worthless persons, from all parts of the world." At New Harmony, the prince's sympathies were reserved entirely for what he called the "ladies and gentlemen of quality." He was dismayed, for instance, to see that a gentleman scientist such as Thomas Say had developed calluses from "the unusual labor" he was obliged to perform in the community garden. After speaking with some of the wealthier communards, the prince claimed that "in spite of the principles of equality which they recognize, it shocks the feelings of people of education, to live on the same footing with everyone indiscriminately, and eat with them at the same table."[*]

At the weekly community dances, partners were sometimes chosen by lot.[†] Marie Fretageot, a French educator who arrived aboard the *Philanthropist*, took it upon herself to shelter the community's "delicately brought up" young women from the "tatterdemalions" and "democratic dancers" who might have the nerve to request a waltz. Naturally, Prince Bernhard approved. He recalled the saga of one of those young ladies, a Philadelphian named Virginia, who was brought almost to tears when her pianoforte practice was cut short by her assigned shift in the dairy. (The cows evidently shared her displeasure. To protest the amateur tuggings of their highborn milkmaid, one stepped on her foot and another slapped her face with a muddy tail.)

While Ms. Virginia had come to New Harmony in flight from an "unhappy attachment," most of the wealthier colonists were drawn by a sincere commitment to Owen's rhetoric of equality. As a consequence, their frustrations with communal living conflicted awkwardly with their stated ideals. In a letter to a friend back home, Sarah Pears, the wife of a wealthy Pittsburgh trader who had come to New Harmony with her husband and seven children, wrote: "No one is to be favored above the rest as all are to be in a state of perfect equality. Oh, if you could see some of the rough uncouth creatures here, I think you would find it

---

[*] Even the most idealistic upper-class Europeans were startled by the egalitarian American dinner table, and not just at utopian colonies. En route to Nashoba, Frances Trollope was startled when her servant was seated "very nearly opposite [her]" at a small Tennessee hotel. During his first week in the United States, William Owen noted in his diary that "all the Americans seem to consider themselves your equal (the tavern keeper often mixing in conversation)."

[†] This system may have had its origins in Owen's own childhood. Owen, noted Edmund Wilson, "was to look back all his life on a dancing school to which he had been sent as a child and where he had seen the disappointment of little girls who had not been able to get partners, as a veritable place of torment."

rather hard to look upon them exactly in the light of brothers and sisters. I am sure that I cannot in sincerity look upon these as my equals and that if I must appear to do it, I cannot either act or speak the truth."

Mocking Owen's dream of a classless society, outside critics had fun with the New Harmonites' pursuit of "perfect equality" and Owen's mechanistic theory of "character formation." "Some of the married women had prettier children than others—and this was a source of inequality," read one satirical report. "Some were without children at all, and sorely envied their more happy next door neighbors, whose pretty little curly-pated machines were playing themselves into perfectibility on the lawn before their doors. . . . [Owen] had serious thoughts of cutting off all the women's noses, to bring them to a level."

Distinctions of faith proved even more persistent than distinctions of class. While Owen is often identified as an atheist, his writings make frequent reference to a Creator or Supreme Power. His quarrel was with sectarianism, what he called the "geographical insanities" of organized religion.* Owen was confident that sustained exposure to the light of Reason would cause such superstitions to "gradually and imperceptibly die away." In the meantime, the Constitution of the Community of Equality had guaranteed everyone's right to "every facility for exercising those practices of religious worship which they may prefer." The two large churches built by the Rappites were in constant use by preachers representing the usual broad palette of American Protestantism and a handful of more obscure faiths. On any given Sunday, a New Harmonite could hear the gospel from a Baptist, a Methodist, a Unitarian, a New Light evangelist, a visiting Shaker, or a Swedenborgian.

The community's utopian intentions and its founder's reputation also attracted a large number of atheists and what were then called "freethinkers." Robert Jennings, a former Universalist minister from

---

* The theory of "character formation" also put Owen at odds with the concept of original sin and the idea that each person is morally responsible for his or her behavior.

Philadelphia who had reinvented himself as a preacher of "natural religion," gave regular public lectures against "the dominion of faith."
The day after a well-attended sermon by a famous Baptist, Jennings
took the pulpit of the old Rappite church to offer a long, erudite rebut-
tal.* Although Jennings did not name the Baptist, the previous evening's
sermon was clearly his subject. According to one observer, the Baptist
was thoroughly "out-preached." After leaving New Harmony, the minister wrote a harsh indictment of Owenism for the *Pittsburgh Mercury,*
helping to cement the colony's growing reputation as a den of infidelity.

Exaggerated tales about the colony of blasphemers filled conservative and religious papers. The *Philadelphia Gazette* even denounced New
Harmony in rhyming verse, offering their readership an oddly Seussian
dose of brimstone. The poem, published in January 1826, describes
Satan emerging from a hole in the North Pole, mounting an ice floe,
spreading his wings to form a sail, and cruising south toward Indiana.

He had heard that a number of people were going
To live on the Wabash with great Mr. Owen:
He said to himself, "I must now have a care,
Circumstances require that myself should be there.

I know that these persons think they are impelled,
And by power of circumstances all men are held, . . .

Since Adam first fell by my powerful hand,
I have wandered for victims through every known land,
But in all my migrations ne'er hit on a plan
That would give me the rule so completely o'er man. . . .

Inquisitions I've founded, make kings my lies swallow,
But this plan of free living beats all my schemes hollow."

---

* Jennings left the community in 1826 and cofounded the Franklin Community, a
short-lived Owenite colony in Rockland County, New York.

Thrilled by what he discovers at New Harmony, Satan hurries back
to the North Pole. In preparation for a stampede of damned Owenites,
he orders his imps to "widen the hole!"* Such shrill attacks on Owen's
well-meaning, overwhelmingly Christian community only reinforced
his long held belief that religion was the most divisive force in society.

Splintering

When the third constitution was ratified—the one granting Owen authority to get New Harmony onto a sound financial footing—some of
the fissures that had been spreading through the community came to
the surface.

During the winter of 1826, a faction of about one hundred Methodists decided to break off from the colony to start their own community.
They were weary of Owen's antireligious talk, and they thought they
could do better on their own. To avoid a prolonged conflict, Owen
leased them a large tract two miles north of the main village. They built
nine cabins and began farming collectively. They called their settlement
Macluria, in honor of William Maclure. (Evidently they did not realize
that Maclure shared Owen's low opinion of organized religion.) Since
the Maclurians did not have any major doctrinal problem with what
was being attempted at New Harmony, their new constitution was almost identical to the one they had left behind, although they did withdraw female suffrage.

A month after the Maclurians left, a group of British-born farmers
who were frustrated with the agricultural incompetence of their fellow
colonists did the same. Again, Owen offered a generous severance: four-

---

* In the poem, Satan emerges from the hole, "Discovered by Symmes at the freezing
North Pole." This is a reference to a theory propagated by an American army captain named John Cleves Symmes, Jr. In 1818, Symmes published a pamphlet and
gave a series of well-attended lectures on his belief that the inside of the earth was
hollow and inhabitable. Symmes claimed that there was a hole at each pole through
which the planet's spacious interior could be accessed. Many took the idea seriously.

teen hundred acres of fertile prairie. The farmers christened their breakaway community Feiba Peveli. This peculiar name derives from a "rational system of nomenclature" invented by Thomas Stedman Whitwell, the British architect who did the sketches of Owen's parallelogram. Under Whitwell's scheme, lines of latitude and longitude are associated with certain letters of the alphabet, so that a place's name encodes its geographic coordinates. The results tend toward the tongue-twisting. New York City becomes Otke Notive; London is Lafa Vovutu; and New Harmony is Ipba Veinul.*

Neither the Maclurians nor the Feiba Pevelians repudiated Owen's basic vision. They simply intended to conduct the same experiment with a smaller, more homogeneous population. Owen, who was incapable of accepting bad news, chose to interpret the departures as the further propagation of the New Moral World. He described Macluria and Feiba Peveli as satellites of New Harmony and referred to them as Community Two and Community Three, respectively.[†]

Perhaps the most disruptive faction of dissidents was a group of young intellectuals who were referred to as "the Literati." The members of this informal group, including both William and Robert Dale Owen, were so devoted to New Harmony's founding mission of total equality and utopian transformation that they grew impatient with the watered-down idealism of their fellow colonists. To assert their egalitarian feelings, the Literati dressed in the utopian costume first conceived

---

* Many utopian-minded reformers have instituted hyperrational schemes of measurement and nomenclature. The savants of the French Revolution, for instance, replaced a hodgepodge of archaic weights and measures with the metric system's handy groups of ten. Not surprisingly, the Shakers were early metric enthusiasts. John Quincy Adams even identified the system's adoption as a sign of the coming millennium. The utopian effort to symbolically restart history has also led to various calendrical innovations. The Khmer Rouge and the French Jacobins both instituted calendars that situated their revolutions at "year zero." For a time, the *New Harmony Gazette* used "First Year of Mental Independence" in its datelines.

† At least one spin-off community *was* a direct and diametric response to Owenite communism. Modern Times, an anarchist colony founded on Long Island by New Harmony's former bandleader, Josiah Warren, was formed to promote a doctrine of radical "individual sovereignty."

aboard the *Philanthropist*. The women wore knee-length dresses tied at the waist with a sash over loose trousers that tapered at the ankle. The men dressed in loose white pantaloons, a collarless shirt, and a small collarless coat. One colonist observed that the men's costume, baggy all over and cinched at the waist by a wide belt, tended to make a wide man look like "a featherbed tied in the middle." Adopted by diehards such as Frances Wright and the Owen boys, the costume designed as the raiment of the new fraternal order became a semaphore of aristocracy.

The Maclurians and Feiba Pevelians started their breakaway communities from the ground up. In the process, they drew off some of New Harmony's most energetic and competent farmers. By contrast, the Literati sought to take over a central portion of the main village and to exclude those members with lackluster enthusiasm. In doing so, they were attempting to remedy the community's founding error: Owen's commitment-blind admissions policy. By operating at the center of New Harmony, they hoped that their example would revitalize the drifting, unwieldy utopia. In other words, they intended to reform New Harmony in precisely the way that New Harmony was meant to reform the world. To some, however, this looked like nothing less than an upper-class coup. Rather than surrender the heart of the village, Owen offered the Literati a rough section of nearby woodland. Realizing that they would have to break virgin ground—felling trees, clearing stone, turning thick prairie sod—the young enthusiasts relented.*

A Hydra of Evils

The nationwide jubilee that began with the second coming of General Lafayette reached its zenith on July 4, 1826, the fiftieth anniversary of the adoption of the Declaration of Independence by the Continental Con-

---

* The tendency of zealous youths to demand a purifying return to first principles became almost a perennial disturbance at the small American utopias.

gress.* At New Harmony, while a heavy summer rain fell on the Wabash valley, everyone gathered in the community hall to hear Owen deliver a long holiday oration titled "A Declaration of Mental Independence." Even by Owen's usual incendiary standards, it was a barn burner.

Standing before the entire community, Owen began with a few words about the world historical importance of the speech he was about to deliver: "This event is likely to prove . . . as important as any which has occurred in ancient or modern times." In deference to the holiday, he then praised the success of the American Revolution, "when the inhabitants of the new world attained the power to withdraw from the control of the old world." But, Owen claimed, the American Revolution was incomplete. The founding generation may have secured "political liberty," but the "prejudices" of their day prevented them from bringing their struggle to its logical end point—namely, overturning "the arts and mysteries by which the few have so long held a pernicious, despotic sway and control over the many."

Humanity remains enslaved, Owen declared, by "a trinity of the most monstrous evils that could be combined to inflict mental and physical evil upon [the] whole race." The first of these evils is private property, which sets people against one another, causing "the industrious [to experience] privations and the idle [to be] overwhelmed and injured by wealth." The second monstrous evil is organized religion, which keeps "the world in continual wars, and massacres" and turns man into a "superstitious idiot," afraid of "nonentities created solely by his own disordered imagination." The final evil in Owen's unholy trinity is the institution of marriage, which he described as an alloy of religion and property, intended to enslave women, cement class distinctions, and concentrate wealth among the few.† "The revolution . . . to be now effected," Owen declared, "is the destruction of this hydra of evils."

---

* It was also the day on which both Thomas Jefferson and John Adams, the intellectual rivals of the American Revolution, died in their respective beds.
† In a speculative aside, Owen posited that it is "almost certain" that marriage was cooked up by the same jerks who invented private property and organized religion. It was designed, he explained, to create and defend aristocracy and to "keep their

Throughout his speech, Owen repeatedly implied that words, specifically his words, will be sufficient to destroy the property/faith/matrimony hydra. "I have calmly and deliberately determined . . . to break asunder the remaining mental bonds which for so many ages have grievously afflicted our nature, and, by doing so, to give forever FULL FREEDOM OF THE HUMAN MIND." Simply by saying the unsayable and thereby unleashing the power of a new truth, Owen claimed that he had secured humanity's liberation "beyond the power of recall." A later generation of American utopians would describe this vision of mental revolution as a "shift in consciousness."

In 1630, preaching belowdecks on the flagship *Arbella,* John Winthrop famously paraphrased the Sermon on the Mount to exhort his flock of seasick Puritans to make themselves "a City upon a Hill" in the New World. Two centuries later, Owen summoned the same logic and the same metaphor: "This light is now set upon a hill, for it will increase daily, more and more, until it shall be seen, felt, and understood, by all the nations of the earth." For both Owen and Winthrop, the point of placing their respective cities upon a hill was not that the hilltop is a nice place to live; the point was that the hilltop can be seen from the surrounding lowlands. As Winthrop told the Massachusetts-bound Pilgrims, "The eyes of all people are upon us."

If the American public had taken their eyes off Owen's small city in Indiana, the widely circulated "Declaration of Mental Independence" recaptured their attention. The force of Owen's blasphemy and the boldness with which he co-opted a quasi-sacred day of national remembrance shocked people. Alongside Owen's well-known antipathy toward religion and capitalism, his new critique of matrimony added a lurid undertone to the public perception of New Harmony. Less than two years earlier, Owen had been the honored guest of four presidents.

---

children apart from the multitude." Owen allowed that a just marriage is theoretically possible, but he said that it is exceptionally rare and that it requires a man and woman to come together as complete equals, "solely with a view to their happiness."

Now, in 1826, his colony was routinely described as a "brothel" and a "whoredom." In the words of one historian, many Americans came to perceive New Harmony as "a compost of all heresy, all licentiousness, all the excesses of the French Revolution, all the anti-Christian theories of the Illuminati—in short, Satan's Kingdom on earth."

Getting Into the Old Style

Unsurprisingly, Owen's speech did little to soothe the growing tensions within the colony. While the New Harmonites continued to split into factions, they struggled with their most intractable problem: paying the bills. The community experimented with various schemes to boost productivity. For a time, each person's working hours were posted in a public place. This proved dangerously invidious. Next, they tried assigning each job a predetermined number of hours. This plan was thrown out when it became obvious that some accomplished as much in an hour as others did in a day. In the pursuit of both fairness and productivity, bylaws and subcommittees proliferated, further sapping esprit de corps.

During the Preliminary Society, Owen technically owned the entire village of New Harmony. The mortgage on the land, the buildings, the livestock, and the tools were all in his name. It had never been clear what this would mean once the community was fully established. Paul Brown and other radicals wanted Owen to turn over everything, including his savings, to "the community." But who constituted "the community"?

In the middle of March 1826, Owen surprised everyone by trying to sell the town to its residents. He had finally decided that a society in which he and, to a lesser extent, William Maclure owned everything was not sustainable. He proposed that the citizens of New Harmony collectively buy the village from him for $126,500, to be paid over twelve years at 5 percent interest. By making everyone financially responsible for the colony's fate, Owen hoped to energize them. Should

New Harmony fail, the financial hazard, like everything else, would be collectivized. The vast majority of New Harmonites, now fully aware of how difficult it would be for the community to pay for itself, rejected the idea.

As a compromise, Owen selected twenty-four colonists who were still confident in the ultimate triumph of the community and transferred ownership to them. This group, known as "the Nucleus," accepted responsibility for the mortgage payments still owed to the Rappites. Since they carried significant personal risk, the members of the Nucleus were granted control over admissions and the authority to generally run things.

When the financial hazard had been primarily Owen's, the threat of default was fairly abstract. With the exposure spread over a larger group, the question of who was contributing to the success of the community came to dominate daily life. The effect on morale was toxic. Artisans, whose skills brought in cash, felt that they deserved greater compensation than the farmers and unskilled workers whose labor helped feed and house the artisans and their families. The artisans and farmers were united by a shared resentment of the scientists, artists, and teachers. The presence of so many thinkers was integral to Owen's vision and to the excellent education being offered, free of charge, to all of the colony's children, but their contribution to the bottom line was somewhat nebulous.

Although William Maclure was an enthusiastic communitarian, his abiding passion was educational reform. He had successfully created a first-rate school for the community's four hundred children and he did not want to see it fall apart. The dream of a *New Atlantis*–like society of learning and research now seemed immiscible with Owen's agro-industrial communist paradise. In May 1826, less than two months after the twenty-four-person Nucleus assumed financial and administrative responsibility, Maclure proposed dividing the community into three subgroups based on three spheres of labor—one for farmers, one for artisans, and one for educators. Since the scale and diversity of New

Harmony seemed to be the source of its unwieldy finances, Maclure hoped that breaking the community into smaller, more unified units would bring order.

Owen agreed to the proposal and the community voted in its favor. A newly formed "Pastoral Society" leased the fields and livestock and assumed control of the farm. The "Mechanic and Manufacturing Society" leased the workshops and raw materials. And the "School Society," led by Maclure, took control of New Harmony's school buildings (the most valuable real estate) and nine hundred acres of land. Each of the three societies was meant to be fully communistic internally. They would barter their services with one another and conduct intramural trade using special "labor notes."* An overarching "Board of Union" was established to administer interactions among the three groups. By reorganizing New Harmony into a confederation of independent sub-communities, the colonists belatedly tried to imitate the Shaker system of confederated families sharing a single village.

It didn't take long for the three groups to turn on one another. Because the division of property among the separate "societies" was vague, squabbles broke out over who owned what. Seeing the educators as lazy snobs, the members of the Pastoral Society and the Mechanic and Manufacturing Society stopped paying school fees. The farmers paid for services already rendered. The mechanics refused to pay even that.

---

* Creating alternative currencies that pegged value directly to labor (specifically, time spent laboring) rather than market stimuli (supply and demand) was another of Owen's ambitions. When he returned to the United Kingdom, he advocated for the widespread use of such "labor notes." Josiah Warren, New Harmony's bandleader, instituted the use of "labor notes" at the anarchist community of Modern Times and in a cooperative "Time Store" that he established in Cincinnati. At the Time Store, items were priced by the hours spent on their manufacture. A farrier could exchange five hours of horseshoeing for a chair that took five hours to make. If the chair maker didn't need his horse shod, he could collect his five hours' worth of value from someone else and the store would keep an account of what everyone was owed or due. Buckminster Fuller advocated for a similar scheme in 1938, suggesting that an hour of labor become the standard unit of exchange.

The only thing uniting most people was the belief that Owen, who still stocked and controlled the tavern and the general store, was somehow to blame. People called for him to give up control over these two marginally successful enterprises. Eager to accommodate, Owen gave the mechanics a half stake in the general store and turned the tavern over to the farmers, who immediately raised prices.

While Paul Brown accused Owen of profit seeking, calling him a petty shopkeeper, William Maclure faulted Owen for the opposite reason. Maclure believed that Owen's constant infusions of cash had attracted the wrong sort and kept profitable industries from gaining traction. Maclure, who had persuaded many of his scientist friends to follow Owen into the wilderness, now believed that the community's founder was an incompetent manager and "the most obstinate man [he] ever knew." Maclure's main purpose in splitting New Harmony into three departments had been to disentangle his school from the rest of the community. He paid Owen for the land and buildings claimed by the School Society and petitioned the state for his own charter.

The unwinding had its own momentum. The more tense things became, the less the citizens of New Harmony were interested in working toward an abstract notion of the common good. With the end coming into sight, malingering and theft increased. Long-term thinking became difficult. Why build a barn that might never get used? Why plant hay that might never get cut? "'Hope deferred maketh the heart sick,'" wrote the colonist Thomas Pears. "I cannot look forward to another year of difficulty."

Owen, like other communal utopians, had hoped to mimic the cohesion and economic advantages of the family unit on a scale of thousands, thereby releasing the flood of love and abundance that he believed was dammed up by familial isolation and free market blood sport. For this to work, relative strangers would need to feel such intense bonds of mutual aid that they would instinctively subordinate their private desires to public ends. Sectarian communists such as the Shakers and Rappites accomplished this synthesis by uniting beneath a particular account of salvation. It is easier to feel like brothers and sisters when you share a common father (God). Their belief in the imminence of the end of history helped, too. The frustrations of communal living are easier to endure when the end is nigh.

In a diverse, secular community such as New Harmony, the function performed elsewhere by God and the millennium (or the Apocalypse) was occupied by the collective dream of a man-made utopia. Like a magnet held above a scattering of iron filings, Owen's vision of the future briefly pointed the New Harmonites toward a single pole. When the dream of a merry proletarian castle rising beside the Wabash began to dim, the magnet switched off, leaving a thousand separate wills pointing in a thousand separate directions.

Some of the most skilled and motivated members began to leave. Those who stayed were either true believers, many of whom remained by the Wabash for the rest of their lives, or roustabouts hoping to ride the gravy train to its final station. While Owen refused to admit defeat, he started selling parcels of land to anyone who professed an interest in forming a community based on the same general principles as New Harmony. At one point, the *Gazette* claimed that ten such communities were in the works. None came to much. An Ohio operator named William Taylor contracted with Owen to buy fifteen hundred acres of New Harmony "with all thereon," to start his own "community of equality." The night before the sale, Taylor smuggled tools and livestock onto the parcel. Once the deal was signed, Taylor dropped the socialist pretense and opened a distillery.

Individualism and competition were the great scourges that New Harmony was meant to eradicate, but they pulled upon the faltering community with centrifugal force. Members were drawn away by private schemes. "Matters were drawing to a close," one observer wrote. "The greater part of the town was now resolved into individual lots; a grocery was established opposite the tavern; painted sign-boards began to be stuck up on the buildings, pointing out places of manufacture and trade; a sort of wax-figure-and-puppet-show was opened at one end of the boarding-house; and everything was getting into the old style."

Owen had paid $95,000 as a down payment on the village, but he still owed the Rappites two payments of $40,000 each. When Frederick Rapp came to collect the first installment in May 1827, Owen couldn't pay. Maclure, seeing an opportunity to end his strained, legally ambiguous partnership with Owen, offered to cover both installments at once. Rapp accepted and the deed reverted to Maclure. Owen and Maclure then sued each other. (The legal question concerned the extent to which they had ever really been partners.) A court-ordered settlement gave Owen a large cash payout and granted Maclure control over most of the land. The first grand experiment in secular communism slouched toward dissolution as a money fight between two rich idealists.

An air of mutiny prevailed in the village. Movable property was carried off. Cabbages of ambiguous ownership were left to rot in their furrows. Paul Brown, who took a morbid satisfaction in the disorder, wrote that "a pilfering disposition very much prevailed; and scarce a week passed but shirts, handkerchiefs, or stockings, were filched from some persons out of the laundries or yards of the boarding houses." Boys kicked holes in the fences. Since nobody could be bothered to mend them, "swine ranged at pleasure throughout [the gardens], then cows, and next horses." Oneida founder John Humphrey Noyes, a great admirer of the Rappites, lamented that the beautiful village they had built ended up in the bungling hands of Owen. "Ten of [the Rappites'] best years they spent in building a village on the Wabash," Noyes wrote, "not for themselves (as it turned out), but for a theatre of the great infidel experiment."

The most determined communitarians left to join other, smaller Owenite experiments. Quite a few people, unwilling to return to the world of "isolated households," moved into the western Shaker villages. Among them was a brilliant young British Owenite named Frederick Evans, who went on to become the most prominent Shaker of the Jacksonian era. Influenced by his time at New Harmony, Elder Evans led the United Society out of its sectarian isolation and toward an active engagement with "worldly" reform movements such as abolitionism, socialism, feminism, pacifism, and vegetarianism. He corresponded at length with the likes of Robert Dale Owen, John Humphrey Noyes, Leo Tolstoy, and Abraham Lincoln.

In May 1827, the great infidel himself finally threw in the towel. The writing, in the form of crummy tacked-up billboards, was on the wall; the World was back. In three years, Owen had poured four-fifths of his fortune into New Harmony and the community had endured seven official reorganizations. Unwilling to call his experiment a failure, Owen looked upon the small satellite communities that were being established, or which he believed would soon be established, and claimed, absurdly, that "the social system is now firmly established." On the first day of June 1827, he left New Harmony for good, traveling east to New York and sailing for Liverpool.

Afterglow

Many New Harmonites remained within the village. Some set up small homesteads or opened shops. Others joined together in modest communal homes and collectivized farms. Some went on to found new communities elsewhere, adjusting their theories to accommodate whatever they had learned at New Harmony.

The dream of a communistic utopia by the Wabash vanished with Owen's departure, but the small frontier town remained a beacon of socialism, educational reform, and scientific research. At a time when the rift between science and faith was growing, the former mecca of American atheism became a hub for scientific inquiry.* William Maclure and Owen's sons stayed in town, running schools, libraries, and laboratories. Maclure's press printed influential scientific studies. His

---

* In 1846, a visiting Scottish scientist noted that the town, which despite its small size and remote location boasted first-rate schools, a workingmen's library, and abundant research facilities, was almost unique in the entire United States for the absence of churches. The citizens of New Harmony would have been quick to add that they had no saloons, either.

academy was the only public school outside of New England and the first that was open to both boys and girls.

After spending several years traveling the country with Frances Wright advocating for workers' rights, women's suffrage, public education, and birth control, Robert Dale Owen returned to live in Indiana. In 1842, he was elected to Congress, where he drafted the bill founding the Smithsonian Institution. Two decades later, he wrote a celebrated letter encouraging Lincoln to issue a proclamation summarily emancipating the slaves.

Some former community members recalled their time at New Harmony as the happiest period of their lives. Others were heartbroken by its failure, the depth of their disappointment matching the heights of their former hope. Fifteen years after Owen's departure, a Scottishborn printer and Owenite named A. J. Macdonald traveled to New Harmony to interview former community members. "I was cautioned not to speak of Socialism," Macdonald wrote. "The people had been wearied and disappointed by it; had been filled full with theories, until they were nauseated. . . . They seemed ashamed of what they had been doing."

The widely reported tale of New Harmony's final year—a tragicomic morass of freeloading, theft, and ideological bickering—helped precipitate a decadelong chill in the young Republic's utopian fever. By one count, if the sectarian villages are excluded, only a single utopian community was founded between 1827 and 1840. Even so, Owenite ideas remained in wide circulation. Ironically, the foundering of New Harmony may have had too many causes for Owen's vision to completely lose favor. As the historian Arthur Bestor wrote, "In a firing squad, if all the guns are loaded, which man performs the execution?"

"I Have Been Ahead of My Time"

The experiment in New Harmony was only one chapter in Robert Owen's long career as a socialist reformer. Two years after the breakup,

Owen returned to the United States for a series of heavily publicized debates with the evangelist Alexander Campbell. Before a crowd of twelve hundred in Cincinnati, Owen defended the proposition that "all religions are erroneous, and that their practice is injurious to the human race." At the close of the debate, the crowd voted by standing or sitting. Owen lost by a near consensus.

In the United Kingdom, Owen worked for the rights of industrial workers and the establishment of cooperative villages. He was also an early leader of the movement for trade unionism. His faith in an imminent secular millennium never faded. As Owen aged, his philosophical writings—never particularly incisive—devolved into vague, repetitious aphorizing about global unity.*

In his eighties, like so many veterans of the golden age of American utopianism, Owen became an ardent spiritualist, conversing at length with the ghosts of Jefferson, Franklin, Mary Shelley, and Lord Byron. Even his mysticism had an egalitarian bent. The spirit of Owen's old friend the Duke of Kent informed him that there were no ranks or titles in the "spiritual spheres." One of Owen's last tracts, a pamphlet published in 1853 when he was eighty-two, attempted to merge his utopian socialism with his spiritualism. It was titled *The Future of the Human Race; Or a Great, Glorious, and Peaceful Revolution, Near at Hand, to Be Effected Through the Agency of Departed Spirits of Good and Superior Men and Women.*

At the age of eighty-seven, Owen returned to his hometown in Wales after a seventy-year absence. Feeling ill, he took to bed in the house beside his father's old saddle shop. Near death, he assessed his efforts to trigger a millennium of abundance and fraternity. "My life was not useless; I gave important truths to the world, and it was only for want of understanding that they were disregarded. I have been ahead of my time."

On the morning of November 17, 1858, the local vicar came to comfort Owen in his final hours. Lying in bed, the dying man refused to

---

* His late prose resembles the bland slogans that decorate bottles of Dr. Bronner's castile soap: "All ONE!"

pray to a God whose existence he had long doubted. He did, however, invite the priest to sit. Owen said that a few ideas had just occurred to him for how the district around Newtown might be better organized. He asked the vicar to kindly convey his suggestions to the relevant authorities.

THE FOURIERIST PHALANXES

The Lemonade Sea

Les attractions sont proportionnelles aux destinées.
(Attractions are proportional to destinies.)
—CHARLES FOURIER

Four Apples

François Marie Charles Fourier, the French clerk who instigated the most popular utopian movement in American history, had a passion for fruit that bordered on obsession. In a fruit bowl he saw the whole world: the beguiling "irony" of melons (they conceal their ripeness until cut), the glorious diversity of pear species, the exquisitely "transitional" way in which nectarines bridge the gastronomic divide between prunes and apricots. By Fourier's tally, there have been four significant apples in history. The first, of course, was Adam and Eve's fateful nosh—the snack that opened humanity's eyes to good and evil and secured our eviction from the orchards of Paradise.

The second world historical apple was a trophy, the infamous "apple of discord" that triggered the ten-year siege of Troy, bequeathing us this gory ordeal known as Western civilization. As payback for not being invited to the wedding of the sea nymph Thetis and the hero Peleus, the goddess Eris wrought an apple in gold, inscribed it "καλλίστῃ" ("to the most beautiful"), and lobbed it into the marriage party. In a moment of Titanic awkwardness, three goddesses—Athena, Aphrodite, and Hera—reached for the prize at the same time. An impromptu beauty pageant broke out. Paris, the hunky but fainthearted prince of Troy, was selected as sole judge. The three goddesses vied for his favor with gifts. Athena promised wisdom and glory in battle. Hera offered political power. Aphrodite, goddess of beauty, proffered the winning bribe: the love of a married woman, Helen of Sparta, she of the ship-launching face.

The third apple was a humble British windfall. In 1666, young Isaac Newton was strolling through an orchard near his home when he saw an apple fall from a tree. In its direct descent to the ground, Newton observed, as if for the first time, that objects always fall perpendicular to the earth. From this insight he formulated his theory of gravity and its relation to mass.

The fourth and final world-changing apple was the one that Charles Fourier saw on a Parisian menu in 1790, during his first, thrilling excursion to the French capital. He was eighteen, a blue-eyed young man from the provinces with a high forehead and formal manners. The apple cost fourteen sous, the price of a hundred apples in his hometown. Although Fourier was neither the first nor the last tourist to be scandalized by the prices on a Parisian menu, he later claimed that this galling markup opened his eyes to the inherent perversion of competitive markets, setting in motion the most dazzling utopian vision ever set to paper.

Like the previous three, Fourier's apple was merely a catalyst. His distaste for capitalism had been developing since he was a boy. He was born in 1772, less than a year after Robert Owen, in the small city of Besançon. Like Owen's, Fourier's life and ideas were, from the outset, swaddled in cloth—the defining product of early industrialism. His father, Charles Fourier, Sr., was a successful textile merchant and woolen draper. He was determined to bring his only son into the family business, but the boy sensed a conflict between commerce and the reverence for truth that was drilled into him on Sundays. "I was taught in catechism and at school that one must never lie," he wrote, "then I was taken to the shop to be trained at an early age in the occupation of lying, the art of selling."

Fourier was a compulsive, sensitive child. He obsessed over botany and cartography. His bedroom was so crammed with maps and flowerpots that it was difficult to move about. At seven, standing behind the counter in his father's shop, he informed a customer that he, the customer, was being shortchanged. This display of honesty earned Charles a four-handed thrashing by both parents. He was so traumatized that in imitation of Hannibal pledging lifelong enmity to Rome, he swore an "eternal oath" against commerce.

In the summer of 1789, when Fourier was seventeen, a thousand angry Parisians fought their way into the Bastille prison—a hulking stone symbol of royal tyranny. Fourier made every effort to remain aloof from the ensuing revolution, but he came to political consciousness in the shade of its darkest episodes.

A year after the violence erupted in Paris, Fourier moved to Lyon, where, at his family's insistence, he apprenticed with a cloth wholesaler. Like Manchester, Lyon, then the capital of the global silk trade, was a textile town in upheaval. A modest form of globalization—a treaty increasing imports from Great Britain—flooded France with inexpensive cloth, decimating the ancient economy. Formerly independent weavers became wage laborers, beholden to erratic prices set by middlemen speculating on an international market. Even haute couture conspired against the silk workers of Lyon. In the tense years before and during the French Revolution, silk became a perilous mark of wealth. When the chic court of Marie Antoinette began sporting fine Manchester cottons, the style-obsessed aristocracy followed suit. As the Revolution bled south from Paris, wartime austerity quashed the already hobbled silk industry. During the 1790s, half the silk workshops in Lyon closed.

At the start of 1793, Fourier traveled from Lyon to his hometown to collect his inheritance of nearly fifty thousand livres. Hoping to secure an early retirement from the unsavory world of commerce, he made a bold bet. He invested almost all the money in a single order of whole-sale colonial goods—cotton, sugar, and coffee—which he planned to sell in Lyon.

His timing could not have been worse. Lyon was France's second city, but unlike the radicalized capital to the north, it was a center of loyalty to the crown. The revolutionary authorities in Paris assigned a harsh Jacobin administrator to run the city, but in June 1793, Lyonnais counterrevolutionaries rebelled. They deposed the puppet administration, set up their own municipal government, and cut off relations with Paris.

In August, the revolutionary army marched on Lyon, besieging the city for sixty days. As the standoff progressed, the starving Lyonnais ate their horses. At precisely the wrong moment, Fourier's wholesale order arrived. He watched as his bales of cotton were used for barricades and his coffee, rice, and sugar were requisitioned to feed the hungry local troops. In a stroke, his inheritance was gone. For the rest of his life, despite his Hannibalic oath against commerce, Fourier supported himself by working as a bookkeeper, a clerk, and a traveling salesman. "In the end," he wrote as an old man, "I was broken to the yoke, and my best years were lost in the workshops of falsehood."[*]

When Lyon finally fell, the reprisals were brutal. The local guillotine worked overtime. Rather than wash away the gore, the executioners let the city's starving dogs lick the cobblestones clean. When the machine failed to keep pace with the necks of so many traitors, accused royalists were marched to the lip of a mass grave and cut down by cannons

---

[*] Between Fourier's endless attacks on the venality of merchants and the absurdity of patriarchy, it does not take a Freudian to deduce a link between his social theories and his feelings toward his merchant father.

loaded with chain and grapeshot. Hiding in the woods outside of the city, Fourier narrowly avoided getting killed in the chaos.

The name Lyon became synonymous with reactionary sedition. In the fall of 1793, the revolutionary "Committee of Public Safety" voted to raze the wealthy districts of the city. On the cleared land, a column was to be erected bearing a terse epitaph: "Lyon made war on Liberty. Lyon is no more." This was the dark side of the Revolution's utopist ambitions: a belief that the new age required the total destruction of the old. The plan to torch Lyon was never carried out, but the wealthiest homes were destroyed. By the spring of 1793, an estimated 1,880 Lyonnais had been killed.

The following summer, Fourier was drafted into a cavalry unit of the newly formed Army of the Rhine. Without adequate supplies, the force was supposed to hold back the Austrian forces arrayed along the river. Fourier was wholly unfit for the arduous campaign but managed to survive with nothing worse than a broken nose. He was discharged two years later.

By 1799, the final year of the Revolution, Fourier was working for a wholesaler in the southern port city of Marseille. One afternoon he was sent to supervise a crew of men as they surreptitiously dumped an entire boatload of slimy rice into Marseille harbor. Although people were starving throughout France and food costs were already soaring, Fourier's employers had been holding out for even higher prices. When they waited too long, the shipment turned to rot.

Disgusted by the waste and violence that he had seen and generally reeling from the twin calamities of the French and Industrial Revolutions—what Eric Hobsbawm called the "dual revolution"—Fourier resolved to figure out where humanity had gone so wrong.

It is common to attribute utopianism to a surfeit of optimism, but the desire to totally overhaul civilization implies a fairly cynical view of the world as it is. Imagining a perfect future is, almost by definition, a way to organize grievances with the here and now. The year that Fourier supervised the disposal of a shipload of rice, he began to sketch the outlines of his ideal society.

Ascending Vibrations

Descartes began his *Meditations on First Philosophy* (1641) by adopting, or at least attempting to adopt, a position of radical skepticism. Intending to restart the entire project of Western philosophy, he consciously scrubbed every possible assumption from his mind. Out went anything resembling an idea or fact. Some mischievous demon might have planted false thoughts in his consciousness. Out went logic. One plus two might not really equal three. Out went sense data. The eyes and ears can lie; he might be color-blind or drunk. Having thus cleared his mind of empirical and rational content, Descartes could with certitude assert only one thing: that something was still going on in his mind. Even if his thoughts had no relation to external reality, even if he was in the grip of a demonic hallucination, *thinking* was happening. And if thinking was happening, regardless of its epistemic merit, some entity must be doing the thinking: a mind. Upon this firm, if meager, foundation—the famous *Cogito, ergo sum* ("I am thinking, therefore I exist")—Descartes raised an intellectual edifice that would become the scaffolding of modern philosophy.

Charles Fourier's attitude to this sort of thing was: Who gives a damn? Generations of philosophers, he wrote, have packed the world's libraries with noble-sounding "stupidity" while doing "nothing to seek any better arrangement for the union of the sexes and the exchange of industrial products." Their sophistry, in other words, willfully neglects the two spheres that, in Fourier's estimation, define civilization: the family and the marketplace. "Philosophy," Fourier wrote, "pretends to analysis while only writing apologies for civilization. Philosophy is very much the enemy of truth."

Despite this churlish attitude, Fourier imitated Descartes's strategy, attempting to do for "social science" what Descartes had done for epistemology. He tried to commence his inquiry into the state of the world from a position of radical doubt. To properly understand civilization, he believed, every single assumption, no matter how basic, must be set

aside. If a utopian is someone who designs a future society with a minimum of regard for the world-as-it-is, then Fourier's exercise in Cartesian doubt is the purest possible example of utopian thinking.*

Inspired, if not intoxicated, by the scientific and intellectual advances of the eighteenth century, Fourier decided that the mathematical and physical principles that govern the universe must have a social
corollary. Wherever he looked—Newtonian physics, Cartesian geometry, the color spectrum, the chromatic scale—Fourier saw the finger-
prints of a divine watchmaker obsessed with order, regularity, and
harmony. Why would God, whom Fourier sometimes called the Eternal
Geometer, go through all the trouble of creating discernible laws by
which the planets orbit one another and billiard balls collide without
composing a similarly perfect system by which humanity—the jewel of
creation—can live in comfort and harmony? Only human society, especially the society Fourier saw slipping into chaos during the French Revolution and subsequent restoration, seemed to be out of rhythm with
the harmonious music of the universe. In the seventeenth century, Isaac
Newton uncovered the laws of attraction that hold matter together. At
the dawn of the nineteenth century, Charles Fourier set out to discover
"the laws of passional attraction" that hold society together.

The French Republic was in tatters when Fourier's first major work, *The
Theory of the Four Movements*, was published in Lyon in the spring of
1808.† The book is wildly abstruse; Fourier himself called it a "riddle."
It claimed to present a theory of everything—an owner's manual for
creation that explained everything from the formation of minerals, to
the principles of musical harmony, to the life cycle of beetles, to the ins
and outs of human sexuality. In the short volume's introduction, Fourier described the *Theory* as a mere prolegomenon—a teaser of the opus
to come. It was. By the time of his death in 1837, he had written six

---

* Fourier had an easier time setting aside social assumptions than theological ones.
He never seems to have questioned, for instance, his own faith in a benevolent, om-
nipotent Creator who wants humanity to be happy.
† The original printing claimed falsely to be from Leipzig. It is not clear why.

colossal tomes on his "system" and countless sub-tracts on space, rocks, orgies, canals, music, and sea creatures. The sheer volume of prose suggests a thread of madness—the hypergraphia of an epileptic prophet.

The Theory of the Four Movements opens with a thorough accounting of the world's ills—a fat almanac of suffering and discord. "Civilization," Fourier wrote, "is bathing in blood": poverty and disease are rampant; commerce nurtures vice; industrial development debases workers; the new technologies of mass production make life worse for all but a few. Everything is out of whack. "The present social order is a ridiculous mechanism in which portions of the whole are in conflict and acting against the whole."

Fourier supplemented this boilerplate radical litany with several provocative additions. He insisted, for instance, that the nuclear family is an absurd, invidious institution. Like Owen and the Shakers, he regarded the "isolated household" as a bastion of inefficiency, untruth, and selfishness. Presaging Owen's "Declaration of Mental Independence," Fourier claimed that marriage—an institution he never experienced firsthand—is nothing more than a prison built to enslave women and lock both of its captives into lives of deceit, intellectual malaise, and sexual nullity.

Fourier viewed society as a huge mechanism with a single purpose: to stamp out human impulse and sentiment, what he called "the passions." By suppressing the passions, society not only obliterates pleasure, it also dampens productivity and progress. "The passions," Fourier wrote, "are the motor forces, the springs of action in man; they are parts of a unity or a whole, which is the soul or the spirit. God, in implanting in man these impelling forces, must have calculated mathematically their mode of action, their tendencies, and their functions." Fourier proposed to rearrange human affairs so that our God-given "springs of action" could spring freely. When society is arranged according to the laws of "passional attraction," the global interplay of each individual's passions—a complex economy of impulse, repulsion, and desire—will produce a state of social harmony akin to the way in which disparate notes add up to a symphony.* (The comparison to music was not strictly a metaphor. Fourier claimed that the same principles that produce musical harmony will govern the ideal society.)

From this perspective, previous attempts at utopian reform appear to have proceeded backward, by shaping human character to fit ideal social forms. Ann Lee taught that the countless shades of human suffering were rooted in passion, particularly *carnality*. The road to Zion would be paved with trampled instinct. Robert Owen's view was similar. Having followed Locke's empiricism to the limits of reason, he looked upon human character as a "white paper" upon which anything might be written. The rise of his New Moral World was predicated upon the idea that individuals can be shaped, through early education and environmental influences, to fit comfortably into idealized institutions. Each human peg would be lathed to fit a precut social hole.

Fourier worked in the opposite direction. He dreamed of creating social institutions that were adapted to the wild variety of human particularity—jigsawing crazily shaped holes to fit each crazily shaped peg. He understood human nature as a complex array of immutable properties. Society can either adapt to those properties or make a mess by attempting to thwart them. The root of this sociology is the humanistic and fundamentally liberal supposition that the diversity of human desire is a good thing. Whereas most utopians understand human nature as the fly in the ointment of their perfected society, Fourier saw modern society as a glutinous ointment gumming up the wings of human nature.

Social problems that appear to stem from unbridled impulse— greed, murder, war, adultery, and so forth—are in actual fact caused by society's clumsy efforts to repress human passion. Vices, or those things

---

* Fourier defines the term *passional attraction* as "the tendency of the passions, their gravitation to the ends or foci to which they are destined." In other words, every impulse (passion) has a specific function (destiny) in the mathematical organization of the perfected universe. Passional attraction functions like a sort of all-controlling cosmic force that holds the entire universe together.

that we currently call vices, serve vital social functions. Greed is good; lust is good; gossip is good. All of these impulses have a place and a function in God's creation. They turn sour only when we try to stamp them out or exercise them in solitude, in which case they are no better than "unchained tigers." Fourier offers the example of a Russian princess named Lady Strogonoff. While trying to suppress her lust for a young female servant, Strogonoff pricks the poor girl with hat pins, thus tormenting "the person who should have been the object of her pleasure." In other words, the struggle to smother impulse yields an endless harvest of misery.*

Two of Fourier's own passions were taxonomy and list making. Almost all of his ideas are supported by swarms of categories and enumerated lists. (Recall the four apples.) He identifies twelve distinct passions. Five of them, the so-called Luxurious Passions, are linked to the five senses. Our impulse to see, hear, taste, touch, and smell certain things governs the health and pleasure we obtain from the physical world. Another four passions, known collectively as "the Affective Passions," concern our relations with others. These include familism, love, ambition, and friendship. The remaining three passions regulate the operations of the first nine. These "Mechanizing Passions" include the Cabalist Passion, which likes scheming and forming groups; the Butterfly Passion, which demands constant variety; and the Composite Passion, which brings us the greatest happiness by mixing intellectual and spiritual satisfaction. Fourier claimed that every person on earth embodies some specific ratio of these twelve passions, with most people dominated by one or another. By his count, there are 810 possible combinations, or "passional types."

Fourier believed that "destiny" always corresponds to passion. If we detect within ourselves a genuine, uncorrupted impulse to do

---

* With his account of human impulse and its elaborate social suppression, Fourier presaged Freud, who 120 years later would also argue that the sublimation of desire was at the root of civilization's discontents.

something—not as easy as it sounds—it is because that is what we are *meant* to do and eventually *will* do. When everyone abides by the dictates of their own passions and these impulses are properly intermingled, society will achieve harmony. Earth will become the paradise it is destined to be.

Along with his exacting taxonomy of passion, Fourier claimed to have discovered the principles by which societies change through time—a theory of history. According to Fourier, all observable change in the universe follows laws of "ascending vibration" and "descending vibration." Manifestations of this process can be seen in everything from the growth and decline of a single individual, to the rise and fall of great empires, to the geologic history of the earth itself.

Applying this principle to human history, Fourier counts thirty-two distinct stages of social development through which the human race is destined to pass—sixteen ascending stages and sixteen descending. In the first stage, Edenism, primitive man enjoyed a delightful existence uncorrupted by hierarchy or property. Unfortunately, the absence of technology and culture left the men and women of Edenism unfulfilled.* From Edenism, the human race has trudged miserably through the epochs of Savagery, Patriarchate, and Barbarism, until arriving at the present era (number five of thirty-two), which Fourier calls Civilization.

Humanity's ascent up this ladder of historical progress is strongly correlated to the status of women within society. As women gain freedom, particularly sexual autonomy, societies advance. "Social progress and changes of a [historical] period are accompanied by the progress of women towards freedom," he wrote. "Extension of the rights of women is the basic principle of all social progress." The close correlation between the status of women and almost every indicator of progress (nutrition, infant mortality, literacy) is now a basic tenet of

---

* By speculating on the emotional and social life of early humans, Fourier was following in the tradition of the most influential thinker of his time and place: Jean-Jacques Rousseau. Unlike Fourier, however, Rousseau claimed that his noble savages were content with their meager lot of fresh fruit and sex.

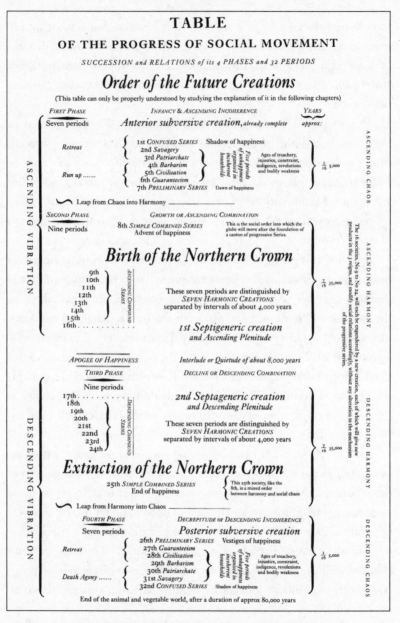

TABLE

OF THE PROGRESS OF SOCIAL MOVEMENT

SUCCESSION and RELATIONS of its 4 PHASES and 32 PERIODS

Order of the Future Creations

(This table can only be properly understood by studying the explanation of it in the following chapters)

FIRST PHASE — INFANCY & ASCENDING INCOHERENCE — YEARS approx:

Seven periods — *Anterior subversive creation, already complete*

Retreat
- 1st CONFUSED SERIES — Shadow of happiness
- 2nd Savagery
- 3rd Patriarchate
- 4th Barbarism
- 5th Civilisation
- 6th Guaranteeism
- 7th PRELIMINARY SERIES — Dawn of happiness

Run up ....

Five periods of unhappiness organised in incoherent households

Ages of treachery, injustice, constraint, indigence, revolutions and bodily weakness

$\frac{1}{16}$ 5,000

Leap from Chaos into Harmony —————

SECOND PHASE — GROWTH OR ASCENDING COMBINATION

Nine periods — 8th SIMPLE COMBINED SERIES — This is the social order into which the globe will move after the foundation of a canton of progressive Series.
Advent of happiness

Birth of the Northern Crown

- 9th
- 10th
- 11th
- 12th — ASCENDING COMPOUND SERIES
- 13th
- 14th
- 15th
- 16th . . . .

These seven periods are distinguished by *SEVEN HARMONIC CREATIONS* separated by intervals of about *4,000 years*

1st Septigeneric creation and Ascending Plenitude

$\frac{7}{16}$ 35,000

APOGEE OF HAPPINESS — Interlude or Quietude of about 8,000 years

THIRD PHASE — DECLINE OR DESCENDING COMBINATION

Nine periods
- 17th . . . .
- 18th
- 19th
- 20th
- 21st — DESCENDING COMPOUND SERIES
- 22nd
- 23rd
- 24th

2nd Septageneric creation and Descending Plenitude

These seven periods are distinguished by *SEVEN HARMONIC CREATIONS* separated by intervals of about 4,000 years

$\frac{7}{16}$ 35,000

Extinction of the Northern Crown

25th SIMPLE COMBINED SERIES — This 25th society, like the 8th, is a mixed order between harmony and social chaos
End of happiness

Leap from Harmony into Chaos —————

FOURTH PHASE — DECREPITUDE or DESCENDING INCOHERENCE

Seven periods — *Posterior subversive creation*

Retreat
- 26th PRELIMINARY SERIES — Vestiges of happiness
- 27th Guaranteeism
- 28th Civilisation
- 29th Barbarism
- 30th Patriarchate
- 31st Savagery
- 32nd CONFUSED SERIES — Shadow of happiness

Death Agony ....

Five periods of unhappiness organised in incoherent households

Ages of treachery, injustice, constraint, indigence, revolutions and bodily weakness

$\frac{1}{16}$ 5,000

End of the animal and vegetable world, after a duration of approx 80,000 years

Left margin: ASCENDING VIBRATION { ASCENDING VIBRATION } DESCENDING VIBRATION { DESCENDING VIBRATION

Right margin: ASCENDING CHAOS — ASCENDING HARMONY — ASCENDING HARMONY — DESCENDING HARMONY — DESCENDING HARMONY — DESCENDING CHAOS

Vertical text right: The 16 societies, No 9 to No 24, will each be engendered by a new creation, each of which will give new products in the 3 reigns, and modify social relations accordingly, without any alteration to the mechanism of the progressive series.

The ascending and descending vibrations of history.

The Theory of the Four Movements *(Cambridge University Press).*
Reprinted with the permission of Cambridge University Press.

development. That was hardly the case in 1808, when poverty and disease were routinely attributed to the easy virtue of lower-class women.

According to Fourier's calculations, the first seven stages of history will take ten thousand years, after which the human race will emerge into the paradisiacal era of Harmony, where we will remain for seventy thousand glorious years. When Harmony ends, this historical process will reverse itself. Human society and all other life on earth will slide back through the seven epochs of "descending incoherence" until the planet stops spinning and all life goes extinct: "End of the animal and vegetable world," as Fourier's chart reads.

Fourier saw Civilization, the chaotic era in which we currently live, as a necessary precursor to the forthcoming paradise. The present epoch (his and ours) is defined by the turmoil of competitive markets and the lonely isolation of the nuclear family. The banker, rather than the chieftain or the soldier, is the signal character of the age. When we ascend from Civilization to Harmony, the wealth and technology that capitalism is so effective at piling up will finally be put to good use.*

As with the twelve passions and the 810 passional types, the numerical specificity of Fourier's theory of history is startling. "The Fourierist number is not rounded off, and in fact this is what gives it its insanity . . . ," wrote Roland Barthes. "Why does our society consider a decimal number 'normal' and an intradecimal number 'irrational'?" This inclination toward precision pervaded everything Fourier did. He seldom left home without a meter stick with which to measure the world around him.

City of Passion

Like Owen, Fourier believed that the best way to speed humanity's ascent into utopia was to build seminal colonies—carefully planned show-

---

* Marx also originally predicted that communism would commence in a highly developed industrial nation such as the United Kingdom or the United States, where capitalism had performed the necessary work of building factories and expanding the industrial proletariat.

cases for the new harmonic order that he called "phalanxes." Each of Fourier's proposed phalanxes will house 1,620 people, twice the 810 possible passional types. They will work and sleep inside a massive edifice called a "phalanstery," which will be twelve hundred meters across, with long wings extending from each side. Unlike Owen's comparatively Spartan parallelogram, Fourier's phalanstery was a decadent mishmash of piazzas, colonnades, caravansaries, and arches, all topped with brightly colored silk banners and surrounded by pleasure grounds.

Within each phalanx, everything will be arranged according to the principles of passional attraction. With two people of each passional type living within each colony, all of life's work will be performed by someone who is "passionally" suited to his or her job. This, along with the same sort of collectivism advocated by Owen and the Shakers, will cause productivity to skyrocket, yielding previously unimaginable abundance. To satisfy the flighty demands of the Butterfly Passion, phalansterians will switch tasks as often as every two hours, dashing from orchard, to loom, to kitchen, to workshop, to concert hall, to school. For a citizen of Fourier's imagined future, Marx's daily cycle of fishing, herding, and criticizing could probably be wrapped up well before lunch, leaving time for another dozen pursuits.

According to the logic of passional attraction, the frequent violation of a certain taboo certifies the illegitimacy of that taboo, rather than any flaw in human nature. So, for instance, the prevalence of marital infidelity evidences the absurdity of marriage as an institution, not the wickedness of the general population.* Fourier claimed that sexuality— like every other expression of human passion—is stifled and perverted in Civilization. So-called civilizees cannot begin to comprehend, let alone satisfy, their own sexual desires or needs.† In the phalanxes of Harmony, the full polymorphous splendor of human eroticism will

---

* Fourier's "Taxonomy of Cuckoldry" lists no fewer than eighty distinct species of cuckold, including the "Health-Conscious Cuckold" and the "Posthumous Cuckold," also known as the "Cuckold of Two Worlds."
† In Fourierist tracts, the words *civilization* and *civilizee* express a level of disdain that recalls Huckleberry Finn's sibilant anxiety about being "sivilized."

flower. Desires that are currently hidden will be celebrated and refined. Homosexuals will freely obey their desires. (Only those attracted to both sexes will attain the highest erotic orders.) Masochists—whom Fourier called "baby doll types" because of the pleasure taken in spanking— will pair up with willing sadists. Even incest, as long as it is between consenting adults, will be socially acceptable. Like Freud, Fourier frankly analyzed his own proclivities, finding himself to be one of the 26,400 earthlings with a "mania" for "Sapphianism"—that is, "the love of lesbians and the eagerness to aid them in every way possible."

Fourier, a man whose closest companions were cats, believed that everything is better in a group. Eating alone may fill the stomach, but it cannot compare with the pleasures of a feast, where the appetite is slightly restrained by social convention (the order and speed at which dishes are unveiled, which fork to use, and so on). Similarly, a solo violinist can express herself with absolute spontaneity, but playing in an orchestra—constraining her technique to harmonize with others—is far more pleasurable. Sex obeys this same principle. Fourier classified group sex as one "of man's natural needs." In the phalanxes of Harmony, specially selected "Pontiffs of Love," aided by functionaries such as "genies, fairies, and other officers of the ministry of the pontiff," will orchestrate vast, elaborately choreographed orgies. Unlike the "confused libertinage" of civilizee orgies, Fourier's imagined Harmonian orgies bring to mind Busby Berkeley's kaleidoscopic choreography. A true harmonic orgy, he wrote, will be "a lasting society skillfully prepared by the ministry of fairies to form amorous scales . . . [that] creates among the initiates a super-tonic founded upon the opposition of two scales of contrasted character; it reinforces everyone's sympathies through a common collective passion, creating a new bond for them all." Such an orgy would demonstrate the vast, syncopated interplay of private impulse that Fourier believed would define social relations within the phalanxes of the future. In Fourier's ideal phalanx, sexual desire, like every other human impulse, will be harnessed to production. Love and pleasure, rather than greed and war, will become the engines of material and scientific progress.

Along with each individual's passional profile, social dynamics will be harnessed to supercharge productivity. Working side by side in the orchard, teams of "passionally aligned" fruit lovers will be driven into the upper branches by a sporting sense of competition, erotic flirtation, and an innate passion for the fruits they pick. Fourier calls this "attractive industry," and he believed that it could make labor not just ardent and pleasurable, but irresistible ("attractive").

In Harmony, even the most seemingly destructive impulses will serve the public good. For instance, young boys, with their disruptive instincts for clamor, military pomp, and getting dirty, will be formed into "little hordes" of garbage collectors. Each morning, these hordes will march out of their phalanstery accompanied by a cacophony of drums, trumpets, and barking dogs. They will wear special "barbaric" uniforms, resembling, one imagines, Fred Flintstone's orange toga. Among themselves, they will speak their own secret rubbish-collecting slang. For extrazealous trash picking, individual boys will be rewarded with medals and military-style honors. "Frenzied by trumpet blasts and roars of approval, intoxicated by unending accolades, the Little Hordes would place their love of filth at the service of the Phalanx," wrote the historian Jonathan Beecher in his monumental biography of Fourier.

Like the Owenites, Fourier was convinced that a single functioning phalanx—a working prototype of the coming utopia—would inspire instantaneous and endless imitation, "owing simply to the allurement of the immense advantages and innumerable enjoyments which this order assures to all individuals." Once a few trial colonies are set up, one Fourierist predicted, "thousands of analogous organizations will rapidly arise without obstacle and as if by enchantment around the first specimens." Phalanxes will then pop up across the entire globe, eventually replacing every other form of human settlement. At the peak of Harmony—the eight-thousand-year epoch known as "the Apogee of Happiness"—every human on earth will live in one of 2,985,984 separate phalansteries. These semi-independent communities will trade surplus goods with one another and communicate by means of carrier pigeon. A central phalanx in Constantinople will house the "Om-

niarch," a leader who will oversee the whole system.* Bureaucrats will
organize intraphalanx festivals, feasts, and orgies devoted to "manias"
that are too exotic to find satisfaction in one's home phalanx. For instance, lovers of vinegar from across the world will form a "gastronomic
cabal" that convenes for international feasts devoted to the tart delights
of heavily vinegared food. Likewise, foot fetishists from every nation
will gather at some predetermined phalanx for immense international
orgies of footsie.

Fourier did not consider this scheme his invention. He was simply
the first person to discern, through close observation and freethinking,
the "Divine Social Code" established by God. Because the system was
perfect and complete, the harmonic future will not require any sort of

Artist Charles-François Daubigny's rendering of a phalanstery.
Note the boys of the "little horde" with their dog-drawn trash wagon.
The Master can be seen resting beneath a tree in the foreground.

Bibliothèque Nationale, Paris, France / Bridgeman Images

---

* Fourier, in his effort to find a sponsor for this scheme, offered to relocate the central
phalanx from Constantinople to Jerusalem if the Rothschild family was willing to
bankroll the construction of a model phalanx.

politics. Each individual phalanx—as well as the global network of interconnected phalanxes—will be a self-sustaining machine, chugging along without any need for interference. Leaders, including the Omniarch, will be mere paper pushers—bureaucrats overseeing the orderly flow of goods and people. The dream of a social order so perfect that governance and power become obsolete is a hallmark of utopian thought. To the utopian, power and coercion are nothing more than symptoms of a disordered society. Even Marx predicted that in the era of postscarcity communism, the state will "wither away," leaving nothing but bureaucracy. In a formulation that would have pleased Fourier, Lenin famously said that in the future, "any cook should be able to run the country."

Although Fourier is remembered as a pioneering socialist—in 1918, the Bolsheviks chiseled his name into a granite obelisk in a garden just outside the Kremlin—he agreed with his near contemporary Adam Smith that self-interest is the basic motor of productivity. The life Fourier describes within his projected communities is filled with races, rivalries, contests, rewards, and honors.* The trick will be to hitch the competitive spirit to the public good. Teams of passionately aligned gourmets will compete with one another to cook the most tasty and nutritious meals. An elite group known as the Sacred Legion will perform unpleasant jobs such as cleaning sewers and digging ditches. For these services, its members will be celebrated like military heroes.

Unlike the Shakers and the New Harmonites, Fourier did not think that communal ownership was either desirable or feasible. Life inside the phalanx will be heavily socialized, but people can still earn and keep property. Fourier's emphasis on individual will and his rejection of collective ownership partly explain his eventual popularity in the United States. To some, his theory seemed to represent a middle path between the demonstrable shortcomings of laissez-faire capitalism and the as-

---

* When he was through with Trotskyism, the critic Dwight Macdonald celebrated this element of Fourierism. "What could be more deadly than the usual post-Marxist vision of socialism as equality and agreement?" he wrote. "Fourier was far more perceptive when he based his Utopia on cabals, rivalry, and every kind of difference."

cetic, anti-individualistic collectivism of Owen and the communitarian religious sects.

Amphibious Servants Plying
the Lemonade Sea

Fourier's theories raise a question about intellectual credibility: How daffy must *some* of a thinker's ideas be for *all* of his or her work to be seen as suspect? Throughout *The Theory of the Four Movements* and Fourier's subsequent writings, humane and refreshingly modern insights about the equality of women, the hazards of unchecked industry, and the virtues of sexual liberty are interspersed with pseudoscientific claptrap about the "copulation" of planets and the inevitability that humans will grow prehensile tails. Many of Fourier's most far-out ideas derive from his conviction that there is a correlation between the arrangement of human society and the "health" of the earth and the cosmos. He regarded the universe as a coherent mechanism created by a beneficent and omnipotent God. Therefore, everything unpleasant that is found on earth must be a glitch in the system. Disease, drought, poverty, extremes of weather, mosquitoes: These things are anomalies, symptoms of the general discord that currently reigns on earth.

In the era of Harmony, when humanity begins treating the globe as it is meant to be treated, disease will disappear and the climate will improve. For Fourier, unlike modern ecologists, "treating the globe as it is meant to be treated" does not mean leaving natural systems alone. It means leveling mountain ranges, irrigating deserts, planting new forests, and digging canals. In Harmony, these sorts of vast earthworks will be a cinch because the application of attractive industry and passional attraction will have exponentially magnified human productivity. Fourier predicts that the expansion of human industry will raise the temperature of the earth's atmosphere, a notion that was surely met with laughter in the 1820s. He claims that this warming of the globe— caused by industrialized agriculture and the reforestation of barren regions—will be a good thing. In the era of Harmony, the entire world will have the warm, dry climate of Italy.

Fourier claims that as the globe warms, a ring of light called "the northern crown" will form over the top of the planet, melting the polar ice, rendering the North Pole inhabitable, and producing a more stable and temperate climate throughout the globe. (Not a thought is spared for rising sea levels, superstorms, or starving polar bears.) As the ice melts, "boreal liquid" will leak into the sea. "In combination with salt," Fourier famously predicted in a footnote, "this liquid will give the sea a flavor of the kind of lemonade known as aigresel." The sea will become lemonade.

As in the biblical account of the millennium, the animal kingdom will take part in the regeneration of earth. Lions will be replaced by docile "antilions" that will serve humans as high-speed, smooth-gated taxi-animals. And along with tasty, potable seawater, the mariners of Harmony will enjoy the assistance of "amphibious servants to pull ships and help in fisheries." According to Fourier, these helpful creatures will replace "the ghastly legions of sea-monsters which will be annihilated by the admixture of boreal fluid and the consequent changes in the sea's structure." Striding proudly through this new world will be a new man—seven feet tall, amphibious, with replaceable teeth and a 144-vertebra tail that terminates in a small hand "as strong as the claws of an eagle or crab."

Fourier's prophecies were not restrained by the limits of the earth's atmosphere. All of creation obeys the laws of passional attraction. Everything, above and below, is part of the same harmonic totality. The galaxy exhibits the same reproductive, passional, and erotic tendencies that humans do. If planets were merely rocks gliding through darkness, Fourier wrote, then "God would appear to be an advocate of laziness." But God is not an advocate of laziness; He is an advocate of passion. Thus, heavenly bodies are as frisky as birds and bees. "Planets can copulate," Fourier wrote, "1st with themselves by means of north and south poles, like plants; 2nd with another planet by means of emissions from opposite poles; 3rd with an intermediary: the Tuberose is engendered from three aromas: Earth-South, Herschel-North and Sun-South."

All this galactic hanky-panky has consequences here on earth. We are stardust—or, more specifically, star hormones: "A planet is an androgynous body, provided with both sexes and functioning as a male through copulations at the north pole, and as a female by those at the south pole," he wrote. "Each substance of the various animal and vegetable kingdoms is the product of an aroma radiated by one of the heavenly bodies combined with that of another. Cattle are born of an aroma sent out by Jupiter; horses of an aroma from Saturn; roses of an aroma from Mercury; carnations of an aroma from Hebe, the eighth moon of Uranus. The operation is roughly similar to that of our gardeners." This, like any good theory, clears up a host of old questions. Comets, for instance, are actually "aromal swarms destined to nourish the sun and the planets, and their approach is a joyful event for all astral bodies."

Some of Fourier's admirers, notably Engels, suggested that these flights of imagination were mere satire or a smoke screen intended to help smuggle Fourier's revolutionary ideas past the censors. There is scant evidence for this interpretation. Fourier seems to have been genuinely convinced that he had figured out everything from the sexual life of the cosmos to the future extinction of giraffes, which it must be admitted are far too gangly for a perfect globe.[*]

Fourier did, however, employ another type of literary subterfuge. To shake off the "scoffers" who would reject his theory without close study, he wrote in an intentionally obscure style. Deeply paranoid of plagiarism, he reasoned that if nobody could fully understand his new science, then nobody could convincingly claim it for his own. *The Theory of the Four Movements* was intentionally opaque—"a Sphinx without Oedi-

[*] Fourier on the connection between giraffes and the truth: "Truth is only beautiful in our society when it is inactive, and the giraffe, by analogy, is only admirable when it is at rest: when it walks or runs it provokes jeers, as truth provokes jeers when it takes a practical form."

pus," he called it—because its publication was meant to test the critical waters before he unveiled his full theory. Some of Fourier's writings certainly prove that he was capable of clear prose. Either way, the subterfuge was unnecessary. Plagiarism was never a big problem, and the critical response to the *Theory* was silence punctuated by a light smattering of laughter.

While Fourier's most wacky reveries have cast a permanent shadow over his reputation as a serious social theorist—no critic has failed to mention the lemonade sea—they have also made him a perennial darling of the avant-garde.* His erotic, Technicolor vision of the future combined with his (sometimes intentionally) humorous prose and liberal view of human diversity have inspired a long roster of artists and poets.†

In the fall of 1822, fourteen years after publishing his first book, Fourier moved from the provinces to Paris. He was fifty, a severe-looking man with swept-back hair, a high, bulbous forehead, and a large aquiline nose bent slightly to the left. In Paris, he hoped to find a benefactor willing to bankroll the construction of the first model phalanx. Until then, he worked as a bookkeeper for an American firm, expanding his masterpiece in the evenings.

Doubt never seems to have visited the crummy garret in which Fourier wrote. His theory, he maintained, was "more important on its own than all the scientific work done since the human race began." It was

---

* Honoré de Balzac, as translated by Jonathan Beecher, spoofed Fourier thusly: "About the age of fifty you will grow a modest tail thirty-two feet long, which you will maneuver with elegance and grace. The moon will have babies, liver pâtés will grow in the fields, the clouds will rain champagne, the frost will be made out of Roman punch . . ."

† André Breton published a surrealist *Ode to Charles Fourier*. The Situationist International lionized him. A New York art collective calls itself the Uranian Phalanstery. In 1962, the Fluxus artist Wim T. Schippers, best known as the Dutch voice of Kermit the Frog, led a camera crew to a beach in Holland, where in front of the assembled media he walked to the water's edge, uncapped a bottle of Green Spot lemonade, and emptied it into the North Sea. More recently, the artist Paul Chan and the writer and artist Guy Davenport have both engaged seriously and at length with Fourier's ideas.

"the only subject of study that reason should sanction." In its wake, all "economic, moral and political theories will need to be thrown away and preparations made for the most astounding, and happiest event possible on this or any other globe, the transition from social chaos to universal harmony."

This messianic confidence makes even Robert Owen, a man who spoke as if the mere utterance of his ideas could reverse millennia of folly, seem positively modest. Despite this fact, Fourier's efforts to put his theory into action, "on this or any other globe," were distinctly passive. Like Owen, he hoped to advance his vision by converting rich and powerful men. In fact, one of those men was Owen. In April 1824, when Owen was about to depart for the United States to purchase Harmonie, Fourier mailed him a copy of his book *Traité de l'association domestique-agricole*. "If you are agreeable," Fourier's accompanying letter read, "I propose to engage myself with you [Owen], at the salary of the least of your clerks, as the individual responsible for the direction of the mechanism." In other words, Fourier, a man whom Owen had never heard of, was offering, for a humble salary, to assume leadership of the community that Owen was about to build. Owen did not read French, but he passed the letter and book to a friend who did. The friend skimmed the book and sent Monsieur Fourier a polite reply: Thanks, but no thanks.

While Owen was able to weave smoothly through the crowd of power brokers at Aix-la-Chapelle, Fourier was known for his total lack of charm. "Under no circumstance and for no reason did [he] ever abandon himself to mirth," a friend recalled. "In the middle of the jokes and merry talk of his friends he maintained a perpetual impassivity and imperturbable composure. . . . Generally it was only by some sally, by some original sortie against the *civilized*, that he would involve himself in conversation. Then everyone might laugh; he alone would maintain his habitual calm and gravity." In portraits of Fourier, a frown the size and shape of a horseshoe consumes the entire lower half of his face, its tips pointing downward toward a ruffled white cravat. Depending upon the angle of one's sympathy, he looks exceptionally sad or exceptionally mean. In the eyes of his young followers, he had the grumpy, brooding charisma that some—perhaps the French especially—tend to associate with genius.

Along with mailing tracts to powerful men—usually tweaking his theory to the interests of each recipient*—Fourier let it be known around Paris that he would be home each day at noon, just in case some millionaire should wish to discuss bankrolling the construction of a model phalanx.

His first real disciple found him. Victor Considerant, an intelligent young man from Fourier's native region of Franche-Comté, stumbled upon *The Theory of the Four Movements* while studying for the entrance exam to the École Polytechnique, an elite school of military engineering outside of Paris. When he arrived in the capital for university, Considerant befriended Fourier and wrote an abridged popularization of *The Theory of the Four Movements*. It was largely because of Considerant's enthusiasm that Fourier gradually gathered around himself a small, devoted coterie of junior intellectuals, many of them engineering students at the École Polytechnique.

An Apostle

Fourier's noontime millionaire never came knocking, but as far as American Fourierism is concerned, someone even better did. In 1828, a year after New Harmony fell apart, Albert Brisbane, the restless, self-serious son of a shopkeeper turned land magnate from Batavia, New York, sailed for France. He was eighteen, thin, and long faced, with a close-cropped neck beard and heavy-lidded eyes. Arriving in Paris full of rosy ideas about continental intellectualism, he enrolled at the Sorbonne to study French poetry and the towering *philosophes* of the eighteenth-century Enlightenment.

---

* When he sent a summary of his theory to the American consul in Paris, Fourier suggested that a phalanx in North America might be a good method of pacifying recalcitrant Native American tribes.

As a young man on his first trip to Paris, Charles Fourier had been awakened to the incoherence of capitalism by an overpriced apple. Four decades later, not long after Brisbane's arrival in Paris, he too was radicalized by a snack. One evening, during intermission at the opera, he stepped outside in his dinner jacket for some fresh air and an ice cream. Ruminating as he licked, Brisbane wondered abstractly how he had come to possess the ice cream in his hand. The cash he had given to the street vendor had been given to him by his father. His father, in turn, had received the money as rent from farmers to whom he leased land in central New York. The farmers got the cash to pay their rent from the wholesalers to whom they sold their wheat. Brisbane realized that the only real labor in this long chain of value was performed by the poor, hardworking plowmen of Genesee County. It was they, he concluded, who had bought his ice cream. "Do I give [the farmers] an equivalent?" he asked himself. "No! Then I get their labor without equivalent, i.e. for nothing." The discomfiting contrast between their toil and his entr'acte *glace* caused Brisbane to realize, apparently for the first time, that "there is a certain class in society [who] lived on the labor of the masses" and that he was a member of that class.

As he worried over large questions about justice and his purpose in the world, Brisbane's lifelong intellectual ambitions began to seem thin, even frivolous. The courses in philosophy and literature that he was taking at the Sorbonne—"a Joseph's coat of all philosophic colors and shapes"— were silent on this sort of thing. He craved something more serious.

Based entirely on what people were saying in Paris, he decided that Georg Wilhelm Friedrich Hegel, then lecturing in Berlin, would be "the final word on wisdom." With Hegel's Idealism as his object, Brisbane took up German and, in the spring of 1829, left Paris for Berlin.[*]

---

[*] En route, he stopped in Weimar to spend an afternoon with Goethe. The ailing poet, three years from his death, wore a long dark cloak, held his huge head with perfect poise, and kept his hands clasped behind his back like a monk. In a tremulous voice, Goethe warned Brisbane, a young man evidently desperate for an intellectual stronghold, of the human tendency to seek out "those theories which are most congenial to the individual character."

———

As one of the only Americans in Berlin, young Brisbane seemed charmingly exotic to German high society. Self-consciously decked out in a flashy purple topcoat, he was welcomed into the homes of diplomats, intellectuals, and Jewish bankers. (Among the latter group, he befriended a frail young piano whiz: the prodigy Felix Mendelssohn.) Brisbane passed many of his evenings in the parlor of the Beer family, where he spent hours watching Hegel, Europe's modern Sphinx, silently playing hand after hand of whist, his gray hair receding and his failing eyes tinted red with focus.

When Hegel's course began in the fall, Brisbane quickly realized that his imperfect German would conspire with the professor's "obscure and wretched manner of delivery" to render the material incomprehensible. Hegel invariably lectured from a prepared text in a monotone, without looking up. When a gong signaled the end of the period, he stopped midsentence, closed his folio, and left. Struggling to keep up, Brisbane hired another professor, the notable Hegelian Karl Ludwig Michelet, for private lessons. Even with Michelet's help, Brisbane grew frustrated with the baroque abstractions of the dialectic. He decided rather suddenly that "he had seen enough of Christian civilization for a while"—an extreme, if understandable, response to Hegelian prose.

Intent on seeing "barbaric civilization," Brisbane traveled east to Turkey and Greece. Having grown up comfortably in lush, prosperous upper New York, Brisbane was disturbed by the crowded poverty, sere landscapes, and open-air suffering that he saw in the East. In both Constantinople and Athens, people seemed to him to be "vegetating in ignorance and apathy" amid an air of "death and stagnation." He estimated that there was more real wealth—by which he meant fertile land, good roads, human energy, and exploitable resources—in his native Genesee County than in all of Greece.

Hegel describes history as a great lumbering force advancing through various stages toward some final absolute terminus as the consciousness of freedom expands. With this view of things ringing in his ears, Brisbane's trip east seemed to him like a form of time travel—a journey backward along a linear track of historical development. In Paris, Vienna, Berlin, Rome, Athens, and Constantinople, he felt as though he were seeing the saga of human progress laid bare, like geologic strata in a road cut.*

After a long loop back through Europe, Brisbane returned to Berlin. His encounter with extreme poverty, not only in Turkey and Greece, but also in the capitals of western Europe, had further cooled his previous passion for literature and metaphysics.† Rapid-fire exposure to a series of wildly different cultures had convinced him of the powerful and direct effect that social institutions have on the lives of ordinary people. But what sorts of institutions would make people's lives better? Ordinary politics did not appear up to the job. Even democracy could not guarantee a wide distribution of prosperity and happiness. At the same time, he was reading the popular "social science" of the French utopian Henri de Saint-Simon. "The idea of a great social reconstruction," he later wrote, "[took] deep root in my mind."

One idle afternoon, three months after returning to Berlin, Brisbane picked up a book that a Saint-Simonian friend in Paris had sent him. It appeared to be a treatise on farming, not usually Brisbane's area of interest. Flipping the book open to a random page, he saw two words printed in large type: "Attractive Industry." The idea expressed in that phrase—and the following few words about "organizing human labor as to dignify it and render it attractive"—struck Brisbane as brilliant in its simplicity. It had a ring of sweeping ambition that aroused his appetite for a grand, world-salvific idea, but unlike the airy metaphysical conjecture he had begun to reject, the words *attractive industry* seemed addressed to the very practical problem that most people do not enjoy

---

* Here, from the perspective of a cosmopolitan nineteenth-century American, is another version of the medieval notion that history travels with the sun, from east to west. By the nineteenth century, this view of things had been supplemented with a strong dose of Orientalism.

† Brisbane eventually came to parrot Fourier's scorn for philosophers and "the emptiness of the highest philosophical speculations."

the labor they are obliged to perform. If labor—"the dreary lot of the masses"—could somehow be made "attractive," Brisbane immediately concluded, everything would change. Scarcity would become abundance. Drudgery would become satisfaction. The curse of Adam would be lifted. "Those two words," he later wrote, "made on me an indescribable impression. I sprang to my feet, threw down the book and began pacing the floor in a tumult of emotion."

Before finishing an entire chapter of the book—*Traité de l'association domestique-agricole, par Charles Fourier* (the same volume Fourier had sent Owen)—Brisbane was dashing around Berlin with the cheaply bound volume under his arm, trying to "convert," as he put it, his high-society friends. "The darkness which had rested on human destiny was dissipated," he wrote, "light began to shine in." Two words: That's all it took.

Impatient to meet the author, Brisbane left Berlin in May 1832. By the time he crossed the French border, he had resolved to translate the *Traité* into English. He found Fourier at number 5, rue Joquelet, the offices of *La Réforme Industrielle*, an eight-page weekly devoted to the advance of his utopian theory. By then, Fourier was sixty, a dyspeptic bachelor living alone in a small apartment crowded with cats and plants. To the wide-eyed young American, Fourier looked just like Dante, or at least a fresco of Dante that Brisbane had seen in Florence.

At the office of *La Réforme Industrielle* (later renamed *Le Phalanstère*), Fourier sat enthroned in a large armchair while young disciples skittered about, taking notes and preparing tracts. Brisbane presented himself with appropriate genuflection and offered five francs a pop for private, biweekly lessons. Fourier, always short on cash, consented.

For the next two years, Brisbane was fully immersed in Fourier's ideas and world. He studied and worked alongside Victor Considerant and the other French disciples. Brisbane never once saw Fourier smile, but he recalled his years in Paris as an immensely happy time—"days of faith and of enthusiasm, when material obstacles were but straws to be blown to the winds before the vehemence of youth under the inspiration of a grand idea!" In the office on rue Joquelet, the glad reign of

Harmony seemed just over the horizon. One afternoon, Considerant burst into the office wearing a red fez. He tossed a donated bag of cash onto the couch and, adjusting the fez, declared, "In twenty years, we shall be in Constantinople!"

Hard Times

In the spring of 1834, like Moses descending Sinai, Brisbane sailed for New York with a valise full of Fourier's writings.

His conversion to the theory had a distinctly religious quality, with the texts themselves assuming a messianic potency. "An ocean of Social Error Flows over Humanity," Brisbane wrote, "but so mighty is Truth, that one drop cast into it will purify and give life to its dead waters. That drop . . . is the principles discovered by Fourier." Fourier himself never came to the United States or had much to do with the remarkable spread of his ideas in the New World.

Back in Batavia, Brisbane began translating, editing, and writing a book on Fourier's theory for an American readership. Fourier's critique of capitalism and his vision of an abundant, cooperative society had arrived on American shores at an opportune moment. Near the end of Andrew Jackson's presidency, after a decade of western expansion, urban industrialization, and heavy foreign investment, the president pushed to pay down the national debt. Extravagant speculation in freshly "cleared" western land had filled federal coffers and created a massive real estate bubble. Jackson, who had successfully waged war against the Bank of the United States, distrusted financial speculation and paper money. In 1836, he tried to throw a bridle over the runaway economy by issuing an executive order requiring all land purchased by speculators to be paid for in gold or silver. The so-called Specie Circular undercut trust in paper currency, rapidly devaluing the blizzard of cash that had been printed by private banks after the Bank of the United States lost its charter.

In 1837, at the start of Martin Van Buren's presidency, a bad harvest in the United Kingdom caused British lenders to call in some of the credit they had extended to American firms. When an overleveraged New Orleans cotton interest collapsed, other companies quickly followed suit. Anxious merchants swarmed New York banks with commercial paper in hand, seeking to exchange it for gold and silver. The banks, already drained of specie owing to Jackson's policies, could not make the swap. Financial panic set in. When crop prices collapsed, the highly inflated value of western land dropped. As credit dried up, unemployment soared. A long, deep recession set in.

The effects of the so-called Panic of 1837, compounded by a second, smaller financial crisis in 1839, lingered into the middle 1840s. The resulting depression, rivaled only by the Great Depression of the 1930s, was the first major interruption in the remarkable, unruly expansion of American capitalism. Widespread unemployment and the sudden destruction of so much wealth lent credence to a growing chorus of voices insisting that a moneyed elite and the free market threatened the purposes of a democratic, egalitarian republic. Hard times sharpened the national interest in reform schemes of every type.

From their respective soapboxes, socialist reformers and millenarian revivalists looked out upon newly attentive faces. In August 1837, a few months after the market collapsed, the Shakers began their most energetic spiritual revival since Lucy Wright's push into the old Southwest. By the 1840s, the revival, known as "Mother Ann's Work," helped bring the United Society to its demographic zenith, with nearly six thousand believers living in nineteen communities.

Charles Fourier did not live to see his ideas take root in the United States. The prophet of the harmonic future died alone in his small Paris apartment on October 10, 1837. His concierge found him slumped beside his bed, dressed in a bathrobe. His devoted followers took a death mask and buried him in a lead-lined coffin in Montmartre Cemetery.

Three years later, in 1840, Albert Brisbane finally published his book on Fourier. Titled *Social Destiny of Man: or, Association and Reorga nization of Industry*, it was intended to "lay before the American public, the profound and original conceptions of Charles Fourier, on the subject of a re-organization of Society." The book surveys Fourier's whole theory but focuses on the doctrine of attractive industry and the pressing need to construct a model phalanx. More than anything that Fourier himself had written, *Social Destiny of Man* was a practical guide to founding a Fourierist phalanx. It would become the bible of American Fourierism.[*]

Brisbane was a keen propagandist. He knew that if Fourier's theory was going to gain traction in the United States, certain adjustments had to be made. His first move was to rebrand the theory, replacing the exotic-sounding "Fourierism" with the practical "Associationism." He also diligently pasteurized the French texts of their more lurid digressions about supertonic orgies and baby doll types. Hundreds of pages on sex in the era of Harmony were left untranslated.[†] Emerson wrote that the working-class men and women whom Brisbane endeavored to convert were protected "by the thin veil of the French language" from Fourier's plan "to secure the greatest amount of kissing that the infirmity of the human constitution admitted." Emerson, a radical in the lecture hall but a puritan in the boudoir, attributed the Frenchman's erotic theories to his nation of origin. "Fourier," he remarked dryly, "was very French indeed."

As it happened, the linguistic veil was too thin. Journalists found their way to the original texts and presented the American public with every kinky detail. In defense of their movement, the leading Associationists pointed out that Fourier was writing about the distant future. It was too fine a point. Like Owen's loudly proclaimed infidelity, Fourier's writings on sex and marriage became a major impediment to the spread of his ideas in the United States.

---

[*] *A Popular View of the Doctrines of Charles Fourier,* published four years later by the New York journalist Parke Godwin, is the most compelling Fourierist book written for an American audience. The material is the same as in Brisbane's book, but Godwin was a better writer.

[†] *Le nouveau monde amoureux,* Fourier's unfinished book on the polymorphous sexuality of life in Harmony, was not published even in France until 1967.

———

By the time *Social Destiny of Man* came out, Brisbane had already begun giving lectures on the wonders of Associationism in Philadelphia and New York. To find a wider audience for the theory, he rented an office in Manhattan, at the intersection of Broadway and Canal. Walt Whitman used to see him around the neighborhood, striding purposefully in a long sack coat. "His step is quick," wrote the poet, "and his arms swing awkwardly, as if he were trying to knock his elbows together behind him. Albert Brisbane the Socialist; the capitalist, too—an odd circumstance for a radical in New York! Somehow or other, he always looks as if he were attempting to think out some problem a little too hard for him."

Working upstairs from Brisbane on Canal Street was an eccentric young Whig journalist named Horace Greeley. Greeley, who had grown up poor in rural New England, was starting to make a name for himself writing about the rights of workers and the dangers of corporate monopoly. A friend of Brisbane's who thought that Greeley was "damned fool enough" to buy into Fourier's theory, suggested Brisbane bring him some literature.

Brisbane carried a copy of *Social Destiny* a few flights upstairs, where he found Greeley bent over his desk, editing a modestly circulating Whig weekly called the *New-Yorker*. Greeley cut a striking figure. He was tall, baby-faced, and nearsighted. Even as a young man, his bald, egg-shaped head was encircled by wispy white hair. He wore a bushy beard that was confined, in the preferred style of nineteenth-century pacifists, entirely to his neck.* Barely looking up to acknowledge his visitor, Greeley accepted Brisbane's proffered book. He promised to look it over that evening on his way to Boston.

When Greeley returned to Manhattan a few days later, he was a

---

* This style, perhaps a stylistic response to the preference of military men for elaborate mustachios and muttonchops, was a common sight at the nineteenth-century utopias. The Shakers, who experimented with the neck beard in the mid-1870s, called the style "throat whiskers."

convert. In the theory of attractive industry, he saw a systematic or "scientific" version of his own general politics—a middle road between laissez-faire capitalism and the anti-individualist communism of Owen and the Shakers. Greeley, who played a prominent role in nearly every progressive cause of his day, saw Associationism as "the Reform which shall embosom almost every other."

In 1841, Greeley folded the *New-Yorker* and founded a daily newspaper called the *New-York Tribune*. Along with news, it published poetry, serialized fiction, literary reviews, and an endless stream of morally feisty editorials, many of them written by Greeley himself. In a crowded media market, Greeley's paper distinguished itself by reporting on the political happenings in Albany and Washington in direct, everyday language. In its pages, Greeley championed little-known writers such as Edgar Allan Poe, Margaret Fuller, Mark Twain, and Karl Marx. At a penny an issue, the *Tribune* was significantly cheaper than its competitors. Working-class readers from New England to the Mississippi subscribed in droves, making the *Tribune* the most popular broadsheet in the country. Greeley, with his odd appearance, humble origins, and distinctive prose style, became one of the most recognizable figures in the country—the straight-talking eccentric from the provinces who gave a voice to working people.

Aside from Brisbane's road-to-Damascus epiphany in Berlin, Horace Greeley's conversion was the decisive event in the history of American Fourierism. An experienced reformer, he helped Brisbane found the Fourier Association of the City of New York and a Fourierist journal called *The Future*. Brisbane paid Greeley $500 a year to print a regular column on Fourierism on the front page of the *Tribune*. Like an advertorial, the columns ran under a disclaimer: "This column has been purchased by the Advocates of Association in order to lay their principles before the public. Its editorship is entirely distinct from that of the *Tribune*." Spurred by these articles, interest in Fourier's ideas exploded. Brisbane began printing pamphlets on Associationism that circulated widely. A bound collection of his *Tribune* columns sold almost ten thousand copies.* At the start of 1843, the *Tribune*'s editorial page officially endorsed both Brisbane and Associationism.

One of the many "passions" that Fourier identified is the drive toward "Unity," the insatiable human impulse to form groups. During the middle third of the nineteenth century, Americans typically belonged to a wide variety of clubs—fraternal orders, Bible study groups, secret societies, drinking lodges, temperance leagues, quilting bees, professional guilds, book clubs. "Americans of all ages, all conditions, and all minds are constantly joining together in groups," marveled Tocqueville in 1831. "When Americans have a feeling or idea they wish to bring to the world's attention, they will immediately seek out others who share that feeling . . . and join forces." In this atmosphere of spirited confederation, a handful of Fourierist clubs was swiftly mustered.

Enthusiasm was highest where the Panic of 1837 had hit hardest. The fledgling industrial corridor that tracked the route of the newly opened Erie Canal across New York State was particularly devastated by the depression. The region, already a hotbed of millenarian evangelism, proved amazingly receptive to the gospel of passional attraction. After a well-attended Fourierist convention in Batavia, one Rochesterian wrote, "All western New York is in a deep, shaking agitation on this subject."

Like the millenarians of the Kentucky Revival, who interpreted the popularity of their camp meetings as proof of God's presence, Brisbane interpreted this "shaking agitation" as evidence of the truth of Fourier's

---

* Because of his endless propagandizing and his connection to Greeley, Brisbane is usually identified by historians as a journalist, a typical sideline for nineteenth-century reformers. Journalism was evidently in his blood. His son Arthur Brisbane became an influential editor and a hugely successful columnist for *Time* magazine and the Hearst papers. When he died in 1936, *Time* described his career as "the most remarkable ever achieved by a writer for the U.S. press." The obituary barely mentions his father, dismissing Albert Brisbane as "a well-to-do parlor radical." Arthur S. Brisbane, Albert's great-grandson, was the *New York Times*'s public editor from 2010 until 2012.

ideas. "Would it not seem that this very general response to, and acceptance of, an entirely new and radically reforming doctrine by intelligent
and practical men, proves that there is something in it harmonizing
perfectly with the ideas of truth, justice, economy and order?"

In the fall of 1842, less than a year after Brisbane's inaugural *Tribune*
column, the first American phalanx got under way. The financial crisis
had left a third of the men in New York City out of work. Inspired by
Brisbane's articles, thirty unemployed machine workers from Brooklyn
pooled their savings, borrowed more, and bought two thousand acres
of woodland abutting a small mountain in the foothills of the Poconos,
in Pike County, Pennsylvania. The land was cheap—$1.25 per acre,
with only $100 down. Calling themselves the Social Reform Unity, the
colonists set to work clearing land and building bridges over the many
small streams that ran through their property. With dreams of a grand
phalanstery, they prepared for a great ingathering of working people.
Their long, detailed constitution conveys the grandiosity of their intentions. Article fourteen, for instance, stipulates that all phalanx money
was to be kept in a specially made safe with seven locks and that the
seven corresponding keys are to be held by seven separate officers. A
cash withdrawal to buy beans in town required a writ signed by the executive council and countersigned by the elected phalanx president.

It is unlikely that the colonists ever had an opportunity to deploy this
elaborate bureaucratic ritual. They were broke from day one, and most
of their time was spent prizing rocks from their frozen fields. Besides a
half-acre garden that had been cleared by an earlier homesteader, their
boulder-strewn land proved unyielding. The members were all manual
workers, but few of them had any farming experience. Having recklessly begun their adventure in November, they were soon hungry, cold,
and in debt. According to one observer, the Brooklynites struggled
"manfully with the rocks, wood, climate and other opposing circumstances, for about ten months; and agreed pretty well [among them-
selves] till near the close." But, as "the means decreased," the "legislating

and chafing increased." They had expected cash and new members to come from Brooklyn, but, times being tight, no support came. The community went bust within the year.

This first, hasty effort to build an American phalanx augured darkly the struggles ahead. By the time the members of the Social Reform Unity were beating their bleary retreat to Brooklyn, far grander schemes were already being hatched.

A North American Phalanx

By the end of 1843, six small, rural phalanxes had been established, most of them set up as joint-stock corporations in which members bought shares. There were two in Pennsylvania (including the Social Reform Unity), two in New York, and one each in Indiana and New Jersey. Many others were in the works. Brisbane, Greeley, and other leaders of the burgeoning movement worried that these small, half-cocked efforts would fail, discrediting Fourier's theory on their way down. The propagandists in New York urged the thousands of new, self-proclaimed Associationists to slow down, pool their resources, scout decent land, and build a proper phalanstery.

Brisbane was the most rigidly doctrinaire of the American Associationists, but even he knew that following Fourier's scheme to the letter would be impossible. Getting 1,620 people—exactly twice the 810 passional types—into a prebuilt phalanstery was not likely. He drafted a more realistic set of guidelines. To truly count as a phalanx, he wrote, a community ought to have at least four hundred members, $400,000 in capital, and two thousand acres of good land located close enough to a city to market its goods and produce. Any community that did not meet these baseline criteria, Brisbane warned, could neither support itself nor allow for the genuine, harmonic operation of passional attraction and attractive industry.

Like Owen's New Moral World, Fourier's vision for global transformation, what he usually called the New Industrial World, hinged on the assumption that a single working model, a brick-and-mortar prototype of the new utopia, would inspire a surge of imitators. In the fall of 1842, hoping to catalyze the formation of that prototype, Brisbane and Greeley drafted a constitution and began selling stock for a projected "North American Phalanx," to be located somewhere outside a major northeastern city.[*]

A few months later, without consulting Brisbane or the officers of the Fourier Association of the City of New York, a group of sixty Associationists from Albany and Troy, New York—carpenters, tradesmen, shopkeepers, and their families—declared themselves the North American Phalanx and bought a 673-acre farm in Red Bank, New Jersey, just across the harbor from Brooklyn and lower Manhattan. Brisbane worried that the upstate group lacked the numbers or cash to establish a proper phalanx. Even so, he decided to support them and bought stock in the NAP, as the colony became known. Horace Greeley did the same, lending his celebrity to their effort by serving as their vice president.

During the summer of 1843, the group moved onto their land and began farming. Within a year, the initial group of sixty had expanded to one hundred. They were led by Charles Sears, a friend of Brisbane's. Rather than constructing a grand phalanstery, they moved into two pre-existing farmhouses and a few small, temporary dwellings. They built a sawmill, a gristmill, and a few small workshops and concentrated on getting their farm established. Like almost every other utopian community of the era, the NAP was short on farmers, but they consulted with the Shakers about the best agricultural practices for a collective society and their fertile land was soon yielding a profitable surplus. Most of their income came from selling produce and flour in Manhattan. After a year of thrift and hard work, the community paid down much of their mortgage.

---

[*] A remarkable fact about this and other joint-stock phalanxes is that, at the outset, the general optimism about their success ran so high that stock was sold to speculators who did not even intend to join one of the communities. Some investors clearly saw their support as philanthropy, but others apparently considered the imminent New Industrial World to be a hot investment.

Despite its modest size, the NAP, which sat just across the water from a huge polyglot metropolis, had one of the most diverse populations of any American utopia. At least twelve different religious denominations were represented. Brisbane, who wanted the community to serve as a national showcase for Fourierism, repeatedly urged them to expand. Demonstrating prudence where Robert Owen had not, the members of the NAP resisted his advice and kept admissions to a trickle. For twelve years, despite steady turnover and a long waiting list of applicants, the phalanx never grew beyond 120 members.

The women of the NAP voted in all community matters. Many of them wore baggy pants under knee-length skirts, in the "Turkish style" that was soon to be advocated by temperance and women's rights activist Amelia Bloomer. Child care, usually provided by older women, was collective and free. As at New Harmony, the young, single phalansterians enjoyed unusually relaxed relations with one another. Dances and concerts were frequent. For Fourier's birthday, they held a ball at which people wore costumes representing the various stations of historical ascent from Edenism to Harmony.

One of the most alluring promises of life "within association" was an improved diet. Fourier, an unabashed sybarite (at least on paper), placed food at the very core of his utopian vision. "In Harmony," he prophesied, "each person will be assured five good meals a day, not including the interludes (or feasts of transition), which will consist of four light snacks of about five minutes each, or the harmonious reunions, where less than two hours' time is generally spent in dining, appropriate to the season and to each individual's taste." In the harmonic future, sugarcane, raised on a newly verdant African savanna, will replace wheat as the global staple. Harmonian chefs will prove their worth by preparing 810 dishes for each of the 810 "passional types." Once the state has become obsolete, a benign variety of nationalism will persist in the form of international, *Iron Chef*-style cook-offs—a harmonic alternative to war.

Although the members of the NAP never scaled these heights of harmonic cookery, they ate much better than their working-class peers in "civilization." As at the other small utopias, meals were eaten communally at long tables in a large dining room. There was a special table for vegetarians. The colonists ordered from an extensive menu, and the cost of whatever they ate was recorded and debited from individual accounts that were replenished by labor on the farm or in the kitchen or in one of several light industries. (This system was designed to prevent abstemious communards from resenting their hungrier peers.) Fourier would have been pleased that the community planted seven thousand fruit trees and built a special fruit-canning "seristery" (Fourier's term for a structure housing the work of a particular category of labor, or "series").

The NAP had its own school, including a kindergarten, still very much a novelty in the 1840s. For adults, foreign-language classes, scientific and philosophical lectures, and lessons in Fourier's theory were offered for free. The community maintained a large library. Greeley and Brisbane came to speak regularly, as did other luminaries such as Emerson and Margaret Fuller.

In 1844, the community hosted Robert Owen, who had come to the United States to visit his sons and to check in on the new burst of utopian activity inspired by Fourier's writings. Fourier and Owen, who were born just eleven months apart, disagreed about many things, but they had remarkably similar ideas about the ideal way to bring on a new and perfected social order. Fourier believed that Owen lacked a basic understanding of pleasure, claiming that the New Moral World was too Spartan to ever take hold. He did, however, admire Owen's success at New Lanark. In Fourier's schema of historical evolution, he placed *Les Owenistes* a half step ahead of the wretched civilizees.*

For his part, Owen never admitted much debt to Fourier (or anyone else), but there was at least one volume of Fourier's writings in circulation at New Harmony. When the *Philanthropist* was stranded in ice,

---

* In the 1820s, when Fourier heard of Owen's intentions to inaugurate a communal experiment in the United States, he was guardedly optimistic. "If [Monsieur Owen] appreciates the plan of *compound action,* in which passionate and industrial ties are combined, then Civilization is over and done with."

Robert Dale Owen passed his evenings studying the theory of passional attraction. In his diary, he noted that Fourier's system was "a strange and most original production, containing many excellent ideas, but mixed up with much which is, I think not practical." Interestingly, Owen's eldest son was particularly taken with Fourier's "masterly" theories on early education, a subject that his father considered a particular specialty.*

In many respects, it is remarkable that Owen's New Moral World and Fourier's New Industrial World were conceived in total isolation from each other. The simultaneity of these two visions—though not the American efforts to implement them, which were staggered by a decade—indicates the broader intellectual currents that fed into both theories: a post-Enlightenment belief in limitless progress; a distaste for revolutionary insurrection; a faith in the potential of model communities to initiate social change; a belief in the rapid approach of a golden age; and an overarching conviction that a true and perfect "science" of society exists.

City of Refuge

One regular visitor to the North American Phalanx was a Unitarian minister named George Ripley. Ripley, the son of a wealthy farming family from Greenfield, Massachusetts, graduated from Harvard Divinity School in 1826, the same year that New Harmony fell apart. A stocky, patrician-looking man with curly hair, dark eyes, and gold-rimmed spectacles, Ripley was a popular minister. After Harvard, he assumed the pulpit of a small, stone box of a church on Purchase Street in Boston. His style of ministry—placid, questioning, shot through with erudite charm—contrasted sharply with the emotional, conversion-oriented revivalism that was then sweeping the United States.

Ripley sermonized in a philosophical mode, dwelling more on ethics than hellfire. His habits of mind and social milieu were far more literary

---

* Robert Dale Owen's diary is written in English, but he switches to German whenever he criticizes his (non-German-reading) father or comments on good-looking women.

than theological. The first meeting of the vaunted Transcendental Club took place in his living room, in 1836. The club's loose membership was drawn from Ripley's circle of friends. It included his wife, Sophia (née Dana), his cousin Ralph Waldo Emerson, Amos Bronson Alcott, Henry David Thoreau, Margaret Fuller, and Orestes Brownson. This much mythologized group of Yankee intellectuals was basically a migrating tea symposium with overlapping interests in liberal Unitarianism and Romanticism, Kant and Swedenborg, Goethe and Coleridge, Hegel and the Vedas. Ripley, Emerson, and Fuller cofounded and coedited *The Dial*, the philosophical and literary review that broadcast the group's sensibility and thought—much of what came to be called "transcendentalism"—to a national audience.

Transcendentalism grew out of the confluence of several intellectual currents, but it initially took shape as a rift within the Unitarian Church. Dissatisfied with what Emerson called "the cold corpse Unitarianism of Harvard College," the men and women who would come to be called transcendentalists sought an understanding of faith that was more personal and more vital. Following the lead of British and German Romantics, the transcendentalists elevated private spiritual intuition above arcane dogma and theological argumentation. By conceiving of the divine as immanent, by locating God in the soul of the individual and within the totality of nature, they blurred the traditional boundary between Creator and creation. "Within and Above are synonymous," Emerson wrote in 1834. While this sort of thing scandalized the old-guard Unitarians at Harvard—who, incidentally, had waged their own rebellion against Puritan Congregationalism a few decades earlier—there was very little irreverence in what the transcendentalists said and wrote.*

---

* For the old guard, one annoyance was the new generation's effort to "rationalize" scripture by claiming that faith did not require a belief in the miraculous suspension of natural laws. One needn't believe in the multiplication of fish or the strolling over water; the words of Jesus are sufficient miracle. To Congregationalists and evangelicals peering in from outside, this drama probably looked like one bunch of deistic infidels (old-school Unitarians) squabbling with another group of deistic infidels (more liberal Unitarians)—in other words, like Sodom censuring Gomorrah.

The earnest search for an authentic faith and ethics pervaded their every poetic sally.

They came to be called transcendentalists because, as Ripley put it, they believed "in an order of truths which transcend the sphere of the external senses. . . . [We] maintain that the truth of religion does not depend on tradition, nor on historical facts, but has an unerring witness in the soul." In other words, the most important things in life can be known without the assistance of the senses or traditional institutions. They might be called deists, but unlike many deists, they did not generally suppose that reason is the surest path to truth. This epistemic stance, which rejects traditional sources of wisdom and grounds the highest order of truths upon the inner contemplation of unfettered individuals, could not help but produce rebellion, both spiritual and social.

There have been moments in American history when the default first step of anyone interested in social reform was to found a magazine, or draft a political candidate, or organize a march, or occupy a public space. During the 1840s, anyone with new ideas about how the world ought to work inevitably considered rounding up a group of fellow travelers and buying a farm on which to nurture, and from which to broadcast, their particular vision. Communes (a word not yet in circulation; they were called communities, associations, or phalanxes) were founded by free lovers, nonlovers, vegetarians, communists, abolitionists, anarchists, Swedenborgians, atheists, spiritualists, Adventists, and teetotalers. For every community that broke ground, a hundred were sketched on paper. "We are a little wild here with numberless projects of social reform," Emerson wrote to Thomas Carlyle in 1840. "Not a reading man but has a draft of a new community in his waistcoat pocket." The notion of advancing a cause by founding a community made particular sense in the United States. The Republic itself, especially its founding mythology as a city upon a hill, could be understood as a set of new ideas made manifest as a physical community. At meetings of the Transcendental Club, there was often general talk of founding a community that would foster a more egalitarian, "poetical" existence. Besides, they already had a quarterly.

At the time, the appeal of communalism as a mechanism of reform was burnished by the ongoing prosperity of the religious communalists. In *The Dial*, Sophia Ripley wrote an effusive dispatch from the village of the Society of Separatists of Zoar, a sect of German communists similar to the Rappites. At a Zoarite village in Ohio, Ripley found "oppression nowhere and abundance everywhere." Like visitors to the Shaker villages, she marveled at the "exquisite neatness" and "purest whiteness" of everything from the separatists' curtains to their bread. Communalism, Ripley proclaimed, offered the women of Zoar a degree of comfort and leisure that was elsewhere reserved for the wives of rich men.

Of course, no sect offered a more compelling example than the Shakers. By the time the transcendentalists began discussing communalism, the United Society had become a seemingly permanent part of the New England landscape. The eleven villages in the East stood quiet sentinel, passively asserting the possibility of a radically different form of society. By then the Shakers were even looked upon with a measure of respect, as somewhat queer guardians of old Yankee virtue. In 1839, George and Sophia Ripley toured several Shaker communities and were struck by the pious, cooperative life they witnessed. The young Nathaniel Hawthorne, a close friend to both Ripley and Emerson, also spent time with the Shakers, eventually setting two of his lesser, bluntly allegorical stories at the immense village in Hancock, Massachusetts. Despite a general allergy to religious protocol, Hawthorne was impressed. "On the whole, they lead a good and comfortable life . . . a man could not do a wiser thing than to join them."* Charles Dana, a young Harvard Fourierist and Ripley acolyte, wrote that "the idea of

---

* Hawthorne's view of the United Society soured later in his life. He eventually described them as a "filthy set." George Ripley underwent a similar shift, calling the United Society "a detestable, miserly, barren aristocracy, without a grain of humanity about it."

founding a society of associated families was strengthened considerably by the experience of the Shakers, and this argument was constantly brought forward in the meetings of those engaged in studying the subject."

Among the Yankee intelligentsia, the appealing example set by the rural sects dovetailed with an increasing distaste for city living. As the Northeast rapidly urbanized, its sooty industrial cities became, for many, the chief emblem of a corrupt, alienating society. Following the lead of their Romantic-era British counterparts, the writers of New England's literary renaissance idealized the pastoral life of their yeoman neighbors. The American farmer, Emerson wrote in *The Dial,* is "the Caesar, the Alexander of the soil. . . . Innocence and Justice have written their names on his brow."* In a later number of the same magazine, the education reformer Elizabeth Palmer Peabody, Hawthorne's sister-in-law and the proprietor of a popular Boston bookshop, wrote that "a true life, although it aims beyond the highest star, is redolent of the healthy earth. The perfume of clover lingers about it. The lowing of cattle is the natural bass to the melody of human voices." These sorts of musings welded the Jeffersonian worship of the freeborn plowman—itself an implicit critique of urban money culture—with poetic notions of a sanctified, simplified life spent stooped among cabbages.

And then along came Fourier. In October 1840, not long after George and Sophia Ripley returned from the western Shaker villages, *The Dial* ran an enthusiastic, unsigned review of Brisbane's *Social Destiny of Man.* "The name of Fourier," it read, "may be placed at the head of modern thinkers, whose attention has been given to the practical evils of society and the means of their removal." However, the reviewer warned, it would be wise to separate Fourier's "general principles" from the details he uses to illustrate them, "many of which may be so adapted to the

---

* Thoreau is a notable exception. In *Walden* he calls the American farmer a serf, forced to eat the soil.

French character, as to prejudice their reception with persons of opposite habits and associations."

That same month, at a gathering of the Transcendental Club in
Emerson's parlor, Ripley stood to say that the time had come for the
group to put their high-flown ideas to the test. He suggested they pool
their money, buy some land, and start a community. By farming cooperatively and living simply, Ripley enthused, they would have plenty of
free time to write and think (a miscalculation about farm living made by
generations of urban intellectuals). Along with farming, they could start
a school in which to test some of the unorthodox pedagogical ideas they
had been kicking around. Maybe they would even make a little money.
At the very least they would escape the mercantile hubbub of Boston to
live, as Thoreau wrote of his time by Walden Pond, "deliberately."

The previous summer, the Ripleys had vacationed at a dairy farm
near the village of West Roxbury, nine miles outside Boston. The property, owned by the Ellis family, was beautiful—175 acres of rolling pastureland abutting a pine forest with views of a gentle bend in the Charles
River. Through the middle of a central meadow ran a small stream for
which the place was named: Brook Farm. It was for sale, and Ripley
suggested to his friends that they buy it.

In the early spring of 1841, George and Sophia Ripley, Nathaniel
Hawthorne, and a small group of like-minded men and women made
a down payment. By May, thirteen of them had relocated to the property. They moved into the large house that sat at the top of the long
meadow overlooking the distant river. The building, which they dubbed
the Hive, was shaded by an ancient sycamore. The downstairs parlor
housed Ripley's extensive library. The kitchen and dining room were
large enough for the whole community to eat together.

The Brook Farmers, as they began to call themselves, may have been
influenced by all the talk of "association" issuing from Brisbane and the
Tribune, but they did not set out to form a phalanx. They knew about
Fourier from Brisbane's columns and book, but when they sat around

the stove that spring in West Roxbury, there was no talk of attractive industry or passional attraction. In fact, soon after Ripley proposed buying the property, *The Dial* endorsed the endeavor while explicitly rejecting any connection to Fourier. "Our imagination rebels against [Fourier's] attempt to circumvent moral freedom, and imprison it in his Phalanx."* Instead, *The Dial* described Brook Farm and its ambitions in Christian terms. The new community would be "a reorganization of society itself, on those very principles of love to God and love to man, which Jesus Christ realized in his own daily life." Tapping into the era's pervasive millenarianism, the author equated the inauguration of Brook Farm with a (very, very) broadly conceived notion of the millennium as a revolution in virtue: "For each man to think and live on this method [of mutual aid] is perhaps the Second Coming of Christ." Even so, no particular religious dogma, except perhaps the antidogma dogma of liberal Unitarianism, held sway at Brook Farm. The community's first constitution prohibited any sort of religious test for membership.

More than any other nineteenth-century utopian community, the first year at Brook Farm resembles the modern image of a commune. The early members were middle-class intellectuals and reformer types—Harvard grads, feminists, musicians, poets, health foodists, liberal Unitarians, socialists, and abolitionists. Hawthorne called them "a knot of dreamers." Their ambitions were more aesthetic than economic or programmatic. They aspired to merge three separate institutions—a farm, a school, and a home—into one harmonious whole. They intended to proceed by intuition and consensus. On their modest Arcadia, they set out to build, as they put it, "paradise anew"—milking cows in the morning and writing blank verse at night by the fire.

The biggest names in the Transcendental Club didn't join. Emerson, the living axis around which New England intellectual life turned, had initially been enthusiastic about the idea. Like Ripley, he was some-

---

* The need for this denial of allegiance shows the influence that Associationism already had by 1841. You could not speak of forming a community without people thinking of Fourier.

times frustrated with the navel-gazing mind-set of his transcendentalist cohort. The practicality of Ripley's plan—the thought of actually *doing* something—appealed to him. But when the time came to join up, his need for privacy and his reflexive distaste for what he called "communities of opinion" kept him on the sidelines.* Having helped encourage the idea, he felt guilty about not pitching in, telling Ripley that his decision had been reached "very slowly and, I may almost say, with penitence."† While he never officially joined, Emerson was a frequent guest at the Farm. Thoreau also stayed away, coming only for a few short visits. He was less ambivalent than his friend Emerson: "I'd rather keep bachelor's hall in hell than go to board in heaven." The brilliant Margaret Fuller, America's first female public intellectual and a close friend to many of the founding Brook Farmers, didn't join either, believing from the outset that Ripley's scheme would fail. Like Emerson, she visited often, taking a carriage from Boston to the Farm to read aloud from early drafts of her latest work and to be worshipped by the rapt young women of the community.‡

The transcendentalists did not tend to advocate any particular economic doctrine, but they worried in a general way about the moral and aesthetic fallout of capitalism. In an 1837 address at Harvard, Thoreau, a graduating senior, described "the commercial spirit" as a national illness: "It infuses into all our thoughts and affections a degree of its own selfishness; we become selfish in our patriotism, selfish in our

---

* From "Self-Reliance": "Well, most men have bound their eyes with one or another handkerchief, and attached themselves to some one of these communities of opinion. This conformity makes them not false in a few particulars, authors of a few lies, but false in all particulars. Their every truth is not quite true. Their two is not the real two, their four not the real four; so that every word they say chagrins us and we know not where to begin to set them right."
† In his diary, Emerson was more dismissive. "I have not yet conquered my own house . . . ," he wrote. "Shall I raise the siege of this hen coop, and march baffled away to a pretended siege of Babylon? It seems to me that to do so were to dodge the problem I am set to solve, and hide my own impotency in the thick of a crowd."
‡ To some communitarians, the refusal of these notables to join up was a mark of egotism. "[Ripley] went to work like a hero," wrote John Humphrey Noyes, "while Emerson stood by smiling incredulity."

domestic relations, selfish in our religion." That same year, Emerson told the Cambridge Phi Beta Kappa Society that "public and private avarice make the air we breathe thick and fat. . . . Young men of the fairest promise, who begin life upon our shores . . . are hindered from action by disgust which the principles on which business is managed inspire, and turn drudges, or die of disgust,—some of them suicides."

Ripley shared these views. He hoped to make Brook Farm a place where "the pressure of competitive institutions" could be toned down— "to substitute," as he put it, "a system of brotherly cooperation for one of selfish competition." But he did not seek to abolish private property. "The evils arising from Trade and Money," he wrote, "grow out of Social Organization, not from an intrinsic vice in the things themselves." The Brook Farmers were emphatically not communists in the Shaker or Owenite mold, but, as one of them put it, they hoped to found "a city of refuge for men and women who refused to be absorbed by money making."

In one way or another, all the nineteenth-century utopias animated the tricky negotiation between individualism and communalism that defines civic life.* For the millenarian sects—the Shakers, the Perfectionists, the Rappites—the obvious desirability of collectivism over individualism was a matter of scriptural imperative. To them, private liberty was hardly a value worth preserving. Elsewhere, things were less clear-cut. George Ripley was particularly keen to synthesize the two poles of this dialectic. He was not a radical by nature. As an undergraduate at Harvard, he had been shunned by his classmates for refus-

---

* The word *individualism* actually came into common usage in the United States as a slur, meaning something like selfishness or egotism, but worse, since it describes a social trend, not a personal failing. Owen wrote, "There never has been an old principle to be abandoned, that produced so much evil as the principle of individualism is now effecting throughout society." For both the Associationists and the Owenites, it was an antonym for socialism. The American Fourierists picked up the term and used it to describe the outlook that they saw at the root of every social problem. It was Emerson who redeemed the word, designating it a virtue, not a vice. Thanks largely to Tocqueville, the word has come to name one of the most essential American traits. Franklin Roosevelt called individualism "the great watchword of American life."

ing to join the "custard riots" that occasionally broke out over the lousy food in the commons. He arrived at Brook Farm carrying the intellectual baggage of transcendentalism, including its reverence for the moral and spiritual intuition of the solitary person. For some transcendentalists, this emphasis on private contemplation led to an active social disengagement. Thoreau made his stand on the shore of Walden Pond. Emerson remained at his farm, writing that "no law can be sacred to me but that of my own nature." Addressing himself to a hypothetical do-gooder seeking contributions, he famously asked, "Are they my poor?"

For George Ripley, this moral exaltation of the individual was counterweighed by a nagging sense of universal brotherhood—an impulse toward what we would now call "social justice." Before he left his pulpit on Purchase Street, he told his congregation, "I cannot witness the glaring inequalities of condition, the hollow pretention of pride, the scornful apathy with which many urge the prostration of man, the burning zeal with which they run the race of selfish competition, with no thought for the elevation of their brethren. . . ." Ripley's response to Emerson's hypothetical philanthropist would have been an unequivocal "Yes"; they were his poor. Ripley believed that the community at Brook Farm could prove that the dichotomy between freedom and mutual aid is illusory—that personal liberty and collectivism can both be had in abundance. In a letter to the head of the Owenite and communistic Skaneateles Community, he wrote: "The great problem is to guarantee individualism against the masses, on the one hand, and the masses against the individual, on the other. In society as now organized, the many are slaves to a few favored individuals in a community. I should dread the bondage of individuals to the power of the mass." Ripley believed that the total abolition of private property would "so far destroy the independence of the individual, as to interfere with the great object of all Social Reform,—namely . . . the substitution of a race of free, noble, holy men and women instead of the dwarfish and mutilated specters which now cover the earth."

The Brook Farmers' effort to steer between the Scylla of tyrannical collectivism and the Charybdis of unrestrained individualism took shape
in the economic foundation they laid for the colony. Like most of the
Fourierist phalanxes being mustered at the same time, Brook Farm was
set up as a joint-stock corporation. The founding members all bought
shares for $500, guaranteeing them lifelong membership and a 5 per-
cent annual return. Those who could not afford stock could compen-
sate with extra labor. Children raised at the farm would gain automatic
membership when they turned twenty. Everyone under ten or over seventy got free room and board. There were to be no servants or household staff. (The fact that this latter rule had to be written indicates the
class of members initially attracted to Brook Farm.) Men and women
had equal rights. All members were entitled to a "social minimum" of
shelter, clothing, nourishment, and health care. Education and culture—in many ways the raison d'être for the entire enterprise—came
free. Once you paid for your bed, one member wrote, "the Greek and
Latin, the aesthetic philosophy, the singing and dancing were thrown
in."

The Brook Farmers aspired, as Ripley wrote Emerson, "to combine
the thinker and the worker, as far as is possible, in a single individual . . .
to prepare a society of liberal, intelligent, and cultivated persons, whose
relations with each other would permit a more wholesome and simple
life." Everyone was expected to perform some manual labor, most of
which was on the farm. Like many of the communards of the 1960s
and 1970s, the early Brook Farmers were long on theory but short on
agricultural know-how. For some, the sheer novelty of farmwork was
sustaining, at least for a season or two. Soft-handed Nathaniel Hawthorne, thirty-seven and fresh from a stultifying job in the Boston Cus-
tom House, spent a spring and summer at the community reveling in his
first taste of physical labor. Although his family in Boston was disturbed
by the thought of their prodigy doing menial chores, Hawthorne wrote
home about the joys of milking and shoveling manure. He marveled at
the appearance on his body of previously unknown muscles and signed
at least one letter home: "Nath. Hawthorne, Ploughman."

Although the Brook Farmers' plan to reinvent themselves as plowmen-intellectuals was principally about creating a more wholesome, spiritually unified existence, it was also tinged with a leveling economics. At Brook Farm, unlike pretty much anywhere else, physical and mental labor were equally compensated: $1.00 per day, at first. "If Democracy was the sublime truth which it was held up to be," wrote one Brook Farmer, "it should be raised up from the sphere of politics, from the sphere of law and constitutions; it should be raised up into life and be made social. The principle of equality, which allowed every man's vote to be as good as that of every other man, should be extended so that in society and in social life the same principle of equality should be applied throughout."

Genteel Bostonians may have been perplexed to see their peers mucking stalls, but they took to the idea more easily than the actual farmers of West Roxbury. Despite the fact that many Brook Farmers were clergymen, their Congregationalist neighbors regarded the colonists as libertine infidels and, more damningly, inept farmers. *The Blithedale Romance,* Hawthorne's tenderly satirical novel about the community, recounts the contempt of the locals. "They told slanderous fables about our inability to yoke our own oxen, or to drive them afield when yoked, or to release the poor brutes from their conjugal bond at nightfall . . . that the cows laughed at our awkwardness at milking time. . . . Finally, as an ultimate catastrophe, these mendacious rogues circulated a report that we communitarians were exterminated, to the last man, by severing ourselves asunder with the sweep of our own scythes! and that the world had lost nothing by this little accident."

They weren't as bad as all that, but the community's boarding school, rather than its fields, was the main source of income. The Brook Farm Academy, which served the boys and girls of the community as well as the children of liberal, prosperous New Englanders, was divided into an infant school, a primary school, and a prep school. The latter focused on grooming boys for admission to Harvard or Williams, where they generally scored exceptionally well on their entrance exams. Occasionally a "rusticated" (suspended) Harvard boy might pass his six-month sentence studying and working at Brook Farm. Margaret Fuller's younger brother, Orestes Brownson's son, and Emerson's nephew were all students. There were also international students—the children of aristocratic Spaniards, Filipinos, and Cubans.

Courses were offered in math, literature, music, dancing, geology, botany, and agriculture. The academy's guiding principle was to let students pursue their own intellectual passions. Most courses were elective, and there were seldom regular hours for class. Sophia Ripley, a tall, hardworking, intellectual woman with a Yankee Brahmin pedigree, ran the school with tireless devotion. She taught German, Italian, history, and a class on the *Divine Comedy*. Her husband taught philosophy and math.

Charles Dana, an energetic twenty-three-year-old from New Hampshire, taught Greek and German when he wasn't fulfilling his duties as headwaiter in the dining room or editor of the Brook Farm paper. Dana had been turned on by transcendentalism at Harvard, where he studied German to read Kant and Friedrich Schelling. He was forced to leave Harvard after damaging his eyesight by, he claimed, staying up all night with a badly printed edition of the just released *Oliver Twist*. Dana became Ripley's right hand in the day-to-day operations of the community.

In addition to their studies, students at the Brook Farm Academy were required to spend some portion of their day laboring for the community, for which they were paid ten cents an hour. The boys typically worked in the fields; the girls helped in the kitchen. Since most of the students came from well-off families, it was often their first experience of physical labor.

Within a year, the community had outgrown the existing buildings. To accommodate the swelling population, the colonists built several small homes around the property. The Ripleys and their library left the Hive for a smaller, hilltop house known as the Eyrie. Even with the new structures, the colony was packed. As at New Harmony and the North

American Phalanx, the sheer diversity and intimacy kept things exciting. "There were farmers and artists among the members," recalled one early historian, "workingmen and Brahmins, girls with hazel eyes and extravagant moods, several Harvard students, an English Baronet's son, a Spaniard, two Filipinos, the son of a Louisiana planter."

Conversation was constant. Under every tree someone was arguing the rights of women, the genius of Beethoven, or the social message of the Gospels. "There were never such witty potato-patches and such sparkling cornfields," reported *Harper's*. "The weeds were scratched out of the ground to the music of Tennyson or Browning."

A craze for letter writing possessed the colonists. Jokey, erudite notes passed constantly from room to room. On clear nights, people would gather in the meadow for an ad hoc astronomy class. The community, which was closer to a major city than most utopias of the era, kept two wagons constantly traveling back and forth to Boston with people and supplies. Brook Farmers went into town to hear the symphony, borrow books, and attend abolitionist meetings. When it was warm, young communards skipped the nine-mile carriage ride back from Boston in favor of a long moonlit walk.

This intensely convivial atmosphere did not suit everyone. The first wave of Brook Farmers had signed up for an Arcadian idyll. By August 1842, "Nath. Hawthorne, ploughman," had had his fill of shoveling manure. "Oh, labor is the curse of the world, and nobody can meddle with it without becoming proportionally brutified!" he wrote home. "Is it a praiseworthy matter that I have spent five golden months in providing food for cows and horses? It is not so." The real problem was that he wasn't getting any writing done. Hawthorne returned to his old life in Boston, later writing Emerson that he regretted not "see[ing] it out to the finish."

The departure of one semifamous writer did little to hamper the intellectual energy at the community. On any given Saturday, Emerson would ride out from Concord to read aloud from his latest essay or Ripley would lecture on Spinoza or Kant. Horace Greeley was also a regular guest, preaching collectivism to the choir in his raspy falsetto. In his diary, Charles Dana kept a catalog of meaningful literary quotations, preserving a snapshot of what Brook Farmers were reading and discussing. There are quotes from Coleridge, Wordsworth, Carlyle, Longfellow, Schiller, Goethe, Spinoza, Virgil, Horace, Cicero, Thucydides, Euripides, and Swedenborg.

The Fragrance of Unseen Flowers

Within Dana's somewhat predictable private canon, two names stand out: Charles Fourier and Victor Considerant. By late 1843, with more than a hundred people living at Brook Farm, copies of *The Phalanx*, the Fourierist paper edited by Albert Brisbane in Manhattan, were circulating through the library in the Eyrie. Some colonists, most notably Ripley and Dana, began riding into Boston for Associationist lectures.

In the pages of *The Phalanx*, the Brook Farmers followed the rise of the North American Phalanx and the remarkable spread of Fourierism across the country. By 1844, just two years after Brisbane's first *Tribune* column, twelve separate phalanxes had been inaugurated. Among the grandest and most successful was the Wisconsin Phalanx, located at the center of a wide valley in the western part of the Wisconsin Territory. The community started with eighty people but grew to include nearly two hundred. Many of them were "*Tribune*-reading Yankees" who had settled on the frontier. They were joined by a large influx of western revivalists, mostly Baptists and Methodists. The community built a sawmill and a modest wooden phalanstery. On their prairie estate, the members of the Wisconsin Phalanx instituted a modified version of Fourier's elaborate scheme for organizing agricultural and industrial workers into specialized, rotating cohorts. They established a free school, banned alcohol, raised cattle, and planted the prairie with buckwheat, potatoes, and turnips. Within a year, the phalanx had its own post office and was clear of all debt.

Around the same time that the Wisconsin Phalanx formed, a group of Fourierists from Rochester founded the Clarkson Phalanx on fifteen hundred acres of fertile grassland by the shore of Lake Ontario, in western New York. An 1843 Fourierist convention in Rochester had spawned multiple divergent factions. Five separate phalanxes had their start in the Rochester area. The members of the Clarkson Phalanx were those men and women who, compared with other Rochester Associationists, were "most determined to follow as near the letter of Fourier as possible." The colony was largely under the direction of Hicksite Quakers, members of a liberal, breakaway group of Friends—followers of Elias Hicks—who a decade earlier had been active in the western Owenite communities.* When the colonists "numbered Israel" in April 1844, they had 420 resident members, among which almost every Christian denomination was represented. There were even a few Catholics, a self-proclaimed atheist, and a group of Perfectionist defectors from the Oneida Community. (This liberalism had its limits. The community's self-census pointedly notes the absence of Mormons and Millerites.)

Not far to the east, in the winter of 1844, another group of Rochester Associationists bought the abandoned Sodus Bay Shaker Village, which for ten years had served as the geographic bridge between eastern and western Shakerdom.† The 260 members of the Sodus Bay Phalanx subdivided the old meetinghouse into bedrooms and brought the

---

* Elias Hicks, who died in 1830, claimed that human impulse was not the work of the devil. He preached that God "gave us passions—if we may call them passions—in order that we might seek after those things which we need, and which we had a right to experience and know." Obviously, this version of Christianity squared nicely with Fourier's theory of God-given passional attraction.

† The United Society was still thriving in 1844 when the Sodus Bay Phalanx was established. In fact, the Shakers were near their demographic peak. The reason they had abandoned Sodus Bay Village in 1836 was that, at the time, they had been given to believe the state of New York planned to dig a canal through their land to link Sodus Bay to the new Erie Canal. The Shakers sold the village and moved its inhabitants, livestock, and movable property to a new village in nearby Groveland, New York. They even dug up and transported the remains of those Shakers who had died at Sodus Bay. The canal, however, was never built.

noisy rhythms of communal life back to the Shakers' rusted-out sawmill and shaggy, overgrown orchards.

That same year, 250 people who had come together following a "Fourier Congress" in Pittsburgh set out for the wilds of eastern Ohio. On a twelve-hundred-acre hay farm, they founded the Trumbull Phalanx, by far the most successful of the four phalanxes eventually founded in Ohio. The Trumbull colonists commenced with soaring enthusiasm and a high sense of purpose. "We have been shown by the Columbus of the new industrial world [Fourier] how to solve the problem of the egg," declared Nathan Meeker, a recent Oberlin graduate and founding member. "A few caravels have adventured across the unknown ocean, and are now, at the dawn of a new day, drawing nigh unto strange shores, covered with green, and loading the breeze with the fragrance of unseen flowers."*

By the end of 1844, nineteen separate phalanxes were planted across the northern half of the United States. Most were born out of regional enthusiasm that had been whipped up by the *Tribune* and local conventions. A few, particularly those in western New York, attempted to support one another by forming loose confederations.

Manhattan, where Greeley, Brisbane, and others continued to raise money and crank out propaganda, remained the intellectual and financial hub of Associationism. As small, underfunded communities kept forming, Brisbane worried that the enthusiasm was spilling over too broad an expanse, dissipating and morphing as it spread across the continent. He was intent on herding the scattered communities into a unified movement capable of producing at least one full-scale phalanx—a New World proving ground for the grand theory.

---

* Meeker, one of the most articulate participants in the Fourierist movement, went on to become an editor at Greeley's *Tribune*. In the 1870s, obeying his employer's famous dictum "Go West, young man," he moved with his family to northern Colorado to help found a cooperative farming community known as Union Colony, later renamed Greeley in honor of its financial and moral benefactor. Meeker was later employed as a federal Indian agent. In 1879, he wound up on the wrong side of what came to be known as the Meeker Massacre when Ute Indians killed him and ten other men.

Transcendental Phalanx

The Brook Farmers watched these developments closely. As the Fourier excitement swept through reformist circles in Boston, some of the leading members of the community began to feel dissatisfied with their isolated life of fellowship and self-discovery. After three years in West Roxbury, with the nation still mired in an economic depression, they began to regard their retreat from the madding crowd as somehow unchristian or, at the very least, a touch dilettantish.

A Harvard-trained minister named William Henry Channing, a good friend of many Brook Farmers and the nephew of the great Unitarian theologian William Ellery Channing, had begun actively recasting Fourier's utopian socialism as a program for practical Christianity—a roadmap, plotted by God and discovered by His prophet Charles Fourier, by which humanity would inaugurate the glad millennium foretold in the Old and New Testaments. Channing served informally as Brook Farm's pastor. During his Sunday services in the nearby pine woods, the colonists would stand in a circle, holding hands in a symbol of "universal unity." Like Ripley, Channing preached a social gospel, locating sin not only within individuals, but also within corrupt social institutions.

Fourier's description of Harmony—an era in which abundance will flow, fearsome animals will become gentle, and man will cease to study war—sounds very much like the Bible's description of the millennium (only with more orgies).* "Association," declared *The Phalanx,* "will fulfill the glorious prophesies of inspiration, and bring down upon earth the kingdom of Heaven." Channing and others believed that the holy city of New Jerusalem was coming and that it would be called a phalanstery.

To hasten the harmonic millennium, Channing founded the Boston-based Religious Union of Associationists and began printing *The Present,* a paper that blended Fourierist propaganda with a Unitarian social gos-

---

* Unlike the millennium, Fourier's Harmony will eventually unwind and all life on earth will devolve during the long era of "descending chaos."

pel. This morally dense mixture was leavened with a generous dash of Swedenborgian mysticism. Even more than Brisbane's *Phalanx* or Greeley's *Tribune*, Channing's *Present*, printed just down the road from West Roxbury, helped steer some of the leading Brook Farmers toward Fourier.

Channing was hardly the only American to see the symmetry between Fourier's utopian vision and Christian eschatology. It was not by chance that the high tide of Associationism coincided with the millenarian excitement of the Second Great Awakening. According to Carl Guarneri, the leading historian of the Associationist movement, "American Fourierism took shape at a time when expectations of an impending millennium had become so pervasive as to be almost an assumption."[*] By the time Brisbane imported the theory from France, the Republic was well kindled with vaguely defined millenarian expectation. It proved a powerful accelerant to Fourier's ideas.

Prior to the eighteenth and nineteenth centuries, most literary accounts of utopia depicted the perfect society as existing in some remote place—a jungle-hidden El Dorado or cliff-bound Shangri-la. By contrast, the utopias sketched by Owen and Fourier, like the utopia depicted in scripture, were not places but *times*, imminent epochs of peace, equality, and abundance.[†] This shift in emphasis—from utopia as an undiscovered *somewhere* to a forthcoming *somewhen*—is explained partly by the fact that by the end of the eighteenth century, nobody reasonably dreamed of stumbling upon new civilizations. Deprived of blank space on the map, the utopian daydreamer, like the theological daydreamer, turned toward the blank space on the calendar. More significant, this shift in thinking reflects the fact that industrial, post-Enlightenment

---

[*] In an 1843 letter to the *Tribune*, the abolitionist John Collins wrote, "That the Paradise of Eden is to be regained at some point or other, there are but few who doubt. By what peculiar means this Heavenly boon is to be secured is yet altogether problematical."

[†] Such visions have sometimes been called euchronias (good *times*) rather than utopias/eutopias (good *places*). Of course, in addition to a temporal utopia (the millennium), the Bible includes two geographically bound utopias: the walled-in Garden somewhere near the region of Eden and that cloudy utopia *above*.

man believed, as people seldom had before, that history was a tale of progress—that humans could reshape the world. Change was no longer something that just happened to us. The utopian *somewhen* was a paradise that we would build for ourselves.

Nobody was keener to bring Brook Farm into the Associationist fold than Albert Brisbane. His motivation, beyond the usual evangelical impulse, is obvious. The principal impediment to the triumph of Fourierism, at least as Brisbane saw it, was the fact that much of the American public, at least the portion that had heard of Fourier, perceived Associationism as the frivolous, if not toxic, creation of a loopy French atheist. Conservatives and evangelicals routinely described the Associationist movement as a clear and present danger to "Christian civilization." Even liberal Bostonians were uneasy about the spread of Fourier's ideas. Writing in *The Dial* in 1844, Elizabeth Palmer Peabody, who had earlier rhapsodized about the pastoral life and the smell of clover, confessed a "vague horror connected with [Fourier's] name." She admitted knowing very little of his actual writings but thought of Fourier's scheme as an "enormous parasitic plant, sucking the life principles of society, while it spread apparently an equal shade, inviting man to repose under its beautiful but poison-dropping branches, . . . a catholicon of evil." This sort of impression—which rhymes closely with twentieth-century fears about the "evil tree" of communism—was precisely what Brisbane needed to overcome if the United States was going to become ground zero for the harmonic millennium. Brisbane knew that the support of the Brook Farmers would lend celebrity and respectability to the movement. The famous, blue-blooded Yankees in West Roxbury could help dispel the popular view of Fourier's theory as an insidious schema of Gallic decadence. (Of course, to a large portion of the population, the Brook Farmers themselves seemed like shaggy-haired deists hung up on disturbing notions such as the equality of women and the sudden abolition of slavery.)

At first glance, Fourier's utopian program and Yankee transcendentalism make for odd bedfellows. Transcendentalism, especially as it has been fossilized in the prose of the Concord men Emerson and Thoreau, celebrates self-reliance, individual union with the spirit, personal freedom, and solitary contemplation of the eternal forms reflected in nature. Fourier, by contrast, sought global transformation through a voluptuary existence in bustling grand hotels. The transcendentalists eschewed material concerns for knowledge of things unseen; Fourier obsessed over costumes and dinner menus. Daily life at Brook Farm was defined by a poetic denial of all structure; the life within Fourier's imagined phalanxes was scheduled to the minute.

But besides these differences in aspiration and style, the union between Fourierism and Brook Farm was a natural one. On the most basic level, the Brook Farmers already assumed the basic premise of all utopianism: namely, that the present organization of social relations—*the system*—needed a total overhaul. "[We] were pretty well agreed," Hawthorne wrote, "as to the inexpediency of lumbering along with the old system any further." More generally, the Brook Farmers, like Fourier and his apostles, aspired to a life of intense personal liberty and social cooperation. Fourier's theory seemed to offer them all the advantages of communalism with none of the enforced equality that they viewed as a threat to liberty. The notion that *individual* passions, freely expressed, can be harmonized to produce a *collective* good seemed to solve the riddle that Ripley had posed for himself and his community: how to liberate "the many [that] are slaves to a few" while avoiding "the bondage of individuals to the power of the mass."

For Ripley in particular and Americans in general, this was the special appeal of Associationism. Unlike Shakerism and Owenism (or, later, Icarianism), Fourier's vision, at least in its pure theoretical form, was a communitarian scheme grounded entirely upon the vital, spontaneous expressions of the individual. On paper it offered the best of both communism—equality, fraternity, the dissolution of power relations, economies of scale—and liberal individualism—the freedom for everyone to rise to his or her own level, unhampered by the needs and sentiments of others. Ripley wrote that "by identifying the interests of the many and the few—the less gifted and the highly gifted—

[Associationism] secures the sacred personality of all, gives to each individual the largest liberty of the children of God."

Finding his own notions reflected back at him with a pleasing mathematical precision, Ripley slipped easily into Fourier's lyrical vocabulary of harmony, vibrations, and series. Life within Association, Ripley wrote, would be "in perfect union with the nature of man; to which every chord in his sensitive and finely vibrated frame will respond; which will call forth, as from a well-tuned instrument, all those exquisite modulations of feeling and intellect, which are aptly termed by Plato, the 'music' of his being."

In April 1844, Albert Brisbane convened a national meeting of Associationists at Clinton Hall, on Astor Place in Manhattan. The purpose of the convention was to bring order and doctrinal coherence to the movement and to find some way of confederating the rapidly proliferating phalanxes. The conventioneers also took the opportunity to publicly and officially distance themselves from the more "speculative" aspects of Fourier's philosophy. New York journalists Parke Godwin, Horace Greeley, and Brisbane led the proceedings, but two Massachusetts men sat on the rostrum: George Ripley and Charles Dana. They were there to celebrate Brook Farm's official reorganization as the Brook Farm Phalanx.

Like the majority of twentieth-century communes, Brook Farm had begun as an essentially inward-facing institution. The Brook Farmers were united by a desire to forge a miniature commonwealth within, but insulated from, a corrupt society. By retrofitting the community as a phalanx, they turned their focus outward. Brook Farm, declared the community's new, Fourierist constitution, "has hitherto worn, for the most part, the character of a private experiment, and has avoided rather than sought the notice of the public. The deep interest in the doctrine of Association which now fills the minds of intelligent persons everywhere, indicates plainly that the time has passed when even initiative movements ought to be prosecuted in silence. . . . We wish, therefore, to bring Brook Farm before the public."

Charles Dana, probably the most ardent Associationist in West Roxbury, had faith in the full speculative sweep of Fourier's vision. He believed that the conversion of Brook Farm would help trigger the physical and social regeneration of the earth. "Our ulterior aim," he wrote, "is nothing less than Heaven on Earth, the conversion of this globe, now exhaling pestilential vapors and possessed by unnatural climates, into the abode of beauty and health, and the restitution to humanity of the Divine Image, now so long lost and forgotten."

A more mundane reason for Brook Farm's conversion can be found in the community's ledgers. By the time Brisbane came to West Roxbury preaching the New Industrial World, the colony was nearly broke. A basic fact of rural economics dogged Brook Farm along with almost every small utopia of the era: The first few years of establishing a farm are by far the most expensive and labor-intensive. Purchasing land and tools, clearing stone, plowing up hard virgin land, planting orchards, building enclosures and mills: These are all up-front costs. Only later, once the soil is loose and the trees have begun to bear fruit, can a farm yield any sort of profit.* At Brook Farm, this situation was aggravated by a series of expensive construction projects required to house the rapid influx of members.

With men like Hawthorne daydreaming at the plow, Brook Farm's fields may have been "witty" and "sparkling," but they were never terribly fruitful. Even with expert cultivation, the farm would probably never have been a great success.† There was a reason the property had originally been a dairy, rather than a hay or vegetable operation. The soil was flinty and interspersed with large outcroppings of puddingstone conglomerate. Despite spreading the fields with plenty of swamp muck (they couldn't afford much manure) and building a greenhouse to

---

* Fourier foresaw this problem. His unrealistic solution was that each phalanx should be fully bankrolled by a wealthy benefactor who could carry the community through its vulnerable early years. Ideally, he hoped that the entire physical infrastructure of a phalanx would be completed before the first person moved in.

† The community did have an excellent head farmer, a former printer and friend of Emerson's named Minot Pratt.

extend their growing season (another pricey start-up cost), the Brook Farmers were unable to raise a profitable harvest. Instead of selling vegetables, they went to Boston to buy them. Because of the poor soil and limited manure, the hay they grew for sale was of the lowest quality and fetched a low price. While the academy and a smattering of light industries brought in some income, the community was operating at a loss. By wedding their fortunes to the vibrant Associationist movement and its wealthy benefactors, the Brook Farmers hoped to secure a measure of solvency.

The story of Brook Farm's conversion into a Fourierist phalanx is usually told as a decline from an age of gold to an age of iron or, in the words of one early historian, a shift from poetry to prose. Miles Coverdale, the narrator of Hawthorne's *Blithedale Romance,* described the community's embrace of Fourier's ideas as a sort of original sin. After leaving the community, he reflected that "the experiment, so far as its original projectors were concerned, proved, long ago, a failure; first lapsing into Fourierism, and dying, as it well deserved, for this infidelity to its own higher spirit."

In 1844, the year of the switch, sixty-seven people joined the community. As new members arrived, some of the old ones departed, lamenting as they went the end of their "severance from the world" and complaining about Fourier's rigid scheme. Emerson expressed the view of some when he wrote that Fourier "had skipped no fact but one, namely Life." The new members were, on the whole, less wealthy and less educated than the founders. Many were drawn from northeastern workingmen's associations and Fourierist clubs. Some had been participants in an 1843 "Social Reform" conference in Boston that was organized to simultaneously promote abolitionism and the "truths of social science discovered by Charles Fourier." These new members lent the community a more politicized, working-class aspect. The historian Carl Guarneri describes the conversion of Brook Farm as "a deliberate tradeoff of charm for social relevance."

The change in culture was most obvious among the women. Some of the early colonists were among the best-educated women in the United States—peers and friends of Elizabeth Palmer Peabody and Margaret Fuller. They arrived in West Roxbury with a clearly defined sense of women's rights. By contrast, many of the new female members were the wives of tradesmen, with scant exposure to "social science," let alone George Sand or Sappho. At Brook Farm, these women generally went to work in the kitchen or laundry. Some of them came to resent the women of the pre-Fourierist era, many of whom taught in the school and engaged confidently with the intellectual life of the community.

John Codman, a seventeen-year-old who arrived with his family just after the conversion, thought of the pre-Fourierist incarnation of Brook Farm as little more than a holiday retreat for upper-class literati. To Codman and his peers, the departing members looked like a pack of snobs—"extinct volcanoes of Transcendental nonsense and humbuggery"—who could not countenance living with anyone who did not read Greek. "There were philosophers enough in it," he said of the early years. "There were plenty of sweet, charming characters and amateur workmen in it, but the hard-fisted toilers and brave financiers were absent." Such a place might have been fun, but it would never transform the world.

The community's convivial, intellectual atmosphere did not evaporate when it became a phalanx. People still gathered in the kitchen in the evening to debate big ideas and play euchre while the next day's bread baked. Groups still took picnics into the woods or to the edge of the Charles River to read poetry and paint watercolors. A group of young men pooled their savings and bought a little sailboat with which to cruise up and down the river. Musical performances, usually by local talent but sometimes by international stars visiting Boston, were practically a daily event. John Dwight, who served as head music teacher, claimed that the brown piano in the Eyrie was best suited to German music, and the community developed a special affection for Beethoven.

The high population of young singles often lent the newly minted phalanx a flirtatious, summer camp atmosphere. Love letters flew from room to room in torrents. At least fourteen marriages originated at Brook Farm. For those unlucky in love, there were dinnertime meetings of the RLSG (Rejected Lover's Sympathy Group). After dinner— usually simple fare such as salt pork, beans, brown bread, and milk— the cleaning up was done by the younger colonists. Like good Fourierists, they turned the chore into a contest, seeing who could wash dishes fastest. When the dining room was clean, they sometimes pushed aside the tables and benches to make space for fiddle-accompanied dancing.

As at the other small utopias of the era, the Brook Farmers (both before and after the conversion) adopted an unofficial and faintly bohemian uniform. While their sisters in Boston were trussed up in heavy Victorian gowns, the women of Brook Farm wore light muslin dresses and broad-brimmed straw hats. Some wore bloomers. They tended to grow their hair long, wearing it down and braiding it with ivy and flowers. Although many of the men had been natty Bostonians just a few months earlier, at the community they took to wearing raggedy farmer's trousers, high boots, workman's tunics, tasseled hats, and brightly colored chintz shirts with floppy Byron collars. Ripley set the style for men's grooming, letting his hair and beard grow long. "In outward show," Hawthorne recalled, "we looked rather like a gang of beggars, or banditti, than either a company of honest laboring-men, or a conclave of philosophers." One young, long-haired Brook Farmer was pelted with rocks while standing on a Boston pier.

The letters and reminiscences of some colonists give the impression that life within the community was one continuous laughing party. Nicknames flourished. There was "Judge," "Professor" (Charles Dana), "the Admiral," "Old Solitary," "the Omniarch" (Ripley), "Monday," "Peppercorn," and, for a man obsessed with Andrew Jackson, "General." An epidemic of punning or "double-enders" swept the community. Question: "What sort of man is that long-haired fellow opposite?" Answer: "He is good in the *mane*." Or: "Mrs.____ is a regular steamboat." "Yes, I know it; she goes by steam—*self'steam*." After a punchy coffee party during which Ripley, Dana, and Brisbane exchanged round upon round of punning toasts, one Fourier-minded communard noted that "our entertainment was a regular series, ascending gradually from a few jokes to the highest spiritual emotions, and gradually descending again."

Attractive Industry

Although many of the self-proclaimed phalanxes that sprang up in 1843 and 1844 had only the most tenuous connection to Fourier's theories, the Brook Farmers were well versed in the master's doctrines. Every Sunday evening they held a "Fourier meeting," at which they reviewed specific aspects of his sprawling philosophy. These were later supplemented with Monday and Thursday classes on Fourierism led by Ripley. After the conversion, the Brook Farmers began weaving Fourierist jargon and logic into their daily lives. When two young women had a crush on the same boy, one wrote that "ours is not the evil rivalry which abounds in 'the world,'—But the true rivalry of Association:—we are friends and rivals." The same young woman lamented the excessive "cabalism" of a particular clique. Outsiders were known as civilizees. John Colson, the community's shoemaker, named his son Charles Fourier Colson. With so much Fourier talk in the air, someone joked that the boy's first word would probably be "Association."

In keeping with Fourier's plans to combine agriculture and industry, the colonists began to focus seriously on manufacturing. They set up workshops to produce shoes, window sashes, blinds, and doors. The stream that cut through the main meadow was too narrow to provide reliable rotary power, so the community installed a brand-new steam engine in the cellar of a workshop where a single horse, yoked to an axle, had previously turned a gristmill. A machine had entered the garden. The clatter and hiss of its pistons no doubt drowned out the "natural bass" of lowing cattle.

To run the new industries, the community required a new type of member: "Men and women," as one Brook Farmer put it, "with only practical, everyday talents, able to be honest and make shoes and sew garments; to strike with a sledge and a blacksmith's arm . . . but who had never read Goethe and Schiller, and, possibly, neither Shakespeare."

In his theoretical effort to render labor "attractive," Fourier confronted the same paradox that Robert Owen attempted to unravel. The rapid advance of industrial technology at the start of the nineteenth century generated unprecedented levels of wealth and productivity while making life worse for many, if not most, workers. Fourier and his disciples claimed that almost every social ill could be traced to the misapplication of labor. Fix the workday and everything else will fall into place. "Industry can be rendered attractive!" Brisbane wrote. "Let this great and practical reform be once effected, and three-fourths of the evils, which oppress mankind, will be done away with as if by a magic influence."

At Brisbane's urging, the colonists instituted a version of Fourier's complex system of "Groups and Series," albeit on a much smaller scale. A group, in Fourier's scheme, is a collection of seven to ten people who share "a common taste for a particular function." The combination of several groups loosely bound by a general category of labor forms a "series," such as a farming series or manufacturing series. Fourier believed that uniting people with similar temperaments into small teams would create a sporting, productivity-boosting sense of solidarity within each group and a similarly productive spirit of competition among the different groups.

In Fourier's idealized phalanx, the scale and complexity of these groupings is staggering. For instance, the Pear Grower's Series will include thirty-two groups of workers, each cultivating those varieties of pears to which they are passionally attracted. Among the thirty-two groups, eight will specialize in cultivating juicy pears; two will focus on quinces and "abnormally hard types"; two will grow soft pears; and for some unknown reason, four groups will specialize in growing "mealy pears." The Brook Farmers, having a relatively limited number of workers and tasks, simplified the scheme. They created one big Pastoral

Series, within which there was a Garden Group, a Haying Group, a Nursery Group, a Dairy Group, and an Orchard Group. A similar system was set up in the school (the Educational Series) and the workshops (the Industrial Series). Each group elected a foreperson, and the members of each series elected a series leader to oversee labor assignments.

Although Fourier, unlike many utopians, never presented his vision of the ideal society in the form of a fictional narrative, his descriptions of the harmonic future are so colorfully specific that they operate more like fiction than any other mode of moral or political suasion. In fact, his prose is a good deal more vivid than much classical utopian fiction. Like the best utopian novels, his descriptions of life in Harmony allow readers to see, in the private theater of the imagination, the type of world that his system will supposedly bring about. His depiction of happy workers "parading outside the phalanx palace, dispersing to the fields and workshops, waving their banners with cries of triumph and impatience," clearly captured the Brook Farmers' imaginations. In a letter to a friend in Boston, one young communard wrote, "Hearing a great hurrah I have just been to the window, and lo! Martin and a group of boys returning from their work,—little Fourierists, with banners flying. The boys are really getting to enjoy their work, and these banners are a grand excitement."

Inspired by Fourier's feminist writings, a group of Brook Farm women pooled their money, ordered wholesale materials, and started a Fancy Goods Group—making capes, collars, caps, and undersleeves to sell in Boston.* They dedicated their profits to "the elevation of woman

---

* As Fourier saw it, the women of Civilization may be better off than their sisters in more "primitive" societies, but they are still in terrible shape. Civilization, he wrote, denies women education, then calls them ignorant; shelters them and calls them weak. In his view, marriage makes most women into "conjugal slaves" and consigns the rest to poverty. In Civilization, every woman is given the same job. While certain women may be *passionally* suited to cooking, cleaning, and child rearing, most could be employed more happily and more productively elsewhere. In the coming era of Harmony, when authentic female passion is loosed upon the world, women will surpass men in every department besides physical strength. Naturally, this assessment

SYSTÈME DE FOURIER.

The Butterfly Passion demands constant variety.

Bibliothèque Nationale, Paris, France / Archives Charmet / Bridgeman Images

forever." Having absorbed Fourier's theory of history, they described
their project in the language of historical ascent: "Raise women to the
equal of man, and what intellectual developments may we not expect?
How the whole aspect of society will be changed." At Brook Farm, as at
New Harmony, commonplace chores such as sewing and weaving were
infused with a sense of high purpose. Acts of collective labor became,
by definition, acts of liberation. "We do live in an atmosphere of our

—————

endeared Fourier to an early generation of feminists and secured the outrage of his
conservative critics.

own . . . ," wrote one member of the Fancy Goods Group. "It is so inspiring, so ennobling!"

To satisfy the Butterfly Passion, the colonists rotated from group to
group and series to series. If a member of the Sash Group grew bored
with sanding window frames, he could switch to the Milking Group in
the Pastoral Series.* In the spring of 1844, Marianne Dwight, a young
Brook Farmer from a well-to-do Boston family, recounted her typical
workday. In the morning, she spent half an hour with the "Waiting
Group," serving breakfast. After clearing and washing dishes for an hour
and a half, she joined the "Dormitory Group," cleaning bedrooms until
eleven. She then changed into nicer clothes and crossed the meadow
to the Eyrie, where she worked in a Sewing Group with other young
women until everyone convened for lunch at twelve thirty. From two
to five thirty, she taught drawing in Pilgrim Hall, a large new building
that was used as a school and dormitory. At five thirty, she returned to
the Hive to set the tables for tea. After tea, she again helped clear tables
and wash dishes. All of this was subject to frequent change. At other
times during her stay at the community, Dwight worked in the garden,
painted lamp shades for sale in Boston, and worked in the Fancy Goods
Group. As cumbersome as this system sounds, 1844, the year of the
conversion, was the first year that Brook Farm turned a profit.

With its population of experienced writers, printers, and editors, Brook
Farm replaced lower Manhattan as the headquarters of Fourierist propaganda. *The Harbinger*, which succeeded *The Phalanx* as the chief organ
of American Associationism, was moved into a newly built two-story
building at the community, and Ripley was appointed its editor in chief.
He filled the pages of the paper with the work of his friends, who also
happened to be some of the country's best-known writers. Horace

---

* This constant changing of jobs may have made labor less arduous, but it seems to
have hurt quality. The windows and doors sold by the community had a reputation
for shrinking due to insufficient seasoning of the lumber.

Greeley, Henry James, Sr., Emerson, and James Russell Lowell were all contributors. The paper's chief concern was the spread of Association-ism, but it also ran fiction, literary reviews, and poetry. The first issue included a translation from George Sand's *Consuelo,* by the wealthy abo-litionist Francis G. Shaw.* John Dwight, Brook Farm's beloved music teacher, contributed reviews of Boston concerts. After leaving the com-munity, he went on to become the most influential music critic in the country. *The Harbinger,* like many individual Brook Farmers, affirmed its commitment to Fourier while rejecting the widespread view of Associa-tionism as a sect or cult of personality. "While we bow to no man as an authoritative, infallible master," the paper's prospectus read, "we revere the genius of Fourier too highly not to accept, with joyful welcome, the light which he has shed on the most intricate problems of human des-tiny."

Despite this caveat, some colonists' reverence for "the genius of Fou-rier" took on a distinctly religious hue. In the spring of 1845, the com-munity threw a party to celebrate Fourier's birthday and "the speedy coming of that era of Harmony and Love and Peace which all the Prophets have announced, and which will be realized in Association." The Brook Farmers filled the dining room of the Hive with flowers from their new greenhouse and strung up banners bearing bright yel-low suns and the slogan "Universal Unity." Fourier's most famous aphorism—*"Les attractions sont proportionnelles aux destinées"*†—was written on the wall with pine boughs. A bust of the master was set before a large glass prism so that the full color spectrum would shine across his stern plaster face. (The lamp that was supposed to illuminate the prism was

---

* Shaw used to ride out to Brook Farm with his young son Robert. During the Civil War, Robert Shaw became a Union army icon, leading the all-black Massachusetts Fifty-fourth Infantry in a heroic but disastrous charge on Charleston's Fort Wagner.
† Translation: Attractions are proportional to destinies. In other words, passion is evidence of destiny. If something—a human, a plant, a planet—is drawn toward some particular condition, that condition is its intended destiny. Our desires, prop-erly understood, can function as a decoder ring for the proper organization of soci-ety. Our God-implanted passions will lead us to perfection.

too weak for the effect to work.) Another artistically minded colonist built a huge white lyre, strung with seven strings, each painted a different color of the rainbow. Both the color spectrum and the musical scale were frequently cited by Fourier as evidence of the divine Law of Series and the mathematical harmony inherent in the universe. Brisbane came for the festivities and shared personal reminiscences about his time in Paris with Fourier. Someone read aloud from the Bible. At the height of the celebration, one ardent Brook Farmer announced the apotheosis of their prophet with a toast: "To Fourier, the second coming of Christ."

Come-outers, Communists, Fruitists, and Flutists

When they weren't actively celebrating Fourier as the Second Coming, the Brook Farmers spent more time talking about what they ate than about the ascending vibrations of supertonic scales. In the 1840s, as in the 1970s, communal utopianism went hand in hand with a general zeal for coarse grains and dietary fads. Many American Fourierists, including a large contingent of Brook Farmers, took up the austere diet preached by the Reverend Sylvester Graham, inventor of the eponymous cracker. Self-described Grahamites abstained from alcohol, meat, and seasoning of any sort. They favored dark, whole-grain bread, even though bread made with finely milled flour was then considered tastier and more healthful. Graham, who traveled the country giving incredibly popular lectures, advocated the exotic practices of daily bathing and tooth brushing. His ideas about health were based upon a vague theory about inflammation that had both physical and psychological connotations. He vehemently denounced masturbation, which he said caused blindness and insanity. He claimed that eating meat and drinking milk produced lust, which he classified as a species of unhealthy inflammation. Not surprisingly, there were "Graham tables" at many of the Shaker villages. At Brook Farm, the Grahamites were monitored by their comrades to see whether they could perform their chores without the benefits of meat. Another Brook Farm pun: "These Grahamites will never make their ends *meat.*" Response: "You may *steak* your reputation on that."

At many of the Fourierist phalanxes of the 1840s, a spare diet was as much a matter of financial necessity as a question of moral hygiene. For some, this imposed asceticism was a point of pride. "If they are willing to endure privations, to eat coarse food, sometimes without meat," one Associationist wrote of his comrades, "they may consider themselves fitted for the transition-period [to Harmony]. But if they sigh for the flesh pots and leeks and onions of civilization . . . they had better stay where they are, and wait for the advent of perfect industrial Associa-tion." In the fall of 1844, to save money, Brook Farm initiated a belt-tightening program that they called "retrenchment." In the crowded dining room of the Hive—where long tables were set with white linens, white plates, and white cups—luxuries such as butter, coffee, tea, meat, and sugar became scarce. (Those in poor health were exempt from the retrenchment diet.) As with many other hardships, the colonists' faith that they were building a new world gave their culinary sacrifices the savor of heroic purpose. "We must drink the waters of Marah in the desert, that others may feed on the grapes of Eschol," proclaimed George Ripley, drawing an analogy between the Brook Farmers' depar-ture from Civilization and the Jews' flight out of Egypt.*

Utopian communities always attract pilgrims seeking an audience for their private enthusiasms. Brook Farm, just a few hours' ride from a major city, hosted more than its share of what one colonist called "come-outers, communists, fruitists, and flutists." This pageant of radi-cals and social innovators forms a fairly comprehensive roster of the

---

* Even during lean times, the Brook Farmers marked special occasions with food. To celebrate a birthday or some notable event in the history of Fourierism, there might be a hot chocolate party, a "candy frolic," a "coffee meeting," a fresh batch of Gra-ham crackers, or even the rare oyster supper.

scattershot, glossolalic yearning for newness that seized portions of the
Republic in the two decades before the Civil War.*

One visitor showed up claiming that sleep was unnecessary and that
he had not slept for a year. When everyone went to bed, he remained
upright in the sitting room of the Eyrie, a lamp burning at his side. In
the middle of the night, an almost equally eccentric Brook Farmer
known as Irish John Cheever looked through the window and spied the
visitor dozing. Hurrying loudly into the building, Cheever apologized
profusely, saying, "I beg your pardon, sir, I did not intend to disturb
your sleep." The guest responded that there was no cause for apology;
he had merely been thinking.

In an early stirring of the nascent Spiritualist movement, Anna Par-
sons, an enthusiastic Boston Fourierist who could not join the community owing to frail health, claimed the gift of "impressibility"—the
ability to "read" the psychology of a dead stranger by touching a sample of his or her handwriting. At Brook Farm, she "read" Fourier using
a letter supplied by Albert Brisbane. Pressing the letter to her forehead,
she channeled the departed master: "If I laugh, it makes me sad. If I'm
sad, it makes me laugh." Brisbane, the only American Associationist to
have had any intimate contact with Fourier, was impressed.

Liberal Unitarianism remained the dominant religious impulse at
Brook Farm, but more arcane spiritual interests thrived, too. The Fourierist boom coincided with the peak of American interest in the teachings of Swedish mystic Emanuel Swedenborg. Swedenborgianism and
Fourierism were so often found in the same place—both popular among
northeastern reformist types—that John Humphrey Noyes declared
Swedenborgianism the "state religion" of Associationism.† Ministers of
the Swedenborgian New Church founded at least two Fourierist Asso-

---

* The critic Gilbert Seldes sketched a composite portrait of the typical mid-
nineteenth-century radical: he was "a comparatively harmless crank, given to fads,
strolling about in white garments, eating nuts, talking of love and beauty."

† There had been Swedenborgians at New Harmony, too. And Frederick Evans, the
Owenite turned Shaker elder, situated Mother Ann at the head of a succession of
spiritual visionaries that included Confucius, Plato, Jesus, and Swedenborg.

ciations: the Canton Phalanx in Illinois and the Leraysville Phalanx in Pennsylvania.

Emerson, who had a brief flirtation with Swedenborgianism, wrote in *The Dial* that "one could not but be struck with the strange coincidences betwixt Fourier and Swedenborg." Like Fourier, Swedenborg claimed that the true nature of God's creation has been subverted and that it can be restored only by bringing human life into accord with certain spiritual realities. Charles Julius Hempel, a German-born homeopath, attempted a full synthesis of Fourier and Swedenborg. His book *The True Organization of the New Church, as Indicated in the Writings of Emanuel Swedenborg: And Demonstrated by Charles Fourier* claimed that the two thinkers illuminate the "scientific" (Fourier) and "spiritual" (Swedenborg) sides of a single coin. Henry James, Sr., was the most well-known American Swedenborgian and also a contributor to *The Harbinger*. Like some of his friends at Brook Farm, James read Swedenborg through a utopian lens, believing that a perfected material world was man's spiritual "destiny."*

Another regular visitor to Brook Farm, and no doubt a habitué of the Graham table, was the education reformer Amos Bronson Alcott. In 1842, Alcott, a staunch vegetarian, visited a school in London that had been founded upon his pedagogical theories. (Because Alcott made a point of never having much money, Emerson paid for the trip.) When Alcott returned to the United States, he was accompanied by the school's founder, the British mystic and reformer Charles Lane. Along with abstaining from all animal products, Lane refused to eat rice or sugar because of their connection to the slave trade. Since he would not burden a horse with his weight, he was obliged to walk the nine miles from Boston every time he visited Brook Farm. And because he could not wear leather, wool, or slave-picked cotton, he made the journey in a linen suit, no matter the weather.†

---

* In *The Metaphysical Club*, Louis Menand quotes William Dean Howells's famous three-word review of James's *The Secret of Swedenborg*: "He kept it."
† Emerson refused to host Lane for Thanksgiving, dreading the Englishman's eulogy for the turkey.

In 1843, inspired by what was happening at Brook Farm but convinced that Ripley's ambitions were "too humble indeed to satisfy the extreme demands of the age," Lane and Alcott founded a small vegan commune near the old Shaker village in Harvard. They called it Fruitlands. The Fruitlandians lived in a single red farmhouse that, aside from a bust of Socrates, contained few creature comforts. They abstained from all animal products and animal labor, refusing even to bridle a horse. (One woman was supposedly ejected for nibbling a bit of fish.) The community included a nudist and a man who refused to eat tubers because any vegetable that grows downward displays questionable ambitions. A Fruitlandian named Joseph Palmer spoke out against the practice of shaving and advocated spiritually cleansing obscenity. "Good morning, damn you," was his preferred salutation. At a time when long beards were not in style, Palmer's bushy whiskers provoked such outrage that he was denied communion and rocks were thrown at his house. When two men tried to shave him by force, Palmer fought back, ending up in jail. (His gravestone, which depicts him with immense facial hair, reads: "Persecuted for wearing the beard.") The most famous alumna of Fruitlands was Louisa May Alcott, daughter of the community's founder and the eventual author of *Little Women*. Dressed in miniature linen bloomers, she and her three younger sisters represented most of the commune's youth population. When Fruitlands fell apart, Lane and his son joined the community of Shakers at Harvard.

The Kingdom of Heaven That Is
to Come on Earth

The steady parade of journalists, well-wishers, and yahoos who passed through the Hive added to the overcrowding that was already Brook Farm's most pressing problem. The existing buildings—the Hive, the Eyrie, and a handful of smaller structures built with both private and communal funds during the first three years—could not accommodate the influx of Associationists. Room assignments tended to be fluid, and families sometimes had to be split up. Nightfall inevitably came with a chaotic scramble for floor space, cots, and quilts. The top floor of the three-story Hive, dubbed Attica, became a stuffy dormitory packed with young men.

On one of his many visits to the community, Albert Brisbane brought drawings by Victor Considerant depicting Fourier's ideal phalanstery. To the most optimistic Brook Farmers, the pictures were like a dispatch from the future, a first glimpse of the millennial abode they intended to build. "I wish you could have seen . . . the pictures that Mr. Brisbane has of a Phalanstery," Marianne Dwight wrote a friend in Boston. "They are magnificent in design, and give one a pretty clear glance at least into the kingdom of heaven that is to come on earth." In a prephotographic era, Considerant's grand, technical-looking drawings—projected straight from the utopian imagination to the page—had a powerful effect. Like Owen's scale model of his parallelogram, the images gave specific shape to the diffuse utopian longing shared by so many Americans.

Early in the summer of 1844, on a high spot overlooking the meadow, the Brook Farmers began digging the foundation for their own phalanstery. The scale of their design was ambitious, but it did not approach Fourier's vision of a Versailles-like palace surrounded by pleasure grounds, fountains, and caravansaries. The Brook Farm phalanstery was to be an immense clapboard rectangle, ringed with wide, multistory porches—a sensible Yankee response to Fourier's Old World fantasy. By July, the cellar was dug and paved.

As small phalanxes sprang to life across the northern half of the United States, Albert Brisbane continued to hope for at least one well-funded, "scientific" phalanx in which to showcase Fourier's theory. With its partially built phalanstery, the Brook Farm Phalanx now looked like a viable contender for that role.

The Brook Farmers, meanwhile, hoped that the building would solve some of their most obvious problems. The existing living arrangements, with everyone housed in small structures spread across the estate, fostered a certain cliquishness and contributed to a cultural divide between single people and families. By getting everyone under one roof in a spacious "unitary dwelling," the phalanstery would knit the community closer together. At the same time, the community's push into various manufacturing enterprises had convinced the colonists that a larger workforce would be needed to make their new businesses profitable. The phalanstery would mean more beds, and more beds would mean more workers. Most immediately, the phalanstery would relieve the pressure of overcrowding, ending the exhausting nightly game of musical beds. "When the Phalanstery is done," enthused Marianne Dwight, "the expansion will be in proportion to the present cramming or condensation."

During the first year at New Harmony, the sense that the *real* community would commence once they moved into their brick parallelogram had kept the community moving forward with equanimity and energy. The slowly rising phalanstery in West Roxbury had the same effect. It gave meaning and direction to the daily life at the community.

Black and Fireless Altars

Even without the phalanstery, the establishment of the Brook Farm Phalanx had achieved much of what Brisbane hoped it would. For those Americans who were not already inclined to view Ripley and Co. as bohemian infidels, the community in West Roxbury helped make Fourier's theory seem less dangerously foreign. Even Elizabeth Palmer Peabody ceased trembling before the "catholicon of evil" and wished the phalanx godspeed: "May it become a University where the young American shall learn his duties and become worthy of this broad land of his inheritance."

While the Associationist movement was burnished by its connection to the community in West Roxbury, Brook Farm's reputation, particularly the reputation of its school, was tarnished by the connection to

Fourier. People who might have sent their children to an academy associated with Reverend Ripley and Nathaniel Hawthorne were less confident about a school that might or might not be connected to a French cult bent on free love. Elizabeth Peabody's sister Sophia, who later married Hawthorne, fretted over the moral influence of a system conceived in the fallout of the French Revolution, when, she wrote, "the people worshiped a naked woman as the Goddess of Reason."

In much the same way, the partnership between the *Tribune* and Fourierism—initially such a boon to Brisbane's movement—became a liability for both. In 1846, during a particularly nasty round of antebellum newspaper wars—a conflict in which everyone buying or selling ink stood to profit—the *Tribune* was routinely tarred for its support of Fourier and the other utopian socialists. The *Morning Courier and New-York Enquirer* called Greeley's paper "the organ of Charles Fourier, Fanny Wright, and R. D. Owen, advocating from day to day the destruction of our existing social system, and substituting in its stead one based upon infidelity, and an unrestricted and indiscriminate intercourse of the sexes."* Greeley wrote to Charles Dana about the toll that his support for Associationism had taken on his personal life: "I have encountered much opposition and ridicule on account of what I have published and the little I have written for Association and have shocked the prejudices of many worthy friends, some of whom have stopped my paper on account of this, and all been chilled in their friendship by my *fanaticism*."†

Because Greeley was a prominent figure in Whig politics, there was political hay to be made by painting any cause with which he was associated in the most sinister colors. Pundits who might otherwise have been indifferent to Associationism cataloged Fourier's most scandalous ideas as a way to bait Greeley. The usual refrain was that Associationists

---

* The *Morning Courier and New-York Enquirer* was edited by a sharp young journalist named Henry Jarvis Raymond. Raymond, who had gotten his start under Greeley at the *New-Yorker* and the *Tribune,* led the media charge against Greeley and Fourierism. In 1851, he founded his own paper: *The New York Times.*
† Greeley gave as good as he got, calling the *New York Sun* a "slimy and venomous instrument of loco-focoism . . . Jesuitical in politics and groveling in morals."

sought to destroy Christianity and the sacrament of marriage. In reality, many prominent Fourierists were happily married churchmen, albeit liberal, antislavery ones. Unlike Ann Lee, Robert Owen, and John Humphrey Noyes, neither Fourier nor his followers ever advocated for the immediate abolition of traditional marriage.

An 1844 lecture delivered by Donald Campbell McLaren, a preacher from upstate New York, captures the sulfurous, hyperbolic tone of many anti-Fourierists. McLaren's polemic—later sold as a slim book under the title *Boa Constrictor: Or, Fourier Association Self-Exposed As to Its Principles and Aims*—oscillates between describing Associationism as frivolous nonsense and declaring it the gravest possible threat to the Republic. God-fearing American women, McLaren proclaims, will not be duped by false promises of social equality. Instead, they will rise up to defend the "citadel" over which the Bible grants them dominion: the home. McLaren tagged the leading Fourierists with that most toxic of American epithets: an elite. "The haughty cabal who make the *Tribune* their platform," he writes, are nothing more than "arrogant reformers" bent on the destruction of American life with *foreign* ideas. They are "daring traitors" who have crawled "lizard-like, [from] the filthiest dregs of Parisian infidelity" and "sworn in conclave on their black and fireless altars" to overthrow America. "No! Ye men of the Tribune! Ye may coax or ye may scold, ye may smile or ye may frown, but American industry, the sprightly, robust nurseling of civilization in this Western World will never be decoyed from the fostering care of its fond and generous nurse, into the skinny arms to be hugged to death on the bony bosom and dry breasts of a dissolute, silly, imported, pauper hag."

Despite such rhetoric, about six or seven thousand Americans eventually lived within a phalanx. Many more—an estimated one hundred thousand—called themselves Associationists. By the end of 1845, twenty-three separate phalanxes had been inaugurated in the United States. Unfortunately, as far as Albert Brisbane was concerned, not one of them counted as a genuine trial of Fourier's theory. They were all too small, or too poor, or too disorganized. As Brisbane tried to nudge the cause forward, he was torn between supporting the struggling communities and focusing on the pursuit of his ideal phalanx. He remained intent on founding at least one colony that was "scientific" (that is, built precisely according to the theory) rather than "patchwork." His talmudic commitment to Fourier's texts did not mix easily with the messy, improvised reality of founding brick-and-mortar communities.*

A Magnificent Temple
of Molten Gold

By the start of 1846, Brook Farm's phalanstery was almost complete. Paid for by the sale of special stock, the building had not arrived, as Brisbane once promised, "like a comet." Instead, construction had repeatedly been put on hold while cash and lumber trickled in. All along, the Brook Farmers kept expecting financial help from the New York propagandists who had steered them toward Associationism in the first place. None came.

In the year and a half since the community's conversion to Fourierism, Brisbane had come to realize that Brook Farm—which started life as something other than a phalanx—could never become the "scientific" Fourierist trial that he sought. Horace Greeley, believing that Brook Farm carried too much debt and that its soil was too poor to sustain a prosperous community, felt the same. Both men were convinced that Brook Farm would not be the place where the full glory of Fourier's theory would finally be proven to the world.

---

* Brisbane's fixation on the minutiae of the master's sacred theory was so extreme that in 1844, when twenty of an eventual twenty-nine phalanxes had been founded and American Fourierism required decisive leadership, he retreated deeper into the labyrinth of the Divine Social Code, returning to Paris for almost a year to study Fourier's theory of music. According to Fourier, music is the only realm of human activity in which mankind has learned to reliably produce the "harmony" that ought to characterize every aspect of life. "The means by which musical harmony is established do not differ from the means by which the highest harmonies in creation are realized," wrote Brisbane.

Since Brisbane now considered Brook Farm a bust vis-à-vis becoming the perfect phalanx, he wanted Ripley and Dana to leave the community and join him on a fundraising lecture tour. In December 1845, he wrote Ripley suggesting that he shut down the Farm and help make a fresh start elsewhere. If they could persuade a hundred rich men to subscribe $1,000 each, Brisbane explained to Ripley, they could finally do the thing right.

At the time Ripley received this letter, he was running himself ragged trying to finish the phalanstery and generally keep Brook Farm afloat. Aside from his wife, Sophia, nobody in the community worked harder. Although Brook Farm was struggling financially, the colonists had reason to believe that flush times were on the horizon. The costly investments of the first few years—the greenhouse, the orchard, the steam engine, the new buildings, the addition of two wings to the Hive, and, most important, the nearly finished phalanstery—were all about to start paying off. Despite all of this, Brisbane wanted Ripley to abandon the community—a real place full of real people who had made real sacrifices—to chase the dream of a "scientific" phalanx.

Ripley refused. From his perspective, Brook Farm was already a qualified success. The colonists had achieved much of what they'd set out to accomplish. They had not transformed the entire earth into a paradise, but on their small slice of New England, they were successfully forging a new type of society, one that was more spontaneous, healthful, egalitarian, intellectual, and fun. Besides, the immense clapboard phalanstery, upon which so many of their hopes were hung, was almost done.

Ripley wrote Brisbane explaining that an infusion of $15,000 would allow Brook Farm to pay down its debts and get onto solid footing. Brisbane responded by saying that the New York backers (Greeley and his friends at the *Tribune*) were focused on supporting the North American Phalanx, a community with which they had more intimate connections. "You might as well undertake to raise dead men as to attain any considerable amount of capital from people [in New York]." Brisbane was locked into the utopian logic of Fourier's theory. He did not want incremental progress or small victories. He wanted a model phalanx that would inspire awe in investors and spawn a thousand imitations, thereby triggering the rejuvenation of all life on earth. Even a happy, healthy, solvent Brook Farm would not do any of those things. As far as Brisbane was concerned, money sent to West Roxbury would be wasted. "Fifteen thousand dollars might do a great deal at Brook Farm," he wrote, "but would it do the thing effectually—would it make a trial that would impress the public?"

Without much hope of outside help, the Brook Farmers kept working on their phalanstery, buying materials when they could. During the coldest part of the winter of 1845–1846, construction was put on hold. The building, standing in the snow with its windows boarded up, was extremely impressive. It was 175 feet long and three stories high. It contained more than a hundred separate rooms. The attic was split up into small bedrooms for singles. The second and third stories were divided into small, three-room apartments for families. These apartments were connected to one another by elevated "piazzas" that ran around the outside of the building and were sheltered by long, overhanging eves. On each floor there were common spaces—a library, a small circular chapel, and a large communal living room. The basement held an auditorium, an industrial-sized kitchen, and a dining room that could seat four hundred. The colonists expected to move in that summer.

On the last day of February, the boards were taken off the windows so that work could resume. The interior carpentry was mostly done, but the walls had not been plastered. Exposed to the winter air, the beams and laths were bone-dry. To keep themselves warm, carpenters working in the basement installed a small woodstove.

Three days later, on the evening of March 3, there was a party in the Hive. In high spirits, the Brook Farmers danced waltzes. A little after nine, someone rushed into the crowd shouting that the phalanstery was on fire. Over the noise of laughter and fiddle music, most people did not hear him. Others took it as a joke. The waltzing continued. Moments later, a bright smudge of light could be seen through the thick glass windows of the Hive.

Everyone rushed out into the cold. Tall flames were pouring from the second-story windows of the phalanstery. The crowd ran across the snowy meadow toward the fire, but it was already too hot to enter. They scrambled to save tools, lumber, and windows that were stacked beside the burning building. The shingled roof of the Eyrie, which sat just beside the phalanstery, began to smoke with the heat. The colonists formed a bucket chain and spread wet quilts across the smaller building's roof.

It was a perfectly still night and the flames shot upward in a single, seething column. The glassy snow reflected the light, making the fire visible for miles. The surrounding woods, one observer recalled, "shone magically to their minutest twigs, in lead, silver and gold." It was like full daylight on a winter night. Seeing the distant light, fire companies in Newton, Jamaica Plain, Brookline, and West Roxbury hitched up their engines and started for Brook Farm. Neighbors came running with buckets.

While everyone watched in stunned silence, the roof collapsed. Then came the walls and beams. Finally, the newly built stone chimneys toppled inward. Melting window glass tinted the flames blue and red. Marianne Dwight was spellbound by the beauty of the conflagration. The burning phalanstery, she wrote, looked like "a magnificent temple of molten gold."

It took an hour and a half for the first fire engine to arrive over the snow-covered roads. By then, the phalanstery was a smoldering heap. Ripley invited everyone into the Hive for coffee and fresh bread. He apologized for not having more to offer. At least, he joked, nobody could provide a warmer reception.

In the following days, with the wet, sour smell of ash clinging to everything, an eerie sense of calm prevailed. Work went on as usual. Some even claimed to feel a sense of relief. The costly phalanstery, two years in the making, had come to represent the community's strained relations with the national Associationist movement. Perhaps its destruction was divine intervention. Construction had been budgeted at $10,000, and $7,000 had already been spent. Because the building was incomplete and there had not been a stove inside it until three days before the fire, it was not yet insured. The Brook Farm Phalanx, already stretched thin, was bankrupted.

Although a sense of optimism persisted into the spring and summer, the financial situation could not be ignored forever. On any farm, autumn is a time particularly devoted to the future. It is the season for cover cropping and putting up preserves. The abundance and busyness of summer distracted the colonists from the question none of them wanted to ask. When the days shortened, it could not be avoided: Would the community survive? For whom were they chopping all this wood and pickling all these beets?

As it had at New Harmony, the mere prospect of collapse undermined morale. The promise of a glorious future, held precariously in the collective imagination like a handful of water, soothes the countless tiny annoyances and trials of communal living. When that promise slips away, things unwind quickly. Some colonists drifted off without saying good-bye. Others took jobs in Boston, returning to the community only on weekends. Their visits dwindled until they ceased to come at all. In the minds of most members, Brook Farm had become a moral crusade. They gave it up sheepishly, making excuses to Ripley as they left.

As the trickle of departures turned into a full-scale exodus, members who had brought furniture with them carried it off. Piece by piece, the rooms emptied. The smaller homes on the property were boarded up. Ripley's private library, one of the best in Massachusetts, was sold to cover debts. "It was like a knotted skein slowly unraveling," young John Codman wrote of the dissolution. "It was as the ice becomes water, and runs silently away. . . . It was like the apple blossoms dropping from the trees. It was as the herds wind out to pasture. It was like a thousand and one changing and fading things in nature. 'It was not discord. It was music stopped.'"

Some Brook Farmers moved to the NAP or other phalanxes. A few, already primed for a new beginning, joined the rush for gold that was beginning in the West. A small group, including Sophia Ripley, who had never shared her husband's enthusiasm for Fourier, eventually converted to Catholicism, following Orestes Brownson in what one colonist described as "a minor stampede Romeward."

For many Brook Farmers, reentry into the World proved uneasy. Marianne Dwight worried that she could never again be happy amid "the conventions of civilization." "None but a Brook Farmer can know how chilling is the cordiality of the world," she wrote. "It does seem as tho' in this wide waste of the world, life could not possibly be so rich as it has been here."

At the end of the summer of 1847, Brook Farm was transferred to a board of trustees who auctioned off the estate. It was later converted into an almshouse. The Ripleys, who had sunk all their money into the project, were broke. With support from Horace Greeley, *The Harbinger* was relocated from Brook Farm into a room at the top of the Tribune Building in Manhattan. Ripley remained editor, and he and Sophia moved into a small apartment in Flatbush, Long Island (now Brooklyn).

Greeley had already hired the Ripleys' good friend Margaret Fuller to serve as the *Tribune*'s book reviewer. He sent her to Italy, where she served as America's first female foreign correspondent.* Greeley also hired young Charles Dana to serve as his paper's managing editor. The year after Brook Farm was sold, Dana went to Europe to cover the revolutions of 1848, in which the French Fourierists played a part. In Paris, Albert Brisbane introduced Dana to Karl Marx. Dana found Marx so impressive that he hired him as correspondent for the *Tribune*.†

---

* In 1850, on her way back to the United States, Fuller and her new husband, Giovanni Ossoli, an Italian marquis turned republican revolutionary, along with their year-old son, Angelo, died when their ship sank just one hundred yards off Fire Island, New York. Thoreau scoured the shoreline for their remains. Only the infant's body was recovered.

† A decade later, in 1862, Greeley fired Dana for hiring too many radical reporters. When Marx heard the news, he wrote Engels complaining that "that old jackass with the face of an angel [Greeley] seems to have been behind it all."

When Dana returned to the United States, he became an influential abolitionist. During the Civil War, he held a prominent post in Lincoln's War Department. After the war, he became editor of the *New York Sun*.

In the fall of 1849, *The Harbinger* folded because of the declining interest in Associationism. Ripley joined his old Brook Farm comrades on the staff of the *Tribune*, beginning a long, celebrated career as a literary critic. With his modest salary, he and Sophia gradually paid down every cent of the community's debts.

Many people connected with the experiment in West Roxbury believed that history would someday vindicate their efforts. "Never did I feel so calmly, humbly, devoutly thankful that it had been my privilege to fail in this grandest, sublimest, surest of all human movements," wrote William Henry Channing after a visit to the shuttered commune. "Were Thermopylae and Bunker Hill considered successes in their day and generation?" Miles Coverdale, Hawthorne's fictitious Brook Farmer, reflected on the breakup of the community from a distance of several years: "More and more I feel we struck upon what ought to be a truth. Posterity may dig it up and profit by it."

Even Emerson, who had been dismayed over Brook Farm's conversion to Fourierism, conceded that the communards had "made what all people try to make, an agreeable place to live in."

All comers, even the most fastidious, found it the pleasantest of residences. It is certain that freedom from household routine, variety of character and talent, variety of work, variety of means of thought and instruction, art, music, poetry, reading, masquerade, did not permit sluggishness or despondency; broke up routine. There is agreement in the testimony that it was, to most of the associates, education; to many, the most important period of their life, the birth of valued friendships, their first acquaintance with the riches of conversation, their training in behavior. . . . It was a perpetual picnic, a French Revolution in small, an Age of Reason in a patty-pan.

Music Stopped

New phalanxes continued to be established for the rest of the 1840s, but the bust in West Roxbury was a major blow. "The end of Brook Farm was virtually the end of Fourierism," wrote John Humphrey Noyes, a close and intelligent observer of the whole movement. "The enthusiasm of hope and victory was gone." Toward the end of the 1840s, the national economy bounced back with amazing vigor. As financial opportunities for working people proliferated, the appetite for radical cooperative experiments waned. The rush for land and fortune in the West siphoned off many of the same people who, a decade earlier, might have been stirred by the adventurous, utopian rhetoric in *The Harbinger*. Even some diehard Associationists were lured westward by Dakota gold.

At the same time, northeastern reformers began finally waking up to the urgency of the abolitionist cause. Much of the enthusiasm, cash, and ink that had flowed into the phalanxes of the 1840s was redirected southward and into the Free Soil fight in the West. In the long prelude to war and emancipation, the fight to abolish slavery gradually eclipsed every other progressive cause.

By the end of the 1840s, the northern half of the Republic was littered with defunct or foundering phalanxes. Most of them had been, in Noyes's words, a "brood of unscientific and starveling 'picnics.'" The community that hung on longest was the North American Phalanx, the rebellious offspring of western New York's Fourier craze and the *Tribune*-based propagandists in Manhattan. Despite an abundance of applications, the members of the NAP kept their community small, ignoring pressure from their backers in Manhattan to expand into a more "scientific" trial of Fourier's theory. The community's 120 members settled into a happy, stable existence in their modest three-story phalanstery.

In the early 1850s, Marcus Spring, a Quaker abolitionist and one of the wealthiest members of the NAP, called for the community to adopt something like Fourierism-lite: "an intermediate position between the North American Phalanx and ordinary society." He found considerable support, and in 1853, the community split. Thirty people followed Spring down the road to Perth Amboy, New Jersey, where they built a grand stone phalanstery and founded the short-lived Raritan Bay Union. Not long after the split, in September 1854, a fire at the NAP destroyed workshops, mills, the main office building, and a large harvest of wheat and corn. The damage was estimated at $14,000. When the community's insurer declared bankruptcy, Greeley offered to cover the losses. The fire, however, had exposed a long simmering division within the community. The two factions could not agree on whether to rebuild on the same land or to start over elsewhere. In 1855, twelve years after its founding, the stockholders of the North American Phalanx voted to sell off the estate and go their separate ways.

La Réunion

While the American Fourierists spent the 1840s struggling to build a viable phalanx, their French counterparts—mostly university students and young radicals—focused on propaganda and the critical study of Fourier's theory. There were a few European efforts to build a phalanx, including one in French Algeria, but nothing on a par with the proliferation of Fourier-inspired, worker-built communities that sprang to life in the United States. In the proud tradition of European revolutionary societies, the Fourierists in Paris sometimes seemed more like a religious sect than a political movement. They developed elaborate costumes, rituals, and an arcane theoretical vocabulary. They spoke of their brilliant, sullen leader as the Second Coming. "First came Jesus Christ," went one French slogan, "then Fourier."

Victor Considerant, who assumed leadership of the movement after Fourier's death in 1837, gradually steered the cause in a more explicitly political direction. By the late 1840s, he was one of the most prominent socialists in France, working actively to undermine the July Monarchy and advocating against more militant communists for a bloodless, democratic transition to socialism. After taking part in the revolution of

1848, Considerant was elected to the Constituent Assembly of the re-
formed French Republic.

A year later, following protests by French radicals over their government's decision to attack the short-lived Roman Republic, there was a
harsh crackdown on socialists. Albert Brisbane, who happened to be in
Paris when the "terrible rumpus" began, rushed to the offices of the
Fourierist daily (by then called *La Démocratie Pacifique*) to hide the master's sacred manuscripts and tear down the caricatures of the newly
elected president, Louis Napoleon, that were pasted all over the walls.
Considerant took part in an abortive uprising and was forced into hiding. He shaved his immense Fu Manchu, dressed as a fisherman, and
fled to Belgium.

Brisbane caught up with Considerant in Brussels and persuaded him
to come visit the North American Phalanx. After six weeks in New Jersey, the two men decided to merge the French and American branches
of the movement for one final try. True to form, they started from
scratch. They took a steamship down the Mississippi, bought horses,
and rode overland into north Texas. Atop limestone bluffs overlooking
the Trinity River, Charles Fourier's two most ardent apostles plotted
one last phalanx.

Considerant returned to Belgium to raise funds and recruit volunteers.
To whip up support, he wrote a book-length proposal published under
the title *Au Texas*. The "European Society for the Colonization of Texas"
easily recruited twenty-five hundred members. In 1855, an advance
team of one hundred men arrived on the outskirts of the small village
of Dallas, in an area that Considerant had described as a "wild Eden."
They cleared land and planted crops. Fourierists began arriving from
across the Atlantic. The community, which they called La Réunion,
soon had more than 350 residents. There were a few Americans among
them, but most were French, Belgian, and Swiss.

Because the newly formed state of Texas was eager for white settlers,
the colonists had expected to receive a generous land grant. Instead,
they were met with outright hostility. The nativist Know Nothing Party

had gained national prominence agitating against foreigners, Catholics, and socialists. La Réunion was crowded with all three.

The fact that the community was supported by Horace Greeley, by then closely identified with the abolitionist cause, convinced some Texans that the phalanx was being built as a haven for escaped slaves. While the colony made no public statements about slavery, Considerant's antislavery writings were easily found. Just before La Réunion was established, an editorial in an Austin paper tried to scare them off. "We are always pleased to have industrious immigrants come among us," it read. "There is one class, however, that we are opposed to. . . . This class is of that Propagandist school which in France and in parts of the United States has and is seeking to sap the foundations of society. The socialist desires to destroy individual rights in property . . . for he holds it as a primary principle in his creed, that no individual has a right to accumulate property for himself." If there was any doubt about what sort of property was most under threat, the article continued: "The socialist is an abolitionist everywhere. . . . It is part of his creed. . . . We note this advent of socialism in Texas [the founding of La Réunion] as foreboding us no good; and we wish them to have a fair understanding before they reach our soil, that as a political sect our whole people are against them."

The Know Nothings might have saved their breath. The sere Texas wilderness proved even less hospitable. Considerant's "wild Eden" was lush and temperate in February, but by summer, the underfed, overdressed European artisans began to flag. They were short on water and besieged by rattlesnakes and grasshoppers. Their soil was chalky, and a freak summer cold snap wiped out their first planting.*

By 1858, the phalanx slid into shabby chaos, with many colonists making their own plans. In 1859, La Réunion dissolved. Its members dispersed. Many of them, including Considerant, settled elsewhere in Texas.†

---

* The colony might have thrived if they had tried digging rather than plowing. The commune sat atop a large and highly valuable limestone deposit.
† The Reunion Tower in downtown Dallas is named for the phalanx.

Strange Land

Ever since Fourier published *The Theory of the Four Movements* at the anxious, future-gazing start of the nineteenth century, his vision of the harmonic future has been derided as the work of a madman. Even some of his most approving critics have classified him as an artist—a dealer in genius, deeply humane phantasmagoria—rather than a social reformer. Yet Fourier's ideas inspired his American acolytes to pursue, with limited success but great practical energy, such radical innovations as public education, female equity, fair wages, workers' cooperatives, farm collectives, and a modest sexual liberation. The Associationists' dream of teeming, merry communities of equality might have been a pie in the sky, but the stumps they dug up and the phalansteries they built were all very real.

Like everyone, the Associationists wanted to make more comfortable lives for themselves. But they also intended to make a more just and satisfying world for everyone. However misguided their efforts, their labors were fundamentally altruistic. Mass thinking and mass action in service of abstract, unproven theories comes with obvious risks, but the powerful influence of Fourier's ideas shows how an appealing, well-elaborated vision of the future—a utopia, in the simplest sense—can move a large, diverse group of people in a single, noble direction.

Since Fourier's death, some of his wildest prophecies have come true. More than a century before the formation of the Civilian Conservation Corps or the Peace Corps, Fourier foresaw the formation of "industrial armies" assigned to dig irrigation ditches, plant trees, and perform large-scale public works for the common good.* Even more outlandish, he predicted that humans would eventually shape the globe for our own convenience—by, he suggested, carving canals through

---

* Unlike the young men of the CCC, when the "soldiers" in Fourier's industrial army go out to plant a new forest, their morale will be buoyed by the sexual ministrations of nubile camp followers. Like the industrial soldiers themselves, these erotic attendants will be highly honored in their home phalanxes for their service to humanity.

Suez and the Isthmus of Panama. He rightly predicted that human industry would warm the atmosphere, causing the poles to thaw. He also
foresaw the rise of mechanized agribusiness and the decline of the family farm. His "Harmonian Court of Love," in which individuals are al-
gorithmically paired for romantic and sexual liaisons, sounded
preposterous in the middle nineteenth century. Today it is the banal
reality of online dating (eHarmony). Since Fourier made his prophecies
on a timescale of millennia, the jury is still technically out on most of
his predictions. Maybe someday we *will* ride quaggas and antilions
through the temperate cane fields of the Sahara.

Fourier accurately predicted the exponential increase in humanity's
ability to achieve material ends: the explosion of productivity brought
about by new technologies and sources of energy. What he did not
foresee—what his singular reverence for the human species made it impossible for him to see—was that those advances could be achieved
without a more fundamental reorganization of social relations. He assumed that we would use our newfound material superpowers to oblit-
erate poverty, shorten the workday, eliminate drudgery, cease making
war, eat better food, make more music, find more genius in our children, play more games, and have more and better sex. Most of all, he
expected cooperation to replace competition as the default mode of
economics and social interaction. Fourier was convinced that our innate
conviviality and diversity—the boggling variety of human desires, all of
which he saw as equally legitimate—would transform this vale of tears
into a festival of love.

His imagination was ceaseless. So was his affection. The lemonade
sea may be a chimera, but the future is a strange land. Picturing it, however imperfectly, requires a strange mind.

ICARIA

People of the Book

It is indeed time that hatred were forgotten;
That all people rallied under a single flag;
The way to salvation for us is smooth
The great liberty of which humanity dreams,
Like a new radiant sun, rises
On the horizon before us.

—ICARIAN POEM

Victor Considerant was not the first Parisian radical to glimpse utopia in the green, vacant wilds of east Texas. On November 14, 1847, a month after George and Sophia Ripley left Brook Farm, the front page of *Le Populaire,* a communist weekly printed in Paris, bore a peculiar headline: C'EST AU TEXAS! (IT'S IN TEXAS!).

Ten weeks later, before dawn at the piers of Le Havre, sixty-nine Frenchmen filed aboard the *Rome,* an American-built steamer with three masts of large, square-rigged sails. As the ship pulled away, thousands waved from the shore, cheering au revoir.

Standing at the stern rail, dressed in matching gray caps and black velvet tunics, the men sang a newly written anthem to the tune of "La Marseillaise":

Arise, workers stooped in the dust,
The hour of Awakening has sounded.
To American shores the banner is going to wave,
The banner of the holy community.
No more vices, no more suffering,
No more crimes, no more pain,
The august equality advances itself:
Proletariat, dry your tears.
Let us go to found Icaria,
The happiness of Humanity.

These solemn pilgrims were the handpicked avant-garde of an immense exodus of French communists to the New World. Icaria, as they called the "holy community" they were going to establish on American shores, was to be modeled on a make-believe place, the happy island nation described in *Voyage en Icarie* (*Travels in Icaria*), a bestselling utopian romance published in 1840 by Étienne Cabet, a communist parliamentarian and the publisher of *Le Populaire*.

After a seven-week crossing, the *Rome* docked in the Port of New Orleans. From there, the communists traveled upriver by steamboat to Shreveport, where they set out on foot toward the Trinity River valley. It was there, not far from the village of Dallas, that they intended to build their utopia. Tens of thousands of self-styled "Icarians" remained behind in France, poised to make the crossing once ground had been broken.

At least that was the plan.

The Good Icar

Étienne Cabet was born in Dijon on the first day of 1788, one year before the outbreak of the French Revolution. His father was a cooper—a strong-armed, red-cheeked Burgundian who built oak casks for Burgundy wine. He was precisely the sort of citizen artisan who was supposed to form the backbone of the new French Republic. His cooperage was filled with boisterous talk of *égalité* and the royalist defeat at Valmy. Toasts were shouted and drunk to Maximilien de Robespierre. Young Étienne came to political consciousness during the rollback of the Revolution's gains, first under Napoleon's empire and then during the restoration of the monarchy. While he shared Fourier's powerful aversion to revolutionary gore, he idolized the stark moral certitude of the Jacobins.

Cabet had poor vision and scant interest in barrels. Instead of apprenticing in his father's shop, he went to the university to study medicine, later switching to law. He graduated just as France fell back under the rule of conservative Bourbon monarchs—first Louis XVIII, then Charles X. The young lawyer became active in the republican underground. During a particularly harsh period of royalist crackdowns, he developed a reputation for defending dissidents.

By the late 1820s, Cabet was in Paris, leading the ascetic life of an underpaid radical lawyer. He had grown into a stern-looking man, built more like a cooper than an advocate, with large eyes, a broad forehead, and a wide face framed by thick muttonchops. Through some of his republican clients he had been recruited into the Charbonnerie, an antiroyalist secret society more or less led by the Marquis de Lafayette.

In July 1830, students and workers built barricades in the streets of Paris to protest a new set of repressive ordinances signed into law by King Charles X. Cabet led an insurrectionary committee that helped organize the demonstrations. The king underestimated the level of discontent and left Paris to go hunting. In his absence, the demonstrations grew. Soldiers who had been called out to hold the line began to mingle with the demonstrators. The protests had begun with relatively modest demands: the repeal of several new laws and the dismissal of the king's prime minister, the Duke of Polignac. Sensing their strength, the people in the streets of Paris called for Charles's abdication.

The radicalized workers and students who gave energy to the demonstrations wanted a fully restored republic. Protest leaders such as Cabet and Lafayette suggested a more realistic compromise: Charles should cede the throne to his cousin Louis Philippe, the popular, relatively liberal Duke of Orléans. On the last day of July, Lafayette and Louis Philippe stepped onto a balcony of the Hôtel de Ville in Paris. In front of an immense crowd, the aged general wrapped the young duke in the Tricolore and embraced him. It was an odd sight: a monarch-to-be draped in the flag of the Revolution. Thus anointed, Louis Philippe was accepted by the demonstrators. The press called him "the King of the Barricades." Charles had no choice but to surrender his throne.

As one of the leaders of the July Revolution, Cabet received an audience with the new king.* Without much diplomatic nicety, Cabet urged Louis Philippe to immediately expand suffrage and loosen restrictions on the media. The king was evidently annoyed by the tone of this counsel. He "rewarded" Cabet for his role in the uprising by sending him as far from Paris as possible: appointing him prosecutor-general in Corsica. That fall, Cabet sailed for Bastia with a mandate to reform the Corsican legal system. He was installed in a large villa overlooking the Mediterranean and the coast of Italy.

To the surprise of many of Louis Philippe's supporters, "the King of the Barricades" strictly censored the opposition press and purged his government of many of the liberals who had helped put him in power. Cabet followed these developments from Corsica, frustrated by his remote posting. "In ordinary times," he wrote a friend, "I should gladly pass a few years here. But today, considering the state of France and Europe, to be away from my country cannot be anything but a penance to the ardent soul of a patriot like me, who is continually thinking of his country." After a year of cushy exile, Cabet ran for a seat in the Cham-

---

* Cabet's support for the Duke of Orléans was not mere political expedience. As early as 1827, he had called for a liberal, constitutional monarchy led by Louis Philippe and buttressed by freely elected assemblies and a free press.

ber of Deputies (the lower house of the Parliament), representing Dijon. He won his race and sailed back to France.

Unlike his utopian contemporaries Robert Owen, Charles Fourier, and John Humphrey Noyes, all of whom were too far-out for any sort of traditional political life, Cabet moved easily through the shifting currents of left-wing French politics.* He stood for office as a moderate, advocating a weak monarchy hemmed in by democratic institutions. But as the government of Louis Philippe became increasingly reactionary, Cabet evolved into a full-throated republican, taking his seat in the chamber among the radicals and turning his considerable energy to full-time king baiting.

Publicly aligning himself with the discontented working class, Cabet became secretary-general of the Association for the Free Education of the People, an organization founded by university students to provide free classes to Parisian workers. Under Cabet's leadership, republican-tinged courses were slipped in among the usual offerings in math and zoology. Cabet also wrote a popular history of the July uprising. The book, which focused on the betrayals of Louis Philippe, was officially condemned, further burnishing his radical profile.

In the summer of 1833, Cabet founded *Le Populaire*, a newspaper trumpeting the values of the first revolution: universal suffrage, women's rights, liberty, equality, and brotherhood. Like a more radical version of Greeley's *Tribune*, Cabet's paper addressed itself directly to working people in simple, emotional language. In Paris, newsboys dressed in red, white, and blue uniforms sold it on the street. *Le Populaire* distinguished itself from other radical periodicals by calling for social justice while emphatically denouncing class warfare and insurrection: "We wish, not that the class which up to now has been dominant should be crushed and humiliated," said the paper's prospectus, "but that the people should be raised to the height which the dignity of man and that

---

* Marx singled him out for his "practical attitude" to communist revolution.

of the citizen demand." Circulation climbed quickly until the paper was
the most widely read republican broadsheet in France. The seventh edition sold twelve thousand copies in Paris alone. Cabet, the precocious
son of a barrel maker, had become a working-class hero. When he rode
in Lafayette's carriage to the funeral of a mutual friend, a crowd
chanted, *"Vive Cabet! Vive Lafayette!"*

Cabet responded to his popularity with increasingly inflammatory articles and speeches in the Chamber of Deputies. In a January 1834
edition of *Le Populaire,* he wrote an article titled "The King's Crimes
Against Humanity," in which he claimed that Louis Philippe was "resolved, if necessary, to have Frenchmen shot, gunned down in the
streets." Accusing the king of a willingness to murder French citizens
was a clear violation of libel and sedition laws. As a publisher, a legisla-
tor, and a lawyer, Cabet must have known in advance the consequences
of what he'd written. He was tried for sedition, indicted, and sentenced
to either two years in prison or five in exile. At the urging of his mistress,
Delphine Lesage, with whom he had a daughter, Cabet chose the latter.
He left Paris for Brussels in the early spring. The Belgians, fed up with
sheltering French agitators, ejected Cabet immediately. He rerouted to
London.

City of Words

Cabet and Lesage got married in England. The small family lived off a
modest pension supplied by French supporters. Cabet spent his days in
the grand, domed library of the British Museum, where he wrote a history of the French Revolution that focused on the heroic conduct of the
Jacobin hard-liner Maximilien de Robespierre.

In the winter of 1835–1836, sitting at his assigned carrel in the library, Cabet read a short book with a long title: *De optimo reipublicae statu,*
deque nova insula Utopia. Utopia, as it is usually known, had been published
three centuries earlier, in 1516, by Thomas More, a thirty-eight-year-

old lawyer, a middling diplomat, and one of London's two undersher-
iffs.* More had a knack for sophisticated wordplay. He wrote in Latin,
the preferred language of sixteenth-century churchmen, but he filled
his little book with Greek puns. "Utopia," the name he gave to the fictional nation that is his book's subject, is itself a pun. The tail end of the
word comes from *topos,* meaning "place" (as in topography), but the
prefix can go two ways. Read aloud, the "u" sounds like the Greek prefix *eu,* meaning "good" (as in euphoria). So Eutopia means Goodplace.
But "u" is also the Latin transliteration of the Greek prefix *ou,* which
negates whatever it precedes. So Utopia equals Notaplace. The tension
within More's pun, between Goodplace and Notaplace, haunts the history of utopian thought. Are narratives of the ideal state, More's included, merely a way to organize our complaints and aspirations about
the here and now? Or is the Goodplace a real possibility?

Like other scholars of his generation, More endeavored to merge the
intellectual glories of pagan antiquity with the dogmas of Roman Catholicism. A poem on the first page of *Utopia* (attributed to the poet
"Windbag Nonsenso") declares that the book is a response to the *Republic,* Plato's dialogue on the nature of the ideal state. "Plato's *Republic* now
I claim / To match, or beat at its own game."

More's response to Plato unfolds in two parts, written at different
times. The first is a dialogue on the proper role of the philosopher, a
direct nod to the structure and subject of the *Republic.* The second part
is modeled loosely on a classical travel narrative. It recounts a conversation in the garden of an Antwerp hotel between a character named
Thomas More, his friend Peter Gilles, and a bearded, sunburnt explorer
named Raphael Hythloday.

After eating lunch, the three men settle onto a turf-covered bench to
talk. Hythloday tells More and Gilles about how he sailed for the New
World with Amerigo Vespucci. When Vespucci doubled back for Eu-

---

* In 1935, to honor More's scholarship, his energetic persecution of Protestants, and
his eventual martyrdom, the Vatican promoted Sir Thomas More to Saint Thomas
More.

rope, Hythloday continued sailing southward. (Even in the 1500s, Europeans apparently associated the ideal society with the Americas.) After dipping below the equator, Hythloday came upon a densely populated, crescent-shaped island about two hundred miles wide. An isthmus once connected the island to the mainland, but the natives dug it up. The perfect society evidently requires some form of moat. The

Frontispiece of Thomas More's *Utopia*.

small nation, a federation of fifty-four nearly identical municipalities, is called Utopia in honor of the wise King Utopos, who briefly ruled the Utopians and established their unusual laws.

King Utopos's most significant innovation was the abolition of private property. There are no economic classes in Utopia. As a result, everyone works; there are none of the idle gentry who constituted England's ruling class at the time More wrote. Most of the Utopians live in neatly arranged cities and work a gentle six-day week in highly efficient, nationalized workshops. From time to time, they rotate to the countryside to serve two-year shifts on collective farms.

Equality in all things is their chief civic ambition. The Utopians regard private property as the self-evident root of almost all social discord. "The one essential condition for a healthy society [is] equal distribution of goods," Hythloday explains. "For, when everyone's entitled to get as much for himself as he can, all available property, however much there is of it, is bound to fall into the hands of a small minority, which means that everyone else is poor. And wealth will tend to vary in inverse proportion to merit. The rich will be greedy, unscrupulous, and totally useless characters, while the poor will be simple, unassuming people whose daily work is far more profitable to the community than it is to them."

When the Utopians are not at their jobs, they occupy themselves with lifelong education, communal entertainment, and high culture. They relish wholesome, sensual pleasures—perfume, music, health food, and lots of sex—but they look down upon pointless displays of material wealth. Civic values are reinforced with clever strategies of social conditioning. To curtail the irrational and troublesome desire for rare minerals, the Utopians use golden chamber pots, give their children jewel-encrusted rattles, and shackle their prisoners with gilded chains. In this way, they ensure that no right-thinking Utopian adult would ever covet gold. When foreign dignitaries parade through the capital in heaps of jewelry, onlookers mistake them for clowns or slaves shackled by golden chains.

Surprisingly, given More's later career as a Catholic zealot, the religious atmosphere in Utopia is diverse, tolerant, and mild. The Utopians look down on any sort of fanaticism or asceticism.* Most of them believe in some form of benign, unitary deity, but they seldom express or proselytize that fact. A Utopian is permitted to evangelize his faith only if he does it "quietly, politely, and by rational argument." Until Hythloday arrives, they know nothing of Christianity.

More, unlike many of his imitators, chose not to suspend the laws of human nature in his idealized state. Life in Utopia is pleasant, but it is not perfect. Despite excellent socialized medicine, the Utopians still suffer death and disease. And while equality and abundance have dramatically diminished criminality, some Utopians are still tempted to break the rules. When they do, the consequences are severe. While the Utopians abhor violence, they sometimes go to war. But since they find no glory in combat, they pay foreign mercenaries to do their fighting for them. Most shocking, they keep slaves, many of whom are convicted criminals.

Two decades after More wrote *Utopia*, at the age of fifty-six, he found himself rather suddenly on the wrong side of the English Reformation. Desperate for a male heir, Henry VIII sought to annul his marriage to Catherine of Aragon and marry her lady maid Anne Boleyn. When the pope forbade the annulment, Henry cut the Church of England's ties with the Vatican. By then, More was one of the king's closest advisers and a passionate opponent of the Protestant heresy that was spreading on the continent. He tried and failed to keep England bound to Rome. Formally unhitched from the Vatican, Henry divorced Catherine, married Anne, and named himself head of the Church of England. Thomas More might have made peace with the new order, but he held firm, conspicuously absenting himself from Anne's coronation. In 1534, he was locked in the Tower of London, where he had previously sent many Protestants. More claimed to enjoy the ascetic simplicity of prison life,

---

* More himself was known to wear a horsehair girdle that scored him so deeply, blood seeped through his outer tunic. When he did not feel sufficiently mortified by his hair shirt, he whipped himself.

but his incarceration didn't last. In the summer of 1535, he was be-headed before a large crowd on Tower Hill.*

More's *Utopia* created a template for an entire literary genre, that meters-long shelf of books describing life in the perfect society. Like *Utopia,* these books typically recount the adventures of some wide-eyed explorer as he stumbles upon a delightful yet unknown nation or planet. As the narrator ambles about, chatting up the locals and taking in the sights (often falling in love with some winsome utopian lass), he usually describes in detail what life in the newly discovered nation looks like. How do the utopians get to work? What color are their costumes? How are their streets cleaned? How do they vote? What's for dinner? Plot and character are usually beside the point. The *topos* is protagonist. Un-like many subsequent utopias, the original *Utopia* is shot through with humor and irony. An enduring testament to its humane ambiguity is the fact that political and religious boosters of every possible stripe have found their ideas reflected back at them in the happy faces of More's Utopians.

The whole point of writing a utopian narrative—instead of, say, a technical tract on the advantages of collectivized agriculture or an ab-stract defense of capital-letter virtues such as Equality and Justice—is that fiction can render ideas visible in the mind's eye, allowing the reader to judge the author's notion of the ideal society by the most inti-mate criterion: Would I want to live there? That was certainly the expe-rience of Étienne Cabet as he read *Utopia* in the British Museum. More's account of a minutely planned, propertyless society converted Cabet from democratic republicanism to full-blown utopian commu-nism. "It was the *Utopia* of Thomas More," he later wrote, "which first decided me to study the communistic system. From its first lines this system impressed me so that I closed the book to collect my own thoughts in meditations that led me to the most complete conviction. I adopted my plan and began to draw it up."

---

* A year later, having delivered a daughter, Elizabeth I, and a stillborn son, Anne Boleyn suffered the same fate.

Cabet commenced his study of "the communistic system" with Robert Owen. Owen's environmental determinism—his insistence that man is entirely formed by his surroundings—appealed to Cabet. Like Owen, Cabet had risen far above his origins, thanks in large part to the attentions, during his youth, of a few literate, broad-minded adults. The notion that character is shaped by circumstance reflected the personal experiences of both men.

Cabet contacted Owen, who was then living in London. They became friends, meeting repeatedly throughout Cabet's five-year exile. Owen's determinism carried Cabet toward the idea that the key to a perfected society consists in submitting man's imperfect nature—apparently the sole stumbling block between here and paradise—to the right sorts of surroundings. Like Owen, Cabet believed that competitive industrialism was a curse, but that industrial technology opened the way toward equality and abundance. "The progress of industry makes the establishment of community easier today than ever before; the current and limitless productive power by means of steam and machines can assure equality of abundance," he wrote. In other words, after millennia of struggle, the time was finally right for utopia.

Borrowing More's template and adopting many of Owen's ideas, Cabet set to work on a new book. The result, *Voyage en Icarie,* describes life in the fictional land of Icaria. If the novel had not had such a powerful influence on so many lives, it would be easy to dismiss. Like More, Cabet uses the loose, ambling structure of a travelogue. But unlike More's slim, witty volume, *Voyage* is a slog—humorless, dense with cliché, and very long. The book purports to be the diary of an Englishman named Lord William Carisdall, "one of the wealthiest lords" and "handsomest men" to ever grace the British Isles with his "noble character." Carisdall travels to a remote island off the western coast of Africa, where he discovers Icaria, a techno-communist paradise with the combined population of France and England.

In Icaria, there is no private property or money. Food, shelter, clothing, and all of life's comforts are produced and distributed by the state.

Men and women are considered equal and receive the same comprehensive public education, although women do not vote. When an Icarian family runs low on food, they place a specially designed container
into a specially designed niche outside of their specially designed apartment. When they return home after a day working in collective workshops, they find their bin topped off with healthful victuals. The sources
of Icarian abundance are technological innovation and the fact that
everyone works for the wealth of the republic. There are no idle rich or
landed aristocracy to draw off the wealth of the nation. As a result of
these reforms, many old occupations have been rendered obsolete. In
Icaria there are no domestic servants, cops, informants, middlemen,
soldiers, gunsmiths, or bankers.

For six hundred pages, the novel follows Carisdall as he travels
around the island, wondering blandly at Icaria's wondrous wonders. In
Icaria, "all the children are charming, the men vigorous and handsome,
the women enchanting and divine . . . all the social and political institutions bear the hallmark of reason, justice, and wisdom. Crime is unknown there. Everyone lives in peace, pleasure, joy and happiness. In a
word, Icaria is truly a second promised land, an Eden, and Elysium, a
new earthly paradise." Whatever is not "wondrous" is "splendid" or
"awe-striking." One early critic noted that "there is such a debauch of
virtue in Icaria that a two-fisted encounter between a pair of rascals
would bring a reader the desired sigh of relief."

A romantic plot—a blushing, star-crossed flirtation between Lord
Carisdall and a comely Icarian named Dinaïse—provides the skimpy
armature on which Cabet hangs his detailed descriptions of Icarian
sanitation, medicine, agriculture, public transportation, education,
journalism, clothing, and cookery. Alas, it turns out that Icarians are
forbidden from marrying foreigners. Shucks for Lord William.

Throughout, the dialogue is unfailingly stilted. When Carisdall first
grasps the basics of Icarian communism, he is *shocked:*

"But this is COMMUNAL OWNERSHIP OF GOODS!" I
exclaimed.

"Precisely," said Valmor's grandfather. "Does such a community frighten you?"

"No, but people have always said that it is an impossibility."

"Impossible! You shall see . . ."

Yes, he shall. Everything in Icaria is "ingeniously arranged," perfectly symmetrical, sparklingly clean, and harmoniously uniform. Every urban annoyance has found its solution. The sidewalks are well lit and protected by glass awnings. The dogs are muzzled. The horses shit only where they are supposed to. Like Ann Lee and Robert Owen, Cabet believed deeply in the social power of the broom—the faith that a tidy environment produces tidy citizens.

The history of Icaria, as it is unfolded for Carisdall by an Icarian scholar named Dinaros, reads like a collaboration between V. I. Lenin and W. E. Disney. Like Utopia, the country is named for its founding tyrant. "The good Icar" began life as a common carter but grew to be a hero of cartoonish virtue. "From earliest childhood he could not see another child without running to caress him, kiss him, and share with him the little he had. . . . At a fire that daunted the bravest onlookers, people were terrified to see Icar throw himself into the flames and, clothing afire and right hand badly burned, emerge with a child in his arms." In 1782, Icar led an uprising against the wickedly named Queen Cloramide and her scheming prime minister, a one-eyed, hunchbacked aristocrat named Lixdox. After the revolution, Icar seized power and established a system of collective and centralized labor wherein every Icarian works for the common weal. All the men vote to elect provincial councils, the National Assembly, and a small executive chamber that enacts the assembly's will. Like Cincinnatus, who saved Rome and then hurried back to his plow, the good Icar set this flawless republic in motion and then stepped aside.

Icaria is divided into a hundred equally sized provinces, each of which is made up of ten communes. Each commune and each province has a capital city at its center. At the very center of the country is the

main capital, Icara. The city, an idealized version of Paris, is a perfect
circle bisected by a river. In the middle of the river is a circular island
covered in gardens and a palace.*

Through the wide, spotless streets of Icara, Icarian workers ride
around in high-tech omnibuses. Smaller carts, drawn by dogs of "remarkable size and strength," deliver daily coal rations. For long trips,
people travel by hot-air balloon, train, or submarine. Their costumes
are designed by a committee who studied all the clothes in the world to
find the most lovely and useful outfits. "There is not a single shoe or hat
that has not been discussed and adopted according to a model." The
standardization of women's apparel has eliminated all "jealousy or co-
quetry."

As the Icarians labor to produce the necessities of life, scented
breezes and Muzak ("harmonious, soft music produced by an invisible
machine") are piped into their workshops to keep them calm and cheer-
ful. Much of the hardest work is done by machines. Describing an immense, highly mechanized clock factory, Cabet writes, "You would
think you were seeing an army regiment; such is the high degree of
order and discipline there." Indeed, almost everything about Icaria
brings to mind a well-scrubbed barracks. At lunch the workers sit down
at communal tables to eat food designed by a committee of expert nu-
tritionists. A great deal about life in Icaria is conveyed by the fact that
the bathroom in every Icarian home features a poster indicating the
ideal temperature and duration for a bath.

Every aspect of life is centralized. Equality in all things is the guiding
principle. Cabet does not deny that humans are born with varying gifts,
but, as one Icarian asks, "Should reason and society not repair the inequality produced by blind chance?" The Icarians think that "the satisfaction experienced by the person whose talent makes him more useful
[ought to be] enough in itself." Even so, like Fourier, Cabet made con-

---

* All of this reflects the metric fetish of the French Revolution, a fantasy of order and
geometry laid over land and people without regard for natural or social topography.
Lewis Mumford, the great historian of cities, rightly notes that islands formed by
rivers are never circular.

cessions to the human appetite for individual distinction. Rather than wealth and power, the Icarians compete for ribbons, trophies, titles, and odes. But unlike in warmongering Europe, in Icaria heroes are more likely to be found in the lab than on the battlefield. As one Icarian tells Carisdall, "All our young girls like to sing a charming song in honor of the young, gallant kitchen designer." Every Icarian latrine comes equipped with a statuette honoring the woman who invented a fantastic air freshener.

With state-baked bread comes state-run circuses. The Icarian work-day ends at one o'clock, and the Icarians spend their afternoons in study and relaxation. At night they gather for extravagant public "entertain-ments," dazzling spectacles involving fireworks and thousands of per-formers choreographed to reinforce the central Icarian virtues: reason, equality, and selflessness.

In Icaria—unlike Ann Lee's Zion, Owen's New Moral World, or Fourier's Harmony—the nuclear family remains the building block of society. Every Icarian is expected to marry. Divorce is easily obtained, but prompt remarriage is expected. Celibacy is frowned upon, and adultery is punished harshly.

Cabet placed a strong emphasis on the democratic nature of his communist neverland. While the Icarians seem to live in an almost con-stant state of voting, many of the social institutions that dazzle Lord Carisdall sound darkly totalitarian on this side of the twentieth century. "The republic," boasts one Icarian, "was able to rewrite all the books that were imperfect—a national history, for example—and to burn all the old books judged to be dangerous or useless." Even art is carefully regulated. "Just as in Sparta they did away with ill or deformed children at birth, here we throw in the darkness of the abyss, without a second thought, all productions unworthy of being illuminated by the rays of the god of the arts." They have just one national paper and one local paper for each province and commune. Like everything else, these pa-pers are controlled by "the people," that is to say the state, that is to say a bureau of specialized bureaucrats, that is to say a small group of pow-erful (democratically elected) men. In 1922, Lewis Mumford observed that "there was more of Cabet than of Marx perhaps in embryonic Soviet Russia."

One of two opposing criticisms is typically leveled at utopian writers and reformers. The first is that they think too little of individuals. The utopian, according to this line of thought, sees people as passive cogs in the machinery of the state who, for a guarantee of comfort and peace, will suffer any indignity. The implication of this critique is that the utopian sees all humans as basically uniform. Here is the hinge on which utopia flips and becomes dystopia: that drizzly, well-intentioned metropolis in which citizens cue up like drowsy cattle for a daily dose of soma and vitamin-enriched bread. The second, seemingly inverse, critique is that the utopian thinks too highly of individuals. With moony optimism, he sees everyone as inherently selfless or, at the very least, reasonable. Once people are shown that their self-interest is identical to the general interest, they will never shirk their chores, cut in line, or take more than they need. The common denominator between these two critiques is that the utopian somehow fails to grasp the complexity and variety of human desire. Probably the most concise rebuke of the classic conception of utopia is this: My Best Possible Society is not the same as your Best Possible Society.* It would be unfair to judge a political theorist by the quality of his fiction. A great leader needn't be a great artist. But the abundant literary deficiencies of *Voyage*—its wooden characters and torrents of cliché—signaled its author's limitations as a thinker and, eventually, a political leader. The case of Étienne Cabet shows that a rotten novelist and an obtuse statesman—in the end, a petty tyrant—share a crucial flaw: the total inability to imagine the minds of others.

---

* The philosopher Robert Nozick, champion of the "minimal state," illustrated this notion with a thought experiment. Try to imagine a single utopia suited to the desires and needs of the following people: Hugh Hefner, Emma Goldman, Yogi Berra, Moses, Elizabeth Taylor, Peter Kropotkin, your parents, Ayn Rand, Ted Williams, Thomas Jefferson, H. L. Mencken, the Lubavitcher rebbe, and you. Nozick might have been speaking directly to Cabet when he wrote that "no one should attempt to describe a utopia unless he's recently reread . . . the works of Shakespeare, Tolstoy, Jane Austen, Rabelais and Dostoevsky to remind himself of how different people are."

Workers' Paradise

In the spring of 1839, Cabet's exile expired. He returned to Paris and published his novel. During his absence, French interest in communism had surged. Tensions between underfed workers and the bourgeois-backed government of Louis Philippe were running high. Secret clubs and socialist "banquet societies" had proliferated. The crown's response was predictably extreme. Gatherings of workers were broken up and

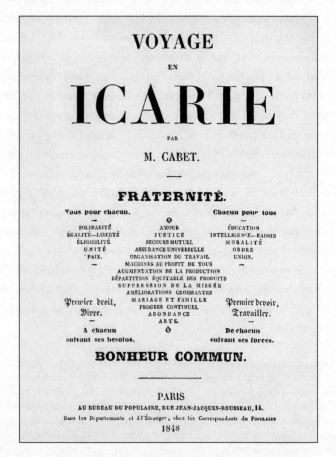

The cover of an 1848 edition of *Voyage en Icarie*.

radical literature was seized. Agitators and communists were rounded up and imprisoned. Official anxiety was sufficiently high that Cabet was briefly detained at the border when he came back from the United Kingdom.

In this uneasy environment, *Voyage en Icarie,* which advocated for communism without any mention of guillotines, barricades, or confiscated estates, became an instant hit. Cloaked in fiction and freighted with bourgeois sentiments about religion and family, Cabet's ideas slipped past the censors. Very soon, according to one historian, "almost every workingman in France had heard [of *Voyage*] even if he had not read it." In the next eight years, the novel went through five editions. Although the first edition was cautiously published under a pseudonym, all subsequent printings bore the author's name in large capital letters.

Back in Paris, Cabet resumed stewardship of *Le Populaire,* printing it now as a monthly. Rather than the arcane and/or militant communism and anarchism on offer elsewhere, Cabet's paper ran sentimental tales of industrial oppression, depicting meek, virtuous workers and craven fat cats against a backdrop of Dickensian poverty. Cabet printed heart-rending letters sent to him by struggling workers throughout France. Some readers seemed to think that Icaria was a real place. They wrote in asking how to get there.

The defining feature of what came to be known as "Icarian communism"—the thing that set it apart from Fourierism, then flourishing under the leadership of Victor Considerant, and other, more militant strains of socialism—was Cabet's strict insistence on respect for the rule of law. Like Owen, Cabet did not think the transition into utopia would require any sort of conflict. He believed his political conclusions were so self-evident that, given time and information, everyone, even the callous bourgeois shop boss, would see the light.

The practical or political extension of this belief was Cabet's faith that genuine republicanism would be a necessary and sufficient cause of a property-free society. "Communism and Republic," he wrote, "[are] one and the same thing." Once the base of suffrage is wide enough, citizens will vote themselves into material equality. The idea that democracy and material equality are nearly interchangeable made particular sense in the shadow of the French Revolution, during which the broad distribution of rights was often described as the first step toward a general economic leveling.

Since Cabet believed that all democrats are embryonic communists, he hoped to unite the myriad factions of French dissent—republican, socialist, militant, Saint-Simonian, Fourierist—under one Icarian banner. With such unanimity in mind, he endeavored to make his movement as inoffensive as possible. In *Le Populaire,* Cabet advocated "civic courage," by which he meant that the Icarians, as his followers had started calling themselves, must be law-abiding and morally wholesome. Terrorism, scandal, secrecy, or skullduggery of any sort could be used by those in power as a pretext to quash dissent.

Icarian clubs sprang up throughout France. Workers gathered to read aloud from *Voyage,* share copies of *Le Populaire,* and sing Icarian-themed songs set to popular tunes. Most Icarians were neither proletarians nor rural peasants. According to demographic research by the historian Christopher H. Johnson, the vast majority were skilled urban artisans. Some were weavers, smiths, and cabinetmakers. Almost half were tailors or shoemakers.* Few of these people worked in factories, but the sudden rise of industrial production threatened their traditional, guild-learned trades. (It is somewhat surprising that these skilled craftspeople were turned on by the Icarian dream of assembly lines and high-tech mechanization.) Cabet's vision of an urban workers' paradise—a place where universal suffrage, diminished working hours, and social equality were combined with traditional family values—offered an appealing alternative to the grim industrial future many artisans saw on the horizon. The self-styled Icarians were people who craved a radical

---

* The philosopher and historian Jacques Rancière argues that, at least in France, clothing-related trades have tended to produce more than their share of radicals because tailors and cobblers endure daily, pride-bruising encounters with the bourgeois. This theory makes particular sense in the case of the Icarians because they wrote as much about their desire for the dignity of full citizenship as they did about any sort of economic equality.

social reorganization but feared a chaotic redistributionist uprising at the hands of the unskilled rabble. Unlike the intended readers of *The Communist Manifesto,* they had quite a bit more than their chains to lose. Not surprisingly, given the fact that the movement was inspired by a novel, the Icarians were almost all literate. Unlike the Fourierists, however, few of them were students or intellectuals. Cabet's folksy, golden rule morality was central to the appeal of Icarianism.

Citizen Christ

As the movement grew, Cabet's chief subject became the affinity between communism and Christianity. He did not belong to any particular denomination. He was a deist who sometimes referred to the Creator, Enlightenment style, as capital N "Nature." But, like Fourier, Cabet had just enough faith to assume that humanity was somehow *meant* to live well. "It is impossible to admit," he wrote, "that man was destined to be unhappy on this earth." This assumption that history moves toward perfect happiness echoes Owen's secular millenarianism and the harmonic eschatology preached by Christian Fourierists such as George Ripley and William Henry Channing. All of them believed, as their contemporary Saint-Simon put it, that "the golden age of mankind is not behind, but before us."

When Cabet called himself a Christian, he meant that he was a follower of Jesus of Nazareth, whom he considered a mortal, world-changing philosopher. For Ann Lee, Joseph Meacham, and John Humphrey Noyes, the Bible endorsed (or maybe mandated) communal ownership. Cabet went further. For him, Christianity was indistinguishable from communism. Like the other nineteenth-century utopians, he drew particular inspiration from the book of Acts' account of collectivism in the early Jesus movement. "Communal ownership of goods," Cabet wrote in the preface to the second printing of *Voyage,* was "proclaimed by Jesus Christ, by all his apostles and disciples, by all the fathers of the church and all the Christians of the early centuries."

Cabet read the New Testament as a record of social revolution. In an era of rank exploitation, Jesus smashed the banks and called for a thorough reorganization of society in which the poor ("the least") would come first and wealth would be an obstacle to salvation. "Jesus Christ came to bring a new law, a new social principle, a new system of organization for society which he called the Reign of the Kingdom of God, the New City," Cabet wrote. "Christianity for the Apostles, for the first Christians, for the Fathers of the Church, was Communism," he wrote in *Le vrai Christianisme suivant Jésus-Christ* (1846). "Yes, Jesus Christ was a Communist."

In Cabet's analysis, the miracles recounted in the Gospels—the water walking and wine multiplication—were a literary subterfuge, invented by the comrades of the sandal-clad artisan from Galilee to slip their ideas past Roman censors and wealthy Jews. This reading of the New Testament had obvious appeal to a man who had hidden his own communist manifesto between the covers of a schmaltzy romance.

Christ was not the only historical figure whom Cabet identified as a communist. Like a John Bircher run amok at the library, he found fellow travelers on nearly every page of the Western canon. Part 2 of *Voyage* features an appendix of great communists. Some are obvious: Fourier, Owen, Thomas More, Plato. Others are less so: Confucius, Apollonius, Zoroaster, Plutarch, Locke, Hobbes, Hume, Benjamin Franklin, Montesquieu, Robespierre, and Napoleon. Even Adam Smith makes the list. "The majority of all western thinkers," Cabet claimed, "especially those who are the light and honor of the human race, adopted the communistic system and if all of them were today to rise from the graves for a Congress under the presiding of Jesus Christ, this Congress would proclaim itself for [communism]."

The Icarian movement spread rapidly during the 1840s, especially in smaller provincial cities where a lagging economy and reactionary police raids galvanized left-leaning artisans. In 1843, reporting for Robert Owen's newspaper in Manchester, Engels wrote, "The French Icarian Communists are estimated at about half a million, women and children

not taken into account."* (In a passing swipe at the less numerous Fourierists, Engels added, "A pretty respectable phalanx, isn't it?") This es-
timate is certainly high. Christopher H. Johnson, whose methods are
considerably more scientific than those of Engels, approximates that by
1846, there were one hundred thousand active Icarians in seventy-eight
of France's one hundred departments. Either way, there were enough
of them for the French police to crown Cabet the *chef des communistes*.

As his popularity rose, Cabet's rhetoric, like the rhetoric of Owen
and Fourier before him, became increasingly messianic. In the minds of
his followers, the idea of Icaria—like Zion, the New Moral World, and
Harmony—was woven into the ancient narrative of millennial anticipation: the end of suffering, the righting of wrongs, the coming of New
Jerusalem. The movement took on religious overtones. Cabet was her-
alded as "the successor to the works of Christ." The Icarians called him
"dear and venerated father" or, simply, "Papa." Cabet, who always had
an inflated sense of his own genius, did not discourage them.

The New Hebrews

Cabet had initially hoped to lead a coalition of communist workers and
bourgeois democrats to turn France into an Icarian-style state through
electoral politics. But as his following grew among the working class,
bourgeois supporters fell away. At the same time, anticommunist sentiment began to heat up throughout France. Self-proclaimed Icarians
were fired from their jobs or had their workshops boycotted. Priests
denounced Cabet from the pulpit. One cleric burned a copy of *Voyage*.
Cabet's arrest or exile began to look far more likely than any hope of
voting France into communism.

Cabet had long opposed the colonization schemes of the Fourierists,

---

* Engels found it odd that the Owenites denounced religion in pious old England
while Cabet and his followers cloaked their communism in Christianity despite living
in "a nation celebrated for its infidelity."

but in 1847, amid mounting hostility, he changed his mind. He decided that Icaria, like any utopia worthy of the name, required a blank piece of land. In May of that year, he announced in *Le Populaire* that it was time for the Icarians—"the New Hebrews," he now called them—to "conquer the Promised land, create a new Paradise on Earth." He did not say where.

Cabet wrote to Robert Owen for advice. After the collapse of New Harmony, Owen had briefly considered starting a second colony in Mexico. When the Mexican government withdrew their offer of free land, the plan had unraveled. Owen still had connections in the region, and he put Cabet in touch with William Peters, an American socialist and land agent who had been hired by the recently annexed state of Texas to find settlers.[*]

In the fall of 1847, Cabet sailed to London to meet with Owen and Peters. Texas, which had joined the United States two years earlier, was eager for white pioneers. Peters proposed that the Icarians sign a deal entitling them to three thousand acres of highly discounted land in the Trinity River valley. There was a catch. Most homesteaders tended to favor regions where land was cheap but where some settlement had already occurred. So rather than offer the Icarians a single, contiguous tract, Peters proposed that they take their land in family-sized allotments of 320 acres, laid out in a checkerboard pattern. Each Icarian-owned plot would therefore be surrounded on four sides by land held back by the Republic of Texas to be sold to future immigrants at a premium. Peters's proposal further stipulated that the Icarians had to begin building homes on half of their plots within a year. If they failed to reach that deadline, they would have to pay full price for the land.

Even if the Icarians had been experienced homesteaders, rather

---

[*] Not long before Cabet contacted Owen, Peters had urged Owen to start a New Harmony–style colony in Texas. Owen, who was then preoccupied with the growing British labor movement, declined.

than urban cobblers and tailors, it would have been almost impossible for them to satisfy their contractual obligation to build so many homes in such a short span of time. And even if they somehow managed to get to Texas and build the required homesteads, it would still have been impossible for them to realize their collective vision of Icaria on land interspersed with non-Icarian settlers. Cabet, however, was undeterred. Like so many other European visionaries, he was enchanted by his impression of North America as an Edenic void—a place where history might be restarted. Drawn in by Peters's descriptions of the lush Trinity River valley and eager to quit the hostile political scene in France, he signed the contract.

Brimming with enthusiasm, Cabet sailed back to Paris and announced— first things first!—contests to design an Icarian costume and write an Icarian anthem. In a specially printed pamphlet, he announced that he had purchased "a new Eden"—a million acres of lush countryside with the "salubrious" climate of Italy. In fact, he had conditional ownership of three thousand noncontiguous acres of scrubland.

Cabet began reviewing candidates for the first convoy. Each volunteer was required to be fluent in Icarian philosophy. He also had to contribute six hundred francs for supplies and transportation. Some Icarians were angry about this steep financial requirement, the equivalent, for the average skilled artisan, of six months' wages. To stoke enthusiasm, Cabet printed accounts of the other utopian communities in the United States. In *Le Populaire*, he described the prosperity of the Rappites, the Shakers, and the New Harmonites. He even mentioned a certain *"Brouck-Tarm, sous la direction du prédicateur unitaire Ripley."*

Many devoted Icarians were skeptical about the new plan. Until that point, the movement had focused on reforming France. Shipping off to a distant wilderness was a very different prospect. While some Icarians were distressed by Cabet's change of course, the Fourierists applauded the plan. Unlike the Icarians, Fourier's French followers had spent a decade contemplating transatlantic colonization. When Cabet announced his plan to build Icaria in Texas, a few Fourierists signed up. The French government also liked the plan. What could be better than a mass self-deportation of communists?

Those Icarians who embraced the scheme did so with a religious fervor. Some had already begun to think of Cabet as their savior; now Papa was leading them to the promised land. "Your idea to realize Icaria gives me new life," a shopkeeper from the northeastern city of Nancy wrote to Cabet, "for death is preferable to life in today's wretched society. Though my establishment is well patronized and I have numerous customers, I long for nothing more than the moment we leave for Icaria."

On February 3, 1848, the handpicked avant-garde of sixty-nine men gathered at Le Havre for a pre-departure banquet. Cabet led them in a call-and-response oath. "Do you persist in declaring that you know perfectly the system and principles of the Icarian Community? Do you adopt, above all, the principle of Fraternity and Community? Are you resolved to endure all weariness and privation, to brave all danger, in the general and common interest? Is your acceptance, in your eyes, a genuine choice? Do you vow to put yourself under control of the Director, as I vow to consecrate all my existence to the realization of the Community based on Fraternity?" The following morning, decked out in their velvet costumes and singing their newly written *chant du départ*, the men boarded the *Rome* and steamed out into the Atlantic. Cabet remained in France to raise funds and organize the subsequent departures. He would make the crossing once ground was broken in Texas.

The Icarians sailed in a spirit of high adventure. They were convinced that their colony in Texas would fulfill the long-defaulted promises of the Revolution of 1789. "We leave full of joy," wrote one Icarian as he left his home in Bordeaux, "for we go to establish the kingdom of God on earth, to put into practice the three regenerative principles of Liberty, Equality and Fraternity that the France of the Republic inscribed on all its monuments; and full of hope because we believe that the *entente cordiale* between all soldiers of the democracy, the politicians, the socialists and the communists, will see to it that these three liberating words will be engraved in all our hearts as they are on our monuments. Then, and only then, will you have a true social Republic, that Republic beloved of the poor and of those who suffer. And we, in establishing it in all its purity on the virgin soil of Texas, will help you to prove to all classes and all races that the practical brotherhood which our dear and venerated father . . . always preached, is not an empty ideal."

At the end of March, as the *Rome* cruised into the Port of New Orleans, the Icarians standing on deck heard the blast of a cannon. It had been fired, they soon learned, by celebrating French Louisianans. Revolution had broken out in Paris after a group of parading workers had refused to disperse before a small detachment of soldiers. While affixing a bayonet to his musket, one of the soldiers fired into the crowd. (It was probably an accident.) In the chaos that followed, other soldiers opened fire. When the racket was over, fifty-two people were dead. Enraged Parisians flooded the boulevards, overturning buses and cutting down trees to form barricades. When they surrounded the palace, Louis Philippe abdicated his throne and fled to the United Kingdom. The uprising in France helped trigger similar uprisings across the continent. It was the start of Europe's "Spring of Nations." News of Louis Philippe's abdication had crossed the Atlantic by a faster ship. Having quit monarchist France with revolutionary dreams, the Icarians arrived in New Orleans to learn that an actual revolution had broken out while they were at sea. Some of the colonists immediately sailed back to France, eager to join the fray.

The rest remained in New Orleans, intent on Icaria. A small group set out for Texas. Adolphe Gouhenant, a handsome Icarian sign painter, led the expedition. The colonists had been led to believe that they could travel most of the way to the so-called Peters concession by riverboat. In fact, the river carried them only as far as Shreveport. From there they commenced a long overland journey through a roadless wilderness.

The trip was a disaster. The pilgrims got lost several times. The ox-cart carrying their supplies broke down. They had to ford swollen rivers on improvised log rafts lashed together with their own belts. Provisions ran low. At one point, fourteen Icarians shared a single boiled pigeon for dinner. A few of them died from a combination of dysentery, starvation, and malaria. One man was killed by lightning. Their only doctor went mad. Amid all of this, documents were discovered in the luggage of Adolphe Gouhenant that exposed him as a paid spy for the recently deposed Louis Philippe and a Jesuit to boot. He was shorn of his beard and long blond hair and sent off into the wilderness.[*]

The twenty-six Icarians who survived reached their allotment in early June and immediately began raising crude log cabins and planting wheat. They worked hard, but their inexperience showed. They sank their only plow too deep into the dense turf, snapping the blade. In August, they discovered that the Texas climate was anything but "salubrious." By the end of the summer, they had framed thirty-two cabins. When the long-awaited second advance guard showed up—now just twenty-two men—they found their comrades malnourished, snakebit, and half-dead with dysentery. In total, eight Icarians died in Texas. The survivors, feverish with malaria and sunstroke, limped back to New Orleans to intercept the shiploads of Icarians that continued arriving from France. The Peters concession was abandoned for good.

Meanwhile in Paris, Cabet was distracted from the exodus he had initiated by the revolution breaking out around him. The uprising in France decimated the lists of Icarians waiting to immigrate to Texas. Less than a year earlier, Cabet had written that the Icarians "have no doubt of being able to unite more than a million co-operators!" After the king's

---

[*] The facts are murky, but according to at least one historian, Gouhenant may have been innocent. Amazingly, he survived his banishment. In 1853, when Albert Brisbane and Victor Considerant rode through Texas scouting locations for La Réunion, they met him. By then Gouhenant was running a combination dance hall/art gallery/Masonic lodge/photo studio in Dallas. His tale of Icarian cruelty must have been satisfying to Considerant, who had a very dim view of Cabet and his followers.

abdication and the jubilant declaration of the Second Republic, only a few thousand remained. Why go all the way to Texas to build a democratic, communist state when one might be imminent in France?*

In *Le Populaire,* Cabet printed a "Manifesto of the Icarian Communists" that was pasted up throughout the country. It was a pointedly moderate statement, clearly intended to calm widespread anxiety about a violent, worker-dominated co-option of the revolution. The document urged French communists to support the bourgeois-dominated provisional authorities and made several relatively moderate demands of the nascent government—namely, the abolition of taxes on certain necessities, press freedom, and the right of workers to organize. Most shocking, Cabet announced that he was abandoning his Texas scheme to help form the new government.

When the revolution took a sharp anticommunist turn, Cabet was denounced as an enemy of the Second Republic. He ran for his old seat in the Parliament and lost. In April, the new government circulated a pamphlet that read, "Down with the Communists, Death to Cabet." In May, police raided the offices of *Le Populaire.* They found a few guns and arrested Cabet.

Once he was released, Cabet turned his attention back to Texas. In December, he boarded a paddle steamer bound for New York, leaving his wife and daughter in Paris. On the last day of 1848, during a heavy snowstorm, he arrived in Manhattan. After a banquet thrown in his honor by Horace Greeley, he sailed south to New Orleans.

In a cluster of brick homes on Saint Ferdinand Street, Cabet found nearly five hundred Icarians. They were split into two factions. Two hundred of them were enraged at their once beloved Papa for sending them into the wilderness and then abandoning them. After an angry confrontation, they returned to France and promptly filed suit against

---

* What was actually imminent, in a matter of months, was the election of Napoleon III as president, his coronation as emperor, and the inauguration of the Second French Empire. In the power vacuum created by the uprising, the forces advocating for dramatic social reorganization—the followers of Saint-Simon, Fourier, and Cabet among them—proved too diverse to form a stable bloc of advocacy.

their former leader, claiming that he had taken their money under false pretenses. The remaining 280 were still committed to the cause of Icaria. They rallied behind Cabet and began scouting for a new site.

Nauvoo

Late that winter, the Icarians made a down payment on the center section of Nauvoo, Illinois, a tidy, prosperous city built on the eastern bank of the Mississippi River by Joseph Smith and his Latter-day Saints.

At the time, the Mormons had a great deal in common with the other communal millenarians active in the United States. Like Ann Lee and George Rapp, Smith taught his followers that the millennium was due to commence and that the United States would be its locus. Writing in Nauvoo in 1842, he claimed that "Zion will be built upon this continent; that Christ will reign personally upon the earth, and that the earth will be renewed, and receive its paradisiacal glory." Like the communal utopians, the early Mormons drank deeply from the book of Acts' account of collectivism in the first-century Jesus movement. The Book of Mormon (1830)—which Smith claimed to have transcribed from "Egyptian characters" engraved onto golden plates that he found buried in a hillside in Manchester, New York—describes the history of a group of Jews who sailed west from the Arabian Peninsula around 600 BC and settled in pre-Columbian North America. Jesus supposedly visited these people sometime after his execution in Jerusalem. During his time amid these seafaring Hebrews (the ancestors, according to the Book of Mormon, of some Native Americans), Jesus organized their society in imitation of the apostolic community back in Judea. Closely echoing the language of Acts, the Book of Mormon (4 Nephi 1:3) records that "they had all things in common among them; therefore there were not rich and poor, bond and free, but they were all made free, and partakers of the heavenly gift."

Within a year of organizing his first congregation, Smith institutionalized this business of having "all things in common" with a form of religious socialism known as "consecration and stewardship." Each new convert turned over ("consecrated") his material wealth to the church. In return, the church granted the individual a lifelong lease ("stewardship") over that portion of the consecrated property that was required for the "support and comfort" of a single family. In this way, one Mormon's surplus could be used for the support of other Latter-day Saints or to bankroll the operation and expansion of the church. It was a system intended to strengthen communal bonds and curtail excessive disparities in wealth. But unlike Shaker communism, in which all property was technically communal, the Mormon system allowed for a large degree of practical individualism and private enterprise.*

The Saints and the Icarians were both peoples bound together by a book. Smith, like Cabet, offered his followers a sprawling, colorful narrative of life within a faraway egalitarian society. (Of course, the Latter-day Saints, unlike the Icarians, regard their book as historical fact.) In the winter of 1830, Smith had a revelation concerning the Old Testament patriarch Enoch, who, Smith claimed, founded Zion, a city so righteous that its residents were transported to heaven without passing through death. Smith believed that God wanted him to build a new Zion—a holy city to shelter the chosen people. The following summer, the Mormons gathered in Jackson County, Missouri, to build their Zion. Two years later, hostile Missourians drove the Saints out of Jackson County. The Mormons started over in nearby Clay County, but the attacks continued. In 1839, the Saints decided to leave Missouri altogether. Smith selected a new spot on the Illinois side of the Mississippi,

---

* Even before Smith died, the church softened its interpretation of this law, merely requiring Saints to tithe a chunk of their material wealth to the church and to "consecrate" their time and labor to the spread of Mormonism. Later, certain small Mormon settlements, notably the town of Orderville in southern Utah, adopted a thoroughgoing communalism that would have been familiar to the Shakers, Rappites, or Oneida Perfectionists. The Orderville Saints ate together, wore matching clothes, lived in uniform homes, and held no private property.

near the small village of Commerce. He named the site Nauvoo, a Sephardic transliteration of the Hebrew for "to be comely." Once again, the Saints began to build their Zion.

Within a few years, there were twelve thousand Mormons living in Nauvoo. They built homes, shops, and a university. At the center of town, they laid out a large, open quadrangle and built a towering limestone temple. At its peak, Nauvoo rivaled Chicago as the largest and most prosperous settlement in Illinois. From there, Smith issued divinely inspired injunctions, sent missionaries throughout the nation and across the Atlantic, commanded a standing army, and planned a run for president of the United States.

In 1844, tensions with the "gentiles" in the region and among the Mormons themselves once again came to a head. Smith and his brother Hyrum were arrested for conspiring to destroy the printing press of an opposition newspaper and charged with treason. While awaiting trial in the Carthage jail, they were shot and killed by a group of men in blackface.

After Smith's death, Brigham Young fended off several rivals for leadership of the church. Within two years, he orchestrated the Mormons' remarkable exodus out of the United States and into the Great Basin. There, by a brackish sea in the lunar high desert, the Latter-day Saints were finally able to build their Zion.

On March 15, 1849, three years after the Mormons left for Deseret, Cabet and almost three hundred Icarians arrived at Nauvoo from New Orleans aboard a northbound Mississippi steamer. They walked a mile inland and surveyed their new home: the large, central portion of the abandoned Mormon city. The houses and shops arrayed around the temple in the main city square had been vacant for almost three years. Despite evidence of fire, rot, and theft, it was not hard for the French communists to see the faint outline of the glorious city they intended to build.

In Nauvoo, the Icarians finally began to thrive. Drawn by Cabet's glowing reports—now slightly more accurate—recruits came from

France. Within two years there were 365 Icarians living in the community. They turned the Mormons' old arsenal into a workshop and
spruced up the storefronts and homes around the temple square. They
built a large two-story community hall and refectory. Each Icarian family was assigned a small apartment and a set of simple, uniform furnishings.

By 1855, five hundred Icarians were living in Nauvoo. Clustered
together in the center portion of the town, they represented a quarter
of the total population of Nauvoo. Most of them were French, but
there were also Germans (at least sixty-five), a handful each of Italians,
Swiss, and Swedes, and one Briton. A few colonists, such as Emile and
Annette Baxter, a French-born couple from Connecticut, arrived as
American citizens.

Like most of the new recruits, the Baxters were avid socialists. Before
coming to Icaria, they had visited the fledgling Oneida Community but
were put off by John Humphrey Noyes's peculiar religious notions. After
learning about the community in Nauvoo, most likely from the *Tribune*,
Emile Baxter wrote to Cabet professing their faith. "Pardon me, Monsieur, if I begin so bruskly to declare first of all our conversion to your
Voyage en Icarie a fact." The Baxters were better educated than most Icarians. Emile, who worked in the textile trade, had attended the University of Edinburgh. Annette, whom her husband described as "even
more Icarian than I," studied at the Sorbonne and a women's seminary
in Hartford.*

Like all utopian pioneers, the people who went to Nauvoo viewed
the move as a personal resolution. Not only would the new place be better; in the new place *they* would be better. Every utopian venture is eventually interpreted as a referendum on human nature. Is our corruption
inherent, or is it merely the effect of a poorly organized society? Emile
Baxter, like his comrades at Brook Farm and New Harmony, expected

---

* Before the Baxters moved to Illinois, Cabet wrote Emile asking him to meet with
Tribune editor and Brook Farm alum Charles Dana to inquire about arranging an
exchange of newspapers between New York and Nauvoo.

the Icarian experiment to settle the debate—"to prove to the world," as
he put it, "man's *innate goodness*."

The work in Nauvoo was intense. A six a.m. bugle call started each
day on a martial note. Although women and men were officially equal
in Icaria, traditional spheres of labor remained intact. Right out of bed,
the men all took a single shot of whiskey before heading for the fields
and workshops. The women tidied up their apartments, then went to
various assigned stations at the laundry, in the kitchen, or at the loom.
Unlike the ornate costumes of their fictional counterparts—"the finest,
most delicate, most ravishing fabrics, colors, and shapes"—the uniform
adopted by the Icarians in Nauvoo was simple: blue cotton pants and
white shirts for the men; white bonnets and cotton dresses worn over
loose pantaloons for the women. To the amusement of their neighbors,
some Icarians wore anachronistic wooden shoes known as sabots.

The entire community ate together, sitting ten to a table in their
large refectory, the walls of which were painted with Icarian slogans.
When they first arrived in Nauvoo, the food was basic, mostly bread,
soup, and water. In miniature homage to the technological marvels described in *Voyage,* they installed a mechanical trolley to carry dishes back
and forth between the dining room and the kitchen. The community
leased two thousand acres of farmland, much of it already improved by
the departed Mormons, and planted wheat and vegetables. They also
raised sheep and cattle. As the former tailors and cobblers learned to
tend stock and drive a plow, their meals improved. Craving a taste of
home, they planted a vineyard.

The promise of wholesome, high-quality mass entertainment—
bourgeois culture for the workingman—was central to the appeal of
Cabet's vision. As one fictional Icarian says: "You have certainly seen in
no other nation as many marionette theatres, pantomimes, and above
all Punch and Judy shows that delight the children. You will never see
such lovely entertainments elsewhere because here the republic directs
them and spares no expense to make them charming in every way. Nor
will you see elsewhere so many wonderful plays, as we call them, where

physics, electricity, light, chemistry, astronomy, and conjurers of all sorts produce more wonders than have ever been seen before." In Nauvoo, on a stage at one end of the refectory, the Icarians produced a constant series of plays, concerts, and operettas. A thirty-six-piece orchestra provided the music for their frequent dances. Like everything else in Icaria, these entertainments were intended to serve the overarching project of communizing society. A committee previewed each performance to "carefully eliminate all that could have a demoralizing influence." The community's American neighbors came in droves to watch Icarian plays and hear Icarian concerts.

On warm weekend days, Papa Cabet would often lead the communists in a procession out of the village, singing Icarian anthems as they walked. At a scenic spot overlooking the Mississippi, they would spend the day picnicking on ham and radishes, collecting berries, swimming (men only), and dancing quadrilles and waltzes to the music of their orchestra.

As at New Harmony, the intellectual life at Nauvoo outshone anything available for hundreds of miles. The Icarian library held more than four thousand volumes, making it the largest in Illinois. Learned colonists offered regular evening lectures, and every Sunday, in lieu of church, Cabet led the community in the *Cours Icarien*, an ongoing seminar on the themes in his novel.

While the Icarians, unlike so many of their utopian contemporaries, regarded the family as the ideal base unit for their society, they still tried to shelter children from the supposedly retrograde influence of their parents. To almost all the nineteenth-century utopians, young minds held the same promise as the vacant North American wilderness: the chance to make a definitive break from the past.* Specifically, Cabet hoped to rear a generation for whom communism was second nature.

As in the fictional Icaria, the Nauvoo colonists regarded education as "the basis and the foundation of the whole of [the] social and political

---

* In the *Republic*, Socrates suggests evicting everyone over ten from the city so that the citizens of the new, ideal state are "free from the ethos of their parents."

system." Like Owen, Cabet was convinced that "man is evidently per-fectible through experience and education." From the age of four on-ward, Icarian children lived and studied together in a single dormitory, visiting their parents' apartments only on weekends. Boys and girls re-ceived the same education, one that focused as much on the cultivation of character as it did on spelling and arithmetic. Cabet himself gave the children regular lessons on the golden rule and brotherhood of man.

The white temple built by the Mormons was by far the most impres-sive building in Nauvoo, a prominent frontier landmark that was visible from ten miles away. The Latter-day Saints had scrambled to finish its construction even as Brigham Young organized their departure for Utah. Just before the Icarians arrived, someone torched the building, gutting its interior. Expressing different priorities from those of the de-parted Saints, the Icarians began to renovate the temple as a massive school. In 1850, while a crew worked on the building, a tornado toppled much of what remained, almost killing several Icarian masons. Rather than repair the damage, the community harvested the limestone to build a new two-story school on the same site.[*]

A French Revolution in Small

In the spring of 1851, Cabet returned to France to face the charges of fraud that had been filed against him by disaffected members of the avant-garde. Because the community in Nauvoo partly depended on donations sent by supporters in Europe, Cabet needed to maintain his good legal standing in France. When he arrived in Paris, he immedi-ately turned himself over to the police. During the ensuing trial, Cabet served as his own attorney, arguing persuasively that the deed for the land in Texas, the existence of the community in Nauvoo, and his own relative poverty all proved that financial gain had never been his inten-tion. He recalled the proceedings with characteristic immodesty. "More

---

[*] The LDS temple was rebuilt in 2002.

than once [I] brought tears to the eyes of [the] judges; and the public ministry itself was constrained to present [me] a solemn vote of thanks in the name of society, for the great service [I] had rendered." The solemn vote of thanks seems unlikely, but he was acquitted.

By chance, Cabet's trip to Paris coincided with an attempted coup in the National Assembly, and he was sought in a dragnet of the usual suspects. After a month in hiding, he was arrested. He promised to leave France immediately and was released. Following a brief stopover in London, Cabet sailed for the United States, reaching Nauvoo at the end of July 1852, more than a year after he left.

Upon his return from France, Cabet felt that the community had stalled. Like all utopias, Icaria existed simultaneously as an actual place and as an idea carried in the minds of its citizens. As long as the village in Nauvoo seemed to be approaching the imagined Icaria, however slowly, life within the community was harmonious. The concept of utopia may be fundamentally static, but on the road to utopia, forward motion is the only option.

In Cabet's absence, productivity had fallen off and people had begun to accumulate private possessions. Some of the women had started wearing makeup. Before the widespread introduction of railroads, it was easier for farmers on the frontier to store, ship, and sell barrels of whiskey than the bushels of corn or wheat from which it was made. The Icarians made and sold good corn whiskey. It was one of their most profitable businesses. During Cabet's long absence, some of the men had begun drinking far more than their sanctioned daily eye-opener. This cut into liquor sales and took an overall toll on productivity and discipline. With less cash coming in, the community's finances were tight.

Convinced that his followers had lost sight of their world high calling, Cabet tightened his grip. To refocus the community, he inaugurated what Robert Sutton, author of the definitive history of the Icarian experience in the United States, called "a moral purge." He banned drinking, smoking, and hunting and fishing for sport, all of which were beloved Icarian pastimes. He also orchestrated the excommunication of two couples for the crime of conceiving children out of wedlock. To increase the production of salable goods, he demanded silence in the workshops. Cabet's belief that the community in Nauvoo was going to catalyze a global revolution had led him into a paradox. Joy was not the business of Icaria; the colonists had something more important to attend to: the joy of all people. The "purpose" of Icaria, Cabet declared, was not "the interest and happiness of its members," it was the interest and happiness "of humanity as a whole." The present must be sacrificed on the altar of the future.

From the time of their arrival in Illinois, the Icarians had thought of the village in Nauvoo as temporary. As soon as they had decided to leave France, the dream of Icaria had become the dream of building a new society from scratch. Their paradise was not meant to be built upon the ruins of someone else's Zion. In the fall of 1854, Cabet petitioned the United States Congress for an enormous land grand: fifty to one hundred and fifty "sections" (between forty-two thousand and ninety-six thousand acres) of wild prairie in Adams County, Iowa. In his application, Cabet downplayed the community's radical ambitions. The Icarians, he wrote, sought the land—an expanse "sufficient to construct one or several communes or cities"—"not as communists," but as immigrants devoted "to making an experiment in the interest of humanity in general." He assured the legislature in Washington that "whatever it may be, your decision will not be prejudicial for or against the question of Communism." As Owen had when he addressed Congress, Cabet connected the Icarian program with the ideals of the American Revolution. He even implied that Uncle Sam somehow owed the communists for historical services rendered. "We Icarians, your brothers in heart as in opinion, are perhaps that portion of the French nation which best represents our Fathers who fought with you . . . for Independence and Liberty."

While they awaited a response from Washington, life in Nauvoo grew increasingly tense under the strain of Cabet's high-handed efforts to galvanize his community. In the fictional Icaria, the transition from monarchy to democratic communism had taken fifty years of gradual reform, including the establishment of state-run workshops, a steeply graduated inheritance tax, and the reeducation of the young. But when the communists decided to build Icaria in the New World, they abandoned this cautious timetable, succumbing to dreams of instantaneous paradise. When that paradise proved illusive, their disappointment turned bitter.

As grumbling about Cabet's reforms increased, so did his paranoia about threats to his leadership. Before sailing for Texas, the Icarians had spoken of Cabet as their messiah. In France, most of them had known him only through his novel, his editorials, and his fearless opposition to the crown. Five years of physical proximity—especially the pungent, elbowy, round-the-clock proximity of communal living—had changed that. "The prestige was gone," wrote one colonist. "[We] had discovered that he was fallible, and began to consider him as a man."

Insecure about the devotion of his followers, Cabet cultivated a network of spies to keep him informed about who was saying what. He even persuaded the assembly to pass a rule against complaining. He ceased distinguishing between the community and himself. In Cabet's mind, obedience to him was synonymous with Icarianism. "If one is an Icarian," he wrote a friend in France, "one will obey willingly: if one hesitates, one is not an Icarian. . . ." Or as the Sun King put it: *"L'état, c'est moi."*

The community began to split between the self-proclaimed "Cabetists," those for whom Icaria and its founder were inseparable, and those who now saw Cabet's autocratic leadership as an impediment to their collective dream.

The most vigorous Cabetists tended to be among the newer members. For them, Cabet was still the good Icar—an infallible moral beacon. The dream of Icaria—a vision potent enough to have drawn them across the ocean, away from everything safe and familiar—remained indistinguishable from the author of *Voyage*. Most of the veterans of the Texas debacle, however, aligned themselves with the opposition. Long

years of labor and privation had eroded their religious devotion to
Papa. They saw how Cabet's personality contrasted with the values enshrined in his novel. Their disillusionment was like waking from a
dream, and they resented Cabet in proportion to their former devotion.

Under the informal leadership of a carpenter named Jean Baptiste
Gérard and a clerk named Alexis Armel Marchand, the opposition
tried to diminish Cabet's authority in the assembly and to soften some
of his new draconian rules. In response, Cabet dug in. In a reckless effort to test his followers' loyalty, he tried to amend the Icarian constitution to extend the term of his presidency from one year to four and to
grant the president greater authority to make appointments. The majority of Icarians voted against him. For Cabet, it was a jarring rebuke.

The colony's persistent money troubles added to the sense of crisis. Like
many of the phalanxes of the 1840s, the Icarians were badly overin-
vested in land. Congress denied Cabet's petition for a land grant, but,
unable to resist the lure of inexpensive virgin prairie, the Icarians had
purchased three thousand acres in southwestern Iowa anyway. The decision was a prime example of what John Humphrey Noyes called "socialist land mania," the tendency among nineteenth-century utopians
to express their exuberance for the dawning millennium by buying
overlarge sections of cheap wilderness. The possibility of owning vast
tracts of virgin land exerted an irresistible hold on the utopian imagination, especially for those utopians arriving directly from the crowded
Old World. In Noyes's estimation, this "land mania" caused the collapse of many of the Owenite and Fourierist communities.

Having bought the land in Iowa, the community in Nauvoo began
dispatching small rotating groups of settlers to farm it. The land, which
ran along the bank of the East Nodaway River, was fertile, well timbered with walnut trees, and dense with game. It was also incredibly
remote. The five-hundred-mile round-trip from Nauvoo by wagon over
the Mormon trail took a month. The nearest outpost where provisions
such as sugar and salt could be purchased was a hundred miles away. In

this rolling wilderness—in summer, a leaning ocean of grasses; in winter, a desolation of snow and wind—a few Icarian men established a rough outpost of dirt-floored cabins. They planted wheat and corn, began raising livestock, and built a gristmill.

Meanwhile, the situation in Nauvoo continued to deteriorate. By the spring of 1856, it was as if two separate communities were living side by side around the temple square. Both the Cabetists and the opposition, now called the Majority, filled their own newspapers with hysterical propaganda denouncing their opponents. When members of the Majority got control of the school, the Cabetist teachers were fired. In the refectory, the two factions ate at separate tables, glaring at each other across the room. Even the little children became viciously partisan. Both factions tried to persuade the colony's supporters in France that *they* represented the true Icaria. On this score Cabet had an advantage. His wife, who had never made the crossing to the United States, helped run the dwindling Icarian bureau in Paris.

Toward the end of the summer, physical violence seemed imminent. Cabet surrounded himself with loyalist bodyguards. Small scuffles broke out over food. Members of the Majority burned Cabet in effigy. As things unraveled, some colonists left. "We had come to Nauvoo to make a paradise on earth and we had made a Sheol," wrote one departing Icarian. "I thought of searching for happiness elsewhere." After Majority men prevailed in an open election, the Cabetists went on strike, refusing to work. In response, the Majority occupied the refectory, refusing to feed the strikers. A sign quoting Saint Paul was nailed to the locked door: "If any will not work, neither let him eat." When members of the Majority went out to dig potatoes, they wore loaded muskets strapped to their backs. Cabetists marched on the refectory, waving revolutionary banners. After they bashed in the door with axes, members of the Majority offered bread for the striking women and children. The Cabetists accepted the loaves, stuck them onto the tips of pikes, and paraded through town.

It is not clear whom all this revolutionary theater was meant for. There was no middle ground. Even before the avant-garde had shipped out for Texas in 1848, Icarianism had begun to blur the line between a political movement and a religious sect. Each side in the conflict at Nauvoo saw their opponents as traitors to a sacred cause. The stark, black-and-white morality of the community's founding text—its depiction of a struggle between truehearted communists and their wicked opponents—proved to be a tainted inheritance: an open invitation to fundamentalism. Citizens felt it was their duty to constantly judge one another's Icarian-ness. Everyone was either a loyal soldier under "the banner of holy community" or a selfish, "individualist" traitor. This outlook flowed directly from the principles laid out in *Voyage*. As one fictional Icarian happily boasts to Lord Carisdall, "All our citizens are required to oversee law enforcement and to pursue or denounce the persons whose misdemeanors they witness."

Cabet had become the leading socialist in France by preaching a well-mannered, bourgeois-friendly strain of communism. Now, at the age of sixty-eight, he stood at the head of a bitter, if absurdly petite, insurrection on the edge of the American frontier. Fed up, the non-Icarian residents of Nauvoo called out the sheriff. For some of the communists, his arrival at their town within a town came as a relief. They had begun to worry that they might be driven from Nauvoo by the same people who had chased off the more numerous, better-armed, better-organized Latter-day Saints. After the sheriff restored order, the mayor of Nauvoo visited Cabet and told him to leave town.

On September 27, 1856, the Majority voted to expel Cabet. A month later, he and 179 loyalists sailed north up the Mississippi for Missouri, where they planned to commence building the *true* Icaria.

Two days after they arrived in St. Louis, Cabet's chambermaid brought him the wrong breakfast. In a fit of anger, he suffered a stroke and died. His followers were crushed. They had given up everything for Icaria, and in their minds, Cabet and Icaria were indistinguishable. They believed that he had died as a martyr for communism, murdered by the traitors to Icaria. They dressed him in his Icarian cape and tunic, cut a lock of his hair for a relic, and buried him in a south St. Louis graveyard.* One addled young German Icarian took his own life.

Messiah-less, the exiled Icarians took out a mortgage on a few hundred acres in Cheltenham, Missouri (now part of St. Louis), and tried to re-create the communal life they had known in Nauvoo. Despite cash sent from the office in Paris, they slipped into debt. At one point, in an effort to make more money, their de facto leader, a young lawyer named Benjamin Mercadier, attempted to reorganize the community as a Fourier-style joint-stock phalanx. The men, most of whom were artisans with salable skills, began taking jobs in St. Louis. When the Civil War broke out, many of them joined the Union army. After six hard years, the Cheltenham Icaria dissolved.

Purification

In the wake of Cabet's departure, life in Nauvoo returned to a quieter, shabbier version of normal. The political drama was over, but the departing faction had carried off much of the community's meager wealth. A national recession that began in 1857 was spreading up the Mississippi River valley, drying up the market for Icarian-made goods. By 1860, the colonists could no longer pay both of their mortgages. They sold the village in Nauvoo, loaded whatever they could onto prairie schooners, and went west to start anew on their land in southwestern Iowa, near the small village of Corning.

Some Icarians saw the move as a blessing. Icarian communism, the faith that had inspired their extraordinary labors, was turning inward, becoming less of an economic creed than a system of moral perfection. It was no longer the world they were trying to remake; it was themselves. Jules Prudent, a former jeweler who had been one of Cabet's most vocal antagonists in Nauvoo, described the exodus to Iowa as a

---

* So that his followers could give him a second, grander farewell, Cabet was later exhumed and reburied.

purification: a way for the communists to free themselves from the rot of individualism. The farther they got from France, from fair-weather communists, and from the temptations of a selfish, individualistic society, the better. In Iowa, a land entirely innocent of culture, history, and non-Icarians, they would truly burn their boats.

In Nauvoo, the Icarians, like all the other utopians of the era, had lived in small apartments within larger "unitary dwellings." In Iowa, they opted for single-family homes. It was a small but significant decision. One by one, the rough cabins made of log and turf were replaced with small, whitewashed houses of milled lumber arrayed around a large communal refectory and school. By establishing an agricultural commune of private homes, the Icarians had effectively abandoned the vision of an urban industrial paradise described in *Voyage*. At the same time, their newfound isolation deepened the community's commitment to the ideology at the heart of Cabet's book—a faintly mystical communism that equated individualism with sin and collectivism with sanctity.

Copies of *Voyage* still circulated through radical circles in Europe, bringing a trickle of converts from France, Switzerland, and Germany. A few Americans also joined. John Dye, a printer who had lived at Oneida and with the Shakers, ran the community's printing press. William Moore, another lapsed Shaker, served briefly as the community's lead horticulturist. Alcander Longley, perhaps the most persistent utopian socialist of the era, joined with his family in 1867. As a teenager, Longley had lived at Ohio's Clermont Phalanx, where his father was a founding member. He then joined the North American Phalanx, before attempting to start Fourierist colonies in Indiana, Michigan, and Ohio. Along the way, he intermittently published *The Communist,* a paper devoted to encouraging cooperation among the various small utopias of the era.*

---

* The Longleys eventually left Icaria to found their own Icarian-style community in Missouri. That community, called Reunion (not to be confused with La Réunion in

As it had in Nauvoo, education, entertainment, and high culture remained at the center of life in Iowa. The community maintained a well-stocked library and a well-practiced orchestra. Every other Saturday, they staged an operetta. Amazingly, given the bitter expulsion of Cabet, they still gathered each Sunday to study his writings in the *Cours Icarien*. A visitor from the Oneida Community was surprised to find that the communists still spoke of Cabet as their apostle. Each February, the colonists celebrated the 1848 departure from Le Havre with plays, waltzes, prairie-grown wine, and a solemn rendition of the *chant du départ*.

The Civil War finished off the anemic Icaria in Cheltenham, but it was a boon to the community in Iowa. By the time the fighting started, the communists had raised a herd of more than six hundred merino sheep. When Union purchasing agents came through southern Iowa, the Icarians signed lucrative contracts to supply wool to the Army of the North. The windfall allowed them to pay down the debts that had been stalking the community since the Texas disaster.

New Icaria, Young Icaria

After a quiet, prosperous decade on the prairie, Icaria was again riven by ideology. By the 1870s, there were fewer than one hundred people in the community. Half of them, mostly the older Icarians, were content with the quiet, stable communal life they had finally achieved. The younger Icarians—both the grown children of the first colonists and new recruits—had other ideas. Calling themselves Progressives, they tried to revive the community's slumbering utopian spirit.

In the spring of 1871, amid fears of a return to monarchy following a disastrous war with Prussia and the collapse of Napoleon III's Second Empire, radicalized workers seized control of Paris and established an

---

Texas), fell apart because half the members supported traditional marriage while the other half were advocates of free love.

autonomous, collectivist government: the Paris Commune. After less than three months, the French army (the Versaillais) marched on Paris, crushing the Commune and killing twenty thousand Communards in the process. By then, the small Icarian colony in Iowa had become a faint legend among some French radicals. Four fugitive Communards who had fled to New York City wrote to the community seeking admission. The Icarians wrote back, saying that they did not want any new members. But before the applicants could receive the reply, three of them had already started west. When they arrived in Corning, they were accepted as probationary members.

Fresh from the Paris barricades, the men made natural allies for the young Icarian Progressives. Inspired by the rhetoric of the Commune and the formation of the First International, they were eager to restore Icaria to a position of experimental importance in international communism, to remake the small prairie village into a beachhead in the global struggle against capital (and the church).

The Paris Commune had celebrated women's liberation and established full women's suffrage. The Progressives now wanted to do the same at Icaria, where, despite decades of rhetoric about female equality, women still could not vote in the assembly. They also wanted the community to admit more members, issue a definitive statement of atheism, and begin actively propagandizing Icarian communism in American cities. To pay for all of this, they wanted to supplement the farm's income with an increase in manufacturing. The self-proclaimed Conservatives who ran the assembly—gray-haired farmers in wooden shoes and blue overalls—no longer had much interest in such lofty ideas. They were more concerned with corn yields and the price of wool.

Neither camp had the two-thirds majority required to expel their opponents or force their agenda. Anger mounted until, once again, it was as if two communities were sharing a single estate. The stark moral logic of Icarian communism and the overheated rhetoric of the Paris Commune bred factionalism, making compromise impossible. As it had in Nauvoo, the disagreement quickly blossomed into an existential battle between truehearted Icarians and "individualistic" pretenders.

The tension erupted in petty sabotage. "This was a real war, even though there was no bloodshed," recalled Marie Marchand Ross, whose father and eldest brother were Conservatives but whose other brother was a leading Progressive. "Families were divided and the opposing factions treated each other like enemies and spoke to one another only in anger." There was a politically motivated tussle over a jar of jam. Buckets of opposition milk were kicked over. Fruit trees were stripped. A Conservative cook intentionally wilted the lettuce bound for the Progressive half of the dining hall. And in a distinctly Gallic act of sabotage, a cup of sand was added to a half-cooked kettle of Progressive foie gras. "This could not fail to cause a general gnashing of teeth," recalled one combatant, "but there was nothing to be done about it."

The decisive conflict was almost purely symbolic. The dooryard vegetable gardens attached to each small house were a source of pride and pleasure for older Icarians. To the Progressives they revealed creeping individualism, proving "the old party's lukewarm zeal for communism." This disagreement about sunflowers and zucchini became a proxy for the broader struggle over the enfranchisement of women and the true purpose of Icaria. Emile Péron, one of the new arrivals from Paris and a leader among the Progressives, told the assembly that the private cultivation of vegetables and flowers was an affront to Icarian ideals. Either the gardens had to go or the community must split in two. When the older group refused, the Progressives left the assembly in silence and declared a strike.

In August 1878, the two parties faced off before the Adams County Circuit Court. Addressing a jury of Iowan farmers, the lawyer for the Progressives tried to get Icaria dissolved on a technicality.* The lawyer for the Conservatives responded by telling the jury that the younger party comprised dangerous Communist radicals. The court sided with

---

* He argued that the community had violated its charter by engaging in manufacturing rather than just agriculture. It was an ironic case for the Progressives to make since they were the ones who hoped to expand the community's manufacturing operations.

the Progressives, legally dissolving Icaria and appointing trustees to manage the breakup.

The Conservatives sold the Progressives their stake in the community in exchange for a large piece of land, cash, and the assumption by the younger group of $8,000 in debt. Using logrollers, the older colonists skidded eight frame houses a mile away from the village to a small, lush valley at the far edge of the original holding. They wrote a new constitution, built a new refectory, and called their community New Icaria.

The Progressives remained on the original site, renaming it Young Icaria. They abolished the presidency, gave women the vote, and relaxed admission standards. Coverage of the trial brought an influx of socialist seekers to Young Icaria, and membership briefly climbed to seventy-two.

Three years later, a Young Icarian barber named Armand Dehay left Iowa for California. In San Francisco, he found an active community of socialists, one of whom, Émile Bée, had been an Icarian during his youth in France. Along with Dehay's father-in-law, a Saint-Simonian socialist named Jules Leroux who had been exiled from France, Bée and Dehay bought a ranch on the Russian River near the village of Cloverdale, north of San Francisco.* At the Santa Rosa courthouse, they filed a certificate of incorporation declaring their intention to found a colony "to prove to our fellow man that a community based on solidarity is reasonable and possible." To their comrades shivering through the win-

---

* In France, Leroux and his brother, the philosopher Pierre Leroux, had both been devotees of Saint-Simon, members of the Legislative Assembly, and leaders in the 1848 revolution. After Louis Napoleon's 1851 coup, they fled France for the island of Jersey off the coast of Normandy, where they befriended fellow exile Victor Hugo. When a general amnesty was granted, Pierre returned to France, where he was an early organizer of the Paris Commune. Jules immigrated to the United States, settling in Kansas, where he started a socialist monthly called *L'Étoile du Kansas* (*The Star of Kansas*). Among the paper's main benefactors was his friend the novelist George Sand.

ter back in Young Icaria, they mailed envelopes stuffed with green leaves and flowers—a compelling invitation west.

In 1883, many of the remaining Young Icarians went to California to join Dehay and Leroux at a community they christened Icaria-Speranza. On the pale, grassy hills of Sonoma County they planted wheat, peaches, and forty-two acres of Malbec, Riesling, and Zinfandel grapes.

The fifty-five members of Icaria-Speranza expected a large payout from the liquidation of their holdings in Iowa, but most of the profits were soaked up by debt collectors, lawyers, and a half-baked scheme by Emile Péron to import Percherons from Normandy. By 1886, the members of Icaria-Speranza started going their own ways. Some remained in Sonoma County, forming the French American Wine Company.

Back in Iowa, the thirty aging communists in New Icaria plodded on, continuing to practice the scrupulous equality in all things that had become their sole religion. When they became too old to handle the haying and plowing, they hired local men. By then, their children were mostly gone, some to the settlement in California, others out into the World.

For half a century, through every possible species of hardship, the Icarian settlers in the United States clung to the ideals enshrined in Cabet's depiction of a happy, communist neverland. Starting from scratch, always chasing the utopian dream of beginning at zero, was practically built into their theory. They did it seven times—in Texas, Nauvoo, Cheltenham, Corning, New Icaria, Young Icaria, and Icaria-Speranza. Taken as a single movement, Icaria was the longest-lived secular utopia of the nineteenth century. Even after the colonists expelled Cabet and abandoned any hope of re-creating the urban workers' paradise depicted in *Voyage*, they pursued the novel's vision of a righteous, semimystical collectivism. In Icaria, communism was not just the means to a happy, just society; it was an end in itself—a state of moral exaltation.

On February 3, 1895, the forty-seventh anniversary of the departure of the avant-garde from Le Havre, the handful of communists still living in New Icaria gathered in their dining hall for their annual elections. They went around the table taking nominations for the presidency, but nobody was willing to assume the job. They were all too old, too tired. Instead of electing officers, they voted to dissolve the community.

It took three years to sell off the property. In 1898, eight geriatric Icarians, the final remnant of what had once been the largest and most hopeful radical movement in France, locked the heavy white door of their refectory and moved into town.

ONEIDA

Kingdom Come

The sin-system, the marriage-system, the work-system, and
the death-system, are all one, and must be abolished together. Holiness, free love, association in labor, and immortality, constitute the chain of redemption, and must come
together in their true order.

—JOHN HUMPHREY NOYES

Burned

On the evening of April 5, 1815, people on the Indonesian island of
Sumatra heard the faint, rumbling sounds of a distant naval skirmish.
To the east, on the island of Sulawesi, the noise was more distinct. Brit-
ish soldiers stationed there could make out the low, intermittent crack
of cannon fire interspersed with the stuttering report of small arms.
Assuming that a merchant ship was under attack by pirates, British of-
ficials dispatched the *Benares,* an armed cruiser operated by the East
India Company, to find and engage the enemy.

For three days, the crew of the *Benares* sailed from harbor to harbor
looking for the pirates. Failing to find any sign of a battle, they returned
to port. Two days later, the clamor resumed, louder and more frequent.
Within the heavy walls of the British fort, plates and cups rattled.

The next morning, the sky went black. "By noon complete darkness covered the face of the day," wrote Thomas Stamford Raffles, captain of the *Benares*. "I never saw anything to equal it in the darkest night."

There had not been any skirmish. The noise came from the island of Sumbawa, a full sixteen hundred miles from Sumatra, where Mount Tambora was erupting.* Despite the volcano's remote location, more than ten thousand people were killed by its eruption and the tsunami it caused. Twenty-four cubic miles of debris were launched into the atmosphere, blotting out the sun for hundreds of miles. The cloud of sulfurous ash spread, dimming the sun over most of the Northern Hemisphere. Byron commemorated the cataclysm with the poem "Darkness" (1816): "I had a dream, which was not all a dream. / The bright sun was extinguish'd, and the stars / Did wander darkling in the eternal space, / Rayless, and pathless, and the icy earth / Swung blind and blackening in the moonless air; / Morn came and went—and came, and brought no day."

In New England, where the founding Brook Farmers were still in short pants, a mysterious red haze hung in the air all summer. The next year, 1816, was freezing. The press called it "Eighteen Hundred and Froze to Death" and "the Year Without Summer." In early June, six inches of snow fell on northern New England, killing tender young crops. Farmers worked through the night to replant. When more snow fell in July and August, the second planting was wiped out. In some parts of northern New England, there were twelve consecutive months of ice and snow. Freshly shorn sheep froze to death standing up in the fields.

In Europe, the cold weather caused food shortages, famines, and riots. In the United States, the farmers of New England's hill-country villages were the hardest hit. Even without Tambora's eruption, the first

---

* By way of comparison, the fact that Tambora's eruption was heard clearly on Sumatra is equivalent to the citizens of Lincoln, Nebraska, hearing a noise made in New York City.

quarter of the nineteenth century was a trial for the region. In 1811, powerful floods washed away mills and drowned cattle. In 1812 and 1813, "spotted fever" (meningitis) felled 3 percent of Vermonters. In 1826, a plague of grasshoppers devoured harvests. During "the Year Without Summer," when corn would not grow, some farmers starved. Countless others were ruined.

The victims of these disasters were the children of the Great Awakening—the descendants of the Puritans. They saw the hand of God in everything. To them, this punishing concatenation of natural disasters seemed like divine judgment. Worn down, farmers from the scrabbly, overfarmed uplands of western New England pulled up stakes. Like dust bowl Okies pouring into California's verdant Central Valley, an exodus of poor Yankees moved west across the Hudson River, toward the deep, alluvial topsoil of New York's broad, green western valleys. Entire New England villages were packed up, carried west, and reassembled in western New York. Beset by famine, floods, locusts, and pestilence, these God-fearing refugees arrived in their promised land with an apocalyptic cast of mind.

At first, western New York did seem like a land of honey and milk. The Erie Canal, begun in 1817 and completed in October 1825, painted a wide stripe of prosperity all the way across the state. By linking the Great Lakes to the Hudson, the canal connected the frontier to the port of New York City and the world. On the morning of its opening, cannons were arrayed at intervals along the canal's route and down the Hudson to New York City. Starting in the west, a triumphant booming signal dominoed its way from Lake Erie to the Atlantic coast and back in three hours and twenty minutes. In the decade before the telegraph, it was a thrilling conquest over time and space.

The canal shortened the time it took to cross New York from a matter of weeks to a matter of days. The cost of transporting freight from the frontier to the coast was cut dramatically. The man-made river carried more than twice as much cargo as the Mississippi. Barges laden with Manchester calico, Chinese china, machine parts, and European immigrants traveled west, passing eastbound boats riding low with lumber, salt, and flour.

Although the canal transformed the national economy, its strongest impact was on the section of New York through which it passed. Along with the jobs created by the work of digging and paving the waterway, countless factories sprang up along the canal's route. Towns such as Utica, Buffalo, and Rochester boomed.*

The social and economic changes taking place along the canal route were an amped-up version of what was happening throughout the Republic. The Yankees in western New York came from small communities of subsistence agriculture. In their old life, the life of their parents and grandparents, family members worked side by side on a single plot of land. They raised a few animals, worked a patch of corn, spun their own woolens, milled their own grain, and made their own shoes and soap. There was little distinction between working hours and nonworking hours. Folding money, when they had any, was for a new kettle, a bottle of patent medicine, a Bible. Life was almost entirely dependent on one's land, labor, and the weather. Ideas, other than those about sin and rain, were scarce.

Things were different in the canal zone. Work and life began to separate. Men went to earn wages on large farms or in small factories. Women stayed home, raising children, keeping house, and taking in piecework. Grown sons (and to a lesser extent grown daughters) traveled away from home to find work. The entire country was shifting rapidly from a rural agricultural economy to an urban industrial economy. In western New York, that transformation seemed to be happening overnight.

The manufactories that sprang up along the canal required capital to buy large machines. Cash-cropping farmers needed loans to buy huge tracts of land. Investors in lower Manhattan paid hard cash for

* Over the course of the 1820s, the populations of those three cities increased by 183 percent, 314 percent, and 512 percent, respectively.

wheat that had not even germinated. Working people in remote places were suddenly entangled in financial markets as far off as London. The canal showed the world a man-made river. Now something called the national economy entered the lives of ordinary people like a man-made version of the weather: a vast, unpredictable force with limitless power over daily life.

The Panic of 1837 derailed western and central New York's vigorous economy. When the inflated price for commodities plummeted, the region slipped into a depression. The sudden downturn was as mysterious as the red haze caused by Tambora's eruption. As the historian Michael Barkun wrote, this rapid transition from natural disaster to man-made calamity gave the citizens of western New York "a special receptivity to millenarian and utopian appeals." The new world demanded new ways of living.

In a place increasingly in the thrall of money and material progress, an alternate set of aspirations blossomed. During the late 1820s and early 1830s, hundreds of thousands of Americans converted to new evangelical denominations in a nationwide paroxysm of faith that came to be known as the Second Great Awakening. The excitement that had carried the Shaker gospel over the Alleghenies at the turn of the century had come east.[*] And once again, talk of the millennium was front and center.

Lay preachers saw "signs of the times" everywhere. They parsed each weird line of that ancient monster parade known as the book of Revelation and watched for clues in the weather, the Vatican, the Congress, even in the distant power struggles of the Ottoman Empire. This sort of horizon gazing was especially common in the newly settled counties of western New York, a place where ideas moved fast and the world seemed to be transforming on a daily basis. The historian Whitney Cross called the canal a "psychic highway."

---

[*] At the time, nobody would have called western New York "the East." It was still the frontier.

———

The new religious excitement spilled out of traditional churches, spawning small denominations by the dozen. Circuit-riding evangelists blanketed upper New York. At rollicking tent meetings, they summoned souls to Christ, telling Americans that salvation was in their hands. Western New York was so crowded with revivals that Charles Grandison Finney, the signal voice of the Second Awakening, dubbed it "the Burned-over District"—a place where the smell of brimstone seemed to hang in the air and scant fuel (sinners) remained to feed the revivalist blaze.* In 1830 alone, more than one hundred thousand western and central New Yorkers were "born again" into the new millenarian churches.

Spiritual and social innovation were fully intertwined. The future-facing citizens of the Burned-over District were at the vanguard of almost every nineteenth-century reform movement. The region was ground zero for abolitionism, feminism, the temperance movement, anti-Masonry, Shakerism, and a wide array of utopian communalist schemes. During the 1840s, the region was home to the country's highest concentration of Fourierist phalanxes. At least ten were planned; seven were actually built.

Mormon prophet Joseph Smith, whose family moved from Vermont to Ontario County during "the Year Without Summer" as part of the Yankee diaspora, became the most successful of the region's many revelators. He described the district as a place of "unusual excitement on the subject of religion . . . an extraordinary scene . . . a strife of words and a contest about opinions."

In 1843, on the eve of Fourierism's tidal surge into western New

---

* The geographic boundaries of the Burned-over District are debatable. Whitney Cross, the region's most celebrated chronicler, defined the district as all of New York west of the Catskills and Adirondacks. As far as religious excitement goes, the far west of the state was certainly the most active area. When other social and communitarian experiments are taken into account, the relevant area expands to include the whole middle swath of New York.

York, people in the region were enthralled by the apocalyptic calculations of an unassuming local farmer named William Miller. Miller, a
veteran of the War of 1812, had no formal theological training, but in
1831 he read the book of Daniel and, using a variety of ancient calendars, calculated that Christ was scheduled to return to the earth sometime between March 1843 and March 1844.* Miller's announcement of
the imminent Second Advent struck a chord in a time and place where
many people expected the end of history to arrive at any minute. To
spread the word of the coming rapture, the "Millerites" held large revivals and printed illustrated posters outlining their apocalyptic math.

When Jesus failed to show during his allotted time, one of Miller's
followers recalculated using a different, older Hebraic calendar, granting the Son of Man an extension until October 22, 1844. On that day,
as many as fifty thousand Americans gathered outside to be beamed
heavenward. Many of them had sold their homes and left their fall
crops to rot in the field. Some had sent money to the federal government, paying off previously dodged taxes. When nothing happened, the
press gleefully chronicled the "Great Disappointment," reporting erro-
neously that the believers had donned white "ascension robes" to meet
their Maker.

Primed for heaven, thousands of Millerites were set adrift. One
group sent word to New Lebanon requesting a Shaker mission. They
formed a substantial harvest for the western New York villages. Others
filed into the phalanxes that were just then springing up around Rochester. A few started their own small communes. The largest and most
lasting spin-off of Miller's movement was the Seventh-day Adventist
Church, whose members still claim that October 1844 was a pivotal
moment in the unfolding saga of the end times.

---

* Daniel is an Old Testament book of prophecy written in Aramaic that purports to
describe the visions of a Jew named Daniel during his captivity in Babylon. It is now
widely believed to have been written four centuries after the events it describes. In his
visions, Daniel sees the resurrection of the just and the establishment of God's Kingdom of Heaven on earth.

A widely distributed poster depicting William Miller's
calculations concerning the end of days.

Future Perfect

Three years after the Great Disappointment, a fresh millenarian excitement arrived in the heart of the Burned-over District. At the very center of New York State, twelve miles south of the Erie Canal, John Humphrey Noyes, a man whose thinking about the end of history developed partly in opposition to Millerism, established the Oneida Community, the most remarkable utopian experiment in American history. At the community's peak, three hundred Oneida "Perfectionists" lived an intensely intimate, intellectual existence in a rambling, Italianate mansion. They saw their community as an earthly branch of the Kingdom of Heaven, a sort of portal through which the millennium would come to earth. Under the influence of their utopian forebears, the Perfectionists renounced private property, raised their children collectively, embraced gender equality, perfected a novel form of birth control, experimented with every health fad of their day, pursued rigorous self-improvement, practiced a complex system of free love, and initiated an unprecedented experiment in eugenics.

Even more than Robert Owen's New Harmony or Étienne Cabet's Icaria, Oneida is the story of one man's evolving vision of the perfect society. John Humphrey Noyes was born in Vermont in 1811. His father's side of the family had been in New England since 1634, when they made the crossing from England. John Noyes, Sr., studied and then taught at Dartmouth before moving to Brattleboro. There, he married Polly Hayes, the tall, red-haired daughter of a tavern keeper from a prominent Vermont family. When their neighbors began migrating west across the Hudson, the prosperous Noyes clan stayed in Vermont, settling in the Green Mountain village of Putney. John Sr. was elected to Congress and, in 1877, while Polly Hayes's son was running his radical experiment in upstate New York, her nephew Rutherford moved into the White House.

Much of the energy of the Second Great Awakening came from

women. In many of the new evangelical churches, they outnumbered men two to one. Polly Noyes was among them. In 1831, she dragged her skeptical eldest son to a four-day revival in Putney. John Jr. was twenty, a gangly, gray-eyed, ginger-haired young man. Fresh from Dartmouth, he was apprenticing at the law firm of his brother-in-law. With a head full of Byron, common law, and intellectual swagger, he went to the revival for the same reason that many people go to church—to please his mother. He wore bell-bottom pantaloons, fancy square-toed boots, and a fashionable pyramid-shaped hat.

For two days, Noyes regarded the hysterics around him with smug undergraduate detachment. On the third day, a strange calm came over him. That night he couldn't sleep. Soaked with sweat, he lit a lamp and reached for the Bible. The familiar sentences of the New Testament seemed to glow on the page, lambent with urgency. On the fourth and final day of the Putney revival, John Humphrey Noyes pledged his life to the Word. "Hitherto, the world," he wrote in his diary, "henceforth, God!"

His instincts were still academic. His first move was to take up Hebrew grammar. Within a month he was enrolled at the prestigious Andover Theological Seminary. It was a bad fit. With the restless zeal of a fresh-saved convert, Noyes disdained Andover's staid, orthodox Congregationalism and the faculty's attachment to Calvinist dogma.

Calvinism was the shipboard religion on the *Mayflower*. It was the founding American faith. Two of its central pillars are the conviction that humankind is irrevocably tainted by sin and that salvation and damnation are fixed, predestined. During the American expansion into the West, the belief that any freeborn (white, male) American could forge his own destiny was rapidly becoming the central myth of the Republic. This sense of possibility was at odds with the deterministic Calvinist account of salvation.

The revivalists of the Second Great Awakening offered a message that was better suited to the willful American citizenry. The whole purpose of a revival is to save unsaved souls. It is logically incompatible with the dogma of predestination. Under the new teaching, American sinners no longer dangled helpless above the fiery pit. The levers of salvation were in their hands.

Noyes was an enthusiastic exegete, but he loathed the detached "professional" spirit of Andover's young churchmen in training. While his peers quibbled over hermeneutic minutiae, he buzzed with the kinetic intensity of the Putney revival. "My heart was fixed on the millennium," he wrote, "and I resolved to live or die for it."

After a year, he transferred to the comparatively progressive program at Yale, where the faculty were not so uniformly arrayed against the new Awakening. Noyes threw himself into his studies with renewed intensity. He also helped found an abolitionist group and preached in one of the city's black "free churches."

As he studied, Noyes found himself drawn to the ancient Christian doctrine of Perfectionism. In orthodox Christian theology, moral corruption is understood as the essential human condition. No human has been "perfect" (without sin) since Adam and Eve ate from the Tree of Knowledge. Perfectionists, by contrast, believe that a living Christian can be wholly freed from sin in this life and thus significantly closer to God. Some Perfectionists go so far as to claim that being a Christian *requires* total salvation from sin. The debate is as old as scripture. Matthew (5:48) says: "Be ye perfect." John (1:8) says: "If we claim to be without sin . . . the truth is not in us."* For a Perfectionist, being saved is to undergo a distinct transformation in the eyes of God. Some Perfectionists believe that this transformation exempts the perfected from the moral regulations that govern the unredeemed. Within the crowded spiritual marketplace of the Second Great Awakening, several strains of Perfectionism had begun to gather converts. The various groups were identified by their headquarters. There was "New Haven Perfectionism," "Oberlin Perfectionism" (a less extreme position associated with Charles Grandison Finney), "New York Perfectionism," and, eventually, "Oneida Perfectionism."

---

* Augustine, with his account of humanity as a lusty, prideful race, irrevocably corrupted by the Fall, deserves most of the credit for lodging the anti-Perfectionist position into orthodox Christianity. Calvin, with his doctrine of "total depravity," hammered the point home.

This rise in Perfectionist theology paralleled a broader intellectual reorientation. Beyond the canvas big tops of the revivalists, a secular interest in social and individual "perfection" flourished.* Secular perfectionism, which provides the groundwork for utopianism, is the belief that progress—in matters scientific, artistic, moral, economic, medical, social—has no upper limit and that the world is approaching some ideal state.† It is impossible to fully unbraid the sacred and the secular threads of American perfectionism. They inform each other and stem from the same general sense about how the world works. Within the person of John Humphrey Noyes, they were wholly inseparable.

All of the nineteenth-century communal utopians spoke in the language of perfectionism. For the Shakers, perfection was a matter of melding individuals into a unified "body of believers" and keeping the imperfections of the World *out*. Their fastidious stone walls were a rampart against the fleshpots of Babylon. Robert Owen claimed that his hyperrational scheme was a mechanism of "endless progressive improvement, physical, intellectual, and moral, and of happiness, without the possibility of retrogression or assignable limit." Fourier wrote that under his scheme, humans "will be elevated to perfection of body and mind." Cabet felt much the same. "Man," he wrote, "is evidently perfectible through experience and education."

While most religious Perfectionists spoke of man's perfectibility as a private spiritual enterprise, the communal utopians regarded perfection, including perfection of the soul, as an inherently collective project. Fourier claimed that the passions he identified will produce harmony when they are expressed in a crowd, whereas in solitude, human nature will "entice us only to evil." A Shaker theologian wrote that the indi-

---

* To limit confusion, I'll use capital P "Perfectionism" to describe the specific Christian dogma that endorses the possibility of living without sin. Lowercase p "perfectionism" will describe the broader, secular notion of individual or social perfectibility.
† John Rawls, who was no fan of this sort of thinking, concisely defines perfectionism as "the sole principle of a teleological theory directing society to arrange institutions and to define the duties and obligations of individuals so as to maximize the achievement of human excellence in art, science, and culture."

vidual who seeks transcendence alone is like a foot separated from a body.

Sin No More

On a freezing Thursday evening in late February 1834, John Humphrey Noyes left the apartment he shared with his younger brother Horatio and hurried across New Haven toward the Orange Street Chapel, where he was scheduled to deliver a sermon. Noyes, then in his second year at Yale, was convinced that the Bible promised the possibility of total, sinless salvation. What he did not yet understand was how such salvation might be attained. Desperate for an epiphany on a par with his conversion in Putney, he had been up for nights poring over the Bible. Vanquishing sin could not simply be a matter of restraint or flawless behavior. Even sinful thoughts are an offense to God, and nobody can prevent the mind from wandering. He concluded that spiritual perfection must be more than rule following; it must be a mystical state, a purifying brush with the divine. Something that happens *to you*.

Stepping into the warmth of the chapel, Noyes removed his overcoat and then sat at a desk facing the congregation. The sparse assembly looked back in silence at their young volunteer minister. Reading calmly from prepared notes, Noyes gave a simple, perplexing sermon: "He that committeth sin is of the devil." Having offered this single line from the book of John, Noyes then insisted on its literal meaning: If you sin at all, you are not a Christian. He stood, pulled on his coat, and walked back into the cold.

Lying in his bed that night, Noyes received the purification he had been craving. "Three times in quick succession a stream of eternal love gushed through my heart, and rolled back again to its source. Joy unspeakable and full of glory filled my soul. All fear and doubt and condemnation passed away. I knew that my heart was clean, and that the Father and the Son had come and made it their abode." He was perfect. Like Ann Lee, who understood her jailhouse vision of Eden as the dawn of a new dispensation for all of humanity, Noyes interpreted his private epiphany as a cosmic event, a decisive step toward the millennium.*

The next morning, one of Noyes's classmates showed up at his apartment. He had heard the Orange Street sermon and wanted to know what Noyes meant by his claim that anyone who sins is of the devil. Humanity is defined by sin; God loves us despite our corruption. To preach that a Christian cannot sin would be to "unchurch" oneself. When Noyes simply repeated what he had said the night before, the frustrated seminarian put it squarely: "Don't you commit sin?"

Knowing that his reply would "plunge [him] into the depths of contempt," Noyes answered firmly: "No."

Word of this heresy flew across the Yale campus. Incredulous young men packed the Noyes brothers' rooms, quizzing John on his alleged sanctity. Even for the relatively forward-thinking faculty at Yale, this was too much. They revoked Noyes's preaching license, expelled him, and suggested that he leave New Haven. He was unfazed. "I have taken away their license to sin and they go on sinning. So, they have taken away my license to preach, I shall keep on preaching."

Kicked out of the Congregationalist Church and unmoored from institutional Christianity at the age of twenty-three, Noyes boarded a sloop for New York City. He took a room in a boardinghouse near Canal Street and, over the next three weeks, became completely unhinged. Tormented by visions of devils and angels, he did not eat or sleep. In a spell of paranoia, he wandered lower Manhattan by night. Test-driving his newfound sanctity, he drew close to sin, tasting his first hard liquor and preaching to stoned prostitutes in the narrow alleys of Five Points. One afternoon, he became certain that he was dying. He returned to the boardinghouse, lay down in his cot, and awaited the end. When the terror passed, Noyes felt reborn—purified. Satan had

---

* In the coming decades, his followers would celebrate February 20 as a sort of spiritual solstice: "the High Tide of the Spirit." August 20, the day furthest on the calendar, was considered a dangerous time: "the climax of the flesh."

tested him and he had proven himself invincible. His spiritual perfection was intact. He later recalled that those three weeks alone in New York felt like three years.

At the time, there were several centers of Perfectionism in the Northeast. Noyes visited with most of the leading members of the movement, but he did not join forces with any of them. He believed that God had singled him out as a divine instrument. He could not countenance working beneath another preacher. For a time, he and an old friend printed a paper called *The Perfectionist* in New Haven, but the partnership didn't last. Noyes drifted around the Northeast, preaching his new doctrine to anyone who would listen. He was often broke. At one point he walked for three days from New York City to New Haven without eating. His willowy frame grew emaciated.

Noyes was on the move for almost three years. It was a period, he later recalled, of "vagabond, incoherent service." He was not a particularly passionate preacher. His genius was for conversation and the written word. Like Ann Lee, Noyes possessed a weird, otherworldly charisma that, among a certain kind of seeker, inspired complete devotion. As he traveled, he accumulated a modest flock.

Noyes returned to Putney to stay in 1836. His brother George and his sisters Harriet and Charlotte all came to regard John as their spiritual leader. Their mother held out for a while, but after months of daily sermonizing—"bullying," she called it—Polly Noyes acknowledged her eldest son as her spiritual "father." (The rest of the family never embraced John's teachings, thus splitting the Noyes clan into two camps.)

When John Sr. died in 1841, Noyes and the three siblings he had converted pooled their inheritance and bought land adjoining the family farm. By then, some of Noyes's other converts had gathered in Putney. Gradually, this small group of Perfectionists organized themselves into a loose community, which they called the Putney Bible School.

Noyes was torn between an urge to hit the road as an evangelist and the desire to build up a strong, stable congregation in Putney. This dilemma, between spreading the Word and living the Word, would never be fully resolved in him, but he settled on a compromise. He would stay with his followers in Putney and broadcast the Perfectionist gospel with a free newspaper, *The Witness*. Even more than most of the ink-stained reformers of his day, Noyes put great stock in the power of newsprint to change the world. The Perfectionists sometimes lived on thin potato soup, but they never skimped on ink or paper.

Noyes's decision to remain in Putney was partly a reaction against revivalism, particularly the hyped-up mass hysteria of the Millerite movement, to which the Putney community lost a few members. Noyes wanted, he wrote, to put Perfectionism on a "permanent basis, not by preaching and stirring up excitement over a large field . . . but by devoting myself to the particular instruction of a few simple-minded, unpretending believers."

By the winter of 1843, there were twenty-eight adults and nine children living on the Noyes family farm. Like the early Brook Farmers insisting that their plan had no connection to Fourierism, Noyes claimed that his ambitions were neither utopian nor socialistic. The Putney community was a prayer group and a publishing operation, not an "association." That gradually changed. In 1846, as he later wrote, "the little church at Putney began cautiously to experiment in Communism." The believers already studied together, farmed together, prayed together, worked together, and ate together. Now they began to hold all their property in common, too.

Like most communitarians of the nineteenth century, the Putney Perfectionists took inspiration from the social and economic arrangements of the primitive Christian Church as described in the book of Acts. Noyes believed that the first community of Jesus followers were theological Perfectionists but that their true, early Christianity had been lost at the close of the age of the apostles. Since that time, Christendom has been stuck in a long dark age that Noyes called "the Apostasy." By imitating the spiritual communism practiced by the first Christians, Noyes intended to revive true Christianity, thus initiating the long forestalled promises of the millennium. As with all religious sects, it is impossible to draw a clear distinction between the Perfectionists' spiritual inspirations and their workaday needs. Along with Noyes's reading of Acts, the practical necessities of rural living probably helped spur the believers into communism.

Noyes's defining quality was a total refusal to acknowledge any division between theory and practice. Every idea that popped into his head was immediately transmitted into experiment. He understood his own spiritual perfection as a sudden, mystical experience—a union with that which is metaphysically perfect (God). Although that experience freed him from the taint of original sin, it did not translate into worldly infallibility. Social perfection—the building up of the millennial kingdom— would not come like a flash. It would be a process, requiring hard thinking, trial and error, and a great deal of human creativity.

Like all utopians, Noyes had little regard for the way things are usually done. He overthrew long held customs with remarkable ease. When it occurred to him that the practice of eating three hot meals a day subjected women "almost universally to the worst of slavery," he simply stopped it. The thirty-odd members of the Putney community ate one sit-down meal in the morning and then foraged for themselves from an open pantry "as appetite or fancy may suggest." The door to the pantry was marked with a card bearing the motto "Health, Comfort, Economy, and Woman's Rights." Later, when the Perfectionists had more money, they went in the opposite direction, experimenting with Fourier's eight-meal-a-day schedule.

It was not by coincidence that the Perfectionists began forming themselves into a commune just as American Fourierism reached its zenith. The Putney community was directly inspired by Brook Farm, which collapsed the same year the Perfectionists began formally organizing themselves as a community. Although Noyes had a revivalist's distaste for the coolheaded abstractions of Unitarian theology, he regarded George Ripley as a moral and intellectual titan. To Noyes, the continuity between what he was doing in Vermont and what the Fourierists were doing else-

where was self-evident. The community in Putney, he wrote, "drank copiously of the spirit of [Brook Farm's] *Harbinger* and of the socialists."

For their part, the leading Fourierists regarded the Perfectionists as
sincere, if slightly addled, comrades. In the winter of 1846, two Brook
Farmers visited the community in Putney to lecture on Fourierism.
After returning home, they reported in *The Harbinger* that the Perfectionists were "well-meaning people, ardently longing for a divine order
of society," but that their fixation on spiritual matters kept them from
appreciating "sufficiently the influence of social institutions." Not surprisingly, the Brook Farmers suggested that the Putney communists
would benefit from reading more Fourier.

In his own paper, Noyes responded to this assessment by saying that
his community certainly admired Fourier, but only as one of several
influences. "On many points [Fourier's] philosophy well agrees with our
principles," he wrote. "But we can say nearly the same of the Shakers."
Noyes believed that Fourier's philosophy—which, like most Americans,
he received via Brisbane, Dana, Ripley, and Greeley—focused too
much on social arrangements while neglecting the importance of the
individual. He believed that "social perfection," which for him was synonymous with the millennium, had to commence with the cultivation
of the soul, not social structures. The Fourierists, he wrote, were pro-
ceeding backward—"trying to build a chimney by beginning at the
top." Noyes called his community a "spiritual phalanx."

The Fourierists, Owenites, and Icarians all tapped into a pervasive belief that some sort of man-made golden age was about to commence.
The Perfectionists, like the Shakers, combined this sort of general millenarian optimism with a specific story about the Second Advent and
the prophesied reign of heaven on earth. Most American Christians
were divided over whether Christ would return before or after the millennium.* Noyes offered a surprising third option: Christ had already

---

* The technical terms for these two views are "premillennialism" (Christ will come
before the millennium) and "postmillennialism" (Christ will come after the millen-

returned and left again. Noyes believed that the Second Coming had been in AD 70, when Roman legions marched on Jerusalem to suppress a Jewish uprising and sacked the Second Temple. The notion that Christ would return just four decades after his death certainly fits with what he told his followers, at least according to the Gospels. "Verily I say unto you," Jesus says to his brother and two other men in the Gospel of Matthew (16:28), "there be some standing here which shall not taste death till they see the Son of man coming in his Kingdom."

For Noyes, the fact that Christ had already made his promised return did not mean that the "resurrection state" of the millennium had already begun, only that it was now possible for individuals to attain spiritual perfection and begin the work of perfecting society. The Savior had done His part of the saving. It is up to humanity to finish the job.

There is an inherent conceptual tension between Christianity and utopianism. In one sense, the dream of a man-made utopia is a Promethean blasphemy. How can anyone presume to devise a better world than the one created by a well-meaning, all-knowing, omnipotent God? Even if humans could radically improve the world, should they? The Bible says that man is destined to live in a world of sin and death until God transforms earth into a paradise. Terrestrial life is meant to be a vale of tears—a difficult qualifying round for the one true utopia: heaven. Noyes's belief that the Second Coming had happened in the first century allowed him to slice through this theological knot. The only reason the earth is not yet a paradise is that true Christianity (Perfectionist, communist) was lost at the end of the apostolic age. Since the Putney Perfectionists were the only people who understood the true nature of redemption, it was up to them to commence building an earthly branch of the Kingdom of Heaven. Noyes further claimed that the apostolic community of the first century was still intact in a higher sphere. He believed that the fulfillment of the millennium would some-

---

nium). Premillennialists generally believe that paradise will arrive as a big, cataclysmic event. Postmillennialists incline toward the view that the millennium will be established gradually through the work of living Christians.

how involve bringing his community into union with those first Jesus worshippers. He felt a particularly intimate fellowship with that apostolic latecomer Paul.

What made Noyes a utopian, rather than a raving seer like William Miller, was that he combined these supernatural beliefs about the end of history with a highly practical plan for realizing his vision. By creating an entirely new type of human community—one that enacts the biblically enumerated promises of the millennium—Noyes planned to trigger the long forestalled reign of heaven on earth. (This could be called fake-it-till-you-make-it millennialism. If you act as though it is the millennium, it will become the millennium.)

To spread the new millennial order, the Perfectionists intended to use the same basic strategy employed by their utopian contemporaries. They would build a single small utopia—a seminal prototype of the coming paradise. Its example would be so appealing that others would rapidly imitate it. Eventually, the entire world would take up the new system. Presto: heaven on earth.

But first, Noyes needed to figure out precisely what life in the millennium would look like. What, as he put it, would be the "social privileges" of life in the "resurrection state"?

Marriage Supper of the Lamb

Although his name was eventually synonymous with libertine sexuality, young John Humphrey Noyes was skittish around women. As a junior at Dartmouth, he confided to his journal that he "could face a battery of cannon with less trepidation than I could a room full of ladies." Debilitating shyness was a family tradition. Out of sheer bashfulness, all four of John Sr.'s brothers had married women already named Noyes—cousins or "kin of some degree."

While Noyes was still in New Haven, not long after his conversion to Perfectionism, he overcame his trepidation long enough to fall in love with an intelligent, dark-eyed Free Church congregant named Abigail

Merwin. She was eight years his senior. Their spiritual connection was intense, and she became Noyes's first real convert.

Merwin's family disapproved of her peculiar young suitor. When Noyes left New Haven to travel and preach, Abigail renounced the new faith. When he came back to visit, she refused to see him. Noyes carried a torch for Merwin for the rest of his long life. Even at the height of the Oneida Community, when he had more lovers than anyone could be bothered to count, Noyes periodically dispatched missionaries to try to coax his first love back into the fold.

One likely reason Merwin's family drew her away from Noyes was that by the time he began calling himself a Perfectionist, that designation already had certain unseemly connotations. Perfectionists, it was widely understood, used their self-declared sanctity as a license for sexual adventure.* To Noyes, a young man sometimes hampered to the point of paralysis by his moral scruples, such an idea was alarming.

At the start of January 1837, Noyes learned that Abigail Merwin had married another man. Reeling, he wrote a long, speculative letter to his friend and fellow Perfectionist David Harrison.

> I will write all that is in my heart on one delicate subject, and you may judge for yourself whether it is expedient to show this letter to others. When the will of God is done on earth as it is in heaven [that is, in the millennium] there will be no marriage. Exclusiveness, jealousy, quarreling have no place at the marriage supper of the Lamb. . . . I call a certain woman my wife. She is yours, she is Christ's, and in him she is the bride of all saints. She is now in the hands of a stranger, and according to my promise to her I rejoice. My claim upon her cuts directly across the marriage covenant of this world, and God knows the end.

---

* A concern that has always hovered around the theology of Perfectionism is whether being "without sin" means *I am perfect so I do not desire anything sinful* or *I am perfect so no matter what I do it is not a sin*. The idea that divine grace comes with amnesty from moral statutes is known as "antinomianism," the general notion being "to the pure all things are pure."

David Harrison passed the letter on to Simon Lovett, a Massachusetts Perfectionist notorious for his role in a scandal known as "the Brimfield bundling," in which two attractive young Perfectionist women were found in Lovett's bed attempting to demonstrate their collective triumph over sin. Through Lovett, Noyes's private musings on this "delicate subject" ended up, without a byline, on the front page of the *Battle-axe and Weapons of War,* a radical Perfectionist newsletter that advocated free love.

Noyes, who never once shied from controversy, immediately claimed authorship of the *Battle-axe* letter in his own newspaper, *The Witness.* His tentative belief that monogamy was somehow unchristian—a belief clearly helped into existence by the news that Abigail Merwin was "in the hands of a stranger"—was now public knowledge.* A storm of censure rained down on the Putney believers. Many of Noyes's followers and subscribers abandoned him. He came to interpret the inadvertent publication of his most private thoughts as a divine kick in the pants— God's way of forcing him, long before he felt ready, "to defend and ultimately carry out the doctrine of communism in love." At the time, he was a virgin.

Noyes reflexively buttressed every one of his ideas with scripture. To prop up the concept of "communism in love," he cited the Gospel of Matthew (22:23–30), wherein a Sadducee (a member of a particular Jewish sect) attempts to stump Jesus with a tricky hypothetical scenario. The Sadducee asks the self-proclaimed Messiah what would happen if a woman, obeying the letter of Mosaic law, were to marry seven brothers in succession, from eldest to youngest, and each man were to die without leaving an heir. Which of the seven would be her husband in the resurrection? Jesus responds by saying that she will not be married to any of them: "For in the resurrection they neither marry, nor are given in marriage, but are as the angels of God in heaven." To Noyes,

---

* At the time, Noyes did not admit the link between his heartache and this shift in his theology, but in 1851, he acknowledged that "Abigail Merwin's marriage stimulated me to break up the marriage system."

the upshot of Jesus's answer to the Sadducee was clear. In the "resurrection state," marriage will not exist.

Amazingly, this same exact sentence was used by the Shakers to certify their prohibition on sex. Both the Shakers and the Perfectionists sought to live as though they were already "in the resurrection . . . as the angels of God." The former sect could not imagine sex without marriage. So for them, no marriage equaled no sex. Noyes, on the other hand, heard nothing in Jesus's response about sex, only a prohibition on matrimony. In the "resurrection state," he concluded, sex will be kosher as long as it is not monogamous. This reading seemed obvious to Noyes because, like Fourier, he viewed the "exclusiveness, jealousy, [and] quarreling" intrinsic to monogamy and the "isolated" family as impediments to harmony and universal brotherhood. Such divisive, unchristian feelings could not possibly be part of God's plan for life in the millennium. Besides, the virginal prophet reasoned, why would one of the best things in life (sex) be banned from heaven on earth? "Whoever has well studied the causes of human maladies," Noyes wrote, "will be sure that Christ, in undertaking to restore men to Paradise and immortality, will set up his kingdom first of all in the bed-chamber and the nursery." It is hard to imagine a better testament to the pliancy of sacred texts. The Shakers and Perfectionists looked upon the same sentence in the same translation of the same book; where one group read a commandment to abstinence, the other saw an invitation to erotic bonanza.* As William Blake put it: "Both read the Bible day and night, / But thou read'st black where I read white."

The year after the *Battle-axe* controversy, Noyes set aside his dim view of matrimony to propose to a pious Vermonter named Harriet Holton.

---

* The Latter-day Saints, who found scriptural support for polygamy in the lives of the Hebrew patriarchs, have yet a third interpretation of Jesus's exchange with the Sadducee. Based on a revelation that came to Joseph Smith at Nauvoo, they claim that most marriages are only "for time" (at death do they part), but marriages "sealed" in a Mormon temple last "for time and all eternity." (Doctrine and Covenants 132:15–18)

Holton and Noyes barely knew each other, but she had been electrified by his preaching and had periodically sent him small sums of money to keep *The Witness* in print. His starkly unromantic proposal addressed her as "sister" and invited Holton to be his spiritual "yoke-fellow." He added that they could "enter into no engagements with each other which shall limit the range of our affections as they are limited in matrimonial engagements by the fashion of this world." Apparently this sounded fine to Holton. She consented so quickly that Noyes worried that his fiancée had "imbibed the spirit of Shakerism" and expected a sexless union. She had not; she did not.

Holton's inheritance allowed Noyes to buy a printing press and a secondhand set of type. The newlyweds spent their honeymoon in Albany, picking up the new equipment. When they returned to Putney, Noyes began to teach his followers how to compose articles, set type, and operate the press. "If we can raise up an army of effective writers," he preached, "we shall ere long get ahead of the clergy."

For several years after his marriage, Noyes continued to philosophize dryly about the virtues of nonmonogamous sexuality, but nothing, as it were, happened. Along with every one of his statements about sexual relations in the "resurrection state," he reiterated his initial claim that established sexual mores could be breached only *after* the Kingdom of God was established on earth. Christ may have already come and gone, but the millennium was clearly not yet in full flower. The Second Coming had opened the possibility of spiritual perfection, but the world was not yet perfect.

These caveats did little to stop rumors. The Perfectionists living communally in Putney prized a high level of social intimacy. Within the tight-knit community, tender expressions of Christian love passed frequently between "brothers" and "sisters." The upright citizens of Putney began to wonder what exactly was going on up at the Noyes farm.

George and Mary Cragin, a revivalist couple from New York City, were among the first Perfectionists to join Noyes in Putney. George was a buttoned-up Grahamite who, before his conversion to Perfectionism, had worked as an editor on the *Advocate of Moral Reform*, a paper that tracked signs of "moral decay" such as the rise of pornography and women working outside the home. The *Advocate*, which exemplified a certain strain of female-led, teetotaling, nineteenth-century reformism, singled out Noyesian Perfectionism for special abuse, calling it "a refinement of wickedness which puts papacy to the blush." It was George's wife, Mary, a schoolteacher with passionate religious feelings, who steered the couple toward Perfectionism. Although a surviving portrait of Mary Cragin shows a dour, large-eared woman with severely parted hair and thin lips, Noyes recalled her as being deeply sensuous. He called her a second Mary Magdalene. "Her spirit," he wrote, "[was] exceedingly intoxicating—one that will make a man crazy."

By 1846, Noyes had begun to wonder whether there might be a reciprocal relationship between the coming of God's kingdom and the abolition of marriage. If free love was going to define life in the millennium, maybe free love would help trigger the millennium.

On a pleasant evening in May, Noyes and Mary Cragin took a stroll on the farm in Putney. At a "lonely place" they sat on a rock to chat. "All the circumstances invited advance in freedom," Noyes recalled, "and yielding to the impulse upon me I took some personal liberties. The temptation to go further was tremendous. But at this point came serious thoughts. I stopped and revolved in mind as before God what to do. I said to myself, 'I will not steal.' After a moment we arose and went toward home. On the way we lingered. But I said, 'No, I am going home to report what we have done.'"

Back at the main house, Noyes and Cragin sat down with their spouses to discuss the incident as a group. After some hesitation, Harriet Noyes and George Cragin, both of whom had already expressed a special spiritual affection for each other in letters, consented to go along with what their spouses had commenced. All four agreed to merge their two marriages into a single union. "The last part of the interview was as amicable and happy as a wedding," Noyes recalled, "and the consequence was that we gave each other full liberty."

The practice of what Noyes dubbed "complex marriage" soon

spread, first to the Noyes siblings and their spouses and then to a few other central members of the community. They considered it a logical extension of the intense collectivism they had cultivated. They already had communism in the kitchen and the workshop. Now they had it in the bedroom. To the small circle of initiates, Noyes counseled "Bible secretiveness." They should not lie, but they could withhold the truth.

This fledgling experiment in sexual liberty was hardly a swinging free-for-all. Only two-person heterosexual couplings were permitted. Every liaison had to have the consent of Noyes and all other relevant parties. Secrecy was strictly forbidden, as was monogamy, which the Perfectionists derisively called "special love." The arrangement was indeed *complex*.

In the coming decades, as more and more people were wed into the communal marriage, the philosophical and theological underpinnings of complex marriage became more elaborate. The Perfectionists eventually came to identify sex as the holiest of human acts—simultaneously an expression of love for God, a path to transcendence, a medium of spiritual edification, and a means of dissolving the covetousness and isolation that reign in the World.

The Region of Easy Rowing

Group marriage was actually Noyes's second erotic innovation. Like Ann Lee, who took up her "cross against the flesh" in the wake of several wrenching stillbirths, Noyes began to experiment with family planning after Harriet delivered four premature infants, all of whom died quickly. (They had one surviving child, a son named Theodore.) In 1844, two years before John's first dalliance with Mary Cragin, he and Harriet began practicing "male continence"—sex in which the man does not climax, within or without.

The genesis of male continence goes back to New Harmony. In 1831, Robert Dale Owen, still resident at his father's shuttered utopia, wrote an influential pamphlet titled *Moral Physiology* that created a scandal by distinguishing between sex for pleasure ("amative") and sex for reproduction ("propagative"). Owen suggested that when pleasure is the main object, people ought to practice coitus interruptus (withdrawal).*

Noyes reviewed Owen's pamphlet approvingly in his own paper. "It is as foolish and cruel," he believed, "to expend one's seed on a wife merely for the sake of getting rid of it as it would be to fire a gun at one's best friend merely for the sake of unloading it." But unlike Robert Dale Owen, Noyes was too committed to the Bible to endorse "spilling" one's "vital powers." Along with coitus interruptus, this ruled out the "French method" (condoms) and masturbation, which Noyes called "the most atrocious robbery of which man can be guilty; a robbery for which God slew Onan."

Along with Owen's pamphlet on birth control, Noyes studied Shaker texts on abstinence. He was keen to underscore the doctrinal similarities between the seemingly opposite practices of his community and the Shakers. "The 'system' of Male Continence," he insisted to a skeptical public, "has more real affinity with Shakerism than Owenism. It is based on self-control, as Shakerism is based on self-denial."

Noyes explained the practical operation of male continence with a vivid analogy:

The situation may be compared to a stream in three conditions, viz., 1, a fall, 2, a course of rapids above the fall, and 3, still water above the rapids. The skillful boatman may choose whether he will remain in the still water, or venture more or less down the rapids, or run his boat over the fall. But there is a point on the verge of the fall where he has no control over his course; and just above that there is a point where he will have to struggle with the current in a way which will give his nerves a severe trial, even though he may escape the fall. If he is willing to learn, experience

---

* The publication of Robert Dale Owen's treatise on "the population question" is still considered a watershed moment in the history of family planning. Owen père, who had been greatly interested in Malthus and the specter of overpopulation, later helped introduce the vaginal sponge in England.

will teach him the wisdom of confining his excursions to the region of easy rowing, unless he has an object in view that is worth the cost of going over the falls.

Having uncoupled pleasure from procreation, the Perfectionist men and women spent the next few decades collectively refining their skills in the bedroom. Lingering in "the region of easy rowing," it turned out, greatly extended sex. While the Perfectionist men diligently avoided "the propagative crisis," the women of the community reportedly enjoyed satisfying orgasms during hour-long bouts of lovemaking. According to one woman's recollection, the preferred sexual position within the community was with the man beside or behind the woman, so he could pleasure her with his hands. At a time when the subject of female eroticism was entirely taboo, Perfectionist women were encouraged to speak frankly about their likes and dislikes.

Trample Under Foot the Domestic and Pecuniary Fashions of the World

On the evening of June 1, 1847, Noyes announced an important shift in his thinking about how the millennium would begin. "The Kingdom of God," he told his assembled community, "will be established here not in a formal, dramatic way, but by a process like that which brings the seasonal spring." As human society approaches perfection, the millennium will gradually blossom. As far as Noyes was concerned, his small community in Putney had already gone a long way toward that end. "We have been able to cut our way through the isolation and selfishness in which the mass of men exist, and have attained a position in which before heaven and earth we trample under foot the domestic and pecuniary fashions of the world. Separate households, property exclusiveness have come to an end with us." The fact that the Perfectionists had successfully overcome so much of what was wrong with the world—monogamy and private property, in particular—proved that, in a subtle way, the kingdom had *already* come. "Is not now the time," Noyes asked, "for us to commence the testimony that the Kingdom of God has come?"

By then, the Perfectionists had developed the habit of voting on almost everything. After Noyes's sermon, he asked the community to consider an unusual resolution. Therefore be it resolved: "The Kingdom of Heaven has come." The vote in favor was unanimous. And so it came to pass that the glad millennium foretold by the Hebrew mystics was kicked off American style—by a show of hands. At the precise moment that the vote was taken, a clap of thunder shook the house. The Perfectionists took it as divine affirmation; the millennium had begun.

A month later, a Putney woman named Harriet Hall who had been bedridden for eight years with a mysterious ailment sent for Noyes. Hall could not walk and could barely see. The slightest movement caused her great pain. For three hours, Noyes and Mary Cragin prayed and spoke with her about salvation. Enthralled, Hall told Noyes that she would do whatever he commanded. He ordered her to sit up. She did. He told her to stand. She did. Mary Cragin raised the window shade, and for once, the daylight did not hurt Hall's eyes. News of this miraculous cure—the most compelling of several faith healings attributed to Noyes—spread among New York and New England Perfectionists, helping secure Noyes's position as the leading man of American Perfectionism.

In the wake of this widely reported cure, the citizens of Putney began turning against the Perfectionists. Matters were made worse when one of Noyes's brothers-in-law attempted to convert a local fifteen-year-old named Lucinda Lamb—one of "the flowers of the village." Lamb's father, who originally consented to her worshipping with the Perfectionists, suddenly changed his mind. Around the same time, a local Methodist minister named Hubbard Eastman began agitating against the community. He wrote a thick volume titled *Noyesism Unveiled: A History of the Sect Self-Styled Perfectionists,* which identified Noyes as "a hideous monster of iniquity" and called his small community "as corrupt and shameless as THE MOTHER OF HARLOTS AND ABOMINATIONS."

Noyes then made a crucial misjudgment. He tried to initiate Daniel Hall, husband of the faith-healed Harriet, into the privileges of complex marriage. Disgusted, Hall rode to Brattleboro to file a complaint with the state's attorney. A warrant was issued, and on October 26, 1847, Noyes was arrested and charged with having "carnal knowledge" of two women not his wife.

There was a preliminary hearing in the local tavern. After freely admitting to having sex with the women, Noyes was released on a $2,000 bond. Before the actual trial commenced, Larkin Mead, one of John's non-Perfectionist brothers-in-law, learned that the state intended to prosecute Noyes and several of his male followers to the full extent of the law. Mead also heard disturbing rumors of a plan to drive the Perfectionists from Putney by force. Despite the fact that he had personally paid Noyes's substantial bond, Mead advised his brother-in-law to jump bail and leave Vermont at once.* Reluctantly, Noyes conceded. Those Perfectionists who were not originally from Putney scattered, too, awaiting counsel from their fugitive prophet.

Oneida

In a shallow, secluded valley at the center of the Burned-over District, a Perfectionist couple named Jonathan and Lorinda Burt lived on a forty-acre woodlot, bounded on three sides by a wide, bell-shaped curve in Oneida Creek. The land was part of a reserve held by the Oneida tribe

---

* Mead, the lawyer with whom Noyes apprenticed in his early twenties, was married to Mary Noyes, one of the siblings who never accepted John as her "spiritual father." The Meads maintained cordial relations with John, but they were generally regarded as the respectable branch of the family. Their son Larkin Goldsmith Mead was a highly celebrated sculptor; he designed Lincoln's tomb. His brother William was an influential architect—the middle partner in the famous firm of McKim, Mead & White. Their sister Elinor married the critic William Dean Howells.

until 1840, when the state of New York bought it and began selling plots to white settlers. There were a few small farms near the Burts' place, but it was wild, densely forested country. Along with three other couples, the Burts lived much as the Shakers had during the early years at Niskeyuna. They shared two farmhouses and some old Indian cabins, operated a sawmill, and gathered nightly around the flame of their Perfectionist faith.

When Burt heard that the Putney community had been scattered, he invited Noyes to come stay. Noyes, who had previously met Burt at a Perfectionist conference, visited the land and liked what he saw. Compared with the nosy, puritanical village of Putney, the wilderness of central New York—home to Shakers, Mormons, Millerites, Fourierists, and plenty of Perfectionists—was a heretic's paradise, a Penn's Woods for the nineteenth century.

Noyes's abiding sense of biblical drama was aroused by the thought of leading his people into the wilderness. He sent a letter to George Cragin announcing that he had found the perfect place for their "spiritual phalanx." "There is some romance," he wrote, "in beginning our community in the log huts of the Indians." Over time, Noyes wrote, they could build themselves a Perfectionist "chateau." Having just jumped bail in Vermont, he probably noted the convenient proximity of the Canadian border.

On the evening of March 1, 1848—while the Icarian avant-garde crossed the Atlantic—the nucleus of the Putney community arrived by train at the Oneida depot. As a heavy snow fell, they traveled the three miles to their new home by sleigh. Other Perfectionists trickled in over the next few months. They pooled their money, bought the land adjacent to Burt's property, and named their new community the Oneida Association.

Even before the Putney believers showed up, the region around Oneida Lake was a hotbed of Perfectionism. About 40 percent of the subscribers to Noyes's *Witness* lived in the Burned-over District, and three-quarters of them lived within thirty miles of Oneida Lake. When these people heard that a Perfectionist community was being started, many were eager to join. A year after Noyes's arrival, there were a hundred people living on the property. In three years, there were more than two hundred.

The people who came were mostly artisans. Among the first wave were printers, cabinetmakers, tinkers, shoemakers, coopers, bakers, and carpenters. Only a few were farmers. The majority entered the community as families or as couples in their twenties and thirties. New members may have been aware of the scandal in Putney, but most did not know about the doctrine of complex marriage. Whatever drew them to Oneida, it wasn't libidinous curiosity.*

Whereas many of the Owenite and Fourierist communities had been divided over secondary issues such as "Sabbath breaking" and vegetarianism, the Oneida Community was blessed from the outset with a population unified by their strong faith in Noyes's socioreligious doctrines. While small utopias often suffocate under reams of bylaws, Noyes insisted that the proliferation of written rules—what he called "legalism"— was anathema to Perfectionism. He claimed that the descent of Christianity into "the Apostasy"—the long, dark age between the demise of the primitive church and the birth of his own community— paralleled the rise of a bureaucratic, rule-making religious establishment and the subsequent atrophy of the living inspiration.† He believed that written ordinances inevitably muffle the small voice of inspiration that is the only true authority.

Noyes did not have a monopoly on revelation. The Oneida colonists believed that God could speak through the community as a unified whole, that inspiration—or "afflatus," as they called it—was often a collective experience. While Noyes generally had the final word on matters of religious doctrine, most major decisions—what type of home to

---

* In later years, when the community's sexual doctrines were well publicized, the Perfectionists went to great lengths to weed out applicants drawn chiefly by the community's "social privileges." They did not always succeed.

† Noyes found scriptural sanction for this idea in the fact that Saint Paul, in his effort to institutionalize Christianity, basically cleared the books of many Jewish laws. Of course, Paul was also a great font of written, institutional theology.

build, which industries to pursue, where to dig the privy—were settled by lively, community-wide debate. Meetings were held daily, and consensus was the constant goal. As a leader, it was Noyes's habit to appoint lieutenants (both men and women) to oversee practical matters. During the early years at Oneida, John Miller, the husband of Noyes's sister Charlotte, did much of the daily administration of the community, freeing Noyes to think and write.

By the start of 1849, the Oneida Association owned 160 acres of woods, swamp, and pasture. They set up a shoemaking shop, a smithy, new mills, a farm, and a community store. No wages were paid. Room, board, child care, and education were considered compensation for all the labor performed. The early years were lean. The settlers cleared stone from their fields, built walls, and drained the boggy areas near the creek. Food—at first mostly coarse bread, milk, beans, and potatoes— was limited. During the first summer, dysentery swept through the community.

Nineteenth-century American utopianism is often understood as a long, slow conversation between, on the one hand, millenarian sects such as the Shakers and the Rappites and, on the other hand, secular utopians such as Owen, Cabet, and Fourier.* The religious sects—inspired by the Bible's account of primitive Christianity and the practical demands of rural separatism—created a communal prototype that the secular visionaries blended with Enlightenment-born ideas about rational planning, gender equality, and social progress. At Oneida, where the Perfectionists studied both Fourier and the Old Testament, the pendulum swung in the opposite direction; the utopian socialists helped inspire a community devoted principally to spiritual ends.

Noyes saw a direct connection between the rise of his community and the ebb of American Fourierism. "The Oneida Community owes

---

* *Secular,* not atheistic. None of these theorists denied the existence of God, and except for Owen, they all identified themselves as Christians. Their theories are secular because their dominant preoccupation was social reform, not salvation or Apocalypse.

much to Brook Farm," he wrote. "Look at the Dates. Brook Farm deceased in October 1847. The Oneida Community commenced in November 1847. It is a simple case of transmigration, or in the latest language, persistence of force." Later, he called Oneida the "continuation" of Brook Farm. Noyes thought that the utopian socialists had failed for many reasons, but chief among them was their neglect of God. He wrote, "Owen, Ripley, Fourier, [and] Cabet . . . left God out of their tale and they came to nothing."

The Fourierist phalanxes had mostly been organized as joint-stock corporations. The Oneida Community, like the Shaker villages and the various Icarias, opted for "communism pure and simple." Private property was totally abolished. New members sold everything they owned—homes, land, animals—and put the proceeds into a common pot. A record was kept of what everyone contributed, and when a member left, as more than a few did, they were refunded their initial contribution, without interest. The land at Oneida, as well as the livestock, the tools, the linens, and the food, was collectively owned. Even pocket watches belonged to the commonwealth. Unlike at New Harmony and the North American Phalanx, nobody wrote down who ate what. If a woman needed a dress, one was made from the common stock of calico or bought with common cash. When a Perfectionist invented a marketable product, the profits went to the collective. Of course, the most extreme expression of this commitment to radical, all-encompassing collectivism was the sexual communism of complex marriage, in which every adult man in the community was understood to be married to every adult woman.

Brisbane and Ripley claimed that the constraints built into pure communism posed an unacceptable threat to individual liberty. In doing so, they defined freedom in the usual American sense, as the absence of external constraints, what Isaiah Berlin termed "negative liberty." Noyes thought this conception of freedom was wrongheaded. He called it the freedom of the porcupine—the right of people to stay away from one another. As an alternative to the freedom of the porcupine, Noyes offered "the liberty of communism," which he defined as the freedom "to approach one another and to love one another." In a very practical sense, this "liberty of communism" also meant freedom from uncertainty, hunger, and solitude.

Like Ripley, Noyes expected his community to resolve the antithesis between individual liberty and mutual aid. He wrote: "The two great principles of human existence, *solidarity* on the one side, *liberty* on the other, are in their nature harmonious, although the forces concerned in them are apparently antagonistic, like the centripetal and centrifugal forces in nature. They are designed to act upon human life in equilibrium. . . . The philosophy of Christ and of reason, teaches that liberty is the result of solidarity; that we are not to seek liberty directly, but to seek first solidarity, and liberty as the fruit of it."

Noyes used the term *Bible Communism* to describe every aspect of his philosophy, from the abolition of private property to complex marriage. While the coupling of the words *Bible* and *communism* was less jarring before the advent of explicitly "godless" communism, there was already a measure of hostility between socialists and revivalists in the middle nineteenth century.* Noyes found this antipathy baffling. To him, the acquisitive, tooth-and-claw nature of capitalism was patently irreconcilable with the teachings of Jesus and the example of the primitive church. Like every generation of radical Christians, Noyes read the New Testament as a manifesto for upending the existing social order. "When the Spirit of Truth pricked three thousand men to the heart and converted them on the day of Pentecost," he wrote, "its next effect was to resolve them into one family and introduce Communism of property. Thus the greatest of all Revivals was also the great inauguration of Socialism."

---

* This early antagonism was not restricted to the United States or Protestantism. In 1846, while Noyes was introducing Bible Communism in Putney, Pope Pius IX issued a papal syllabus denouncing "that infamous doctrine of so-called Communism which is absolutely contrary to the natural law itself, and if once adopted would utterly destroy the rights, property, and possessions of all men, and even society itself."

———

Inspired by Owen's parallelogram and Fourier's phalanstery, the Perfectionists decided that some sort of "unitary dwelling" was essential to their plan of living as one unified family. In 1848, on a low knoll at the center of their estate, they built a wooden, hotel-sized building. Noyes personally laid much of the foundation. After considering and rejecting the terms *phalanstery* and *communistery*, they decided to call the building "the Mansion House." It was an odd choice for a band of separatists living in the wilderness, but it perfectly fit the building and the lifestyle that the Perfectionists created for themselves over the coming decades.

Winter came before the Mansion House was finished. The entire community moved into a single room on the second floor. In the center of the space, they installed a stove and a sitting area. The rest of the room was divided into small "bedrooms" with sheets hung from ropes. For decades, the communists recalled the cozy winter they spent in "the tent room" as a halcyon age of communal harmony and intimacy. For outsiders, this months-long slumber party provided the germ for the absurd but persistent rumor that the Perfectionists all slept in a single bed.

The Mansion House was expanded over the next ten years. In 1860, the three-story building was torn down and replaced with a larger, red-brick structure, also called the Mansion House. The Perfectionists remained in a nearly constant state of demolition and construction. Like all the other utopians of the era, they realized that the shape of rooms and halls defines the shape of social relations. They rearranged their estate with such frequency that a local carpenter suggested they put their buildings on casters. This never-ending pursuit of the ideal physical domain reflected the community's approach to pretty much everything: ceaseless refinement through trial and imagination.

By the 1870s, the Mansion House was huge—a rambling U-shaped complex with slate roofs and a grand, pillared entrance. The building, which enclosed a small grass quad, had two large towers, a cavernous auditorium, and 475 rooms. It looked (and still looks) like the ivied hub of an elite New England college. Most adults slept in their own narrow,

The Mansion House.

cell-like rooms, but every floor had parlors, reading rooms, and libraries, all of which served the community's architectural maxim that "the balance of inducement should always be toward aggregation and not separation."*

A Two-Legged Animal

To the surprise of the Oneida Community's neighbors, Perfectionist women did much of the carpentry on the first Mansion House. At a time when the male and female spheres of labor were drifting apart, the Perfectionists deliberately mixed things up. Men ironed sheets in the laundry; women hammered iron in the metal shop. Noyes can hardly be

---

* In 1870, for the two hundred adults living in the Mansion House, there were 169 separate beds, usually 1 bed per room. When a bed was shared for the night, it was generally by two women or two men. Noyes believed that men and women should not slumber together. "Their coming together should not be to sleep but to edify and enjoy."

counted as a feminist—he claimed nominal allegiance to Saint Paul's chauvinist statements about man's natural dominion over woman—but he believed that "worldly" society made too much of the innate differences between the sexes. The idealized Victorian woman was a paradoxical mix of fragility and fertility. In almost every respect, the feminine ideal at Oneida was that Victorian lady's opposite number. She was supposed to be intellectually assertive, physically robust, sexually frank, and totally indifferent to mothering.

Noyes partly blamed fashion for exaggerating the physical differences between men and women. Women's dress, he wrote, is "a standing lie [that] proclaims that she is not a two-legged animal but something like a churn, standing on castors!" Not long after the Perfectionists arrived in Oneida, Harriet Skinner (Noyes's sister), Harriet Noyes, and Mary Cragin gathered to design a less churnlike costume for themselves. The result was a long-sleeved blouse and a matching knee-length skirt worn over loose "pantalets." They called it "the uniform of a vital society." After some snickering, all of the women in the community adopted it. This so-called short dress was soon supplemented with elastic sneakers, which, like true utopians, they called "the final shoe." After a group of Perfectionist women were harassed at Grand Central Terminal, the community began to keep a few traditional dresses on hand for traveling.

Despite a midcentury vogue for elaborate updos, the women at Oneida cut their hair shoulder length or shorter, a style then associated with adolescent girls. While their sisters in the World routinely spent an hour arranging combs, pins, and extensions atop their heads, the women of Oneida boasted that they went directly from bed to the breakfast table. "Any fashion which requires women to devote considerable time to hair-dressing," they announced in the community paper, "is a degradation and a nuisance."* Having freed themselves from the

---

* The fashion for short women's hair at Oneida put Noyes's reforming instincts at odds with his beloved Saint Paul. In his first letter to the Corinthians (1 Cor. 11:15–

tyranny of girdles, toe-binding boots, and waist-length hair, the Perfectionist women were able to participate fully in the physically active life of the community.

While the community came under constant attack for its economic and sexual communism, nothing seemed to excite as much outrage as the appearance of female Perfectionists. Among outsiders, it was stated as a matter of settled fact that the women of Oneida were ugly. The evidence given for this supposed homeliness says more about the tastes of the day than the relative good looks of the communists. Compared with the tottering, neurasthenic delicacy that was then regarded as the height of feminine beauty, the hardworking, sports-playing women of Oneida were seen as unattractively tan and hale. Uncorseted, they lacked the stiffness of carriage expected of fashionable women.

The women of Oneida claimed that their outdoorsy, teetotaling, childless existence kept them young. "We women of thirty are often mistaken for Misses [because] we are saved from so much care and vexation." When they read about the new trend of "enameling"—a practice in which the female face was plastered with a rigid layer of putty and then painted over in red and white—they were horrified. "People sneer at our dress, and talk slightingly of our looks, but, alas! They know not what they say. We have no 'heavers,' nor 'plumpers,' nor 'false calves,' nor 'rouge'; and perhaps we don't look as well as your city belle who is puffed and padded and painted; but we are *genuine* from head to foot."

Although the Perfectionists practiced many of the social reforms that were only being discussed elsewhere, they felt surprisingly little kinship

---

16), Paul wrote that it is "a glory" for women to have long hair (and a "shame" for men). As always, Noyes found a work-around. Paul's object, he claimed, "is not ornament but a covering." Since, according to the then popular "science" of phrenology, the libido is housed in the back of the head, Noyes claimed that the Victorian updo was actually less modest than the "down in the neck" style that the Perfectionist women wore.

with secular reformers, even when those reformers were their neigh-bors.* The year that the community moved to Oneida, Lucretia Mott, Elizabeth Cady Stanton, Frederick Douglass, and a group of progres-sive female Quakers met at nearby Seneca Falls for the convention that launched the crusade for women's suffrage. While tracts by the likes of Stanton and Susan B. Anthony circulated in the Mansion House library—and Anthony actually visited the community—the commu-nists insisted that their feminism derived from revelation and their own experimentation, not the "imported ideas" of "worldly reformers." In the 1860s, a group of community women started an "express service" to convey visitors and packages back and forth between the mansion and the nearby train depot. The venture presented local non-Perfectionists with the jarring sight of "unattended" women in sporty dresses and childlike haircuts loading parcels, wrangling horses, and op-erating a prosperous enterprise. The community journal described the venture as a triumph for "women's rights" but put the phrase—a new-comer in the national lexicon—between scare quotes, adding: " 'Wom-an's Rights,' is a term we always prefer to quote as borrowed; it is not indigenous in the nomenclature of the Community."

Like almost all nineteenth-century utopians, the Perfectionists be-lieved that the narrow, superseding loyalties engendered by marriage and the biological family were anathema to progress, particularly fe-male liberation. Owen identified marriage as the main impediment to female equality. Fourier called it "the germ of falsity and immorality." The Shakers, by deed if not declaration, seemed to agree. Noyes hoped that complex marriage would free women from both matrimony and motherhood, thereby revealing capacities obscured by their traditional status as chattel. Under the Oneida system, he wrote, "women are not men's slaves, but loosened from the bondage of marriage, are set free to criticize men and express their own tastes and feelings."

---

* By contrast, Frederick Evans, the New Harmonian turned Shaker elder, was per-fectly happy to strike up alliances with "worldly" progressives on issues such as social-ism, women's rights, abolitionism, animal cruelty, and nonviolence.

The Infantile Population

Complex marriage did away with the idea that women are the property of their husbands. Male continence freed them, for better or worse, from motherhood. The Perfectionists' ongoing effort to prevent insemination did not reflect any sort of Malthusian scruples or religious opposition to breeding. "We are not opposed, after the Shaker fashion or even after [Robert Dale] Owen's fashion, to the increase of the population," Noyes wrote. "We are opposed to *random procreation which is unavoidable in the marriage system.*" In fact, male continence was one of the few things at Oneida that lacked an elaborate theological underpinning. The Perfectionists spoke about birth control in familiar terms. It was a matter of health, practical economy, and women's rights. A community notice from 1858 declared that "child-bearing, when it is undertaken, should be a voluntary affair, one in which the choice of the mother, and the sympathy of all good influences should concur. Our principles accord to woman a just and righteous freedom in this particular, and however strange such an idea may seem now, the time cannot be distant when any other idea or practice will be scorned as essential barbarism."

The community's unusual method of birth control was surprisingly effective. Among roughly two hundred sexually busy adults, there was, on average, about one accidental pregnancy each year, a rate that compares favorably with that of modern birth control pills.* Those few men

---

* Outside critics claimed that the practice of male continence would produce sterile men and physically stunted women. One visiting obstetrician worried about the consequences of depriving so many women of "the sedative and relaxing seminal fluid." To refute these sorts of pseudoscientific claims, the Perfectionists kept exacting health records. In 1877, Theodore Noyes, by then a Yale-educated physician, invited a gynecologist to examine the women of the community for an article in the *American Journal of Obstetrics*. The doctor was surprised to find that the women of the community were exceptionally healthy. He did note two interesting anomalies. Fifty-seven percent of the women who grew up at Oneida began menstruating a full two years earlier than their peers in the surrounding area, and the Perfectionist women were, on average, significantly bustier than other American women.

who were unable to master male continence were paired with those women who were, in the poignant euphemism of the day, "past the time of life." In 1852, the *Circular* boasted that "the increase of population by birth, in our forty families, for the last four years, has been considerably less than the progeny of Queen Victoria alone."[*]

Until 1869, when the community began its experiment in controlled breeding, most of the children at Oneida were brought into the community when their parents converted. They were raised collectively. Infants were reared and nursed by their biological mothers until fifteen months. From then until they turned twelve, they lived in "the Children's House," where specially assigned nurses, teachers, and guardians looked after them. Those babies who were born in the Mansion House, either by accident or by special dispensation, were formally welcomed into the fold with a community-wide naming ceremony. Their biological parents would suggest a name, and then the entire community would approve it in "recognition of the Community sponsorship" of the child.

Parents usually maintained a close relationship with their offspring, but excessive intimacy was discouraged. The sin of demonstrating too much parental attachment was known as "philoprogenitiveness," and it was considered "as blind a passion as ever [romantic] love was represented to be." So-called special love, either between lovers or between a parent and a child, was thought to turn the individual away from God and community. For women, motherhood was considered an overwhelming distraction from "self-culture and the appetite for universal improvement." Of course, many people found these prohibitions painful. Some left because of them. Others welcomed communal loving and communal parenting as a liberation and a means of advancing real gender equality.

Inside the Children's House, young Perfectionists were actively communized. To foster the "Pentecostal spirit," their homemade dolls, wag-

---

[*] The monarch whose fecundity and virtue named the era had nine children.

ons, and hobbyhorses were held collectively in one room. In community publications, the children are invariably described as a "herd" or "flock." They sang together, learned their numbers together, and went boating together at the community's lake house. Adult Perfectionists turned out in big numbers to watch the "weekly ablution of the infantile population."

As the community prospered, the Children's House became increasingly deluxe. A large, steam-heated playroom was outfitted with indoor seesaws, balance beams, swings, and a miniaturized wood shop in which a group of boys attempted to build themselves a "flying machine." During the winter, the children joined the adults in skating on the millpond or sledding on a hill that was specially graded for that purpose. They gave speeches and performances in the auditorium of the Mansion House. On one evening in 1866, for instance, the "small orchestra" performed the Overture of the Spring Whistle, consisting of "fifteen willow whistles, blown in the most violent manner by fifteen ardent little performers." One community critic noted that, "unlike most musical artists, they soon tired of their own music, and began biting the bark off their own instruments."

While the Perfectionists' views on child rearing can sound refreshingly modern (lots of play, no corporal punishment), their pursuit of a perfected collectivism occasionally produced scenes of alarming fanaticism. The children conducted their own sort of self-governance. In 1851, they raised their small hands in support of a series of resolutions denouncing their homemade dolls as a medium of "the mothering spirit": "This doll-spirit that seduces us from Community spirit in regard to helping the family and that prevents us from being in earnest to get an education is the same spirit that seduces women to allow themselves to be so taken up with their children that they have not time to attend to Christ, and get an education for heaven." After a discussion about their "idolatrous" toys, the children voted to put their dolls to the flame. The little boys were particularly "loud in their clamors for the great massacre." Following the vote, a group of nine- and ten-year-old girls stripped their dolls of the bloomer-style outfits they had sewn for them and, one by one, tossed the toys into the woodstove. When the burning was over, "all hands rejoiced in the condemnation."

Well-Aired and in Rapport
with the World

This so-called Doll Revolution took place around the stove of the small satellite branch that the community established in Brooklyn Heights in 1849, just a year after the inauguration of the upstate colony. John and Harriet Noyes, the Cragins, and other core members of the old Putney "family" left the Mansion House to live in two adjacent town houses on Willow Place, just across the East River from Manhattan. Noyes told his converts that the urban residence would afford him "a more quiet place for reflection, and a better opportunity to act upon the Association than a residence directly in it."

The community in Brooklyn supported itself by manufacturing gold chain. Chain making, which could be done by men, women, and children, was an ideal occupation for the small community. "It is a business," Noyes wrote, "that can employ all classes, and in coincidence with the coming in of the 'golden age,' seems an appropriate introduction of the Association, to the mechanical, manufacturing world."

After the printing shop at Oneida burned down, the community newspaper—by then a triweekly called the *Free Church Circular* (later the *Circular*)—was moved to Brooklyn. By transferring his paper and himself to the nerve center of the American media, Noyes hoped to hasten the spread of Bible Communism.

By the early 1850s, the process that he had set in motion at Oneida—the germination and spread of the millennial social order—seemed to be gaining momentum. Along with the satellite commune in Brooklyn, a group of Perfectionists was living quietly on the old Noyes farm in Putney. A fourth, smaller group shared a house and a chain-making shop in Newark, New Jersey. In 1851, the fifth and largest satellite was established on the Quinnipiac River in Wallingford, Connecticut, near New Haven.

Once in Brooklyn, Noyes quickly established contact with the influential Associationists on the masthead of Greeley's *Tribune*. George Ripley, by then resident in Flatbush, and Charles Sears, president of the NAP, came for dinner at Willow Place in July 1850. Ripley, once lean from his labors at Brook Farm, had grown portly. He and Noyes discussed the woeful state of "civilization" and the exemplary communalism of the Apostolic Church. Ripley, who was still mourning the breakup of Brook Farm, told Noyes that the community had been five hundred years ahead of its time. Noyes responded that his colony in Oneida was a thousand years before its time.

For anyone networking on behalf of utopia, the real prize was Horace Greeley. As Noyes well knew, it was the *Tribune*'s eccentric editor who had transformed American Fourierism from the private obsession of Albert Brisbane and a few progressive intellectuals into an influential national movement. In 1851, Noyes learned that Greeley would be attending the World's Fair in London and figured that he should be there, too. As he told one follower, the fair would be "a Congress of all nations, and it seemed proper that the Kingdom of God should be represented." Noyes found out which ship Greeley would be taking to Liverpool and booked himself a cabin directly beneath Greeley's. The voyage, Noyes told his brother, would afford "a natural and favorable opportunity to get into communication with Greeley. [We] will be shut up together on shipboard for two weeks."

The crossing was unusually stormy. Greeley, who was continuously seasick, rode out the waves in the anteroom of Noyes's cabin. The two men discussed everything from Swedenborg to their divergent understandings of the Second Coming. Although they "crossed swords" over the merits of pure communism, Noyes was flattered to learn that Greeley was well acquainted with Bible Communism and the tenets of complex marriage. Ultimately, Noyes's efforts to convert Greeley were useless. The great editor's utopian enthusiasm had been badly bruised by the unraveling of the Fourierist movement. While the *Tribune* was more supportive of the Perfectionists than most papers, Greeley never promoted Bible Communism with any of the vigor he had spent on Fourier's scheme.

The Oneida Community's newfound proximity to the New York media establishment yielded useful contacts, but it also brought unwelcome attention. In January 1852, the *New York Observer* printed the first of several editorials denouncing the "disgusting order of united adulterers." The paper informed its readers that the "total depravity" of the Perfectionists exceeded "the foulest days and darkest places of Roman Catholic iniquity." Even the reviled polygamists in Utah, the *Observer* noted, had the decency to maintain the "distinction of husband and wife." As usual, the girlish haircuts and sporty costumes of the female Perfectionists—"plainly the germ of *bloomerism!*"—raised as much alarm as the community's "concubinage."

Noyes did not seem to much mind this sort of thing. Except for the early days of "Bible secretiveness" in Putney, he tried to operate his community with total transparency. The Perfectionists sent as much honest information into the world as they could, even mailing a detailed account of their beliefs and practices to their congressional representative, the governor of New York, and various upstate authorities. This commitment to the free flow of information is one of the things that distinguishes Oneida from most separatist enclaves or cults. The information went in both directions. While many religious sects strive to curtail the influence of outside ideas, the Oneida communists actively kept themselves "saturated all the time with worldly influences." The community subscribed to 140 separate publications, including *The Nation*, the *Tribune*, the *Evening Post*, *Harper's*, and even a picture magazine or two. The long reading tables in the Mansion House library were stocked with books representing every possible viewpoint. Noyes wrote that he wanted his community to be "well-aired and in rapport with the world."*

---

* Regarding this insistence on transparency, even the *Observer* had something nice to say: "The Oneida Associationists are honorably contrasted with the Fourierists of this city, who refuse to be held responsible for the consequences to which their doctrines inevitably leads." So according to the *Observer's* loose hierarchy of turpitude,

The World, however, wasn't terribly interested in such an open exchange of ideas. Because moral dudgeon plus sex equals hot copy, the *Observer*'s campaign against the community continued and was picked up by other, lesser papers. Support for the Perfectionists came in the surprising form of Henry James, Sr., one of the richest and best-known literary men in New York. James, who was himself the occasional subject of moralizing editorials in the *Observer*, made two visits to Willow Place. Despite a tense exchange with Noyes—each man found the other impertinent—he took to the pages of the *Tribune* to defend the communists against the "flimsy zeal" of their critics. "It appears to me," James wrote of the *Observer*'s crusade, "about as unmanly a sight as the sun now shines upon, to see a great prosperous newspaper . . . gathering together the two wings of its hebdomadal flatulence, 'secular' and 'religious,' for a doughty descent upon this starveling and harmless fieldmouse!"

A Suitable Marine

At the start of the 1850s, "starveling" was only a slight overstatement of the conditions at Oneida. Along with the gold chain business in Brooklyn, the community upstate was selling flour, celery, apples, strawberries, potatoes, shoes, wheel spokes, scuffle hoes, silk thread, and rustic furniture made from twisty, unmilled wood. Despite this diverse array of ventures, the community was barely making ends meet. The Perfectionists were able to raise most of their own food, but the costs of buying land and building the Mansion House were considerable. They needed a reliable stream of income.

Although none of the Perfectionists had much experience with boats, they decided to try shipping. In February 1850, the community

---

Mormons ranked below Catholics but above Perfectionists, while Fourierists (some of whom happened to staff the *Observer*'s chief rival across town) were at the very bottom.

bought a sloop called the *Rebecca Ford* and began transporting limestone down the Hudson River from Kingston, New York, for resale in Brooklyn and Manhattan. Noyes had high hopes for the new business and its role in the coming of the millennium. "If Printing is the most important art as the medium for uttering truth, Navigation properly stands next in importance, as the means of transporting it. With these two arms, a competent and organized Press, and a suitable Marine, truth is furnished for the conquest of the world."

On a bright, warm day in late July 1851, a group of six Perfectionists, including Mary Cragin and a recent convert named Eliza Allen, boarded the *Rebecca Ford* in Brooklyn. They sailed around the bottom of Manhattan and tacked north up the Hudson. The beautiful weather and the "mixed company" gave the voyage the feel of a pleasure cruise. When they docked at Kingston, the men loaded blocks of gray limestone into the hull. Cragin and Allen cooked and read aloud from the Bible.

When the ship was full, they started back down the river with the wind behind them. Just north of Hyde Park, Cragin called the men to eat. Francis Long, the youngest Perfectionist on board, took the tiller while the other three men went below for lunch.

While they ate, a sudden gust filled the mainsail, pushing the sloop hard over. The men ran up to the deck to help Francis Long. Mary Cragin and Eliza Allen stayed below. The *Rebecca Ford* lurched to the side, dislodging the limestone in the hull and pulling the ship farther over. Water rushed in through the portholes and the sloop capsized. The four men, two of whom couldn't swim, leapt from the deck, clinging to whatever they could find. The crew of a passing schooner plucked them from the water as the *Rebecca Ford* sank. Cragin and Allen were still in the cabin.

On the floor of the Hudson, the ship righted itself. At low tide, the top few feet of the mast protruded above the river. When Noyes arrived the next evening, he rowed out into the river and hung a lantern from the tip of the mast to keep vigil over the drowned women. After nineteen days, the sloop was raised. Cragin and Allen were buried near Hyde Park.

The incident had a powerful effect on Noyes. Addressing the community, he called the two women martyrs for Bible Communism. "[They have] the North River for a grave, the sloop for a coffin, and their short dresses for uniforms; enough for any soldier." In death, Mary Cragin replaced Abigail Merwin as the principal idol of Noyes's romantic devotion. "There is no other woman I loved as I did her," he wrote. After Cragin's death, Noyes never again indulged in the type of "special love" that he taught his followers to reject.

Noyes had gone to Brooklyn intending to spread the Kingdom of God using the same communitarian program attempted by Owen, Fourier, and Cabet—building a prototype colony and then encouraging its replication with propaganda. After the sinking of the *Rebecca Ford*, with the community's finances badly strained, Noyes shifted tack. He decided to focus his energy on perfecting Bible Communism in one location. As his son Theodore wrote, he wanted to "see and show how much God can do for man and society on a single spot." The Oneida Community sold its property in Brooklyn and closed the satellite enclaves in Vermont and New Jersey. The scattered Perfectionists convened in Oneida and, to a lesser extent, Wallingford.

As was his tendency, Noyes interpreted his private trauma as a turning point in human history, a station along the ascent into the millennium. The Oneida Community had already defeated "the domestic and pecuniary fashions of the world." Following the shipwreck, Noyes aimed higher. "Mrs. Cragin's death will lead me to overcome death just as Abigail Merwin's marriage stimulated me to break up the marriage system."*

---

* In Genesis (3:22), after Adam and Eve eat from the Tree of Knowledge of Good and Evil, God hustles them out of Paradise, "lest [Adam] put forth his hand, and take also of the tree of life, and eat, and live for ever." By restoring humanity to its sinless, pre-Fall condition, Noyes expected to taste the fruit of that second tree.

Where Every Dish Is Free
to Every Guest

By the 1860s, with three hundred people living at Oneida and Wallingford, the Perfectionists' struggle against "the marriage system" was
going surprisingly well. While moralizing critics described the community as an "orgy" or "brothel" or "harem" or "seraglio" or "whoredom," the Perfectionists insisted upon their own conservatism. Their
erotic delight, they pointed out, came with all the usual pledges and
sacrifices of the marriage bed. Any two Oneida lovers, by dint of their
membership in the community, were obligated to support each other
through sickness and health, to hold all of their wealth in common, and
to care for any offspring born of their coupling.*

During her jailhouse vision in Manchester, Ann Lee came to believe
that sex was humanity's original sin. Noyes had a different theory. He
claimed that Adam and Eve's real offense was shame, as evidenced by
their nude dash behind the shrubbery when they heard God coming.†
"In a holy community," Noyes wrote, "there is no more reason why
sexual intercourse should be restricted by law, than why eating or drinking should be—and there is as little occasion for shame in the one case
as in the other." Sex, as practiced within the community, was understood as a sacrament—"a more perfect symbol of [a union with Christ]
than eating bread and drinking wine," as Noyes put it. Speaking with a
group of (presumably blushing) Shakers at Watervliet, Jonathan Burt

---

* The usual term for what went on at Oneida was and is "free love." The Perfectionists claimed to have introduced that phrase into circulation, and Noyes used it for
many years, including in the Oneida Community's first official "Theocratic Platform." Later, the community disavowed the term to underscore the distinction between complex marriage and other, freer forms of free love. While the Oneida
communists tried to shake off the term *free love*, non-Noyesian Perfectionists, notably
the acolytes of Charles Grandison Finney at Oberlin, started dropping the designation *Perfectionist* owing to its association with the community in Oneida.
† After "Where are you?" Jehovah's second, angry post-apple question is: "Who told
thee that thou wast naked?"

called the human genitals "the highest instruments of praise and worship in the heavenly world." The notion that loving other people is a
way to express and perfect the love of God is hardly radical; the Perfectionists simply removed the distinction between agape and eros.

Noyes claimed that "making of twain one flesh" is a form of spiritual dialogue, "a medium of magnetic and spiritual interchange." Every
adult in the community was loosely ranked according to a system of
"ascending" and "descending fellowship." To hasten spiritual growth,
novices were encouraged to go to bed with those who were more enlightened.* In practice, this meant that the young or recently converted
slept with older, more experienced Perfectionists. Noyes occupied the
top of this pyramid of "ascending fellowship." For years, he considered
it his duty to sexually initiate many of the young women in the community.

It is tempting to interpret this one fact as the true, secret core of the
entire Oneida story, to see everything else—Bible Communism, the
Kingdom of God, the first-century Advent of Christ, all of it—as a
dazzling sideshow to the real business of satisfying a brilliant creep with
a hankering for outspoken tomboys and suppressed orgasms. The relationship between Noyes and the women of the community—their
seemingly genuine attraction to him, his advanced views on female capacity, his apparent lack of interest in any form of sexual monopoly—
thwarts such a simple conclusion. And at Oneida, unlike at so many
other sexed-up religious enclaves, the May–December loving went both
ways. "Spiritually ascendant" older women erotically baptized teenage
boys. Given that the mechanics of male continence were difficult for
young men to master, receiving their sexual education from postmeno-
pausal women offered one practical benefit: there could be no risk of an
unplanned pregnancy.

Once people had adequate mastery over their orgasms, they enjoyed

---

* The idea that wisdom or virtue is somehow sexually transmitted—usually from the
old and wise to the young and nubile—is not unique to Oneida. The most obvious
analogue is the *paiderastia* of ancient Athens.

a good deal of latitude in selecting their own lovers, provided they never showed signs of "exclusive" or "special" love.* "The new command-ment," Noyes preached, "is that we love one another, not by pairs, as in the world, but en masse." Since sex cultivated the spirit, sex with many partners cultivated the broadest spirituality. "Variety is, in the nature of all things, as beautiful and useful in love as in eating and drinking." If two people seemed overly attached to each other and began to refuse other comers, they would probably face criticism. In extreme cases, one lover might be called away to work in Wallingford.

The usual procedure for initiating a tryst was for the man to make his interest known to a third party, typically an older woman. If both parties were in accord, the man would visit the woman's room at bed-time for a "social interview." (In the Perfectionist lexicon, "social" al-most always meant sexual.) This system was meant to serve as a check against secrecy and to allow people to gracefully decline an unwanted invitation. Everyone was theoretically free to decline any lover, but in practice, the system was probably subject to the byzantine power dy-namics of ascending and descending fellowship. If an attractive young person declined some influential older suitor, he or she might be criti-cized for excessive attention to another, younger lover.

Fourier spoke of establishing a "sexual minimum" as a form of erotic welfare for the underpleasured. The Perfectionists likewise tried to en-sure that nobody's needs were neglected. When Noyes believed that the young men of the community were overlooking certain ladies, he urged them to be "liberal and diffusive" in their attentions to the other sex. "Let us consider whether we may not do good, get good, and feel good by drawing nearer than we have to certain worthy young ladies whose charms have not yet been fully appreciated, such as L.B.R. and N." He also reminded them not to forget about their elders. "Let us be heroes in love, and train our hearts to scale the heights above as well as to enjoy

---

* Same-sex couplings were not discussed, let alone sanctioned. However, it does seem likely that a community that blurred rigid Victorian gender norms and offered a form of family life without heterosexual matrimony held a certain appeal for lesbians and gay men.

the beauties of our own level." At one point, Noyes considered staging live sex shows for the spiritual edification of those Perfectionists who were too old or infirm to partake in complex marriage.* The idea never got off the ground.

While these arrangements seem risqué now, they were mind-boggling at the time. Contemporaneous critics could not even bring themselves to *describe* the system they sought to censure. One national incident, wholly unrelated to Oneida, suffices to convey the semihysterical prudery of the middle nineteenth century. The year that Noyes was converted at Putney, all but one member of President Andrew Jackson's cabinet resigned, most of them at the insistence of their wives, in protest over the fact that John Eaton, Jackson's friend and secretary of war, had too hastily married the recently widowed Peggy Timberlake. (There were rumors that Eaton and Timberlake conducted a romance prior to her husband's death.) The so-called Petticoat Affair fixated the nation for months and brought the federal government to its knees.† The year after the scandal, Frances Trollope helped spread the notion that American housewives had taken to draping cloth skirting over the legs of their pianos to conceal the titillating sight of a high-gloss mahogany calf.

Talking Cure

The purpose of the Oneida Children's House was to raise a generation of enlightened Bible Communists who were untainted by the old thinking and old habits of their parents. Until that generation came of age, the Perfectionists needed to build their paradise with secondhand

---

* Fourier had proposed the establishment of "museum orgies" to refine the erotic sensibility of the general population.
† The scandal also had a lasting effect on the Republic. Because the widower Martin Van Buren lacked a moralizing wife, he was free to join President Jackson in his lonely support of the scandal-plagued Eatons, thus securing his place as Jackson's anointed successor.

materials—namely, themselves, ordinary people formed amid the folly of the World. Life inside the Mansion House placed those people under extraordinarily trying circumstances. What could be more volatile than a remote, crowded mansion dedicated to sexual and economic experimentation? Lesser communities have fallen apart over dirty dishes and gardening. How did the Perfectionists—several hundred men and women handicapped by the usual assortment of vices and hang-ups— thrive under such unusual social arrangements?

Part of the answer clearly lies in Noyes's powerful charisma. There is no limit to what a compelling individual can get people to do once he or she is draped in the mantle of divine inspiration. Many people, even nonbelievers, attested to Noyes's disarming intelligence and wide-eyed magnetism. Charisma, however, requires proximity (or some technological approximation thereof), and Noyes spent almost half of his time away from the main community. During the early years, he was often in Brooklyn. Later, he spent much of his time at the Wallingford branch, where the community had established a profitable cutlery works.

Another reason for the Perfectionists' willingness and ability to live under such unusual conditions lies in the nature of the era. For many Americans in the middle of the nineteenth century, the shape of things to come was a question mark. Old ways were crumbling, and nobody could say with much authority what tomorrow would look like. This was especially true in central New York, where the rate of social change was accelerated by immigration, a supercharged economy, and a profusion of new faiths. The indistinct future loosened people's commitment to the mores of their parents. Reasonable people considered ideas that would sound outrageous at other times.

While Noyes's personality and the general uncertainty of the era contributed to the community's success, the biggest reason the Perfectionists were able to maintain communal harmony despite such fraught circumstances was institutional: a form of weekly group therapy that they called "mutual criticism." At Andover Theological Seminary, Noyes's only confidants had been a group of earnest young men who called themselves "the Brethren." Most of them were studying to be missionaries in Africa, the East Indies, and Asia. Among the disappointingly "professional" seminarians, the Brethren came closest to matching John's revivalist fervor. In a spirit of merciless self-improvement, they periodically sat together in a circle and took turns criticizing one another. Each man would sit silently while his classmates searchingly analyzed his every flaw. At Putney, Noyes initiated a similar practice among his followers, and by the time the community relocated to Oneida, regular sessions of mutual criticism had become a central pillar of Bible Communism.

Converts found the experience uncomfortable at first. It is easy to write off the criticism of a single person, but it is nearly impossible to gainsay a chorus of twenty critics. As the Perfectionists got better at mutual criticism, most of them came to regard it as a vital catharsis and an essential means of maintaining the colony's delicate social harmony. It functioned like a cross between confession, performance review, and psychoanalysis, but crowdsourced. The fact that everyone had a turn in the hot seat took some of the sting out of the ordeal.* Praise, or "commendatory criticism," was doled out alongside negative criticism.

In the pursuit of social and individual perfection, no foible was too picayune for the attentions of mutual criticism. One colonist was criticized for being unpoetic, another for reading too little, another for "sauciness of speech." A man identified in the minutes only as "J" was informed that "his whole manner is sensational. He talks for effect and walks for effect, he flourishes his handkerchief for effect; takes out his letters and watch for effect." One man was cautioned that he had "masculinity carried to excess. There is not enough woman in him." A long-winded old Yankee was scolded for his "too frequent mentions of

---

* Only Noyes was exempt from mutual criticism. He bore the brunt of the abundant, unorganized criticism directed at the community from without and decided that that was "whipping enough to keep one man sober." He did say that he would gladly submit to criticism if and when it was offered by Christ or one of His apostles, preferably Paul.

Vermont." Even the smallest communists took part. A report from 1874 records that "the four-year olds have had a round of criticism, themselves acting as critics and good ones too."

Rather than addressing some specific error that hurt the community—burning the biscuits, leaving a gate open, ejaculating—mutual criticism tended to focus on some deeper deficiency that was believed to be the true cause of the trouble. When Francis Long, the young man whose inexperience caused the *Rebecca Ford* to founder, returned to Oneida, he endured a blistering volley of criticism. Rather than discuss his poor performance at the tiller, the community analyzed his "perverse" resistance to kindness, which they identified as a "direct cause" of the tragedy.

In a society with bewilderingly complicated social relations and extremely high standards of conduct, regular sessions of mutual criticism allowed the Perfectionists to police such subjective and contradictory vices as laziness and excessive work, frivolity and self-seriousness. Noyes saw it as a method of governance that combined the best of all other modes. "It is Theocratic, for in recognizing the Truth as King, it recognizes God who is the *source* of all Truth . . . It is Aristocratic, in as much as the best critics have the most power. It is Democratic in as much as the privilege of criticism is distributed to all classes, and the highest attainments and skill in it are open to everyone." Perhaps most important, the regular sessions of mutual criticism allowed the colonists to air the countless minor aggravations that will erode a cooperative colony from within if left to fester.*

Like Shaker confession, mutual criticism was used as a form of spir-

---

* In a contemporaneous report on the community, *The New York Times* offered a more cynical (and silly) account of mutual criticism's role as "the real secret of the prolonged life of the Oneida Community." The *Times* suggested that because everyone was periodically abused with public censure, nobody was willing to leave the community until they could exact revenge (that is, by criticizing their erstwhile critics). The desire to "get square," the *Times* claimed, kept the communards locked into a bitter seesaw of retribution. "That Noyes should have recognized the fact that he could bind his followers together by the bond of mutual hate stamps him as a man of real, if perverted, genius."

itual hygiene. Community members who returned after sojourning in the World were subjected to a vigorous, spirit-scrubbing round of criticism before resuming life in the Mansion House. "It is our spiritual Turkish Bath," boasted one pamphlet. And since the Perfectionists believed in a one-to-one-to-one correlation between spiritual, psychic, and bodily health, they used the "medicine" of mutual criticism to treat many physical ailments. A communard laid up with a bad back or a sore throat could summon a committee to her bedside. Under a barrage of harsh analysis, the patient would apparently begin to sweat profusely. When the criticism-induced fever broke, the patient would supposedly emerge refreshed and healthy. "One secret of its efficacy," the Perfectionists claimed, "is that it stops the flow of thought toward the seat of difficulty and so tends to reduce inflammation. At the same time it has a very bracing, invigorating effect." When an epidemic of croup broke out in the Children's House, the children were gathered in the schoolroom and instructed to tell one another their faults.

Storming Company

As a collective, spontaneous method of enforcing community norms, mutual criticism dovetailed perfectly with Noyes's distaste for written rules ("legalism"), allowing the community to respond nimbly to their constantly evolving values and needs. It was this ability to adapt to changing circumstances—"to reduce sail and shift anchor at a moment's notice," as Noyes put it—that most distinguished the Perfectionists from the other utopians of the era. Inspired by the scientific advances of their day, Owen and Fourier (and to a lesser extent Cabet) spoke about finding, or thought they had already found, a "social science" with the rigid elegance of a mathematical theorem. They assumed that Truth had to come in the form of a *system,* something fixed, internally coherent, reliable, and final. Having drawn up their elaborate cities of words, they sometimes failed to look up from the page to face the shifting ambiguities of life. Noyes, believing that "the disasters of Owenism and Fourierism have not been in vain," intended to profit from that mistake. "It is certainly high time that Socialists . . . should chasten their confidence in flattering theories, and turn their attention to actual events," he wrote. Among other benefits of this outlook, the Perfection-ists' ability to "shift anchor" in response to actual events helped them secure the remarkable wealth that they gradually achieved.

Like almost all nineteenth-century utopians, the Bible Communists dreamed of building themselves a new Eden. They arrived in Oneida intending to earn their living in the most Edenic way possible: by grow-ing fruit. "[We] are destined," wrote one colonist, "to carry fruit cultiva-tion to a development and perfection that the world has no conception of." During their first year on Jonathan Burt's land, the Perfectionists planted thousands of apple, cherry, peach, plum, and pear trees. It was a difficult, expensive enterprise, but one they expected to sustain their utopia in perpetuity.

This dream of a re-creating Eden in central New York was short-lived. Neither the community's soil nor its climate was suited to large-scale fruit cultivation. Surveying the history of other utopian col-onies, Noyes concluded that their almost unanimous commitment to horticulture—an understandable impulse at the soot-smudged dawn of the machine age—had more to do with romantic fantasy than economic reality. Without skipping a beat, the Perfectionists cut their blighted sap-lings for kindling and began looking for a better way to bankroll the Kingdom of God.

Sewell Newhouse, a trapper and blacksmith who migrated from Ver-mont to the Burned-over District as part of the Yankee exodus in 1820, moved to the community during its first summer with his wife, Eveliza. Before converting to Perfectionism, Newhouse made and sold simple claw traps of his own design to local Iroquois trappers. His traps were lighter and more reliable in cold weather than the German-made mod-els that dominated the market. Noyes asked Newhouse to teach a few young colonists his secret technique for tempering the flat spring that sprang the fast jaws of his traps. In short order, the community estab-lished a state-of-the-art trap factory, fitted out with a mechanical roller and power punch driven by Oneida Creek. In the 1850s and 1860s, as Americans poured onto the western frontier, the fur trade boomed. Oneida-brand traps, which ranged from tiny rodent traps to huge moose traps, were the best on the market. Demand was insatiable. While many Americans laughed about William Seward's scheme to purchase Alaska, the Oneida Community considered sending him a gold-plated bear trap.

Excluding the fact that the mostly vegetarian Perfectionists made their living from mammalian carnage, the business was perfectly suited to the community.* Because orders for traps came in fits and starts, the need for labor was erratic. If, for instance, the Hudson's Bay Company put in a large order for beaver traps, a "trap-making bee" could be announced at the daily community meeting. All nonessential labor would be put on hold and everyone would pile into a horse-drawn omnibus and head for one of their two factories. They would work late into the night, welding chain, assembling traps, and packing crates.

These sorts of labor "bees" were common at every utopian colony of the era, but the Perfectionists raised them to an art. They held bees for every large task—brick making, planting, broom corn harvesting, bag stitching, vegetable picking, and fruit preserving. "Working in storm," as they called it, made tedious jobs go fast and gave the communists an economic edge over their neighbors. Neither "isolated" householders nor wage-paying bosses could quadruple or halve their workforce from day to day. The *Circular* regularly trumpeted the efficiencies of the system. Four thousand quarts of strawberries were picked in a single day. A barn was raised in a weekend. A large trap order was filled in one night. One "storming company" was tasked with stitching the bindings of nine hundred religious pamphlets. They ran out of printed matter so quickly that they went looking for other things to sew, turning their needles upon a large heap of flour sacks in need of darning.

---

* One Oneidan, clearly channeling Fourier, claimed that vermin were a sign of an unhealthy globe and that the Perfectionists were right to hasten their extinction.

Laboring in "mixed company"—especially when combined with breaks for cake or brief bouts of fiddle-accompanied contra dancing—helped give tiresome undertakings a flirtatious, festal atmosphere. Under the influence of Fourier, the Perfectionists spoke about harnessing "social harmonies" to make industry "attractive." "We have lately found it pleasant and profitable," they reported in 1855, "to avail ourselves of one of Fourier's suggestions in marching out to our field services with music. . . . This introduction of music to our field work . . . chimes in beautifully with the growing spirit of sport and ardor among us." Taking another suggestion from Fourier, the Perfectionists found that frequent job rotation turned "drudgery into sport" and boosted creativity. A carpenter serving a shift on the cleanup crew invented a new type of mop ringer. A machinist requisitioned to the kitchen built a potato peeler based on the device used in the trap shop for cleaning rust off pieces of iron.

Word of these Fourier-inspired reforms reached the North American Phalanx, prompting some of the leading Associationists to visit Oneida. After being thrown out of France for his role in a botched coup, Victor Considerant came for an extended stay. In Oneida Creek, the Parisian radical fulfilled his dream of catching "an American trout." After his visit, a portrait of Fourier was hung in the Mansion House.

There is a great deal of symmetry between the theories of Bible Communism and passional attraction. Both Noyes and Fourier preached that human impulse, that age-old burr under the saddle of civic harmony, can be harnessed as the "motor force" of a hypercohesive, hyperproductive social order. More specifically, they both believed that sexual passion can fuel solidarity and material progress. "Amativeness," Noyes wrote, "is a mighty passion, and whatever is to be done it will do. If God can apply that passion to the public service, the stronger it is the better." Both men claimed that stifling the free flow of human passion with monogamy, "legalism," and taboos saps society of energy, creativity, and fraternity.

Even more than the Fourierists, the Oneida communists felt a special kinship with the Shakers. Both the Shakers and the Perfectionists re-

garded competitive markets and the nuclear family as inherently anti-
Christian; both sought to imitate the communism of the primitive
church; and both tried to build a distinctive, physical stronghold for the
millennium that they believed their respective doctrines would trigger.
Relations were particularly friendly between Noyes and Elder Frederick
Evans and between the Oneida Community and the four Shaker "families" living at Watervliet. Noyes, who borrowed liberally from the secular utopians, repeatedly identified the United Society of Believers as his
single biggest influence. One Shaker elder wrote that the two sects regarded each other as "noble contestants" in the struggle to establish the
Kingdom of God on earth.

Level Up to the Highest Standard

Ann Lee and her successors made the United Society rich by sacralizing
labor—turning physical work into a medium of worship. Noyes did not
think of work in those terms. For him, labor was always a means to
other ends. But he did something very similar with the work of "self-
culture." The soul might be perfected through faith and grace, but the
perfection of society (that is, the building up of the millennium) would
require diligence and time. Along with the collective work of perfecting
social relations, each individual communist had to endeavor constantly
to make him- or herself worthy of the new millennial dispensation.
Studying grammar, practicing the cello, perfecting your sexual technique, or fine-tuning your personality with dose upon dose of mutual
criticism: These were acts of faith at Oneida, outward expressions of
belief in the dawning Kingdom of Heaven on earth. The Perfectionists'
communism—their collectivized child care, laundry, cooking, manufacturing, governance, sex—gave them the time and liberty to explore
their full potential as individuals.

Most of the colonists entered the community with scant book learning, but the entire community was soon highly literate, proving their
belief that "the tendency in living together is to level up to the highest

standard." Freed from a great deal of domestic obligation (such as parenthood, marriage), the Perfectionists studied chemistry, poetry, geometry, astrology, and philosophy. The library in the Mansion House held almost four thousand volumes, and the reading room was full most evenings. Noyes himself was not a great lover of literature. Science and religion were his subjects. He favored poetry that did what he thought religion ought to—express something spontaneous or ecstatic. William Blake was a particular favorite.

During the winter of 1863, an adult Perfectionist could take his or her pick from among one of two math classes, a lively fifty-member geography seminar, a slew of music courses, or tutorials in Latin, French, and grammar. Math was especially popular. "If anything will arouse persons from their apathy, and awaken their dormant faculties," noted the *Circular,* "it is algebra." One elderly Perfectionist became so

AN EVENING IN THE SOCIAL HALL, ONEIDA COMMUNITY.

Bible Communism in full swing.

absorbed working out an algebraic equation that she missed the meal bell. After everyone else had eaten, she saw a man pulling on his coat and asked if he was skipping dinner. "This caused a general laugh in the room," reported the community paper, "which recalled our mathematician from her abstraction to this mundane sphere, and to the physical wants of the body."

Much of this activity took place in the Community Hall, a grand room at the center of the Mansion House with a large raked stage at one end. It was the closest thing the community had to a church, but it contained no cross or pulpit. With its frescoed walls, mezzanine seating, and heavy red curtains, it looked more like an opera house. At seven thirty each evening, a bell summoned everyone to the hall for the daily community meeting. According to the *Circular*, these gatherings were "partly social, partly intellectual, partly industrial, and partly religious." The colonists would begin by discussing practical matters, perhaps a new initiative in the Children's House or a potential new business scheme. Afterward they might sing a few songs, have a round of waltzing, or read aloud from the *Tribune*. If Noyes was in residence, he might give a "home talk" on Bible Communism or healthy living.

During one of these talks, Noyes explained his evolving view that pleasure was the real purpose of life on earth. "Enjoyment," he said, was "the very business that [God] set Adam and Eve about, AND NO OTHER." With money from traps and other light manufacturing rolling in, enjoyment—in a very particular sense of the word—became the business of the Oneida Community, too. In keeping with the "spirit of improvement" that formed the undersong to everything that went on inside the Mansion House, the communists gravitated toward pleasures that required a high degree of cultivation. They formed bands and orchestras; studied Greek to read Homer; learned astronomy for early morning stargazing; and staged elaborate productions of *A Midsummer Night's Dream* and *Hamlet*. Staying impressively au courant for a bunch of trap-welding separatists in the hinterland, they mounted a production of *H.M.S. Pinafore* less than a year after its London premiere, declaring that Gilbert and Sullivan's depiction of interclass romance and jolly fellowship on the high seas was "a good medium of communism."

Like the men and women of Brook Farm, Noyes hoped to blur the line between aesthete and laborer. He thought that a refined sense of pleasure and beauty would have practical benefits in the coming millennial utopia. "The love of the beautiful could be made to harmonize with and quicken all kinds of manual industry," he wrote. "The artist does not need to be an idler, a dreamer, a mere speculator. It is possible to combine the worker and the artist. We have begun that work here."

Aside from complex marriage, a system designed to strengthen civic bonds by refining and harmonizing private pleasures, the best example of the Oneidans' distinctive conception of pleasure as both edifying and communizing may have been their enthusiasm for one particular activity: croquet. The Perfectionists were so obsessed that they sometimes swept snow from their specially built "croqueterie" to play in mittens and scarves. Noyes, who instinctively devised a theory about everything that crossed his path, claimed that croquet served a special social function, allowing the natural "moderation" of women to temper the male instinct for "very hard striking of the balls." He called the sport "a harmonic cooperation with God."*

The all-encompassing "spirit of improvement" that came to dominate life within the community merged with the Perfectionists' distinctive notions about health to form the most audacious link in the Noyesian "chain of redemption": defeating the "death system." According to scripture, everlasting life, or at least transport from earth to heaven without passing through illness and death, is supposed to be one of the

---

* There was a certain logic to the community's passion for croquet. The game, which came to the United States from England in the 1860s, sparked a minor sexual revolution. The genteel sport was accepted as a respectable coed activity, making it pretty much the only game that men and women could play together in public. For a few years, city parks and country lawns throughout the Republic were overrun with hoops, mallets, and flirting singles. Even the Shakers took up the sport.

perks of life in the millennium. In the early years, many Perfectionists sincerely believed that as the millennium unfolded, they would some-how secure an actual "victory over death." Later, this ambition slid into the more modest goal of delaying death and eliminating aging. "The thought occurred to me," Noyes wrote after a decade in the Mansion House, "whether we could not create an opposite atmosphere—one which would resist and repel the advances of old age, and make it more easy and natural to grow youthful than to grow old and infirm. . . . There is a strong feeling (and it is a worldly imagination) that youth is the bright time of enjoyment; and persons expect after they arrive at a certain age that their enjoyment will decrease—that they will lose their susceptibilities to pleasure. I think this is a false view." In light of this new thinking, one elderly Perfectionist announced that he did not want to be treated like an old man, insisting that "old age" was "nothing but a habit." It is hard to imagine a more extreme example of the utopian disregard for the world-as-it-is. Physical decline, the most immutable human experience, is nothing more than "worldly imagination" and "old-fashioned testimony." Death—like private property, family, and monogamy—is just somebody else's bad idea.

If Mr. Noyes Takes a Pinch of Snuff,
All the Community Sneezes

Having fled Putney for the wilderness isolation of central New York, the Perfectionists experienced something odd: the World came to them. The community had stopped actively promoting spin-off colonies in the late 1850s, but Noyes was still determined, as Albert Brisbane had put it, to make "a trial that would impress the public." In July 1852, at the height of the *Observer*-stoked outcry over complex marriage, the com-munists opened their gates to a skeptical public, inviting people to come in and be impressed. That event, a free "strawberry festival," was the first of countless subsequent picnics, performances, and concerts, all of which were orchestrated for the pleasure of the World.

The outreach worked. The Perfectionists' upstate neighbors gradually became their best defense against periodic attacks by crusading
politicians and churchmen. When the district attorney in Utica agitated
for the community's expulsion, a prominent local businessman wrote
Noyes, promising that "the people in this vicinity will not consent to
have you disperse."

On summer weekends during the 1860s and 1870s, tourists overran
the grounds. Around the increasingly luxurious Mansion House, the
Perfectionists laid down curving gravel walks, neatly edged flower beds,
and wide expanses of close-trimmed lawn. "Few corners of America,"
wrote an English visitor, "can compete in loveliness with the swards and
gardens lying about the home of the Oneida Family." On the Fourth of
July, as many as fifteen hundred visitors would come to tour the property.

In 1870, a new rail spur gave the community its own depot near the
orchard, just a short walk from the Mansion House. The new line shortened the trip from New York City, bringing ever larger crowds. When
trains stopped at Oneida, the conductor would half-jokingly call out:
"Cars stop for fifteen minutes for stealing fruit." From the station, visitors were directed to a reception room in the foyer of the Mansion
House, where they could buy a dinner ticket or request a tour. To the
horror of certain upstate clergymen, even Sunday school classes came
to picnic on the communist lawns and mingle with the oversexed here-
tics. Among the attractions at Oneida, besides the impressive gardens,
were live music, well-stocked libraries, and a stereoscope. On the second floor of the mansion, the community "museum" displayed ancient
Egyptian relics, an Argentine maté set, a mastodon tooth, a samurai
sword, an emu egg, a depiction of a Fourierist phalanstery, and many
other exotic curios.

So many tourists came that the community had to print up a list of
rules: no smoking in the Mansion House, no graffiti, no hotdog carriage
racing on the main circle, no card playing, no fruit stealing, no flower
trampling. Since the Perfectionists didn't drink and were mostly vegetarian, they asked visitors—who were welcome at the midday dinner—

to refrain from bringing or requesting alcohol, tobacco, or meat. "Eggs," a sign in the refectory noted, "can be furnished to those who require animal food." Along with various religious tracts, visitors could buy, for twenty-five cents, a vegetarian cookbook titled *Oneida Community Cooking; or Dinner Without Meat.*

The rustic gazebos and croqueterie were beautiful, but the Perfectionists—with their "short dresses," childish haircuts, and air of sexual transgression—were probably the main attraction. Many visitors were convinced that something sinister lurked beneath the community's sunny appearance. Some cornered Perfectionist children, asking whether they were as happy as they appeared or if they knew who their parents were. Oneida women grew accustomed to being asked whether their hair had been cut by force. The general notion among outsiders was that the Perfectionists were saucer-eyed rubes and that Noyes was a tyrant. The press compared him with Brigham Young or a practitioner of "Mahometanism." "If Mr. Noyes takes a pinch of snuff," went the line, "all the Community sneezes." Some visitors speculated that the community's octagonal stone cistern, about thirty feet around and covered with a turf roof, was some sort of dungeon or satanic altar.

A Perfect Perfectionist

As long as people have dreamed of the ideal society, they have populated it with ideal citizens. But who is that citizen? The idealized Shaker was supposed to be an angel of restraint and transcendence, devoid of sex and will—a blissed-out cog in the serene machinery of Zion. By contrast, Owen and Cabet hoped to fill their respective utopias with jolly, virtuous, right-thinking factory workers. They believed that humanity's disruptive impulses—what Jeremy Bentham called our "mischievous passions"—were nothing more than symptoms of a badly disorganized society. Desire, pride, and personality need not be extirpated, just softened with an overriding sense of fraternity and a calmly calculating rationalism. The ideal citizen of Fourier's Harmony was a very different sort of person: an impulsive, convivial, pleasure-seeking *Übermensch*. Fourier, the most humanistic of all utopians, believed that the average person already contains unfathomable potential for productivity, intelligence, and delight. When social and labor relations are properly arranged, he claimed, this potential will gush forth. In Harmony, "there will normally be on earth thirty-seven million poets the equal of Homer, thirty-seven million mathematicians the equal of Newton, thirty-seven million authors of comedies the equal of Molière, and the same number in all other conceivable talents." (With uncharacteristic modesty, Fourier added, "These are estimates.")

Despite the Oneida Community's emphasis on education and self-culture, the Perfectionists did not associate a proliferation of genius with the coming exaltation of the species. While Fourier awaited millions of Homers and Molières, Noyes claimed that his community never "desired to produce a Byron, a Napoleon, or a Michelangelo." Any system that could "foster abnormal or excessive development in the individual," he believed, "[could do so only] at the expense of the mass." At Oneida, the perfection of the individual was inseparable from the perfection of society at large. The stated purpose of the community's defining institutions—mutual criticism, community of goods, complex marriage—was to simultaneously elevate and knit together "the mass."

All three of these institutions expressed what Noyes called "the plodding spirit," that part of human nature that "is willing to learn little by little." By 1869, after the communists had been plodding toward perfection for three decades, Noyes decided to pick up the pace. He still believed that his community would usher in the millennium, but it was taking longer than expected. At the same time, the revivalist fervor of the early years was cooling, both at Oneida and throughout the wider Republic. To revitalize the community and hasten the perfection of its members, Noyes announced the inauguration of a eugenics program designed to breed an enhanced generation of Bible Communists.

He had been thinking about the "science" of breeding for decades. In 1849, in the "First Annual Report of the Oneida Association," Noyes wrote: "We believe that the time will come . . . when scientific combination will be applied to human generation as freely and successfully as it is to that of other animals." The ability to actually achieve "scientific combination"—as opposed to the "promiscuous scrambling" of the World—was opened by the twin innovations of male continence and complex marriage. In hindsight, Noyes's hat trick of erotic experiments form a chain. Male continence, first inspired by Harriet Noyes's birthing traumas, created the possibility of complex marriage. And it was complex marriage, the community's civically oriented *ménage à trois-cent*, that made their experiment in controlled breeding possible.

Utopia and eugenics share a long history. Plato's *Republic*, the first major Western utopian text, describes a system of selective breeding designed to populate the titular state with the right kinds of citizens. Ever since, controlled breeding has been a regular feature of utopian visions of the future. The specter of state-bred helots has also become one of the most consistent features of modern literary dystopia.

One reason for the timing of the eugenics experiment at Oneida was that the community needed fresh members. Two decades of diligent continence had kept the youth population relatively low. And while there were plenty of applicants from outside, the Perfectionists' hard-won prosperity made it difficult to sort the true believers from the "thousands [who] are ready to rush in for the loaves and fishes." To weed out what Noyes called "Owenites, infidels, spiritualists, irresponsible free lovers, and the riffraff of defunct Communities," the Oneida Community's admission standards had progressively stiffened. The eugenics program, which Noyes dubbed "stirpiculture,"* allowed the Perfectionists to admit members "by another entrance."

At the same time, interest in selective breeding was growing outside of the community. Mainstream enthusiasm would not peak until the 1880s, but Francis Galton—Darwin's cousin and the most influential

---

* From the Latin *sterpes*, meaning "race," and *culture*, as in "cultivation," like horticulture.

booster of controlled breeding—published *Hereditary Genius,* the book
that introduced the term *eugenics,* in 1869, the same year stirpiculture
commenced at Oneida.

Noyes believed that there are two separate forces at work on the development of the human species. One is the slow, imprecise influence
of natural selection, refining the herd, as he put it, "by weeding out its
poorest stock." *On the Origin of Species by Means of Natural Selection* was
published in 1859, setting people on edge throughout Christendom.*
Noyes immediately folded Darwin's theory into his own. "The principles of natural selection and the survival of the fittest," he wrote, "leads
right on to the idea of improvement of man by voluntary selection."
During the 1860s and 1870s, Noyes watched the rising antagonism between Christianity and science with dismay. He regarded science as
"the true handmaid of faith" and saw no reason why education should
erode belief. "I have followed . . . Darwin into his endless genealogies,"
Noyes wrote, "and yet I am as sure now that Christ is king of the world
as I was before science began to swell into infidelity." To the Perfectionists, Darwin's theory offered a biological analogue to their millenarian
utopianism, proving that progress is a natural law—that perfection is
the universal telos.†

Alongside natural selection, the other force that Noyes saw at work
on the development of the species was the direct, supernatural interference of God. Noyes read the Old Testament's genealogies—those endless rosters of begetting—as a record of the Creator's efforts to mate,
cull, and crossbreed humanity in preparation for the millennium. "The
Lord himself has exercised the herdsman's right of selection," Noyes
wrote, "and carried on a course of scientific breeding with reference to

---

* Writing in the *Tribune,* the sensible Reverend Ripley gave Darwin one of his few
early raves in the American press.
† Of course, this perceived analogy springs from a misreading of *On the Origin of Species.* Like the social Darwinists, the Perfectionists imagined moral imperatives between the lines of a descriptive science. Darwin merely claims that natural selection
fits organisms to the shifting particulars of their environment, not that finches are
approaching some perfected state of finch-ness.

the production of a specific result." After most of the descendants of Adam were "set aside as worthless," God focused His attention upon Noah, killing off everyone but his family. Ten long generations later, the Lord switched His attention to the bloodlines of Abraham, picking the pious shepherd to father a new race: the Jews. Noyes carefully documented how God employed the husbandry technique of "close culture" (the inbreeding of close relations to isolate and amplify a desired trait) in His effort to breed "the perfect work"—namely, Christ and His apostles.*

While a stallion might be prized for good teeth and a glossy coat, Noyes claimed that God selected men such as Noah and Abraham for their exceptional spiritual sensitivity—their high levels of "inspiration and obedience."

When the stirpiculture experiment began at Oneida, men and women volunteered singly or in pairs. For a time, selections were made by a six-member committee that included two Yale-educated physicians. Mostly the selections were left up to Noyes and his inner circle. Like breeders of flowers or dogs, the Perfectionists had to choose which traits they were aiming for. While the intelligence and health of the volunteers were taken into account, the main criterion was a highly subjective notion of spiritual inspiration. On the dubious assumption that good sex makes good babies, mutual attraction between volunteers was considered a plus. Practically speaking, the Perfectionists had their ideal target close at hand. "The existence of Noyes," wrote George Bernard Shaw, "simplified the breeding problem for the Communists, the question as to what sort of men they should strive to breed being settled at once by the desirability of breeding another Noyes." Not surprisingly,

---

* Noyes wrote a genealogy showing the frequent coupling of blood relations among Abraham's progeny. Abraham and his wife, Sarah, for instance, had the same father. Likewise, the union of Lot and one of his daughters produced Moab, who was supposedly an ancestor of Jesus. Although Noyes theoretically favored inbreeding, eventually fathering a son with his niece Helen, he made a rare concession to popular sentiment and decided that breaking the taboo against sibling sex—what he called "the last citadel of social falsehood"—would be too much for the benighted American public of the 1870s. Sanctified incest would have to wait.

Noyes personally fathered a sixth of all the "stirpicults." Ultimately, a total of fifty-three women and thirty-eight men were selected. They pledged themselves as " 'living sacrifices' to God and true Communism" and went upstairs in pairs.

Between 1869 and 1879, forty-five "stirpicults" were born.[*] They were raised and nursed by their biological mothers for nine months and then transferred to the nursery of the Children's House, where they were cared for by specially selected teachers and generally fussed over by the entire community. The biological parents renounced all rights of parenthood.

In 1891, after the breakup of the community, Anita Newcomb McGee, a final-year medical student at Johns Hopkins who specialized in gynecology, studied the stirpicults for a report in the *American Anthropologist*. By then, the eldest were twenty-two. McGee found that most of them had been impressive students, with both boys and girls earning scholarships to top universities. With a single exception, all were perfectly healthy. Many were unusually tall. They were highly literate, and when they convened at the Mansion House each summer, they entertained themselves with debate competitions and concerts. With the exception of Noyes and a few other lawyers and clergymen, the volunteer parents had all originally been farmers, laborers, and craftspeople. All but one of the stirpicults (a machinist) pursued nonmanual professions. Among the eldest boys in the group—those for whom a career could reasonably be predicted in 1891—there were medical students, law students, businessmen, a math prodigy, and a successful musician. The eldest girls, in the estimation of Dr. McGee, were also bound for intellectual careers. One was a scholar of Greek at a women's college; another was studying the new kindergarten system. Of course, much, if

---

[*] There were more pregnancies, but some did not come to term, and some that did come to term died in infancy. The stated goal of the experiment was quality, not quantity. The high rate of insemination among volunteers laid to rest worries about the effects of male continence on their reproductive organs. The experiment's rate of infant mortality was less than a third of the rate in the country at large (based on the 1870 census).

not all, of the stirpiculsts' success in life can be attributed to their carefully administered upbringing in the Children's House and the intellectual, self-improving tenor of the community in which they were raised.

Ironically, the stirpiculsts' main "failing" was a distinct lack of faith. Assuming that "inspiration" was somehow inheritable, Noyes had set out to raise a generation of spiritually advanced Perfectionists, men and women who would someday lead various Oneida-like communities when the millennium began in earnest. At the time of McGee's study, however, few of the adult stirpiculsts were regular churchgoers. Only one still considered himself a Perfectionist. Faith, it seems, cannot be bred.

Exile

> So He drove out the man; and He placed at the east of the
> garden of Eden Cherubims, and a flaming sword which
> turned every way, to keep the way of the tree of life.
> —GENESIS 3:24

By the middle 1870s, with stirpiculture in full swing, a recurring throat illness lowered Noyes's voice to a hoarse whisper. His hearing also began to fade. These were grave handicaps for a man who rejected written rules and led entirely by talking. Noyes had always preached that spiritual perfection would lead to a triumph over disease, if not immortality. As late as 1871, he wrote, "We are so near a second coming, or something like it, that I see no death before me, and by that I mean I see no cessation of my active power."* Since he was supposed to be the most spiritually advanced member of the community, Noyes's waning vitality undermined his prophetic authority. It also dimmed the erotic magne-

---

* Should his own physical existence somehow come to an end, Noyes claimed that he would join Christ and His apostles to lead the Oneida Community from the great beyond.

tism that was integral to the soft power with which he held the community together. As with Owen and his multicolored "silent monitors," Noyes's authority rested upon his followers' desire for his warmth and approval. Unlike Owen, Noyes sometimes expressed that warmth and approval in bed—if not personally, then by orchestrating a coveted tryst.

In 1874, James William Towner, a leading member of a small free love community near Cleveland known as the Berlin Heights Society, moved into the Mansion House along with his wife, Cinderella, their three grown children, and seven other members of the collapsed Ohio commune. As a new convert, Towner, a handsome, charismatic lawyer who had lost an eye fighting for the Union army, occupied a fairly low rung on the Oneida Community's unwritten ladder of ascending fellowship. It was an uncomfortable position for a man with Towner's self-regard, and he came to resent the top-down regulation of complex marriage. The Berlin Heights Society had had a considerably freer understanding of free love. Towner thought that consenting adults should have total freedom to choose their own partners and that parents should have sole authority over their teenage children's sex lives.

Two years after Towner's arrival, Noyes encouraged the community to install Theodore, his eldest and only legitimate son, as president of the community. Theodore, then in his midtwenties, was one of Oneida's two physicians. He was popular within the community, but everyone knew that he had returned from Yale with a good deal of doubt about his father's doctrines, if not Christianity altogether.* The community approved his promotion to president, but having a skeptic in a position of authority irked true believers and allowed younger Perfec-

---

* Theodore's skepticism did not extend to the Spiritualist movement, about which he was the community's leading enthusiast. When the Spiritualist craze swept through the Burned-over District and then the country in general, Theodore began leading séances in the Mansion House. The elder Noyes mostly discouraged Spiritualism among followers. He had no doubts about the existence of spirits or their ability to communicate through mediums, but he felt that just because someone is dead doesn't mean they have anything intelligent or useful to say.

tionists who had missed the galvanizing early years to air their own uncertainties about Noyes's inspiration.

During his brief presidency, Theodore tried to reassert centralized control over complex marriage (things had been getting lax) and led an effective but high-handed effort to streamline the community's finances. Combined with the quiet agitation of Towner and those who agreed with him, these initiatives created an air of discord that was previously unknown at Oneida. For decades, Noyes had preached that "philopro-genitiveness" (excessive attachment to blood relations) was antithetical to Bible Communism. His own blinkered nepotism seemed to prove the point.* After eight months, Theodore resigned and his half-deaf father resumed the presidency.

Stirpiculture had been intended to reinvigorate the community with an infusion of fresh vitality—to replace the "the fading word of truth," as one historian put it, with "ablutions of semen." Instead, by introduc-ing an elite subclass—the selected parents—into a society devoted to radical equality, the experiment added to the gathering sense of drift and discontent. Combined with Theodore's effort to tighten control over complex marriage, the breeding program stirred dormant resent-ments about the sexual hierarchies inside the community. When James Towner began to challenge Noyes's authority—first in secret gatherings in the tower of the Mansion House, later at meetings of the whole community—he found considerable support, especially among newer members. Unaccustomed to such dissension, Noyes withdrew from the daily operations of the community, spending more and more time in prayerful communion with Saint Paul.

As if sensing weakness, critics from outside began to circle. In the early 1870s, a shrill, sex-obsessed strain of conservatism was on the march throughout the country. At the start of 1873, Anthony Comstock, the young founder of the New York Society for the Suppression of Vice,

---

* Noyes's nepotism did square with his belief that spiritual "inspiration" was some-how hereditary.

rallied Congress to ban "obscene materials" from the mail, including any information about contraception.* As a uniformed agent of the U.S. Postal Service, Comstock waged war against a broad range of threats to the Christian household: dirty books, suffragettes, family-planning advocates, D. H. Lawrence. Late in his career, he boasted about having pulped 160 tons of literature and having caused fifteen suicides. In a stroke, the passage of the Comstock Act made many of the Oneida Community's foundational texts illegal if they touched a postage stamp.†

The same upwelling of conservative prudery that bore Comstock aloft emboldened a Presbyterian firebrand named John W. Mears to try to abolish the Oneida Community. In 1873, the year that "Comstockery" became federal law, Mears, a professor at Hamilton College just down the road from Oneida, began a scorched-earth crusade against the community. In sermons, lectures, and editorials, and at public meetings of religious leaders, Mears called for the forcible expulsion of what he dubbed "the utopia of obscenity." "The people of Illinois could not endure the immorality of the Mormons, but drove them from Nauvoo in 1846, and compelled them to take refuge in the Great Central Basin, a thousand miles from the outskirts of civilization," Mears fulminated. "Thus polygamy was treated; while the far more corrupt concubinage of the Oneida Community luxuriates at ease in the heart of New York State."‡ Within the community, the avenging minister in his black coat and top hat became a figure of genuine terror. "In the Children's House," Noyes's son Pierrepont recalled, "we learned to hate Judas Iscariot, Benedict Arnold, and Professor Mears as the great triumvirate of evil."

Some of the secular press came to the community's defense, further

---

* If a text Comstock deemed obscene couldn't be found in the mail, he would write to the author under a pseudonym requesting a copy and then prosecute.

† Even the most oblique description of male continence violated federal law because it was "a means of keeping unwanted children from being born." Even well into the twentieth century, historians had difficulty writing freely about the Oneida Community.

‡ In a dismally familiar bit of reasoning, Mears claimed that if complex marriage was tolerated, bestiality would be the next logical step.

inflaming Mears and his allies. An illustration on the cover of the magazine *Puck* depicted a clutch of scowling churchmen gesturing toward the peaceable commune. "Oh, dreadful!" reads the caption. "They dwell in peace and harmony, and have no church scandals. They must be wiped out."[*]

In 1879, Mears and a group of ministers met in Syracuse to devise a legal strategy. They proposed adding the phrase *persons living in concupiscence and adultery* to an existing New York statute against "disorderly persons." In response, the citizens of Oneida and Madison Counties circulated a petition attesting to the Perfectionists' piety, industry, and fair dealing. Even the local Shakers came to the community's defense, calling the marital arrangements at Oneida "vastly purer than some of the most respectable marriages of today." The booming trade in traps, silk, and cutlery had made the Oneida Community a large and popular employer. The Perfectionists paid high wages and provided their employees with housing, child care, and education. When the legislature in Albany proved unwilling to regulate anything as subjective as "concupiscence," Mears lowered his sights. Instead of demanding the total destruction of the Oneida Community—and thus the loss of many good jobs—he called for Noyes's arrest.

The real risk for Noyes was that some disgruntled member of the community would bring charges against him for adultery or having sex with a minor. On June 21, 1879, a headline in the *Syracuse Standard* declared: "COMMUNIST NOYES TO BE ARRESTED AND LEGAL PROCEEDINGS TO BE TAKEN." There is no evidence that an arrest was actually imminent, but by the morning of June 23, Noyes was gone. The previous night, without telling anyone except a few close friends, he crept out of the Mansion House in his socks and caught a train for the Ontario side of Niagara Falls, where he stayed with a family of Canadian Perfectionists.

---

[*] Other papers sided with Mears. The author of an editorial in *The Israelite*, a Jewish weekly from Ohio, wished that it "were within [our] power to wipe from the face of existence this cankerous worm that is gnawing into our social system. . . ." Ironically, the classifieds section of *The Israelite* offered a coupon for a 50 percent discount on "Oneida's finest stainless, stoneware and cutlery."

With Noyes gone, the fault lines that had been forming within the community spread fast. Some Perfectionists blamed James Towner and his supporters for the sudden departure of their beloved father Noyes. Professor Mears's zeal was not satisfied by the disappearance of Noyes. He continued to call for legal action against the community. Complex marriage had always required an incredibly high level of solidarity and equanimity to function smoothly. Under the strain of Noyes's exile and Mears's attacks, it began to fall apart. Nobody knew what should replace it.

Noyes's view was that for the community to continue to enjoy the "social variety" of free love without the religious superstructure of ascending and descending fellowship would be "to go below" the already low plane of "worldly morality." Some Perfectionists agreed that the only suitable alternative to complex marriage was Shaker-style celibacy. After all, it was the egotism and possessiveness of monogamy that they had initially sought to overcome. Others, especially younger communists and those anxious to legitimize the children who had been born at the community, were keen to give one-man-one-woman matrimony a try. From Canada, where Noyes and a group of loyal believers were living in a large stone cottage by Niagara Falls, he reminded his followers of their long history of "shifting anchor" when circumstances impinged upon theory. He agreed to support whatever they decided but suggested that the Perfectionists follow the position of Saint Paul, "which allows marriage but prefers celibacy."

On a hot afternoon in late August 1879, the Perfectionists gathered in the Community Hall. They voted unanimously to conclude their thirty-three-year experiment in free love. To some, the decision was as wrenching and disorienting as any divorce. The communists gave themselves two days to make "sexual 'good-byes.'"

The end of complex marriage accelerated the unwinding of the other distinctive institutions of Bible Communism. Children started sleeping over in their mothers' rooms. Young women let their hair grow. Some made themselves long dresses. Twenty-five couples who had been married before joining the community were formally reunited. Other pairs, often those who had produced a child, got married for the first time. Within four months of the vote to end complex marriage, twenty couples were wed on the stage of the Community Hall. James Towner presided over many of the ceremonies. Professor Mears demanded to see the marriage certificates.

For some Perfectionists, the scramble to couple up was like a painful game of musical chairs. For three decades, they had sustained meaningful sexual and romantic relationships with many different lovers. Years of collective child rearing and stirpiculture made things even more confusing. A young mother might have had a passionate long-standing romance with one man but have a child by another. "Our relations are no longer 'complex,'" one woman wrote to a friend, "but they are dreadfully complicated."

Noyes's old claim that sexual communism propped up economic communism proved correct. In August 1880, a year after the first monogamous marriage was conducted in the Community Hall, the communists voted to "divide and reorganize," turning themselves into shareholders of a profitable corporation. At midnight on the last day of 1880, after a few months of haggling over how to distribute stock, the new arrangements went into effect. Suffixed with that most holy trinity of the American alphabet, the sacred Oneida Community became the earthly Oneida Community, Ltd.

Six hundred thousand dollars' worth of stock was divvied up among the 225 remaining members. Older Perfectionists could opt for a guarantee of health care and comfortable living in the Mansion House instead of a payout. A trust was set aside for the education of all the children. Some members moved out of the mansion. Others remained, paying a modest rent on the rooms they had occupied for years. Eighty-four of the 109 adults who originally founded the community on Jonathan Burt's land remained in the Mansion House until the end of their lives. Anyone who wanted a job with the newly formed corporation got one. For the first time, the Perfectionists received wages for their labor. Some of them had never once handled cash.

Like Adam and Eve looking down to discover that they were nude, some shareholders of the newly formed Oneida corporation were suddenly ashamed of their participation in the country's most famous sex experiment. Reams of community documents were burned.

By the time of the breakup, the community was effectively divided into two camps, those supporting Noyes and those who had rallied behind James Towner. In the final settlement, the pro-Noyes folks, including almost all of the founding members, constituted a strong majority. They inherited most of the stock and therefore retained control of the Oneida corporation and its considerable assets.[*]

Towner and thirty-five of his supporters left Oneida for southern California, settling near the village of Santa Ana. There, the small band of free-loving communists had the odd distinction of helping to found the conservative utopia of Orange County. Towner chaired the committee that set up the county government and served as Orange County's first superior court judge. Although the Townerites continued to receive dividends on their Oneida stock, they asked for their financial statements to be mailed west in plain, unmarked envelopes.

On April 13, 1886, John Humphrey Noyes—the man who taught that community is sacred, pleasure is wisdom, and paradise is ours to build—died in his stone cottage above the thundering Horseshoe Falls. He was seventy-five. Two days later, on a green, early spring afternoon, his body was carried across the border and buried in the shady hillside graveyard behind the Mansion House.

Not long before he died, Noyes reflected on his effort to build an

---

[*] In 1894, Pierrepont Noyes, one of the stirpicults fathered by John Humphrey Noyes, assumed the directorship of Oneida Ltd., staffing it with other stirpicults and building it into the most successful cutlery maker in the United States. Sherrill, the company town that grew up just north of the Mansion House, was imbued with many of the Oneida Community's old progressive and egalitarian values.

earthly paradise. "We made a raid into an unknown country, charted it and returned without the loss of a man, woman or child," he wrote. Exiled from that unknown country, the surviving Perfectionists began a slow, disorienting journey back into the foreign land that they had always called the World.

CONCLUSION

The Future Ain't What It Used to Be

> Everyone forgets that Icarus also flew.
> —JACK GILBERT, "FAILING AND FLYING"

> Glaucon: I understand. You mean that [the just person will] be willing to take part in the politics of the city we were founding and describing, the one that exists in theory, for I don't think it exists anywhere on earth.
>
> Socrates: But perhaps . . . there is a model of it in heaven, for anyone who wants to look at it and to make himself a citizen on the strength of what he sees. It makes no difference whether it is or ever will be somewhere, for he would take part in the practical affairs of that city and no other.
>
> —PLATO, *REPUBLIC*

The Civil War impinged less on the lives of the communal utopians than it did on most other Americans, but it did impinge. At the teetering breakaway Icaria near St. Louis, the promise of Union army wages drew away most of the able-bodied young men. In other communities, particularly the religious sects, there was no question about taking part in the fighting. Nonviolence and nonparticipation were long established articles of faith. At the United Society's two villages in Kentucky, Union and secessionist troops helped themselves to Shaker cattle and roasted them over thousands of pilfered Shaker fence rails. Elder Frederick Evans went to Washington to petition Lincoln to exempt Shaker brothers from the draft. The president granted the exemption, reportedly telling Evans, "You ought to be made to fight. We need regiments of just such men as you." At Oneida, a clerical error saved the Perfectionist men from conscription. (There was confusion over which county the Mansion House occupied.) In general, those communities that were still standing by the 1860s had retreated somewhat from their global ambi-

Two Shaker sisters with saxophones,
Canterbury Village, New Hampshire.

Canterbury Shaker Village Archives,
Canterbury, N.H.

tions, opting instead for a quiet internal exile from the ugly dramas of the Republic.

The war's real effect on American utopianism was indirect. The communitarian movements of the early and middle nineteenth century had been fueled by a widely held belief in the imminence of a new golden age. That faith could not survive forty-nine months of wholesale butchery in familiar cow pastures. The thrum of millenarian optimism that had set so many Americans on the road to utopia went quiet. For those still inclined to regard their days as the end of days, the war replaced John Noyes's garden party millennium with the "fateful lightning" of John Brown's bloody-saber Apocalypse.

While the Shakers, Owenites, Fourierists, Icarians, and Perfectionists had different visions of the coming paradise, they all shared the belief that some specific, ideal social order exists. Whether or not they saw God or Reason or Passion as the author of that ideal order, they proceeded from the assumption that humankind is somehow *meant* to live in utopia. Beneath this assumption was the conviction, born out of the intellectual advances of the Enlightenment, that there exists some knowable, universal "science" of human relations. "It is our Father's beautiful garden in which we are," wrote John Codman after leaving Brook Farm. "I have learned that all is intended for order and beauty, but as children we cannot yet walk so as not to stumble. Natural science has explained a thousand mysteries. Social science—understand the word; not schemes, plans or guessing, but genuine science, as far from guess or scheme as astronomy or chemistry is—will reveal to us as many truths and beauties as ever any other science has done. I now see clearly! Blessed be God for the light!" The utopians had assumed that the arc of history was short and that it would soon bend toward perfection. The chaotic war years, during which all human ingenuity seemed turned to murder, had a predictable impact on that sort of thinking. Such ceremonies of innocence were no longer possible.

In a more practical sense, the Civil War changed the way that most Americans thought about progress. At the start of the nineteenth century, few citizens regarded their remote, anemic government as an especially potent mechanism for social reform. The war and its aftermath changed that, ushering federal and state authority into the daily lives of ordinary people. In the new, battle-born Republic, reformist causes went into politics, often becoming less radical in the process. Abolitionism, formerly the ultraist fringe of the antislavery movement, became federal policy. The moral crusade for temperance became the political cause of Prohibition. And utopian socialism, once indifferent to the councils of government, gave way to political Progressivism and various schools of party socialism.*

Ultimately, the decline of American communal utopianism was less about the defeat of one idea than it was about the triumph of another. As the Republic surged westward, the dream of a transformed, egalitarian social order burned off like mist under the hot rising sun of American prosperity. For some, the rapidly opening West, or at least their idea of the West, became a replacement for utopia—a blankness upon which new futures might be imagined. Despite a few notable exceptions, those imagined futures were very different places from the Shaker Zion, Owen's New Moral World, Fourier's Harmony, Cabet's Icaria, or the Perfectionists' Kingdom of Heaven on earth.

Long before the war, in the young, makeshift Republic where those would-be utopias were planted, the future had seemed up for grabs. People on both sides of the Atlantic expected the final chapter of human history to unfold in North America, but nobody knew with much certainty what exactly it would look like. This hopeful uncertainty loosened the grip of old ideas about how the world works. Society seemed like something to be invented, rather than merely endured.

Toward the end of the century, as buffalo leather was tanned into machine belts for eastern manufactories, dreams of private fortune and

---

* Some of the communal utopians' most utopian initiatives—providing universal education, sheltering the destitute, maintaining free libraries—eventually came to be considered the purview of the state.

the American mythology of heroic individualism were in the ascendant. "The nineteenth century," wrote the critic Greil Marcus, "was when America discovered itself." The United States as an idea had narrowed and stabilized. By the time John Humphrey Noyes was buried behind the Mansion House in 1886, a constellation of distinctly American ideals shone above the Republic. Having assumed that vaunted position, they came to appear fixed, inevitable.

"The American Dream" has never referred to a national destiny: some swell place we are all going together. Rather, it is the distinctly private dream of giving your children more options. By the end of the nineteenth century, the ordinary rate of progress—the erratic, lopsided spread of free market prosperity and the slowly dilating circle of justice and citizenship—seemed like all that most people could hope for. The notion of collectively storming the future was drowned out by the separate ambitions of millions of separate (the utopians would have said "isolated") families. The future would come at its own pace. The busy weekly business of the present was enough.

The next flood tide of American communalism came a century later.* In the late 1960s and early 1970s, after the scene went sour in the East Village, the Haight, and other such places, middle-class youths flocked to the rural counties of Vermont and California, Tennessee and Oregon, New Mexico and Michigan. Like the nineteenth-century utopians, the long-haired communards of the sixties and seventies rejected the prevailing values of their day as morally corrupt and expressed that rejection through the total reconfiguration of their own daily lives.

Despite a great deal of material similarity between the two cohorts, the aspirations of the hippie communards were categorically different from those of their utopian forebears. Although the communalists of the sixties and seventies tried (and often succeeded) to build strongholds of cooperation, pleasure, and consciousness amid the mercantile bustle

---

* There was, of course, plenty of communal experimentation in the century between 1870 and 1970.

of American life, they seldom described their communities as levers of millenarian transformation. Unlike Charles Dana, who left Harvard for Brook Farm, the young men and women who drove north to Humboldt and south to Taos did not claim that their chore wheels and whole grains would somehow trigger the "conversion of this globe, now exhaling pestilential vapors and possessed by unnatural climates, into the abode of beauty and health." Nor did they imagine that their free loving and home birthing would vanquish the "isolated household," let alone establish the Kingdom of Heaven on earth. In general, the twentieth-century communes expressed a secessionist impulse—a leave-taking from the World—not the opening gambit of a new global dispensation.* Their revolution was more personal and, ultimately, far less utopian. The buildings tell the story. The sprawling, Versailles-like fantasies of Robert Owen and Charles Fourier were replaced with the tepees of New Buffalo, the jerry-rigged zomes of Drop City, and the yurts and chicken coops of a thousand small enclaves. The dream of a world-salvific New Jerusalem gave way to an older vision of paradise: a garden of naked innocence, walled off from the fallen world.

A history of utopian experimentation is, by definition, an inner history— less an accounting of what people did than what they had in their heads.

---

* Obviously, the 1960s produced plenty of talk about global revolution. The difference was that it generally came from cities and college campuses, not backwoods communes. What's more, the mechanisms of that imagined revolution were more familiar—marches, political campaigns, propaganda, insurrection, the occasional bank heist. Perhaps the closest analogue to the nineteenth-century utopians were the lysergic cheerleaders at the vanguard of the psychedelic revolution. Some of their high-flown rhetoric echoed the millenarian prophecies of the nineteenth-century utopians. Discussing Fourier's writings in 1842, Albert Brisbane wrote, "An ocean of Social Error Flows over Humanity, but so mighty is Truth, that one drop cast into it will purify and give life to its dead waters." The most hopeful acid boosters spoke in similar terms about the messianic potential of synthetically revitalized consciousness. Their "drop" of Truth was soaked into sheets of paper, not printed upon them, but the general idea was the same: the only thing keeping us from paradise is a thin veil of ignorance. A metric ton of LSD could do the trick: turn on the whole earth and inaugurate the Aquarian millennium.

What most unites the nineteenth- and twentieth-century communalists was their acute dissatisfaction. Nobody risks inventing a new world if they like the one in which they live. The remnants of nineteenth-century utopianism—letters, dinner menus, moth-chewed bloomers, and tumbledown dormitories—add up to a testament of American longing and American discontent. The utopians were driven together by a moral refusal to accept the world as they found it. They believed that human association could offer far more than what they experienced in the villages and cities where they lived. They demanded more fellowship, more pleasure, more learning, more time, more dignity, and more equality. "There is a small number," wrote Horace Greeley, "to whom the old ways, the old purposes of life have become impossible of pursuit—who must breathe freely or be stifled—who cannot live longer to merely personal ends—who will readily dig ditches, if that be the most useful employment which solicits them, but who must do even this heroically, not sordidly, or not at all. They are ready to welcome drudgery, privation, obscurity, but not willing that the covering and cherishing of their own bodies shall be the purpose of their life-long struggle."

This refusal to chase "the old purposes" would be paralyzing without an attendant belief in the human capacity for transformation and a vision of new, better purposes. Traveling around the United States in the period between Robert Owen's retreat to the United Kingdom and Albert Brisbane's triumphal homecoming from Paris, Tocqueville marveled at what he saw as the uniquely American faith in "man's infinite perfectibility." As always, Tocqueville had an explanation: "When citizens are classed by rank, profession, or birth and everyone is forced to follow the path chosen for him by chance, each individual thinks that the limits of human potential are not far off from wherever he happens to find himself. . . . They imagine the condition of the societies of the future as better but not different. And while they acknowledge that humanity has made great progress and may still make more, they believe that certain unsurpassable limits are laid down in advance." By contrast, in the United States, "as castes disappear; as classes come together, and change is evident in men subjected to tumultuous mixing as well as in usages, customs, and laws . . . the image of an ideal and always fleeting perfection presents itself to the human mind." In short, while jostling through a society of (seemingly) limitless possibility, Americans came to believe that "man in general is endowed with an infinite capacity to perfect himself."

Tocqueville doesn't say it, but the present age suggests that this effect works in reverse. As social fluidity coagulates and individuals cease to imagine their own circumstances changing very much, they are less likely to imagine a dramatically improved future for society in general. The future, as an organizing principle for both hope and critique, ceases to exert much pull on the present. The forms of human association come to seem more or less fixed, subject only to incremental improvement or decay.

The aspirations of the nineteenth-century utopians underscore the extent to which we have fallen out of the habit of contemplating that "fleeting perfection." Today, rather than considering idealized futures, we are more likely to look longingly (and selectively) over our shoulder. Americans in particular have made our brief past the repository of all value and virtue—a Kodachrome fantasy of thrift, fresh air, honest labor, and various greatest generations. Instead of articulating extravagant dreams about the future, let alone experimenting with those dreams, we have made our history into a sort of utopia: a high white wall onto which we project our collective longings and anxieties. Even when we talk about the future, we think of the past. The largest super PAC supporting Mitt Romney's 2012 presidential campaign rallied under the koanlike banner "Restore Our Future." Don't just bring back yesterday, bring back yesterday's tomorrow, too.*

When we can be bothered to speculate about the future, our assessments are almost universally grim. Ahead lie swelling debts, moral decay, soaring inequality, peak oil, cultural bankruptcy, dry aquifers, resource-gobbling geriatrics, gnatlike attention spans, a despoiled landscape, and

---

* Yes, there is stark irony in the suggestion that we look to the 1840s to learn how to stop romanticizing our past and start romanticizing our future.

rusting infrastructure. Thanks to anthropogenic climate change, even the weather forecast is bleak. In a century and a half, the prevailing outlook has shifted from jubilantly millenarian to tepidly apocalyptic. None of these predictions are necessarily wrong, but compared with the unmeasured, action-inspiring optimism of the nineteenth-century utopians, it appears that we are experiencing a deficit of imagination.

Without fantasies about the shape of things to come, we are as likely to be led into the future by the almost random process of technological innovation as anything else. Invention mothers necessity, and material progress lurches rudderless, indifferent to anything higher than convenience or the restless appetite for quick satisfactions. As Emerson famously put it in an ode to the Fourierist minister William Henry Channing: "Things are in the saddle, / And ride mankind."

Our present material abundance exceeds even the most fantastical daydreams of the nineteenth-century utopians. A working-class American suburb offers comforts that would stupefy any citizen of the fictional Icaria. But who would call that suburb paradise? "While we are pouring ever increasing intellectual efforts into improving our means, we seem to have given no thought to the ends we serve," wrote the French philosopher Bertrand de Jouvenel. "Every year we are better armed to achieve what we want. But what do we want?"

Uncoupled from utopian ends, even the most incisive social critique falls short. Imagining idealized futures, unburdened by worldly cynicism, begins as a way to catalog social ills and to sift out those values that matter most. But unlike other modes of critique, utopian thinking and experimentation goes further, inevitably generating its own solidarity and enthusiasm, thereby stimulating the numberless private exertions that add up to social progress. The nineteenth-century utopias, "starveling picnics" though many of them were, demonstrate how a thoroughly elaborated vision of a better world can move a diverse group of people in a single direction.

Myths and stories about the past give coherence and energy to a polity. A story about the future—a plot to be fulfilled—can do the same. When the citizens of New Harmony or Icaria believed that utopia was on the horizon, they labored together with remarkable energy, channeling their separate ambitions into a shared vision. "We all work with tireless zeal," wrote a young Icarian named Pech who was assigned to the laundry. "We are doing everything for the love of humanity . . . rather than the love of money, there is no limit to our desire to work." Once the collective vision began to fade, its power became obvious. Suddenly the work was heavier; the soup tasted thinner; and the annoyances were more annoying.

As Socrates suggests toward the end of the *Republic,* the mere contemplation of an ideal polis ("the city we were founding and describing") is a civic act—a means of accessing social and moral truths that might otherwise be obscured by the overwhelming material reality of the world around us. Some of the things that the nineteenth-century utopians got right decades in advance of their fellow citizens—the equality of women, the importance of public education in a democratic society, the need for a social safety net, the edifying vitality of a diverse society, the hazards of unchecked markets—show the social dividends of contemplating idealized futures with a relatively soft commitment to the present state of affairs.

The nineteenth-century utopians did not carry the day. They thought that the world was on the cusp of renewal. They were wrong. The big wooden dormitories were boarded up. The collective gardens went to seed. The loud, merry dining rooms sank into silence. And the sea, despite Fourier's harmonic arithmetic, does not yet taste like lemonade. Their disregard for the world as it is guaranteed that they didn't survive long. Our disregard for the world as it might be could prove just as grave.

Acknowledgments

Amanda Urban made this entire enterprise possible. Without her faith this book would not exist. I am incredibly lucky to have had Jon Meacham as an early champion at Random House. Will Murphy and Molly Turpin read and edited the book with enormous skill. I am deeply grateful for their intelligence, care, and encouragement. Sona Vogel is a brilliant and meticulous copy editor.

A century and a half's worth of journalists, critics, and historians made it easy for a late arrival like myself to wade into this subject. I am indebted to the research and writing of Priscilla J. Brewer, Edward Deming Andrews, Stephen A. Marini, John F. C. Harrison, Arthur Bestor, Lawrence Foster, Carl J. Guarneri, Robert P. Sutton, Lillian M. Snyder, Christopher H. Johnson, Frank E. Manuel, Fritzie P. Manuel, Charles Nordhoff, Robert S. Fogarty, Edmund Wilson, Gilbert Seldes,

Donald E. Pitzer, Spencer Klaw, Robert Allerton Parker, Michael Barkun, and A. J. Macdonald.

I am particularly grateful to Anthony Wonderley, curator of the Oneida Community Mansion House, for both his scholarship and his hospitality; Jonathan F. Beecher, at UC Santa Cruz, for saving me from several embarrassing errors about the lives of Charles Fourier and Victor Considerant; Stephen J. Stein, at Indiana University Bloomington, for his remarkable work on the Shakers and his willingness to help a rank amateur; and Saundra Clem Leininger in Corning, for her efforts to keep the memory of Icaria alive.

This book was written at almost a dozen different desks. The nicest two were Lawrence Rinder's kitchen table in Ukiah and Neal and Karen Latt's picnic table in Orleans. My yearlong berth at Stearns Consulting was less scenic, but it allowed me to pretend that I had a real job. My thanks to Jim Stearns, Kevin Yee, and Christian Cain for keeping me company.

Dana Dart-Mclean made writing seem fun when it had ceased to be. Colter Jacobsen and Jon Jensen straightened me out on a few Latter-day Saints–related matters. Larissa MacFarquhar offered pages of incisive suggestions. I cannot imagine a better reader. Corrine Fitzpatrick applied her fine-tuned poet's ear to the manuscript and provided moral support as I crossed the finish line.

For their love and support, I am forever grateful to my family, Tom Depoto, Jonah Stern, Kathryn Sá-Davis, and Buck Mulligan.

I am daily humbled by the guts, idealism, and work ethic of the men and women who populate the preceding pages. They were giants.

Notes

DARK DAY

xiv   **After hearing Bishop and Wright's account** Andrews, *People Called Shakers,* 19.

xiv   **A few days later, Harlow returned** Francis, *Ann the Word,* 127.

xiv   **"Egyptian darkness"** Andrews, *People Called Shakers,* 19.

xv   **"first-born son in America"** *Summary View,* 35.

xv   **Within a decade, thousands of Americans** Pitzer, ed., *America's Communal Utopias,* 37.

INTRODUCTION: MAN-MADE MILLENNIUM

3   **"A map of the world that does not include"** Wilde, *Soul of Man,* 40.

4   **Francis Bacon is the most notable proponent** Wiener, ed., *Dictionary of the History of Ideas,* vol. 4, 469.

5   **"fresh, green breast"** Fitzgerald, *Great Gatsby,* 180.

5   **"We have it in our power"** Paine, *Common Sense,* 32.

5   **The notion that history, like the sun, travels east** Lester, "A New Geography," in Marcus and Sollors, eds., *New Literary History of America,* 2–6.

6   **"God made me the messenger"** Sargent, Schaer, and Claeys, eds., *Utopia: The Search for the Ideal Society,* 96.

6   **"Thus in the beginning"** Locke, *Two Treatises,* 226.

8   **By the end of the 1840s, twenty-nine Fourierist** Guarneri, *Utopian Alternative,* 408.

10   **To their fellow citizens** Bestor, *Backwoods Utopias,* 47.

10   **"The great utopians"** Manuel and Manuel, *Utopian Thought in the Western World,* 27.

10   **"the sole nexus of man with man"** Carlyle, *Past and Present,* 180.

11   **"only needed to be seen"** Fellman, *Unbounded Frame,* 3.

11   **"The only practical difficulty"** Owen, *New View of Society,* 212.

12   **Mocking Fourier, Owen, and Cabet** Marx, *Selected Writings,* 262.

12   **In volumes 1 and 2** Johnson, *Robert Owen in the United States,* 81.

12   **"Though Marx had pointed out the naïveté"** Wilson, *Finland Station,* 327.

12   **"Even revolutionaries like to have ancestors"** Hobsbawm, *How to Change the World,* 2.

13   **"some practical joker"** McCarthy, *Oasis,* 33.

13 **"what comfort some have"** Bellow, *Augie March*, 392.

14 **"That which produces in the world"** Noyes, *History of American Socialisms*, 71.

14 **"as one man, afire with dedication"** Sutton, *Les Icariens*, 146.

15 **"Seating myself in the venerable orchard"** Noyes, *History of American Socialisms*, 332.

16 **"I expect the sun will rise and set"** Trollope, *Domestic Manners*, 70.

17 **"chilling cordiality of the world"** Orvis, *Letters from Brook Farm*, 41.

17 **"is not to imagine better worlds"** Judt, *Thinking the Twentieth Century*, 304.

17 **"I cannot overcome my fear"** Tocqueville, *Democracy in America*, 759.

18 **"There are men who will kill"** Berlin, "Message to the 21st Century," 37.

19 **"when practice has shown its superiority"** Bestor, *Backwoods Utopias*, 12.

20 **"a French Revolution in small"** Emerson, "Historic Notes of Life and Letters in New England," in *Complete Works*, vol. 10, 364.

THE SHAKERS: AMERICAN ZION

23 **They lived in a small apartment** Dixon, *New America*, 96.

23 **When Lee was little** Francis, *Ann the Word*, 6.

24 **Peasants who had previously** Engels, *Condition of the Working-Class*, 4.

24 **The plump little girl** *Summary View*, 6.

24 **This insolence earned her** Ibid.

24 **For a time she prepared** Francis, *Ann the Word*, 15, 16.

24 **The Wardleys believed** Evans, *Shaker Communism*, 28.

25 **Among those exiled to England** Ibid., 25.

25 **The French Prophets, as they came to be known** Marini, *Radical Sects*, 75.

25 **Slimy, stagnant creeks** Engels, *Condition of the Working-Class*, 51.

25 **The poorest workers** Ibid., 49.

26 **As one commentator later wrote** Adam Ulam, "Socialism and Utopia," in Manuel, ed., *Utopias and Utopian Thought*, 127.

26 **"And there appeared a great wonder"** Bible (KJV), Revelation 12:1.

27 **"as if it were made of embers"** Foster, *Religion and Sexuality*, 24.

27 **On July 14, 1772** *Manifesto*, 193.

27 **"ingenious system for combining"** Ibid., 194.

27 **Three months later** Ibid., 193.

28 **"for disturbing the congregation"** Ibid.

28 **"the most astonishing visions"** *Summary View*, 9.

28 **Lee later argued** Marini, *Radical Sects*, 150.

28 **"Unto the woman he said"** Bible (KJV), Genesis 6:16.

28 **"In the sweat of thy face"** Ibid., 3:19.

29 **"why did not the shame"** Youngs, *Testimony of Christ's Second Appearing*, 37.

29 **"It may easily be determined"** Ibid., 42.

29 **In the afterglow of her vision** *Summary View*, 9.

29 **"saw at once that the candle of the Lord"** Ibid.

29 **"From this time she was received"** Ibid.

29 **"vessel to revive and bring to light"** Ibid., 10.

29 **"Here commenced the real manifestation"** Ibid.

29 **By the early 1770s** Foster, *Religion and Sexuality*, 26.

30 **"While I was sitting there"** *Summary View*, 46.

30 **The tree, the group decided** Andrews, *People Called Shakers*, 13.

30 **"God had a chosen people in America"** *Summary View*, 46.

30 **On May 10, 1774** Andrews, *People Called Shakers*, 13.

30 **The Wardleys and Lee's father** Francis, *Ann the Word*, 80.

30 **When, according to Shaker history** *Summary View*, 19.

31 **A slightly more plausible account** Francis, *Ann the Word*, 83.

31 **"with the wicked at public houses"** *Summary View*, 15.

31 **"She sat down upon the stone"** Sears, ed., *Gleanings from Old Shaker Journals*, 18, 19.

31 **The following year, Lee moved upstate** Andrews, *People Called Shakers*, 15.

31 **The women slept on the ground floor** Ibid.

32 **Lee had seen their arrival** Ibid., 21.

32 **More people camped** Ibid., 32.

34 **One of the first accounts** Stein, *Shaker Experience in America*, 15, 17.

34 **"In the best part of their worship"** Andrews, *People Called Shakers*, 28. [Note: Although Rathbun became an apostate, his account does not differ much from those of more sympathetic observers—for in-

stance, the 1782 observations of William Plummer, as quoted in Francis, *Ann the Word*, 226.]

34 **Eunice Stanton, who followed** Marshall, *Rise and Progress of the Serpent*, 62.

35 **"I have seen the Mother at Niskeuna"** Mackie, *The Gift of Tongues*, 99.

35 **Valentine Rathbun, the convert** Campion, *Mother Ann Lee*, 105.

35 **He left the sect to become** Andrews, *People Called Shakers*, 47.

35 **Rathbun published a pamphlet** Ibid., 44.

36 **In early July 1780** Ibid., 33.

36 **Those who refused to sign** Crain, "Tea and Antipathy," 135.

36 **"Frequent complaints have been made"** Stein, *Shaker Experience in America*, 13.

36 **The men were locked up** Marini, *Radical Sects*, 78.

36 **The state's plan** Andrews, *People Called Shakers*, 33.

37 **Mother Ann was set free** Ibid., 211.

37 **Traveling by foot along the roads** Francis, *Ann the Word*, 304.

37 **Whittaker, who later succeeded Lee** *Summary View*, 44.

37 **During one of her longer stints** Ibid., 12.

38 **Some described a feeling of being dowsed** Marini, *Radical Sects*, 79.

38 **When Mother Ann and the other** Stein, *Shaker Experience in America*, 23, 24.

38 **The sect, which might more properly be called** Ibid.

39 **After he died in 1778** Sears, ed., *Gleanings from Old Shaker Journals*, 3, 4.

39 **A handful of them had traveled to Niskeyuna** Francis, *Ann the Word*, 168.

39 **Word of Lee's presence in Harvard spread** Marini, *Radical Sects*, 96.

39 **Shaker carpenters reinforced the floors** Francis, *Ann the Word*, 191.

39 **The startled citizens of Harvard** Sears, ed., *Gleanings from Old Shaker Journals*, 60.

40 **To the Shakers' antagonists** Andrews, *People Called Shakers*, 44.

40 **Not long after the Shakers' arrival** Sears, ed., *Gleanings from Old Shaker Journals*, 59.

40 **On more than one occasion** Ibid., 41.

40   **Mother Ann may have been** Andrews, *People Called Shakers*, 43.

40   **Lee preached that the Revolution** Francis, *Ann the Word*, 148.

41   **During the summer of 1781** Sears, ed., *Gleanings from Old Shaker Journals*, 61.

40   **In August, the local militia came** Francis, *Ann the Word*, 198.

41   **That winter, the lead Shakers** Sears, ed., *Gleanings from Old Shaker Journals*, 41.

41   **Later that night, when everyone** Ibid., 42.

41   **Back in Harvard that summer** Ibid., 80.

42   **A leader of the mob announced** Ibid., 82.

42   **Men on horseback whipped them** Marini, *Radical Sects*, 93.

42   **"one continued scene of cruelty"** Sears, ed., *Gleanings from Old Shaker Journals*, 87.

42   **"We shall have one meeting together"** Marini, *Radical Sects*, 112.

43   **James Whittaker said that he wanted Shaker life** Ibid.

43   **"Of all the relations that ever I see"** Kanter, *Commitment and Community*, 90.

44   **An experienced Shaker would then be sent** Marini, *Radical Sects*, 100.

44   **Like the secular utopians they would soon inspire** Foster, *Religion and Sexuality*, 30.

44   **Their turbulent two-year odyssey** Francis, *Ann the Word*, 304.

44   **The believers gradually came to conceive** Andrews, *People Called Shakers*, 56, 57.

44   **The scriptural dichotomy** Stein, *Shaker Experience in America*, 68.

44   **Even the secular utopians** Noyes, *History of American Socialisms*, 280.

44   **Lee returned to Niskeyuna looking thin** Francis, *Ann the Word*, 41.

45   **"There are no slovens or sluts"** Sears, ed., *Gleanings from Old Shaker Journals*, 46.

45   **Before joining the Wardley prayer circle** *Summary View*, 38, 52.

45   **It is not clear what killed him** Stein, *Shaker Experience in America*, 32.

45   **"without a struggle or a groan"** *Summary View*, 37.

45   **The *Albany Gazette* carried the news** Stein, *Shaker Experience in America*, 32.

46   **"eunuchs for the Kingdom of Heaven's sake"** Marini, *Radical Sects*, 111.

46   **One of the more extravagant libels** Stein, *Shaker Experience in America*, 77.

46   **In 1840, at the White Water Shaker Village** *Ohio History,* 422.

46   **George Darrow, whose brother David** Stein, *Shaker Experience in America,* 34.

46   **They pooled their money** Marini, *Radical Sects,* 111.

46   **A year after Lee's death** Ibid., 112.

47   **"was as clean as a dining table"** Lossing, "The Shakers," *Harper's New Monthly Magazine,* 167.

48   **"the wisest man that has been born"** Andrews, *People Called Shakers,* 55.

48   **"first in the female-line"** Ibid., 61.

48   **"it will be equal to gaining a nation"** Francis, *Ann the Word,* 214.

49   **"The man cannot gather and build the church"** Marini, *Radical Sects,* 127.

50   **During the twentieth century** Stein, *Shaker Experience in America,* 256.

50   **On Christmas Day 1787** Andrews, *People Called Shakers,* 56, 7.

50   **"There can be no church in complete order"** Youngs, *Testimony of Christ's Second Appearing,* 506.

50   **Within a decade, this verbal covenant** Ibid., 507.

51   **The Shakers found biblical precedent** Ibid., 509.

51   **"And all that believed were together"** Bible (KJV), Acts 2:44, 45; 4:32, 34, 35.

52   ***"Le communisme, c'est le Christianisme"*** Cabet, *Le vrai Christianisme,* xii.

52   **Using a metaphor that evoked** Noyes, *History of American Socialisms,* 192.

52   **"The first people in America"** Morse, *Shakers and the World's People,* 91.

53   **The first communistic colony** Bestor, *Backwoods Utopias,* 277.

53   **"And I John saw the holy city"** Bible (KJV), Revelation 21:2.

53   **When it was completed in 1787** Burks, ed., *Shaker Design,* 5.

53   **Within seven years** Ibid.

54   **The village in New Lebanon** Stein, *Shaker Experience in America,* 44.

54   **By 1796, there were eleven Shaker communities** Priscilla J. Brewer, "The Shakers of Mother Ann Lee," in Pitzer, ed., *America's Communal Utopias,* 43.

54   **Along with meetinghouses** Stein, *Shaker Experience in America,* 44.

56   **At the village in Canterbury** Burks, ed., *Shaker Design,* 13.

56 **Walls built over uneven ground** Ibid., 12.

56 **"The plan, the life, the thought of Mount Lebanon"** Dixon, *New America*, 272.

57 **"split and piled up as neat"** Owen, *Life of Robert Owen, Written by Himself*, vol. 1.A., 154.

57 **"the very dust in the road seemed pure"** Lossing, "The Shakers," *Harper's New Monthly Magazine*, 166.

57 **During one episode** Morin, ed., *Heavenly Visions*, 113.

58 **"Order is the creation of beauty"** *Youth's Guide to Zion*, 12.

59 **"The beauty and glory of the heavenly world"** Promey, *Spiritual Spectacles*, 69.

59 **"plain and without superfluity"** Andrews, *People Called Shakers*, 60.

59 **Stephen J. Stein opens his brilliant** Ibid.

59 **It is somewhat trite to say** Stein, *Shaker Experience in America*, xiii.

60 **"We walked into a grim room where several grim hats"** Burks, ed., *Shaker Design*, 22.

60 **Father Joseph, who reportedly had no "gift"** Fluhman, "Early Mormon and Shaker Visions," *BYU Studies Quarterly*, 99.

60 **New "laboring exercises"** Stein, *Shaker Experience in America*, 48.

61 **Ranks of believers** Burks, ed., *Shaker Design*, 35.

63 **At each of these four levels** Stein, *Shaker Experience in America*, 133, 134, 135.

63 **Aristotle wrote that mutual familiarity** Aristotle, *Politics*, 1326b.

64 **Aristotle makes an allowance** Ibid.

64 **Robert Owen, who modeled his American utopia** Johnson, *Robert Owen in the United States*, 56.

64 **This put him very close to Plato** Plato, *Complete Works*, 1419.

65 **A Shaker brother named Angell** Stein, *Shaker Experience in America*, 53.

65 **The federal census of 1800** Brewer, "Shakers of Mother Ann Lee," in Pitzer, ed., *America's Communal Utopias*, 43, 50.

65 **The guarantee of three squares** Bestor, *Backwoods Utopias*, 43.

66 **Because foundlings and winter Shakers** Stein, *Shaker Experience in America*, 54.

66 **In 1802, word arrived at New Lebanon** Brewer, *Shaker Communities, Shaker Lives*, 32.

66 **"I want you to go with me"** Andrews, *People Called Shakers*, 71.

66 **By late afternoon** Medlicott, *Issachar Bates*, 67.

[Note: Various sources give different numbers of converts. For instance, Brewer, *Shaker Communities, Shaker Lives*, 32, reports twenty-five converts on that particular evening.]

66 **"There was a bright road"** Andrews, *People Called Shakers*, 71; Brewer, *Shaker Communities, Shaker Lives*, 32.

67 **Later that same year** Andrews, *People Called Shakers*, 72.

67 **At a camp meeting in Cane Ridge** McNemar, *Kentucky Revival*, 26.

68 **On the day of the Pentecost** Bible (KJV), Acts 2:13–14.

68 **In the summer of 1801** McNemar, *Kentucky Revival*, 25.

68 **The more people who showed up** Ibid., 26.

68 **"Before he began to speak"** Seldes, *Stammering Century*, 46.

69 **In the frozen predawn blackness** Andrews, *People Called Shakers*, 72.

69 **He was probably sent west** Medlicott, *Issachar Bates*, 62.

69 **The three men traveled on foot** Andrews, *People Called Shakers*, 72.

69 **They were dressed in brown overalls** Ibid., 75.

70 **"Since the falling away of the Apostolic order"** *Ohio History*, 253.

70 **It would be two decades** Stein, *Shaker Experience in America*, 105.

70 **When they asked to address his congregation** McNemar, *Kentucky Revival*, 75.

70 **The next Sunday, Bates and Youngs** Ibid., 76.

70 **"The power of God, revealed in this day"** *Summary View*, 99.

70 **To regain the innocence of Paradise** McNemar, *Kentucky Revival*, 76.

71 **Malcolm Worley, a wealthy local farmer** Stein, *Shaker Experience in America*, 59.

71 **Worley's confession was soon followed** Andrews, *People Called Shakers*, 75.

71 **Although he was an avid revivalist** MacLean, *Richard McNemar*, 4.

71 **"For upwards of 15 years"** Stein, *Shaker Experience in America*, 59.

71 **According to one account** MacLean, *Richard McNemar*, 22, 28.

71 **"We have news of a Zion"** McNemar, *Kentucky Revival*, 80.

72 **By the end of May 1805** Ibid., 85.

72 **He had been selected by Lucy Wright** Stein, *Shaker Experience in America*, 60.

72 **The six elders from New Lebanon** Ibid., 61.

72 **They taught the westerners how to dance** Andrews, *People Called Shakers*, 76, 77.

72 **At $3.00 an acre** Ibid., 79.

72 **Within a year, there were** Stein, *Shaker Experience in America*, 62.

72 **Over the next six years** Ibid., 61.

72 **People threw rocks** Andrews, *People Called Shakers*, 81.

73 **Their horses were branded** Ibid.

73 **"fruits of their unlawful embraces"** Ibid., 91.

73 **All of this abuse** Ibid., 86.

73 **An 1807 Shaker mission** Stein, *Shaker Experience in America*, 62.

73 **Within a decade of the three missionaries' arrival** Ibid., 64.

73 **A decade later, at the time of Wright's death** Foster, *Religion and Sexuality*, 44.

73 **The Ohio villages, in order of their founding** Stein, *Shaker Experience in America*, 114.

74 **Even as Zion sprawled** Marini, *Radical Sects*, 134.

74 **When a draft of Shaker regulations** Stein, *Shaker Experience in America*, 114.

74 **Within six months they authorized** Ibid., 95.

74 **Shakers "should not slip their feet"** Harrison, *Second Coming*, 175.

74 **In fact, there should not be any rugs** Ibid.

74 **No gathering of nuts** Andrews, *People Called Shakers*, 268.

74 **When praying, a Shaker should fold** Ibid., 246.

74 **"My stars!" "My gracious!"** Ibid., 268.

74 **"When you take a piece of bread"** Harrison, *Second Coming*, 175.

74 **"cross your knife & fork"** Andrews, *People Called Shakers*, 183.

75 **Some are laughably obvious** Ibid., 267.

75 **Men and women should not pass** Ibid., 266.

75 **Men's clothes should never be hung** Ibid., 267.

75 **No watching animals have sex** Harrison, *Second Coming*, 168.

75 **"If you commit sin with beasts"** Francis, *Ann the Word*, 263.

75 **"attending to the amour of two flies"** Harrison, *Second Coming*, 168.

76 **By the middle of the 1820s** Stein, *Shaker Experience in America*, 40.

76 **When they counted themselves in 1823** Ibid., 87.

76 **Stephen J. Stein, the leading contemporary historian** Ibid.

76 **Two years later, on thirteen hundred acres** Andrews, *People Called Shakers*, 89.

76 **The population of Zion** Brewer, "Shakers of Mother Ann Lee," in Pitzer, ed., *America's Communal Utopias*, 37.

77 **In the coming decades** Bestor, *Backwoods Utopias*, 41.

77   **"We are the people who turned the world"** Andrews, *People Called Shakers,* 18.

77   **"I will bow and be simple"** Stein, *Shaker Experience in America,* 192.

NEW HARMONY: THE GREAT INFIDEL EXPERIMENT

79   **"The change has come upon the world like a thief in the night!"** Owen, *Life of Robert Owen, Written by Himself,* vol. 1.A., 137.

79   **A little before noon** William Owen, *Diary of William Owen,* 9.

79   **Navigating the rough road** Ibid.

80   **Elder Seth Wells greeted the three men** Ibid.

80   **Two hundred and fifty believers** Ibid., 12.

80   **The women wore long brown gowns** Ibid., 10.

80   **The Shakers were used to visitors** Ibid., 9.

80   **They probably did not know** Bestor, *Backwoods Utopias,* 95.

81   **In Albany, he and his son William** William Owen, *Diary of William Owen,* 9, 51; Bestor, *Backwoods Utopias,* 105, 113.

81   **When he sailed into New York Harbor** Feller, *Jacksonian Promise,* 1.

81   **Lafayette, the last living general** Ibid., 2; Howe, *What Hath God Wrought,* 304.

82   **On New Year's Day 1824** Howe, *What Hath God Wrought,* 304.

82   **"What ideas individuals may attach"** Owen, *New View of Society,* 120.

83   **Arthur Bestor, the most influential historian** Bestor, *Backwoods Utopias,* 3.

83   **Starting in 1818, when he printed** Harrison, *Quest for the New Moral World,* 53.

83   **"neutralize family loyalties"** Ibid., 92.

83   **"conclusive argument against the system"** Owen, *Life of Robert Owen, Written by Himself,* vol. 1.A., 145.

83   **The word *socialism*** Harrison, *Quest for the New Moral World,* 45.

83   **"their idle peculiarities"** Andrews, *People Called Shakers,* 132.

83   **"how much sooner must it be feasible"** Bestor, *Backwoods Utopias,* 39.

84   **"Let us, then, profit by the lessons"** Evans, *Shaker Communism,* 118.

84   **To Greeley, the Shakers' most unpardonable** Ibid.

84   **"The objection [to communism] supposes"** Nordhoff, *American Utopias*, 19.

85   **"uncommonly neat and clean"** William Owen, *Diary of William Owen*, 11.

85   **After a thorough tour of the village** Ibid.

85   **"of Quakers? or Jews? or what?"** Ibid., 14.

85   **Around four in the afternoon** Ibid.

86   **"Then," the Shaker said** Ibid., 15.

86   **"I do not know when"** Ibid., 13.

86   **"The character of man"** Owen, *New View of Society*, 43.

86   **At ten, Owen left home** Johnson, *Robert Owen in the United States*, 14.

86   **From there, he went to Stamford** Manuel and Manuel, *Utopian Thought in the Western World*, 676.

86   **Owen spent his nonworking hours** Owen, *Life of Robert Owen, Written by Himself,* vol. 1, 14.

86   **McGuffog was a Presbyterian** Packard, *Life of Robert Owen*, 23.

86   **"Before my investigations were concluded"** Owen, *Life of Robert Owen, Written by Himself,* vol. 1, 16.

87   **"religious feelings were immediately replaced"** Ibid.

87   **"more varied, extended and singular"** Johnson, *Robert Owen in the United States*, 70.

87   **At age five, he was so eager** Packard, *Life of Robert Owen*, 11.

87   **"habit of close observation"** Ibid.

88   **In 1788, when Owen was seventeen** Harrison, *Quest for the New Moral World*, 152.

88   **In the final three decades** Ibid., 153.

88   **In the slums, the smell of putrefaction** Engels, *Condition of the Working-Class*, 49.

88   **Moldy bread and rancid meat** Ibid., 70.

88   **Flour was cut with gypsum** Ibid.

88   **Bitter gin and "Port wine"** Ibid.

89   **"From this foul drain the greatest stream"** Hobsbawm, *Age of Revolution*, 27.

89   **"Hell upon Earth"** Ibid., 53.

90   **In 1819, a British parliamentarian** Packard, *Life of Robert Owen*, 247.

90   **By 1791, at the age of nineteen** Ibid., 35.

90   **A pound of raw cotton** Ibid., 38.

90 **As Owen began to make money** Wilson, *Angel and the Serpent*, 97.

90 **He began to wonder** Muravchik, *Heaven on Earth*, 34.

90 **In 1799, Owen corralled a group** Packard, *Life of Robert Owen*, 52.

91 **David Dale, a pious man** Ibid., 47.

91 **"indolent, dirty, imbecile"** Johnson, *Robert Owen in the United States*, 25.

91 **"lived in idleness, in poverty"** Owen, *Life of Robert Owen, Written by Himself,* vol. 1, 277.

91 **One contemporaneous biographer** Packard, *Life of Robert Owen*, 64.

92 **Although the mill** Morton, *Life and Ideas of Robert Owen*, 28.

92 **He established strict curfews** Owen, *New View of Society,* x.

92 **At every workstation** Ibid.

92 **Bentham and Owen were friends** Harrison, *Quest for the New Moral World*, 48.

92 **When mills throughout the nation** Packard, *Life of Robert Owen*, 74.

93 **When he returned to New Lanark** Harrison, *Quest for the New Moral World*, 157.

93 **"men and women of a new race"** Muravchik, *Heaven on Earth*, 28.

94 **In 1816, to begin the work** Morton, *Life and Ideas of Robert Owen*, 31.

94 **"without exception, passive"** Owen, *New View of Society,* 19.

94 **Despite Owen's self-proclaimed passion** Owen, *Life of Robert Owen, Written by Himself,* vol. 1, 140.

95 **Reports of Owen's progress** Harrison, *Quest for the New Moral World*, 152.

95 **Between 1815 and 1825** Ibid.

95 **"is not, I apprehend, to be found"** Lockwood, *New Harmony Movement*, 51.

95 **"Mr. Owen the Philanthropist"** Harrison, *Quest for the New Moral World,* 11; Morton, *Life and Ideas of Robert Owen*, 31.

95 **Grand Duke Nicholas of Russia** Muravchik, *Heaven on Earth*, 36.

95 **"the most popular man in Europe"** Lockwood, *New Harmony Movement,* 43.

95 **In 1815, he drafted a bill** Morton, *Life and Ideas of Robert Owen*, 15.

95 **"The employments of these Children"** Owen, *Life of Robert Owen, Written by Himself,* vol. 1.A., 27.

95 **A coalition of mill owners** Ibid., 29.

96 **As for the outlandish notion** Ibid., 28.

96 **"heads of families of their natural control"** Ibid., 30.

96 **"had not the least doubt"** Emerson, "Historic Notes of Life and Letters in New England," in *Complete Works,* vol. 10, 346.

96 **"As soon as they understand the plan"** Owen, *New View of Society,* 212.

97 **In March 1817, while Owen's child labor bill** Packard, *Life of Robert Owen,* 127.

97 **When Owen sat down to testify** Ibid.

97 **When the session ended** Ibid., 129.

97 **Eventually someone stepped out** Bestor, *Backwoods Utopias,* 70; Morton, *Life and Ideas of Robert Owen,* 34.

97 **He resolved to bring his plan** Bestor, *Backwoods Utopias,* 70, 71.

98 **"all the mail-coaches in the kingdom"** Packard, *Life of Robert Owen,* 134.

98 **In August 1817, in front of several thousand** Ibid., 135.

98 **"the fundamental notion of every religion"** Ibid., 139.

98 **By the fall** Bestor, *Backwoods Utopias,* 70.

99 **On September 6** Owen, *New View of Society,* 204.

99 **The letter begins with an ambitious proposal** Ibid.

99 **"You may shut yourselves up in your parks as usual"** Muravchik, *Heaven on Earth,* 39.

99 **"The change from the OLD system"** Ibid., 213.

99 **"To resist the introduction of this plan"** Ibid.

100 **The transition into the New Moral World** Ibid.

100 **"Every social movement, every real advance"** Engels, *Socialism,* 43.

100 **"one of the few born leaders"** Ibid., 40.

100 **"The only real practical difficulty"** Owen, *New View of Society,* 212.

100 **"In the day and hour when I disclaimed"** Ibid., 220.

101 **This letter includes a postscript** Ibid., 226.

101 **"Ere long there shall be"** Ibid., 220.

101 **"Even now, the time is near at hand"** Ibid., 222.

101 **"TRUTH," Owen declares** Ibid., 220.

101 **"THE WORLD APPROVES"** Ibid., 225, 226.

102 **"Not only men of his own class"** Engels, *Socialism,* 42.

102 **"the most amiable, sanguine, and candid of men"** Johnson, *Robert Owen in the United States,* 12.

102 **At the 1818 Congress of Aix-la-Chapelle** Owen, *Life of Robert Owen, Written by Himself,* vol. 1, 186.

102 **"fitted so tightly to his person"** Ibid., 185.

102 **Owen convinced John Quincy Adams** Morton, *Life and Ideas of Robert Owen,* 150.

103 **"do as much for peace as he had previously"** Owen, *Life of Robert Owen, Written by Himself,* vol. 1, 202.

103 **"Mr. Owen is the first philosopher"** Hazlitt, *Collected Works,* 124.

103 **"Lord Wellington," the critic extrapolated** Ibid., 125.

103 **"marked as a Jacobin, a leveler"** Ibid., 126.

103 **In August 1824, a man named Richard Flower** Bestor, *Backwoods Utopias,* 101.

104 **In 1791, Rapp, a Pietist weaver** Berry, *America's Utopian Experiments,* 44.

104 **Like Ann Lee** Karl J. R. Arndt, "George Rapp's Harmony Society," in Pitzer, ed., *America's Communal Utopias,* 61.

104 **He claimed that his church** Ibid., 62.

104 **Between 1803 and 1805** Berry, *America's Utopian Experiments,* 45.

104 **Eight hundred Rappites** Arndt, "George Rapp's Harmony Society," in Pitzer, ed., *America's Communal Utopias,* 67.

104 **Their industries thrived** Pitzer and Jones, *New Harmony Then and Now,* 28.

105 **Rapp may also have sensed** Arndt, "George Rapp's Harmony Society," in Pitzer, ed., *America's Communal Utopias,* 73, 74.

105 **With $250,000** Harrison, *Quest for the New Moral World,* 164.

105 **He was already well aware** Arndt, "George Rapp's Harmony Society," in Pitzer, ed., *America's Communal Utopias,* 91.

105 **Flower offered Owen a bargain** Nordhoff, *American Utopias,* 77. [Note: Accounts of how much Owen paid for Harmonie vary. Harrison (*Quest for the New Moral World,* 174) says that Owen spent $125,000 on the estate and another $75,000 once the community was established. Bestor (*Backwoods Utopias,* 180) reports that Owen paid Rapp $95,000 in April 1825 and then spent a further $30,000 on the "Preliminary Society" and $15,000 on supplies for the New Harmony store.]

106 **"the cradle of the future liberty"** Morton, *Life and Ideas of Robert Owen,* 139.

106 **"Here it is," he wrote** Lockwood, *New Harmony Movement,* 70.

106 **After five weeks at sea** Bestor, *Backwoods Utopias*, 101.

106 **Less than a month after that** William Owen, *Diary of William Owen*, 92.

106 **The second day of 1825 was cold** Ibid.

106 **Afterward, father and son** Ibid.

107 **From the top of a low, conical hill** Ibid., 93.

107 **The Rappites had planted orchards** Bernhard, *Travels Through North America*, 116.

107 **On the gentle slopes** Ibid.

107 **Near the center of the village** Wilson, *Angel and the Serpent*, 42.

107 **"We contemplated with pleasure"** William Owen, *Diary of William Owen*, 93.

107 **The next morning, Owen sat down** Ibid., 94.

107 **That same day he left** Wilson, *Angel and the Serpent*, 111.

107 **"the industrious and well disposed"** Harrison, *Quest for the New Moral World*, 164.

108 **A month after buying the village** Bestor, *Backwoods Utopias*, 111.

108 **President-elect John Quincy Adams** Ibid., 113.

108 **At a meeting at the Dennison Hotel** Ibid., 109.

108 **To satisfy local curiosity** Johnson, *Robert Owen in the United States*, 26.

109 **Even outgoing president James Monroe** Bestor, *Backwoods Utopias*, 111.

109 **"Changes [are] at hand"** Johnson, *Robert Owen in the United States*, 21.

109 **He explained that he had come** Ibid., 32.

109 **"the degrading and pernicious practice"** Ibid.

109 **"the gigantic superiority of union"** Ibid.

109 **Owen explained his belief** Ibid., 31.

109 **"give and secure liberty"** Ibid., 30.

109 **"manfully and promptly step forward"** Ibid., 29.

110 **"unmeaning phrases, forms, and ceremonies"** Ibid., 28, 29.

110 **To preempt charges of blasphemy** Ibid., 45.

110 **Despite this impiety** Bestor, *Backwoods Utopias*, 112.

110 **"The gentle tone of his voice"** Trollope, *Domestic Manners*, 127.

111 **During Owen's second speech** Johnson, *Robert Owen in the United States*, 47.

111 **"every domestic arrangement"** Ibid., 48.

112 **"the future habitation of the human race"** Ibid., 47.

112 **"cultivated like a garden"** Ibid., 49.

112 **"a new machine for performing"** Ibid., 47.

112 **Late in 1825, Owen brought** Bestor, *Backwoods Utopias*, 129.

113 **While Owen traveled through the East** Ibid., 114, 161.

113 **By the time Owen returned to the community** Bestor, *Backwoods Utopias*, 122.

113 **A group of hatters** Lockwood, *New Harmony Movement*, 96.

113 **The chandlery was producing** Bestor, *Backwoods Utopias*, 163.

113 **Packed though it was** Ibid.

113 **Unskilled laborers, many of whom** Ibid., 165.

114 **Owen returned to find the Rappite-built** Wilson, *Angel and the Serpent*, 135.

114 **While the colony was underwritten** Ibid.

114 **A shortage of housing** Bestor, *Backwoods Utopias*, 162.

114 **Rather than laying foundations** Ibid.

114 **He had already picked out a nice flat plot** Johnson, *Robert Owen in the United States*, 50.

114 **"Mechanism and Science," he announced** Owen, *Life of Robert Owen, Written by Himself*, vol. 1.A., 124.

114 **In 1855, Owen's hopes for a mechanically induced** Harrison, *Quest for the New Moral World*, 100.

115 **"When the new arrangements shall be"** Johnson, *Robert Owen in the United States*, 33.

116 **"So soon as we have over-supplied"** Feller, *Jacksonian Promise*, 30.

116 **During the spring of 1825** Pitzer and Jones, *New Harmony Then and Now*, 56.

117 **"The Society is instituted generally"** Lockwood, *New Harmony Movement*, 84.

117 **To get the ball rolling** Sutton, *Communal Utopias*, 6.

117 **As it turned out, pious, wellborn** Wilson, *Angel and the Serpent*, 122.

118 **Caroline and her other two daughters** Ibid.

118 **During the spring and summer of 1825** Bestor, *Backwoods Utopias*, 165.

118 **They did manage to put in a field** Ibid.

118 **Some of the Rappites' well-fertilized fields** Wilson, *Angel and the Serpent*, 126.

118 **The New Harmonites were forced** Ibid.

118 **Many of them, including Owen** Bestor, *Backwoods Utopias*, 218.

118 **Soon after his triumphal trip to Washington** Ibid., 114.

119 **"persons of all ages and descriptions"** Lockwood, *New Harmony Movement*, 85.

119 **Some utopian socialists** Guarneri, *Utopian Alternative*, 375.

119 **To the shame (presumably)** Wilson, *Patriotic Gore*, 341.

120 **"We propose a radical and universal reform"** Codman, *Brook Farm*, 42.

120 **Aside from placing a single notice** Robert Dale Owen, *To Holland and to New Harmony*, 232.

120 **A lithograph Owen printed** Harrison, *Quest for the New Moral World*, 85 (illustration).

120 **By the time Owen arrived in Philadelphia** Bestor, *Backwoods Utopias*, 100.

121 **Exercising his strong instinct** Wilson, *Angel and the Serpent*, 138.

121 **Along with a heavy cargo of books** Robert Dale Owen, *To Holland and to New Harmony*, 237.

121 **Like Owen, Maclure took a radical view** Harrison, *Quest for the New Moral World*, 38.

121 **Along with lending his considerable** Wilson, *Angel and the Serpent*, 138.

121 **He agreed to take charge** Harrison, *Quest for the New Moral World*, 37.

121 **Other members of the Boatload of Knowledge** Robert Dale Owen, *To Holland and to New Harmony*, 237.

122 **"one of the significant intellectual migrations"** Bestor, *Backwoods Utopias*, 133.

122 **"If everybody alleged to have traveled"** Wilson, *Angel and the Serpent*, 137.

122 **A judge in one Pennsylvania river town** Robert Dale Owen, *To Holland and to New Harmony*, 259.

122 **Twenty-four-year-old Robert Dale Owen** Ibid.

122 **Some American towns strung chains** Seldes, *Stammering Century*, 116, 206.

122 **In the evenings** Robert Dale Owen, *To Holland and to New Harmony*, 246.

123 **On January 24, 1826** Wilson, *Angel and the Serpent*, 137.

123 **Owen, who had traveled most of the way** Ibid.

123 **With their benefactor and his brainy retinue** Bestor, *Backwoods Utopias,* 170.

123 **"a certain degree of pecuniary inequality"** Ibid., 173; Wilson, *Angel and the Serpent,* 148.

123 **Now it was happening** Bestor, *Backwoods Utopias,* 171.

123 **"Equality of rights, uninfluenced by sex"** Wilson, *Angel and the Serpent,* 129.

123 **Community of property** Bestor, *Backwoods Utopias,* 173.

124 **Workers within each department** Wilson, *Angel and the Serpent,* 150.

124 **Everyone already living** Bestor, *Backwoods Utopias,* 168.

124 **A notice in the *New Harmony Gazette*** Lockwood, *New Harmony Movement,* 98.

124 **A ring of benches** Bernhard, *Travels Through North America,* 120.

124 **The colonists even invented** Ibid., 118.

124 **Josiah Warren, an accomplished bandleader** Lockwood, *New Harmony Movement,* 135.

125 **They called one another** Ibid., 136.

125 **One visitor recalled** Bernhard, *Travels Through North America,* 117.

125 **"There was something especially taking"** Robert Dale Owen, *Threading My Way,* 245.

125 **Lectures and debates were offered** Bestor, *Backwoods Utopias,* 168.

125 **Under the editorship of William Owen** Wilson, *Angel and the Serpent,* 147.

125 **On Sunday mornings** Bernhard, *Travels Through North America,* 116.

125 **During these Sunday talks** Ibid.

125 **"a general desire throughout society"** Bestor, *Backwoods Utopias,* 12.

125 **"from Community to Community"** Johnson, *Robert Owen in the United States,* 75.

126 **During 1825 and 1826** Berry, *America's Utopian Experiments,* 57.

126 **A decade after the collapse** Ibid.

126 **She and Lafayette were so close** Feller, *Jacksonian Promise,* 11.

126 **Annoyed by such rumors** Ibid.

126 **Her interest in communalism** Noyes, *History of American Socialisms,* 57.

127 **After hearing Owen's speech** Feller, *Jacksonian Promise,* 12.

127 **At New Harmony, she struck upon** Bestor, *Backwoods Utopias,* 219.

127 **The colony would purchase slaves** Seldes, *Stammering Century,* 342.

127 **"an establishment where affection"** Lane, *Frances Wright,* 25.

128 **With Nashoba falling apart** Noyes, *History of American Socialisms,* 71.

128 **In Wright's continued absence** Feller, *Jacksonian Promise,* 81, 82.

128 **Wright gave up on the community** Wright, "Establishment at Nashoba," *New Harmony Gazette,* 164, 165.

128 **"a perpetual trust for the benefit"** Ibid.

128 **The money was spent mostly** Ibid.

128 **"unsexed herself and become"** Bernhard, *Travels Through North America,* 108.

128 **"the priestess of Beelzebub"** Bestor, *Backwoods Utopias,* 221.

128 **For a time, antebellum conservatives** Ibid.

129 **Meanwhile at New Harmony** Bestor, *Backwoods Utopias,* 174.

129 **Just two weeks after the colonists** Ibid.

129 **New Harmony had operated for a year** Ibid., 164.

129 **"He would be responsible"** Ibid.

129 **"aspiring aristocratical spirits"** Lockwood, *New Harmony Movement,* 137.

129 **To some, the fact that New Harmony** Bestor, *Backwoods Utopias,* 165.

130 **"aversion to serious duties"** Brown, *Twelve Months in New Harmony,* 25.

130 **Even though Owen lived modestly** Lockwood, *New Harmony Movement,* 137, 145.

130 **Brown, a living parody** Brown, *Twelve Months in New Harmony,* 101.

130 **The *Gazette,* which was published by Owen** Sutton, *Communal Utopias,* 11.

130 **"Babel-like confusion"** Lockwood, *New Harmony Movement,* 142.

130 **"Ere long," he had prophesied in 1817** Owen, *New View of Society,* 220.

130 **"lazy worthless persons"** Bernhard, *Travels Through North America,* 117.

130 **"ladies and gentlemen of quality"** Ibid., 118.

130 **He was dismayed, for instance** Ibid., 116.

131 **"in spite of the principles of equality"** Ibid., 110.

131 **En route to Nashoba** Trollope, *Domestic Manners,* 41.

131 **"all the Americans seem to consider"** William Owen, *Diary of William Owen,* 16.

131 **"was to look back all his life on a dancing school"** Wilson, *Finland Station,* 89.

131 **Marie Fretageot, a French educator** Bernhard, *Travels Through North America*, 116, 119.

131 **He recalled the saga** Ibid., 117.

131 **"No one is to be favored"** Wilson, *Angel and the Serpent*, 152.

132 **"Some of the married women"** Seldes, *Stammering Century*, 85.

132 **His quarrel was with sectarianism** Harrison, *Quest for the New Moral World*, 86.

132 **"gradually and imperceptibly die away"** Owen, *New View of Society*, 208.

132 **On any given Sunday** Wilson, *Angel and the Serpent*, 118, 130.

132 **Robert Jennings, a former Universalist** Bernhard, *Travels Through North America*, 122; Wilson, *Angel and the Serpent*, 130.

133 **Although Jennings did not name** Wilson, *Angel and the Serpent*, 131.

133 **After leaving New Harmony** Ibid.

133 **The *Philadelphia Gazette*** Lockwood, *New Harmony Movement*, 103.

134 **During the winter of 1826** Bestor, *Backwoods Utopias*, 176.

134 **To avoid a prolonged conflict** Sutton, *Communal Utopias*, 10.

134 **They called their settlement Macluria** Ibid.

134 **Since the Maclurians did not have** Wilson, *Angel and the Serpent*, 153.

134 **A month after the Maclurians left** Bestor, *Backwoods Utopias*, 177.

135 **"rational system of nomenclature"** Lockwood, *New Harmony Movement*, 115.

135 **The results tend toward the tongue-twisting** Ibid., 115.

135 **John Quincy Adams even identified** Feller, *Jacksonian Promise*, 70.

135 **For a time, the *New Harmony Gazette*** Wilson, *Angel and the Serpent*, 27.

135 **Perhaps the most disruptive faction** Bestor, *Backwoods Utopias*, 179.

136 **The women wore knee-length dresses** Holloway, *Heavens on Earth*, 112.

136 **"a featherbed tied in the middle"** Wilson, *Angel and the Serpent*, 147.

136 **Adopted by diehards** Bestor, *Backwoods Utopias*, 179.

136 **By contrast, the Literati sought** Ibid.

137 **At New Harmony, while a heavy summer** Brown, *Twelve Months in New Harmony*, 33.

137 **"This event is likely to prove"** Johnson, *Robert Owen in the United States*, 67.

137 "the arts and mysteries by which the few" Ibid., 69.

137 "a trinity of the most monstrous evils" Ibid., 71.

137 "the world in continual wars" Ibid.

137 "keep their children apart from the multitude" Ibid.

137 "The revolution . . . to be now effected" Ibid., 72.

138 "I have calmly and deliberately" Ibid., 70.

138 "beyond the power of recall" Ibid., 74.

138 "This light is now set upon a hill" Ibid.

139 In the words of one historian Seldes, *Stammering Century*, 83.

139 For a time, each person's working hours Lockwood, *New Harmony Movement*, 120.

139 This plan was thrown out Ibid.

139 During the Preliminary Society Carmony and Elliott, "Seedbed for Utopia," 168.

139 In the middle of March 1826 Sutton, *Communal Utopias*, 10; Bestor, *Backwoods Utopias*, 181.

140 As a compromise, Owen selected twenty-four Bestor, *Backwoods Utopias*, 182.

140 Artisans, whose skills brought in cash Lockwood, *New Harmony Movement*, 160.

140 He had successfully created Bestor, *Backwoods Utopias*, 183.

140 In May 1826 Sutton, *Communal Utopias*, 11.

141 A newly formed "Pastoral Society" Ibid.

141 They would barter their services Bestor, *Backwoods Utopias*, 185.

141 Creating alternative currencies Ibid.

141 Buckminster Fuller advocated Burton, *Paradise Planters*, ix.

141 It didn't take long for the three groups Ibid., 186.

142 People called for him to give up control Ibid., 187.

142 Eager to accommodate Ibid., 186.

142 "the most obstinate man" Wilson, *Angel and the Serpent*, 187.

142 He paid Owen for the land Sutton, *Communal Utopias*, 12.

142 "'Hope deferred maketh the heart sick'" Letter from Thomas Pears to B. Bakewell (March 21, 1826), University of California, Davis, online archive, http://historyproject.ucdavis.edu/lessons/view_lesson.php?id=10.

143 While Owen refused to admit defeat Wilson, *Angel and the Serpent*, 162.

143 **At one point, the *Gazette* claimed** Bestor, *Backwoods Utopias*, 195.

143 **An Ohio operator** Ibid.

143 **"Matters were drawing to a close"** Noyes, *History of American Socialisms*, 41.

144 **Owen had paid $95,000** Bestor, *Backwoods Utopias*, 180.

144 **When Frederick Rapp came to collect** Sutton, *Communal Utopias*, 13.

144 **Maclure, seeing an opportunity** Bestor, *Backwoods Utopias*, 197.

144 **A court-ordered settlement** Ibid.

144 **"a pilfering disposition"** Lockwood, *New Harmony Movement*, 149.

144 **"swine ranged at pleasure"** Ibid.

144 **"Ten of [the Rappites'] best years"** Noyes, *History of American Socialisms*, 33.

144 **The most determined communitarians** Barkun, *Crucible of the Millennium*, 96; Harrison, *Quest for the New Moral World*, 166.

144 **Influenced by his time at New Harmony** Andrews, *People Called Shakers*, 233.

145 **In three years, Owen had poured** Robert Dale Owen, *Threading My Way*, 346.

145 **"the social system is now firmly established"** Wilson, *Angel and the Serpent*, 162.

145 **At a time when the rift between science and faith** Ibid., 191.

145 **In 1846, a visiting Scottish scientist** Ibid.

146 **Two decades later, he wrote** Letter from Robert Dale Owen to Abraham Lincoln (September 17, 1862), University of Evansville online archive, http://faculty.evansville.edu/ck6/bstud/lincoln.html.

146 **"I was cautioned not to speak"** Noyes, *History of American Socialisms*, 42.

146 **By one count** Bestor, *Backwoods Utopias*, 227.

146 **"In a firing squad, if all the guns are loaded"** Ibid., 228.

147 **"all religions are erroneous"** Howe, *What Hath God Wrought*, 446.

147 **In his eighties, like so many veterans** Packard, *Life of Robert Owen*, 232.

147 **Even his mysticism** Morton, *Life and Ideas of Robert Owen*, 145.

147 **One of Owen's last tracts** Owen, *Future of the Human Race*, 1.

147 **At the age of eighty-seven** Harrison, *Quest for the New Moral World*, 7.

147 **"My life was not useless"** Johnson, *Robert Owen in the United States*, 15.

147   **On the morning of November 17, 1858** Packard, *Life of Robert Owen*, 239.

148   **He asked the vicar to kindly convey** Ibid.

THE FOURIERIST PHALANXES: THE LEMONADE SEA

149   *Les attractions sont proportionnelles* Godwin, *Popular View*, 25.

149   **In a fruit bowl he saw the whole world** Barthes, *Barthes Reader*, 364; Beecher, *Charles Fourier*, 234.

149   **By Fourier's tally** Guarneri, *Utopian Alternative*, 15.

150   **He was eighteen** Godwin, *Popular View*, 20.

150   **The apple cost fourteen sous** Guarneri, *Utopian Alternative*, 15.

151   **"I was taught in catechism"** Fourier, *Harmonian Man*, 150.

151   **His bedroom was so crammed** Beecher, *Charles Fourier*, 20.

151   **At seven, standing behind the counter** Fourier, *Harmonian Man*, 150.

151   **A year after the violence erupted** Beecher, *Charles Fourier*, 37.

151   **A modest form of globalization** Doyle, *French Revolution*, 231.

151   **When the chic court of Marie Antoinette** Beecher, *Charles Fourier*, 38.

152   **During the 1790s, half the silk workshops** Doyle, *French Revolution*, 403.

152   **At the start of 1793, Fourier traveled** Pellarin, *Life of Charles Fourier*, 7, 20.

152   **As the standoff progressed** Beecher, *Charles Fourier*, 42.

152   **He watched as his bales of cotton** Ibid.

152   **"In the end," he wrote** Fourier, *Harmonian Man*, 151.

152   **Rather than wash away the gore** Doyle, *French Revolution*, 254.

152   **When the machine failed** Ibid.

153   **"Lyon made war on Liberty"** Ibid.

153   **By the spring of 1793, an estimated 1,880** Ibid.

153   **The following summer, Fourier was drafted** Beecher, *Charles Fourier*, 46, 47; Pellarin, *Life of Charles Fourier*, 24.

153   **One afternoon he was sent to supervise** Beecher, *Charles Fourier*, 52.

153   **Eric Hobsbawm called the "dual revolution"** Hobsbawm, *How to Change the World*, 6.

154 **"nothing to seek any better arrangement"** Fourier, *Theory of the Four Movements*, 3.

154 **"Philosophy,"** Fourier wrote Fourier, *Harmonian Man*, 236.

155 **Why would God** Burton, *Paradise Planters*, 190.

155 **At the dawn of the nineteenth century** Fourier, *Theory of the Four Movements*, 16.

155 **The original printing claimed** Beecher, *Charles Fourier*, 116.

155 **The book is wildly abstruse** Ibid.

155 **In the short volume's introduction** Fourier, *Theory of the Four Movements*, 3.

156 **"Civilization,"** Fourier wrote Ibid., 10.

156 **"The present social order"** Brisbane, *Association*, 33.

156 **"The passions,"** Fourier wrote Fourier, *Harmonian Man*, 37.

157 **Fourier defines the term** *passional attraction* Ibid.

158 **They turn sour only** Charles Fourier, "Of the Role of the Passions," https://www.marxists.org/reference/archive/fourier/works/ch01.htm.

158 **"the person who should have been"** Beecher, *Charles Fourier*, 238.

158 **He identifies twelve distinct passions** Fourier, *Theory of the Four Movements*, xvii.

158 **Fourier claimed that every person** Ibid., xviii.

159 **According to Fourier, all observable change** Ibid., 40.

159 **Applying this principle to human history** Ibid., 40, 41.

159 **"Social progress and changes"** Beecher, *Charles Fourier*, 208.

161 **According to Fourier's calculations** Fourier, *Theory of the Four Movements*, 40, 41.

161 **"End of the animal and vegetable world"** Ibid., foldout chart.

161 **When we ascend from Civilization to Harmony** Godwin, *Popular View*, 40.

161 **"The Fourierist number is not rounded off"** Barthes, *Barthes Reader*, 361.

161 **He seldom left home** Beecher, *Charles Fourier*, 96.

162 **Each of Fourier's proposed phalanxes** Ibid., 243.

162 **They will work and sleep** Ibid.

162 **To satisfy the flighty demands** Brisbane, *Social Destiny of Man*, 121.

162 **So, for instance, the prevalence** Fourier, *Hierarchies of Cuckoldry*, 39.

162 **Fourier's "Taxonomy of Cuckoldry"** Ibid., 10–37.

163 **Homosexuals will freely obey** Beecher, *Charles Fourier*, 303.

163 **Only those attracted to both sexes** Ibid.

163 **Masochists—whom Fourier called "baby doll types"** Ibid.

163 **Even incest, as long as it is** Ibid., 304.

163 **"the love of lesbians and the eagerness"** Ibid., 84.

163 **Similarly, a solo violinist** Fourier, *Harmonian Man,* 266.

163 **"of man's natural needs"** Ibid., 278.

163 **"Pontiffs of Love"** Ibid., 262.

163 **"a lasting society skillfully prepared"** Ibid., 264.

164 **Working side by side in the orchard** Brisbane, *Social Destiny of Man,* 121.

164 **For instance, young boys** Fourier, *Harmonian Man,* 285.

164 **They will wear special "barbaric" uniforms** Ibid.

164 **"Frenzied by trumpet blasts and roars"** Beecher, *Charles Fourier,* 287.

164 **"owing simply to the allurement"** Bestor, *Backwoods Utopias,* 13.

164 **"thousands of analogous organizations"** Ibid., 16.

164 **At the peak of Harmony** Beecher, *Charles Fourier,* 243.

164 **These semi-independent communities** Ibid.

165 **Fourier, in his effort to find a sponsor** Ibid., 480.

165 **For instance, lovers of vinegar** Fourier, *Harmonian Man,* 109.

166 **Although Fourier is remembered** Fourier, *Theory of the Four Movements,* x.

166 **"What could be more deadly"** Macdonald, *Masscult and Midcult,* 9.

166 **An elite group** Guarneri, *Utopian Alternative,* 126.

167 **In Harmony, these sorts of vast earthworks** Fourier, *Theory of the Four Movements,* 175.

167 **Fourier predicts that the expansion** Ibid., 49.

168 **the warm, dry climate of Italy** Ibid., 175.

168 **Fourier claims that as the globe warms** Ibid., 47.

168 **"In combination with salt"** Ibid., 49.

168 **Lions will be replaced by docile "antilions"** Beecher, *Charles Fourier,* 304.

168 **"amphibious servants to pull ships"** Fourier, *Theory of the Four Movements,* 50.

168 **"the ghastly legions of sea-monsters"** Ibid.

168 **Striding proudly through this new world** Beecher, *Charles Fourier,* 340.

168 **"God would appear to be an advocate"** Fourier, *Harmonian Man*, 49.

168 **"Planets can copulate"** Fourier, *Theory of the Four Movements*, 45.

169 **"A planet is an androgynous body"** Fourier, *Harmonian Man*, 51.

169 **"aromal swarms destined to nourish"** Ibid., 49.

169 **Some of Fourier's admirers** Fourier, *Theory of the Four Movements*, x.

169 **"Truth is only beautiful in our society"** Ibid., 283.

169 **"a Sphinx without Oedipus"** Beecher, *Charles Fourier*, 120.

170 **Plagiarism was never a big problem** Ibid., 128.

170 **"About the age of fifty you will grow"** Ibid., 486.

170 **He was fifty, a severe-looking man** Pellarin, *Life of Charles Fourier*, 80.

170 **In Paris, he hoped to find a benefactor** Ibid., 57.

170 **"more important on its own"** Fourier, *Theory of the Four Movements*, 3.

171 **"economic, moral and political theories"** Ibid., 4.

171 **In fact, one of those men was Owen** Beecher, *Charles Fourier*, 368.

171 **"If you are agreeable"** Ibid.

171 **"Under no circumstance and for no reason"** Ibid., 79.

172 **Along with mailing tracts** Pellarin, *Life of Charles Fourier*, 98.

172 **When he sent a summary of his theory** Manuel and Manuel, *Utopian Thought in the Western World*, 645.

172 **Victor Considerant, an intelligent young man** Beecher, *Charles Fourier*, 389.

172 **It was largely because of Considerant's enthusiasm** Ibid., 390.

172 **Arriving in Paris full of rosy ideas** Brisbane, *Mental Biography*, 69.

173 **One evening, during intermission** Ibid., 71.

173 **"Do I give [the farmers] an equivalent?"** Ibid.

173 **"there is a certain class in society"** Ibid., 72.

173 **As he worried over large questions** Ibid., 73.

173 **"a Joseph's coat of all philosophic colors"** Ibid., 73.

173 **"the final word on wisdom"** Ibid., 83.

173 **En route, he stopped in Weimar** Ibid., 79, 80.

174 **As one of the only Americans in Berlin** Ibid., 80.

174 **Among the latter group** Ibid., 81.

174 **Brisbane passed many of his evenings** Ibid., 84.

174 **"obscure and wretched manner"** Ibid., 88.

174 **When a gong signaled** Ibid., 89.

174 **Struggling to keep up** Ibid.

174 **"he had seen enough of Christian civilization"** Ibid., 97.

174 **Intent on seeing "barbaric civilization"** Ibid.

174 **"vegetating in ignorance and apathy"** Ibid., 121.

174 **He estimated that there was more real wealth** Ibid., 132.

175 **Rapid-fire exposure** Ibid., 111.

175 **"The idea of a great social reconstruction"** Ibid., 170.

175 **One idle afternoon, three months after returning** Ibid., 171.

175 **"organizing human labor as to dignify it"** Ibid.

176 **"Those two words"** Ibid., 172.

176 **"The darkness which had rested"** Ibid., 184.

176 **By the time he crossed the French border** Ibid.

176 **He found Fourier at number 5, rue Joquelet** Ibid., 185.

176 **To the wide-eyed young American** Ibid.

176 **At the office of *La Réforme Industrielle*** Beecher, *Charles Fourier*, 292, 443.

176 **Brisbane never once saw** Brisbane, *Mental Biography*, 186.

176 **"days of faith and of enthusiasm"** Ibid., 195.

177 **"In twenty years, we shall be in Constantinople!"** Ibid.

177 **In the spring of 1834** Ibid., 197.

177 **"An ocean of Social Error Flows"** Fellman, *Unbounded Frame*, 3.

178 **When an overleveraged New Orleans** Howe, *What Hath God Wrought*, 502.

178 **Hard times sharpened the national interest** Barkun, *Crucible of the Millennium*, 119.

178 **From their respective soapboxes** Ibid.

178 **The prophet of the harmonic future** Morell, *Sketch of the Life of Charles Fourier*, 14.

178 **His devoted followers** Ibid.; Pellarin, *Life of Charles Fourier*, 111.

178 **"lay before the American public"** Brisbane, *Social Destiny of Man*, iii.

179 **Hundreds of pages on sex** Beecher, *Charles Fourier*, 297.

179 ***Le nouveau monde amoureux*** Ibid., 298.

179 **"by the thin veil of the French language"** Emerson, "Historic Notes of Life and Letters in New England," in *Complete Works*, vol. 10, 354.

179 **"Fourier," he remarked dryly** Ibid.

180   **To find a wider audience** Brisbane, *Mental Biography*, 204.

180   **"His step is quick"** Guarneri, *Utopian Alternative*, 25.

180   **Working upstairs from Brisbane** Brisbane, *Mental Biography*, 204.

180   **Greeley, who had grown up poor** Rourke, *Trumpets of Jubilee*, 260; Burton, *Paradise Planters*, 207.

180   **"damned fool enough"** Brisbane, *Mental Biography*, 204.

180   **Brisbane carried a copy of *Social Destiny*** Ibid.; Rourke, *Trumpets of Jubilee*, 246–48.

181   **"the Reform which shall embosom"** Rourke, *Trumpets of Jubilee*, 274.

181   **In 1841, Greeley folded the *New-Yorker*** Ibid., 261.

181   **At a penny an issue** Ibid.

181   **Working-class readers from New England** Ibid., 268.

181   **An experienced reformer, he helped Brisbane** Sutton, *Communal Utopias*, 25.

181   **"This column has been purchased"** Linn, *Greeley*, 81.

181   **A bound collection of his *Tribune* columns** Sutton, *Communal Utopias*, 25.

182   **At the start of 1843, the *Tribune*'s editorial page** Linn, *Greeley*, 81.

182   **"Americans of all ages"** Tocqueville, *Democracy in America*, 595.

182   **"When Americans have a feeling"** Ibid., 598.

182   **"All western New York is in a deep"** Noyes, *History of American Socialisms*, 268.

183   **"Would it not seem that this very general response"** Ibid., 270.

183   **The financial crisis had left a third of the men** Guarneri, *Utopian Alternative*, 66.

183   **Inspired by Brisbane's articles** Noyes, *History of American Socialisms*, 256.

183   **Article fourteen, for instance** Ibid., 257.

183   **Having recklessly begun their adventure in November** Ibid.

183   **"manfully with the rocks, wood, climate"** Ibid., 259.

184   **By the end of 1843, six small, rural phalanxes** Guarneri, *Utopian Alternative*, 153, 407.

184   **He drafted a more realistic set of guidelines** Brisbane, *Social Destiny of Man*, 350.

184   **Any community that did not meet** Guarneri, *Utopian Alternative*, 123.

185 **In the fall of 1842, hoping to catalyze** Ibid., 165.

185 **A few months later, without consulting** Hayden, *Seven American Utopias*, 156, 157.

185 **Horace Greeley did the same** Noyes, *History of American Socialisms*, 449.

185 **During the summer of 1843** Guarneri, *Utopian Alternative*, 171.

185 **Like almost every other utopian community** Ibid.; Hayden, *Seven American Utopias*, 161.

186 **At least twelve different religious denominations** Guarneri, *Utopian Alternative*, 168.

186 **For twelve years, despite steady turnover** Ibid., 407.

186 **Many of them wore baggy pants** Sutton, *Communal Utopias*, 34.

186 **For Fourier's birthday, they held a ball** Ibid., 36.

186 **"In Harmony," he prophesied** Fourier, *Harmonian Man*, 109.

186 **In the harmonic future** Beecher, *Charles Fourier*, 251.

186 **Harmonian chefs will prove their worth** Ibid.

187 **The colonists ordered from an extensive menu** Guarneri, *Utopian Alternative*, 183.

187 **Fourier would have been pleased** Hayden, *Seven American Utopias*, 160.

187 **The NAP had its own school** Sutton, *Communal Utopias*, 41.

187 **Fourier believed that Owen lacked** Beecher, *Charles Fourier*, 365.

187 **In Fourier's schema of historical evolution** Ibid., 366.

187 **"If [Monsieur Owen] appreciates the plan"** Ibid., 367.

187 **When the *Philanthropist* was stranded in ice** Robert Dale Owen, *To Holland and to New Harmony*, 240, 244.

188 **Interestingly, Owen's eldest son** Ibid., 248.

188 **Ripley, the son of a wealthy farming family** Crowe, *George Ripley*, 42.

188 **His habits of mind and social milieu** Ibid., 76.

189 **The first meeting of the vaunted Transcendental Club** Frothingham, *George Ripley*, 54.

189 **"the cold corpse Unitarianism of Harvard College"** Crowe, *George Ripley*, 63.

189 **"Within and Above are synonymous"** Herwig Friedl, "The Divinity School Address," in Marcus and Sollors, eds., *New Literary History of America*, 245.

190 **"in an order of truths which transcend"** Crowe, *George Ripley*, 75.

190 **"We are a little wild here with numberless projects"** Guarneri, *Utopian Alternative*, 13.

190 **At meetings of the Transcendental Club** Crowe, *George Ripley*, 139.

191 **At the time, the appeal of communalism** Bestor, *Backwoods Utopias*, 33.

191 **"oppression nowhere and abundance everywhere"** Ripley, "Letter from Zoar," *Dial*, July 1841.

191 **In 1839, George and Sophia Ripley toured** Guarneri, *Utopian Alternative*, 81.

191 **"On the whole, they lead a good"** Stein, *Shaker Experience in America*, 217.

191 **"a detestable, miserly, barren aristocracy"** Wilson, *Life of Charles A. Dana*, 40.

191 **"the idea of founding a society"** Ibid., 523.

192 **As the Northeast rapidly urbanized** Barkun, *Crucible of the Millennium*, 137.

192 **"the Caesar, the Alexander of the soil"** Emerson, "Agriculture in Massachusetts," *Dial*, July 1842.

192 **Thoreau is a notable exception** Thoreau, *Walden and Civil Disobedience*, 47.

192 **"a true life, although it aims"** Elizabeth Palmer Peabody, "Plan of the West Roxbury Community," *Dial*, January 1842; Noyes, *History of American Socialisms*, 114.

192 **"The name of Fourier," it read** "Select List of Recent Publications," *Dial*, October 1840.

193 **That same month, at a gathering** Guarneri, *Utopian Alternative*, 83.

193 **The previous summer, the Ripleys had vacationed** Swift, *Brook Farm*, 15.

193 **In the early spring of 1841, George and Sophia** Francis, *Transcendental Utopias*, 37.

193 **The building, which they dubbed the Hive** Brooks, *Flowering of New England*, 242.

194 **"Our imagination rebels"** Noyes, *History of American Socialisms*, 112.

194 **"a reorganization of society itself"** Ibid., 110.

194 **"For each man to think and live"** Ibid., 111.

194 **"a knot of dreamers"** Hawthorne, *Blithedale Romance*, 8.

194 **"paradise anew"** Ibid., 4.

195 **"most men have bound their eyes"** Emerson, *Essential Writings*, 29.

195 **"very slowly and, I may almost say"** Crowe, *George Ripley*, 139.

195 **"I have not yet conquered my own house"** Ibid., 138.

195 **"I'd rather keep bachelor's hall in hell"** Burton, *Paradise Planters*, 95.

195 **The brilliant Margaret Fuller** Ibid., 141.

195 **"[Ripley] went to work like a hero"** Noyes, *History of American Socialisms*, 108.

195 **"It infuses into all our thoughts"** Henry David Thoreau, *Writings of Henry David Thoreau*, 9.

196 **"public and private avarice"** Emerson, "The American Scholar," in *Complete Works*, vol. 1, 114.

196 **"the pressure of competitive institutions"** Swift, *Brook Farm*, 16.

196 **"The evils arising from Trade"** Frothingham, *George Ripley*, 148.

196 **"a city of refuge for men and women"** Orvis, *Letters from Brook Farm*, x.

196 **"There never has been an old principle"** Owen, *Development of the Principles and Plans*, 31.

196 **The American Fourierists picked up the term** Guarneri, *Utopian Alternative*, 104, 381.

196 **As an undergraduate at Harvard** Crowe, *George Ripley*, 26.

197 **"no law can be sacred to me"** Emerson, *Essential Writings*, 26.

197 **"Are they my poor?"** Ibid., 27.

197 **"I cannot witness the glaring inequalities"** Frothingham, *George Ripley*, 74.

197 **Ripley believed that the community at Brook Farm** Crowe, *George Ripley*, 166.

197 **"The great problem is to guarantee individualism"** Codman, *Brook Farm*, 148.

197 **"so far destroy the independence of the individual"** Ibid., 147.

198 **Like most of the Fourierist phalanxes** Guarneri, *Utopian Alternative*, 49.

198 **"the Greek and Latin, the aesthetic philosophy"** Wilson, *Life of Charles A. Dana*, 527.

198 **"to combine the thinker and the worker"** Swift, *Brook Farm*, 16.

198 **Soft-handed Nathaniel Hawthorne** Ibid., 47.

199 **Although the Brook Farmers' plan** Francis, *Transcendental Utopias*, 43.

199 **"If Democracy was the sublime truth"** Wilson, *Life of Charles A. Dana*, 521.

199 **"They told slanderous fables"** Hawthorne, *Blithedale Romance*, 48.

199 **They weren't as bad as all that** Sutton, *Communal Utopias*, 39.

199 **The Brook Farm Academy, which served** Ibid.; Codman, *Brook Farm*, 11.

199 **The latter focused on grooming boys** Burton, *Paradise Planters*, 149.

199 **Occasionally a "rusticated" (suspended) Harvard boy** Wilson, *Life of Charles A. Dana*, 527.

200 **Margaret Fuller's younger brother** Guarneri, *Utopian Alternative*, 49.

200 **Courses were offered in math** Brooks, *Flowering of New England*, 244.

200 **Sophia Ripley, a tall, hardworking** Swift, *Brook Farm*, 59.

200 **Her husband taught philosophy** Brooks, *Flowering of New England*, 244.

200 **Charles Dana, an energetic twenty-three-year-old** Ibid.

200 **He was forced to leave Harvard** Wilson, *Life of Charles A. Dana*, 14.

200 **In addition to their studies** Burton, *Paradise Planters*, 55.

201 **"There were farmers and artists"** Brooks, *Flowering of New England*, 244.

201 **"There were never such witty potato-patches"** Curtis, *Early Letters*, 9.

201 **"Oh, labor is the curse of the world"** Swift, *Brook Farm*, 166, 167.

201 **"see[ing] it out to the finish"** Codman, *Brook Farm*, 20.

201 **On any given Saturday** Brooks, *Flowering of New England*, 244.

201 **In his diary, Charles Dana kept a catalog** Wilson, *Life of Charles A. Dana*, 56.

202 **By late 1843, with more than a hundred people** Guarneri, *Utopian Alternative*, 234.

202 **Some colonists, most notably Ripley and Dana** Burton, *Paradise Planters*, 187.

202 **Many of them were "*Tribune*-reading Yankees"** Fogarty, *Dictionary of American Communal and Utopian History*, 190.

202 **They were joined by a large influx** Sutton, *Communal Utopias*, 31.

202 **The community built a sawmill** Noyes, *History of American Socialisms*, 414.

202 **They established a free school** Ibid.

202 **Within a year, the phalanx had its own** Ibid., 415.

203 **Five separate phalanxes** Guarneri, *Utopian Alternative*, 157.

203 **"most determined to follow as near"** Noyes, *History of American Socialisms*, 272.

203 **The colony was largely under the direction** Ibid.

203 **When the colonists "numbered Israel"** Ibid., 280.

203 **There were even a few Catholics** Ibid.

203 **Not far to the east, in the winter of 1844** Ibid., 286.

203 **The 260 members of the Sodus Bay Phalanx** Guarneri, *Utopian Alternative*, 165, 184.

204 **On a twelve-hundred-acre hay farm** Noyes, *History of American Socialisms*, 328–30.

204 **"We have been shown by the Columbus"** Ibid., 332.

204 **Meeker, one of the most articulate participants** Fogarty, *Dictionary of American Communal and Utopian History*, 75.

204 **By the end of 1844, nineteen separate phalanxes** Guarneri, *Utopian Alternative*, 407, 408.

205 **A Harvard-trained minister** Ibid., 55.

205 **Channing served informally as Brook Farm's pastor** Burton, *Paradise Planters*, 69.

205 **"Association," declared *The Phalanx*** "Celebration of Fourier's Birthday at Brook Farm," *Phalanx*.

205 **To hasten the harmonic millennium** Swift, *Brook Farm*, 222.

206 **This morally dense mixture** Burton, *Paradise Planters*, 187.

206 **Even more than Brisbane's *Phalanx*** Ibid.

206 **"American Fourierism took shape at a time"** Guarneri, *Utopian Alternative*, 73.

206 **"That the Paradise of Eden is to be regained"** Barkun, *Crucible of the Millennium*, 1.

207 **Nobody was keener to bring Brook Farm** Swift, *Brook Farm*, 280.

207 **Conservatives and evangelicals** McLaren, *Boa Constrictor*, 5.

207 **"vague horror connected with [Fourier's] name"** Noyes, *History of American Socialisms*, 513.

208 **"[We] were pretty well agreed"** Hawthorne, *Blithedale Romance*, 47.

208 **"the many [that] are slaves to a few"** Codman, *Brook Farm*, 148.

208 **"by identifying the interests of the many"** Ibid.

209 **"in perfect union with the nature of man"** Crowe, *George Ripley,* 173.

209 **In April 1844, Albert Brisbane convened** Guarneri, *Utopian Alternative,* 232.

209 **The conventioneers also took the opportunity** Ibid.

209 **"has hitherto worn, for the most part"** Noyes, *History of American Socialisms,* 523.

210 **"Our ulterior aim," he wrote** Delano, *Brook Farm,* 372.

210 **A more mundane reason** Noyes, *History of American Socialisms,* 525, 526.

210 **The community did have an excellent** Swift, *Brook Farm,* 185.

210 **Despite spreading the fields** Ibid., 41.

211 **The story of Brook Farm's conversion** Ibid., 115; Burton, *Paradise Planters,* 176; E. M. Halliday, "Our Forefathers in Hot Pursuit of the Good Life," *Horizon,* Autumn 1973, 115.

211 **"the experiment, so far as its original"** Hawthorne, *Blithedale Romance,* 195.

211 **In 1844, the year of the switch** Guarneri, *Utopian Alternative,* 58.

211 **"severance from the world"** Ibid.

211 **"had skipped no fact but one"** Delano, *Brook Farm,* 93.

211 **"truths of social science discovered"** Guarneri, *Utopian Alternative,* 57.

211 **"a deliberate tradeoff of charm"** Ibid., 58.

212 **"extinct volcanoes of Transcendental nonsense"** Codman, *Brook Farm,* 68.

212 **"There were philosophers enough"** Ibid., 26.

212 **People still gathered in the kitchen** Ibid., 52, 60.

212 **Groups still took picnics into the woods** Brooks, *Flowering of New England,* 245.

212 **A group of young men pooled their savings** Ibid.

212 **John Dwight, who served as head music teacher** Burton, *Paradise Planters,* 151.

213 **Love letters flew from room to room** Orvis, *Letters from Brook Farm,* 84.

213 **For those unlucky in love** Ibid.

213 **Like good Fourierists, they turned the chore into a contest** Codman, *Brook Farm,* 54.

213 **When the dining room was clean** Ibid., 94; Orvis, *Letters from Brook Farm*, 5.

213 **Some wore bloomers** Brooks, *Flowering of New England*, 245.

213 **They tended to grow their hair long** Swift, *Brook Farm*, 117.

213 **Although many of the men** Sutton, *Communal Utopias*, 39.

213 **Ripley set the style for men's grooming** Crowe, *George Ripley*, 160.

213 **"In outward show," Hawthorne recalled** Hawthorne, *Blithedale Romance*, 47.

213 **One young, long-haired Brook Farmer** Swift, *Brook Farm*, 65.

213 **Nicknames flourished** Brooks, *Flowering of New England*, 244; Swift, *Brook Farm*, 68.

213 **An epidemic of punning** Codman, *Brook Farm*, 173.

214 **"our entertainment was a regular series"** Orvis, *Letters from Brook Farm*, 76.

214 **Every Sunday evening** Ibid., 12.

214 **These were later supplemented** Ibid., 40.

214 **"ours is not the evil rivalry"** Ibid., 20.

214 **The same young woman** Ibid., 62.

214 **Outsiders were known** Ibid., 69; Brooks, *Flowering of New England*, 246.

214 **John Colson, the community's shoemaker** Orvis, *Letters from Brook Farm*, 36.

214 **They set up workshops** Guarneri, *Utopian Alternative*, 58.

214 **The stream that cut through** Swift, *Brook Farm*, 34.

214 **"Men and women," as one Brook Farmer put it** Codman, *Brook Farm*, 30.

215 **"Industry can be rendered attractive!"** Brisbane, *Social Destiny of Man*, vi.

215 **"a common taste for a particular function"** Beecher, *Charles Fourier*, 233.

215 **For instance, the Pear Grower's Series** Ibid., 279.

215 **They created one big Pastoral Series** Codman, *Brook Farm*, 84, 85.

216 **A similar system was set up in the school** Ibid., 110.

216 **"parading outside the phalanx palace"** Fourier, *Theory of the Four Movements*, 163.

216 **"Hearing a great hurrah"** Orvis, *Letters from Brook Farm*, 42.

216 **As Fourier saw it, the women of Civilization** Fourier, *Theory of the Four Movements*, 148.

216 **"the elevation of woman forever"** Orvis, *Letters from Brook Farm,* 32.

217 **"Raise women to the equal of man"** Ibid., 33.

217 **"We do live in an atmosphere of our own"** Ibid., 96.

218 **This constant changing of jobs** Codman, *Brook Farm,* 208.

218 **In the spring of 1844, Marianne Dwight** Orvis, *Letters from Brook Farm,* 7, 8.

218 **As cumbersome as this system sounds** Guarneri, *Utopian Alternative,* 58.

218 **With its population of experienced writers** Ibid., 237.

218 **He filled the pages of the paper** Sutton, *Communal Utopias,* 26.

219 **The first issue included a translation** Codman, *Brook Farm,* 106.

219 **Shaw used to ride out to Brook Farm** Ibid.

219 **John Dwight, Brook Farm's beloved music teacher** Ibid., 106, 107; Delano, "*The Harbinger* Reviews Its Transcendental 'Friends,'" *Colby Library Quarterly,* 74.

219 **"While we bow to no man"** Codman, *Brook Farm,* 102.

219 **"the speedy coming of that era of Harmony"** "Celebration of Fourier's Birthday at Brook Farm," *Phalanx.*

219 **A bust of the master was set before a large glass prism** Ibid.

220 **Another artistically minded colonist** Ibid.; Burton, *Paradise Planters,* 249.

220 **"To Fourier, the second coming of Christ"** Crowe, *George Ripley,* 181.

220 **Not surprisingly, there were "Graham tables"** Stein, *Shaker Experience in America,* 156.

220 **At Brook Farm, the Grahamites were monitored** Codman, *Brook Farm,* 121.

221 **"These Grahamites will never make their ends *meat*"** Ibid., 173.

221 **"If they are willing to endure privations"** Noyes, *History of American Socialisms,* 339.

221 **In the crowded dining room** Codman, *Brook Farm,* 48.

221 **"We must drink the waters of Marah"** Ibid., 149.

221 **Even during lean times** Orvis, *Letters from Brook Farm,* 63, 72.

221 **"come-outers, communists, fruitists"** Codman, *Brook Farm,* 79.

222 **"a comparatively harmless crank"** Seldes, *Stammering Century,* 201.

222 **One visitor showed up claiming** Codman, *Brook Farm,* 81.

222 **"I beg your pardon, sir, I did not intend to disturb"** Ibid.

222 **"If I laugh, it makes me sad"** Orvis, *Letters from Brook Farm*, 181.

222 **Swedenborgianism and Fourierism** Noyes, *History of American Socialisms*, 550.

222 **And Frederick Evans, the Owenite turned Shaker** Stein, *Shaker Experience in America*, 227.

222 **Ministers of the Swedenborgian New Church** Guarneri, *Utopian Alternative*, 72.

223 **"one could not but be struck"** Emerson, "Historic Notes of Life and Letters in New England," in *Complete Works*, vol. 10, 349.

223 **"He kept it"** Menand, *Metaphysical Club*, 85.

223 **Because Alcott made a point** Burton, *Paradise Planters*, 109.

223 **Along with abstaining from all animal products** Ibid., 110.

224 **"too humble indeed to satisfy the extreme demands"** Lane, "Brook Farm," *Dial*, January 1844.

224 **The community included a nudist** Seldes, *Stammering Century*, 208.

224 **"Good morning, damn you"** Ibid., 216.

224 **The most famous alumna** Ibid.

224 **When Fruitlands fell apart** Stein, *Shaker Experience in America*, 216.

224 **The existing buildings** Codman, *Brook Farm*, 97.

225 **The top floor of the three-story Hive** Swift, *Brook Farm*, 28.

225 **"I wish you could have seen . . . the pictures"** Orvis, *Letters from Brook Farm*, 69.

225 **The Brook Farm phalanstery** Noyes, *History of American Socialisms*, 554.

225 **By July, the cellar was dug** Codman, *Brook Farm*, 194; Swift, *Brook Farm*, 36.

226 **"When the Phalanstery is done"** Orvis, *Letters from Brook Farm*, 48.

226 **"May it become a University"** Elizabeth Palmer Peabody, "Fourierism," *Dial*, April 1844.

227 **People who might have sent their children** Codman, *Brook Farm*, 214.

227 **"the people worshiped a naked woman"** Beecher, *Charles Fourier*, 498.

227 **In 1846, during a particularly nasty round** Swift, *Brook Farm*, 275.

227 **"the organ of Charles Fourier, Fanny Wright"** Linn, *Greeley*, 83, 84.

227 **"I have encountered much opposition"** Wilson, *Life of Charles A. Dana*, 42.

227 **"slimy and venomous instrument of loco-focoism"** Rourke, *Trumpets of Jubilee*, 264.

227 **Because Greeley was a prominent figure** "New York Observer on Association," *Harbinger*, August 15, 1846.

228 **God-fearing American women** McLaren, *Boa Constrictor*, 27.

228 **"The haughty cabal who make the *Tribune*"** Ibid., 11.

228 **They are "daring traitors"** Ibid., 13.

228 **"sworn in conclave on their black and fireless altars"** Ibid., 12.

228 **"No! Ye men of the Tribune!"** Ibid., 9.

228 **Despite such rhetoric, about six or seven thousand** Guarneri, *Utopian Alternative*, 60.

228 **Many more—an estimated one hundred thousand** Ibid.

228 **By the end of 1845, twenty-three separate phalanxes** Ibid., 408.

228 **As Brisbane tried to nudge the cause forward** Codman, *Brook Farm*, 145, 146.

229 **He remained intent on founding** Ibid.

229 **Brisbane's fixation on the minutiae** Guarneri, *Utopian Alternative*, 408, 137; Brisbane, *Mental Biography*, 229.

229 **"The means by which musical harmony"** Ibid., 245.

229 **Paid for by the sale of special stock** Codman, *Brook Farm*, 74.

229 **In the year and a half since the community's conversion** Ibid., 142.

229 **Both men were convinced that Brook Farm would not be the place** Ibid.

230 **In December 1845, he wrote Ripley** Ibid., 144, 145.

230 **Ripley wrote Brisbane explaining that an infusion** Ibid.

230 **"You might as well undertake to raise dead men"** Ibid., 146.

231 **"Fifteen thousand dollars might do a great deal"** Ibid., 148.

231 **Without much hope of outside help** Swift, *Brook Farm*, 37.

231 **It was 175 feet long** Ibid., 36.

231 **These apartments were connected** Codman, *Brook Farm*, 114.

231 **On the last day of February** Ibid., 186.

231 **To keep themselves warm** Ibid.

231 **In high spirits, the Brook Farmers danced** Ibid.

231 **A little after nine, someone rushed** Ibid.

231 **Moments later, a bright smudge of light** Ibid., 191.

232 **It was a perfectly still night** Orvis, *Letters from Brook Farm*, 147.

232 **"shone magically to their minutest twigs"** Ibid.

232   **Seeing the distant light, fire companies** Codman, *Brook Farm*, 193.

232   **Melting window glass tinted the flames** Orvis, *Letters from Brook Farm*, 147.

232   **"a magnificent temple of molten gold"** Ibid.

232   **It took an hour and a half** Codman, *Brook Farm*, 192.

232   **Ripley invited everyone into the Hive** Ibid., 198.

232   **At least, he joked** Ibid.

232   **The costly phalanstery, two years in the making** Orvis, *Letters from Brook Farm*, 148.

233   **Because the building was incomplete** Noyes, *History of American Socialisms*, 554; Codman, *Brook Farm*, 195.

233   **They gave it up sheepishly, making excuses** Burton, *Paradise Planters*, 274.

233   **"It was like a knotted skein slowly unraveling"** Codman, *Brook Farm*, 232.

234   **"a minor stampede Romeward"** Swift, *Brook Farm*, 115.

234   **"the conventions of civilization"** Orvis, *Letters from Brook Farm*, 41.

234   **"None but a Brook Farmer can know"** Ibid., 177.

234   **At the end of the summer of 1847** Swift, *Brook Farm*, 25.

234   **With support from Horace Greeley** Ibid., 138.

234   **Dana found Marx so impressive** Guarneri, *Utopian Alternative*, 336, 337.

234   **"that old jackass with the face of an angel"** Williams, *Horace Greeley*, 227.

235   **During the Civil War, he held a prominent post** Wilson, *Life of Charles A. Dana*, 526.

235   **Ripley joined his old Brook Farm comrades** Guarneri, *Utopian Alternative*, 290.

235   **With his modest salary, he and Sophia** Swift, *Brook Farm*, 137.

235   **"Never did I feel so calmly"** Codman, *Brook Farm*, 254.

235   **"More and more I feel we struck upon"** Hawthorne, *Blithedale Romance*, 195.

235   **"made what all people try to make"** Emerson, "Historic Notes of Life and Letters in New England," in *Complete Works*, vol. 10, 179.

236   **"The end of Brook Farm"** Noyes, *History of American Socialisms*, 562.

236   **Toward the end of the 1840s, the national economy** Guarneri, *Utopian Alternative*, 342.

236 **Even some diehard Associationists** Ibid., 343.

236 **"brood of unscientific and starveling"** Noyes, *History of American Socialisms,* 247.

236 **By the end of the 1840s, the community's** Hayden, *Seven American Utopias,* 173.

236 **"an intermediate position"** Noyes, *History of American Socialisms,* 489.

237 **Thirty people followed Spring down the road** Ibid., 487.

237 **Not long after the split** Guarneri, *Utopian Alternative,* 327.

237 **The damage was estimated at $14,000** Ibid.

237 **In 1855, twelve years after its founding** Ibid.

237 **In the proud tradition of European revolutionary** Johnson, *Utopian Communism,* 207.

237 **"First came Jesus Christ"** Ibid.

237 **Victor Considerant, who assumed leadership** Sutton, *Communal Utopias,* 44.

238 **Albert Brisbane, who happened to be in Paris** Brisbane, *Mental Biography,* 312, 315.

238 **He shaved his immense Fu Manchu** Ibid.

238 **They took a steamship down the Mississippi** Sutton, *Communal Utopias,* 45.

238 **To whip up support** Ibid.

238 **"European Society for the Colonization of Texas"** Ibid.

238 **The community, which they called La Réunion** Ibid.

239 **"We are always pleased to have industrious immigrants"** Guarneri, *Utopian Alternative,* 46.

239 **By 1858, the phalanx slid into shabby chaos** Sutton, *Communal Utopias,* 47, 48.

240 **Unlike the young men of the CCC** Fourier, *Theory of the Four Movements,* 173.

240 **Even more outlandish** Beecher, *Charles Fourier,* 284.

241 **He also foresaw the rise** Guarneri, *Utopian Alternative,* 108.

241 **"Harmonian Court of Love"** Fourier, *Harmonian Man,* 266.

ICARIA: PEOPLE OF THE BOOK

243 **"It is indeed time that hatred"** Sutton, *Les Icariens,* 124.

243 **On November 14, 1847** Shaw, *Icaria,* 23.

243 **Ten weeks later, before dawn** Sutton, *Les Icariens,* 49.

244 **"Arise, workers stooped in the dust"** Ibid., 50.

244 **His father was a cooper** Johnson, *Utopian Communism,* 21.

245 **Toasts were shouted and drunk** Piotrowski, *Étienne Cabet,* 1; Chicoineau, "Etienne Cabet and His World," in Snyder, ed., *Humanistic Values,* 9.

245 **While he shared Fourier's powerful aversion** Piotrowski, *Étienne Cabet,* 129.

245 **By the late 1820s, Cabet was in Paris** Johnson, *Utopian Communism,* 25.

245 **Through some of his republican clients** Ibid., 24.

245 **Protest leaders such as Cabet and Lafayette** Sutton, *Les Icariens,* 7.

246 **As one of the leaders of the July Revolution** Piotrowski, *Étienne Cabet,* 23.

246 **Cabet's support for the Duke of Orléans** Johnson, *Utopian Communism,* 27.

246 **That fall, Cabet sailed for Bastia** Piotrowski, *Étienne Cabet,* 30.

246 **"In ordinary times," he wrote a friend** Ibid.

247 **Marx singled him out for his "practical attitude"** Johnson, *Utopian Communism,* 29.

247 **He stood for office as a moderate** Ibid., 30.

247 **Under Cabet's leadership, republican-tinged courses** Ibid., 35.

247 **The book, which focused on the betrayals** Ibid., 34.

247 **In the summer of 1833** Ibid., 37.

247 **In Paris, newsboys dressed in red, white, and blue** Piotrowski, *Étienne Cabet,* 45.

247 **"We wish, not that the class"** Ibid., 45.

248 **The seventh edition sold twelve thousand copies** Johnson, *Utopian Communism,* 37.

248 ***"Vive Cabet! Vive Lafayette!"*** Piotrowski, *Étienne Cabet,* 46.

248 **"resolved, if necessary, to have Frenchmen shot"** Johnson, *Utopian Communism,* 41.

248 **The Belgians, fed up with sheltering** Sutton, *Les Icariens,* 16.

248 **The small family lived off a modest pension** Piotrowski, *Étienne Cabet,* 51.

248 **In the winter of 1835–1836, sitting at his assigned** Johnson, *Utopian Communism,* 45.

249 **"Plato's *Republic* now I claim"** More, *Utopia,* 5.

249 **After eating lunch, the three men settle** Ibid., 17.

250 **An isthmus once connected the island** Ibid., 49.

251 **"The one essential condition"** Ibid., 44.

251 **To curtail the irrational and troublesome desire** Ibid., 67.

251 **When foreign dignitaries parade** Ibid., 68.

252 **The Utopians look down on any sort** Ibid., 100.

252 **"quietly, politely, and by rational argument"** Ibid.

253 **More's account of a minutely planned** Johnson, *Utopian Communism*, 43.

253 **"It was the *Utopia* of Thomas More"** Piotrowski, *Étienne Cabet*, 69.

254 **Cabet commenced his study** Sutton, *Les Icariens*, 20.

254 **Owen's environmental determinism** Johnson, *Utopian Communism*, 71.

254 **They became friends, meeting repeatedly** Ibid.

254 **"The progress of industry makes the establishment"** Cabet, *Travels in Icaria*, lviii.

254 **"one of the wealthiest lords"** Ibid., 3.

255 **When an Icarian family runs low** Ibid., 47.

255 **"all the children are charming"** Ibid., 4.

255 **"there is such a debauch of virtue"** Piotrowski, *Étienne Cabet*, 75.

255 **"But this is COMMUNAL OWNERSHIP"** Cabet, *Travels in Icaria*, 31.

256 **"From earliest childhood he could not"** Ibid., 175.

256 **In 1782, Icar led an uprising** Ibid., 172.

256 **Icaria is divided into a hundred** Ibid., 19.

257 **In the middle of the river is a circular island** Ibid., 20.

257 **Lewis Mumford, the great historian of cities** Mumford, *Story of Utopias*, 118.

257 **"remarkable size and strength"** Cabet, *Travels in Icaria*, 38.

257 **"There is not a single shoe or hat"** Ibid., 48.

257 **"harmonious, soft music"** Ibid., 92.

257 **"You would think you were seeing an army regiment"** Ibid., 51.

257 **A great deal about life in Icaria** Ibid., 57.

257 **Every aspect of life** Ibid., 33.

257 **"Should reason and society not repair"** Ibid., 80.

257 **"the satisfaction experienced"** Ibid., 83.

258 **"All our young girls"** Ibid., 56.

258 **Every Icarian latrine comes equipped** Ibid., 55.

258 **"The republic," boasts one Icarian** Ibid., 104.

258 **"Just as in Sparta they did away"** Ibid., 41.

259 **"there was more of Cabet than of Marx"** Mumford, *Story of Utopias*, 122.

259 **The philosopher Robert Nozick** Nozick, *Anarchy, State, and Utopia*, 311.

260 **In the spring of 1839, Cabet's exile expired** Sutton, "The Icarians of Corning, Iowa," in *Adaptation of the Icarians to America*, 4.

260 **Secret clubs and socialist "banquet societies"** Johnson, *Utopian Communism*, 68.

261 **Official anxiety was sufficiently high** Piotrowski, *Étienne Cabet*, 122.

261 **"almost every workingman in France"** Holloway, *Heavens on Earth*, 109.

261 **In the next eight years** Sutton, "The Icarians of Corning, Iowa," in *Adaptation of the Icarians to America*, 4.

261 **Back in Paris, Cabet resumed** Johnson, *Utopian Communism*, 78.

261 **Some readers seemed to think** Ibid., 170.

261 **"Communism and Republic"** Rancière, "Why Did the Icarians Leave France?," in Snyder and Sutton, eds., *Immigration of the Icarians to Illinois*, 10.

262 **According to demographic research** Johnson, *Utopian Communism*, 205.

262 **The philosopher and historian Jacques Rancière** Rancière, "Why Did the Icarians Leave France?," in Snyder and Sutton, eds., *Immigration of the Icarians to Illinois*, 9.

263 **Not surprisingly, given the fact that the movement** Johnson, *Utopian Communism*, 156.

263 **He was a deist** Sutton, "Voyage to Icaria: A Message to the World," in Snyder. ed., *Humanistic Values*, 23.

263 **"It is impossible to admit"** Piotrowski, *Étienne Cabet*, 78.

263 **For him, Christianity was indistinguishable** Johnson, *Utopian Communism*, 215.

263 **"Communal ownership of goods"** Cabet, *Travels in Icaria*, lviii.

264 **"Jesus Christ came to bring a new law"** Cabet, "History and Constitution," *Iowa Journal of History and Politics*, 236.

264 **"Christianity for the Apostles"** Sutton, *Les Icariens*, 41.

264 **In Cabet's analysis, the miracles** Johnson, *Utopian Communism*, 94.

264   **Part 2 of *Voyage* features an appendix** Piotrowski, *Étienne Cabet*, 65.

264   **"The majority of all western thinkers"** Ibid.

265   **"a nation celebrated for its infidelity"** Friedrich Engels, "Progress of Social Reform on the Continent," *New Moral World* 19 (November 4, 1843).

265   **Christopher H. Johnson, whose methods** Johnson, *Utopian Communism*, 145.

265   **Either way, there were enough of them** Ibid.

265   **As his popularity rose, Cabet's rhetoric** Sutton, *Les Icariens*, 41.

265   **In the minds of his followers** Johnson, *Utopian Communism*, 175.

265   **"the successor to the works of Christ"** Rancière, "Why Did the Icarians Leave France?," in Snyder and Sutton, eds., *Immigration of the Icarians to Illinois*, 10.

265   **"dear and venerated father"** Ibid.

265   **Cabet had initially hoped** Johnson, *Utopian Communism*, 230, 231.

265   **At the same time, anticommunist sentiment** Rancière, "Why Did the Icarians Leave France?," in Snyder and Sutton, eds., *Immigration of the Icarians to Illinois*, 7.

265   **One cleric burned a copy** Sutton, *Les Icariens*, 44.

265   **Cabet's arrest or exile** Johnson, *Utopian Communism*, 235, 236.

266   **"conquer the Promised land"** Ibid., 238.

266   **Cabet wrote to Robert Owen** Cabet, *Travels in Icaria*, xxiv.

266   **When the Mexican government withdrew** Packard, *Life of Robert Owen*, 215.

266   **he put Cabet in touch** Johnson, *Utopian Communism*, 256.

266   **Not long before Cabet contacted Owen** Ibid.

266   **Peters proposed that the Icarians sign a deal** Sutton, *Les Icariens*, 48.
      [Note: Various sources report various acreages for the land in Texas, depending on what exactly is counted as being part of the "Peters concession." The numbers are further muddled by Cabet's own exaggerations in *Le Populaire*. Albert Shaw (*Icaria*, 33) reports that the deal was ultimately for one million acres. Christopher H. Johnson (*Utopian Communism*, 256) says that the entire concession, presumably including the non-Icarian plots, was ten and a half million acres. Three thousand acres, the number used by Robert Sutton (*Les Icariens*, 48), seems most likely.]

266 **Each Icarian-owned plot** Sutton, *Les Icariens*, 46.

267 **Cabet, however, was undeterred** Ibid.

267 **Brimming with enthusiasm** Ibid., 46, 47.

267 **In a specially printed pamphlet** Ibid., 47.

267 **Each volunteer was required** Rancière, "Why Did the Icarians Leave France?," in Snyder and Sutton, eds., *Immigration of the Icarians to Illinois*, 7.

267 **He also had to contribute six hundred francs** Ibid.

267 ***"Brouck-Tarm, sous la direction du prédicateur"*** Shaw, *Icaria*, 22.

267 **Many devoted Icarians** Johnson, *Utopian Communism*, 243.

267 **When Cabet announced his plan** Ibid.

268 **"Your idea to realize Icaria gives me new life"** Rancière, "Why Did the Icarians Leave France?," in Snyder and Sutton, eds., *Immigration of the Icarians to Illinois*, 8.

268 **"Do you persist in declaring"** Gundy, "Glimpses of the Immigration of French Icarians," in Snyder and Sutton, eds., *Immigration of the Icarians to Illinois*, 25, 26.

268 **The following morning, decked out in their velvet costumes** Sutton, *Les Icariens*, 125.

268 **"We leave full of joy," wrote one Icarian** Rancière, "Why Did the Icarians Leave France?," in Snyder and Sutton, eds., *Immigration of the Icarians to Illinois*, 10.

269 **At the end of March, as the *Rome* cruised** Sutton, *Les Icariens*, 56.

269 **News of Louis Philippe's abdication** Ibid.

270 **The trip was a disaster** Gauthier, *Quest for Utopia*, 17.

270 **At one point, fourteen Icarians** Ibid., 19.

270 **Amid all of this, documents were discovered** Ibid., 17.

270 **He was shorn of his beard** Ibid.

270 **The facts are murky** Johnson, *Utopian Communism*, 282.

270 **In 1853, when Albert Brisbane** Beecher, *Victor Considerant*, 309.

270 **They sank their only plow** Shaw, *Icaria*, 35.

270 **By the end of the summer** Ibid., 33.

270 **The survivors, feverish with malaria** Ibid., 43.

270 **"have no doubt of being able to unite"** Ibid., 21.

270 **After the king's abdication** Sutton, *Les Icariens*, 53.

271 **In the power vacuum created by the uprising** Piotrowski, *Étienne Cabet*, 126.

271   **"Manifesto of the Icarian Communists"** Johnson, *Utopian Communism,* 264.

271   **The document urged French communists** Ibid.

271   **Most shocking, Cabet announced** Ibid., 265; Cabet, *Travels in Icaria,* xxvii.

271   **He ran for his old seat** Johnson, *Utopian Communism,* 278.

271   **"Down with the Communists, Death to Cabet"** Cabet, "History and Constitution," *Iowa Journal of History and Politics,* 222.

271   **In May, police raided the offices** Ibid., 223.

271   **On the last day of 1848, during a heavy snowstorm** Gauthier, *Quest for Utopia,* 7.

271   **After a banquet thrown in his honor** Ibid.

272   **"Zion will be built upon this continent"** Harrison, *Second Coming,* 180.

272   **"they had all things in common"** Book of Mormon, 4 Nephi 13.

272   **Within a year of organizing** Dean L. May, "One Heart and Mind," in Pitzer, ed., *America's Communal Utopias,* 136.

273   **But unlike Shaker communism** Ibid., 141.

273   **Even before Smith died** Ibid., 142.

273   **The Orderville Saints ate together** Ibid., 149.

274   **On March 15, 1849** Gauthier, *Quest for Utopia,* 25.

274   **The houses and shops arrayed** Ibid.

275   **Within two years there were 365 Icarians** Sutton, *Les Icariens,* 165.

275   **By 1855, five hundred Icarians** Robert P. Sutton, "An American Elysium," in Pitzer, ed., *America's Communal Utopias,* 293.

275   **Most of them were French** Gundy, "Glimpses of the Immigration of French Icarians," in Snyder and Sutton, eds., *Immigration of the Icarians to Illinois,* 24.

275   **Like most of the new recruits** Snyder, "A Day in the Life of Emile Baxter," in Sutton, ed., *Adaptations of the Icarians,* 18.

275   **Before coming to Icaria** Ibid.

275   **"Pardon me, Monsieur, if I begin so bruskly"** Ibid., 16.

275   **Before the Baxters moved to Illinois** Ibid., 19.

275   **"even more Icarian than I"** Ibid., 16.

276   **"to prove to the world," as he put it** Ibid., 16.

276   **A six a.m. bugle call started each day** Sutton, *Les Icariens,* 74.

276   **Right out of bed, the men all took** Ibid.

276 **"the finest, most delicate, most ravishing fabrics"** Cabet, *Travels in Icaria*, 49.

276 **To the amusement of their neighbors** Sutton, *Les Icariens*, 73.

276 **In miniature homage to the technological marvels** Vallet, *Icarian Communist*, 24.

276 **They also raised sheep and cattle** Sutton, *Les Icariens*, 65.

276 **"You have certainly seen in no other nation"** Cabet, *Travels in Icaria*, 181.

277 **A thirty-six-piece orchestra** Sutton, "The Icarians of Corning, Iowa," in *Adaptation of the Icarians to America*, 10.

277 **"carefully eliminate all that could have"** Vallet, *Icarian Communist*, 31.

277 **On warm weekend days** Snyder, "A Day in the Life of Emile Baxter," in Sutton, ed., *Adaptations of the Icarians*, 22.

277 **The Icarian library held** Parish, "Who Were the Icarians?," in Snyder and Sutton, eds., *Immigration of the Icarians*, 4.

277 **"free from the ethos of their parents"** Plato (*Republic* VII, 541), *Complete Works*, 1155.

277 **"the basis and the foundation of the whole"** Cabet, *Travels in Icaria*, 74.

278 **"man is evidently perfectible"** Cabet, "History and Constitution," *Iowa Journal of History and Politics*, 234.

278 **From the age of four onward** Sutton, *Les Icariens*, 81.

278 **The white temple built by the Mormons** Vallet, *Icarian Communist*, 20.

278 **In 1850, while a crew worked on the building** Ibid.

278 **Because the community in Nauvoo partly depended** Sutton, *Les Icariens*, 70.

279 **"More than once [I] brought tears to the eyes"** Cabet, "History and Constitution," *Iowa Journal of History and Politics*, 230.

279 **He promised to leave France immediately** Ibid.

279 **Following a brief stopover in London** Sutton, *Les Icariens*, 71.

279 **Some of the women had started wearing** Cabet, *Travels in Icaria*, xxxv.

279 **It was one of their most profitable businesses** Sutton, *Les Icariens*, 74.

279 **"a moral purge"** Ibid., 81.

280 **He also orchestrated the excommunication** Ibid.

280 **"the interest and happiness of its members"** Cabet, "History and Constitution," *Iowa Journal of History and Politics,* 215.

280 **In the fall of 1854, Cabet petitioned** Gauthier, *Quest for Utopia,* 52.

280 **"sufficient to construct one or several communes"** Ibid., 53.

280 **"We Icarians, your brothers in heart"** Ibid.

281 **"The prestige was gone"** Vallet, *Icarian Communist,* 34.

281 **He even persuaded the assembly** Sutton, *Les Icariens,* 84.

281 **"If one is an Icarian"** Ibid., 83.

282 **Under the informal leadership** Sutton, *Communal Utopias,* 62; Shaw, *Icaria,* 55–58.

282 **"socialist land mania"** Noyes, *History of American Socialisms,* 594.

282 **In Noyes's estimation, this "land mania"** Ibid.

282 **Having bought the land in Iowa** Gauthier, *Quest for Utopia,* 45.

282 **The five-hundred-mile round-trip** Ibid., 51.

283 **When members of the Majority got control** Sutton, *Les Icariens,* 95.

283 **Even the little children became viciously partisan** Ibid.

283 **His wife, who had never made the crossing** Gauthier, *Quest for Utopia,* 31.

283 **Members of the Majority burned Cabet** Sutton, *Les Icariens,* 93.

283 **"We had come to Nauvoo to make a paradise"** Vallet, *Icarian Communist,* 36.

283 **After Majority men prevailed** Ibid., 35.

283 **"If any will not work, neither let him eat"** Ibid.

283 **When members of the Majority went out** Ibid.

283 **The Cabetists accepted the loaves** Ibid.

284 **"All our citizens are required to oversee law enforcement"** Cabet, *Travels in Icaria,* 108.

284 **Fed up, the non-Icarian residents of Nauvoo** Sutton, *Les Icariens,* 95.

284 **They had begun to worry** Gauthier, *Quest for Utopia,* 36.

284 **After the sheriff restored order** Cabet, *Travels in Icaria,* xxxvi.

284 **On September 27, 1856** Sutton, *Les Icariens,* 95.

284 **Two days after they arrived in St. Louis** Sutton, *Les Icariens,* 98; Johnson, *Utopian Communism,* 290; Gauthier, *Quest for Utopia,* 36.

285 **So that his followers could give him a second** Gauthier, *Quest for Utopia,* 36.

285 **One addled young German** Ibid., 37; Piotrowski, *Étienne Cabet,* 135.

285   **Messiah-less, the exiled Icarians** Sutton, "The Icarians of Corn-
      ing, Iowa," in *Adaptation of the Icarians to America*, 6.

285   **At one point, in an effort to make more money** Sutton, *Les Icar-
      iens*, 112.

285   **When the Civil War broke out** Ibid., 113.

285   **Jules Prudent, a former jeweler** Rancière, "Why Did the Icarians
      Leave France?," in Snyder and Sutton, eds., *Immigration of the Icarians
      to Illinois*, 12.

286   **In Iowa, they opted for single-family** Gauthier, *Quest for Utopia*, 47,
      59.

286   **John Dye, a printer who had lived at Oneida** Sutton, *Les Icariens*,
      127.

286   **William Moore, another lapsed Shaker** Sutton, "The Icarians of
      Corning, Iowa," in *Adaptation of the Icarians to America*, 9.

286   **Alcander Longley, perhaps the most persistent** Shaw, *Icaria*, 179.

286   **As a teenager, Longley had lived** Bestor, *Backwoods Utopias*, 56.

286   **The Longleys eventually left Icaria** Shaw, *Icaria*, 179.

287   **The community maintained a well-stocked library** Sutton, "The
      Icarians of Corning, Iowa," in *Adaptation of the Icarians to America*, 10.

287   **Amazingly, given the bitter expulsion of Cabet** Sutton, *Les Icar-
      iens*, 123.

287   **A visitor from the Oneida Community** Ibid., 124.

287   **Each February, the colonists celebrated** Ibid., 125.

287   **By the time the fighting started** Vallet, *Icarian Communist*, 38.

287   **By the 1870s, there were fewer than one hundred people** Sutton,
      Les Icariens, 127.

287   **The younger Icarians** Ibid.

288   **Four fugitive Communards who had fled** Vallet, *Icarian Communist*,
      39.

288   **Fresh from the Paris barricades** Gauthier, *Quest for Utopia*, 68.

288   **The Progressives now wanted to do the same** Ibid., 70.

288   **They also wanted the community to admit more members**
      Ibid.

288   **To pay for all of this** Sutton, *Les Icariens*, 130.

288   **The self-proclaimed Conservatives** Gauthier, *Quest for Utopia*, 65.

288   **Neither camp had the two-thirds majority** Ibid., 69.

289   **"This was a real war"** Ibid., 67.

289 **There was a politically motivated tussle** Ibid., 70.

289 **A Conservative cook intentionally wilted** Ibid.

289 **"This could not fail to cause a general gnashing"** Ross, *Child of Icaria*, 90.

289 **"the old party's lukewarm zeal"** Gauthier, *Quest for Utopia*, 73.

289 **Emile Péron, one of the new arrivals** Sutton, *Les Icariens*, 130.

289 **When the older group refused** Ibid.

289 **In August 1878, the two parties faced off** Ibid., 133.

289 **The lawyer for the Conservatives responded** Ibid.

290 **The Progressives remained on the original site** Ibid., 135, 136.

290 **Coverage of the trial brought an influx** Gauthier, *Quest for Utopia*, 92.

290 **Three years later, a Young Icarian barber** Sutton, "Cabetian Orthodoxy," in *Icaria-Speranza*, 33, 34; Berry, "A Granddaughter Reminisces," in *Icaria-Speranza*, 14.

290 **In France, Leroux and his brother** Berry, "A Granddaughter Reminisces," in *Icaria-Speranza*, 5–8; Shaw, *Icaria*, 167.

290 **"to prove to our fellow man"** Gauthier, *Quest for Utopia*, 93.

290 **To their comrades shivering through the winter** Ibid., 92.

291 **In 1883, many of the remaining Young Icarians** Ibid., 94.

291 **On the pale, grassy hills** Berry, "A Granddaughter Reminisces," in *Icaria-Speranza*, 11.

291 **The fifty-five members of Icaria-Speranza** Piotrowski, *Étienne Cabet*, 136; Gauthier, *Quest for Utopia*, 94.

291 **Taken as a single movement** Sutton, "The Icarians of Corning, Iowa," in *Adaptation of the Icarians to America*, 3.

292 **In 1898, eight geriatric Icarians** Sutton, *Les Icariens*, 144.

ONEIDA: KINGDOM COME

293 **"The sin-system, the marriage-system"** Oneida Community, *Bible Communism*, 42.

293 **On the evening of April 5, 1815** Raffles, *Memoir*, 243.

293 **British soldiers stationed there** Ibid., 245.

293 **Assuming that a merchant ship** Ibid.

293 **Within the heavy walls of the British fort** Ibid.

294 **"By noon complete darkness covered"** Ibid.

294 **The cloud of sulfurous ash spread** Howe, *What Hath God Wrought,* 30.

294 **"Eighteen Hundred and Froze to Death"** Ibid., 31.

294 **In early June, six inches of snow** Barkun, *Crucible of the Millennium,* 108.

294 **Freshly shorn sheep** Ibid.

295 **In 1811, powerful floods** Ibid.

295 **In 1812 and 1813, "spotted fever"** Ibid.

295 **To them, this punishing concatenation** Howe, *What Hath God Wrought,* 31.

295 **Worn down, farmers from the scrabbly** Barkun, *Crucible of the Millennium,* 105.

295 **Entire New England villages** Ibid.

295 **The Erie Canal, begun in 1817** Howe, *What Hath God Wrought,* 117.

295 **On the morning of its opening, cannons were arrayed** Ibid., 222.

295 **The man-made river carried more than twice** Ibid., 117.

295 **Barges laden with Manchester calico** Cross, *Burned-Over District,* 56.

296 **Over the course of the 1820s, the populations** Ibid.

297 **The Panic of 1837 derailed** Barkun, *Crucible of the Millennium,* 114–17.

297 **"a special receptivity to millenarian"** Ibid., 8.

297 **They parsed each weird line** Ibid., 50.

297 **"psychic highway"** Cross, *Burned-Over District,* 3.

298 **Circuit-riding evangelists blanketed** Seldes, *Stammering Century,* 102.

298 **Whitney Cross, the region's most celebrated chronicler** Cross, *Burned-Over District,* 4.

298 **In 1830 alone, more than one hundred thousand** Robertson, *Oneida Community,* 3.

298 **During the 1840s, the region was home** Noyes, *History of American Socialisms,* 268.

298 **ten were planned** Guarneri, *Utopian Alternative,* 154.

298 **"unusual excitement on the subject of religion"** Joseph Smith, "Joseph Smith—History," https://lds.org/scriptures/pgp/js-h/1?lang =eng.

299   **To spread the word of the coming rapture** Barkun, *Crucible of the Millennium*, 128.

299   **One group sent word to New Lebanon** Ibid., 96; Stein, *Shaker Experience in America*, 209.

299   **A few started their own small communes** Barkun, *Crucible of the Millennium*, 44.

301   **At the very center of New York State** Michael Barkun, "John Humphrey Noyes and Millennialism," *Syracuse University Library Associates Courier* 28, no. 2 (1993): 14.

301   **His father's side of the family** Parker, *Yankee Saint*, 5.

302   **In many of the new evangelical churches** Howe, *What Hath God Wrought*, 218.

302   **In 1831, she dragged her skeptical eldest son** Parker, *Yankee Saint*, 17.

302   **He wore bell-bottom pantaloons** George Wallingford Noyes, ed., *Religious Experience of John Humphrey Noyes*, Syracuse University Library, Oneida Community Collection, https://library.syr.edu/digital/collections/r/ReligiousExperienceOfJohnHumphreyNoyes/Chap01-09.html.

302   **"Hitherto, the world"** Robertson, *Oneida Community*, 3.

302   **Within a month he was enrolled** Parker, *Yankee Saint*, 18.

302   **With the restless zeal of a fresh-saved convert** Klaw, *Without Sin*, 23.

303   **"My heart was fixed on the millennium"** Seldes, *Stammering Century*, 160.

303   **He also helped found an abolitionist group** Klaw, *Without Sin*, 24.

304   **"the sole principle of a teleological theory"** Cavell, *Cities of Words*, 221.

304   **"endless progressive improvement"** Owen, *New Moral World*, iii.

304   **"will be elevated to perfection of body"** Pellarin, *Life of Charles Fourier*, 29.

304   **"Man," he wrote, "is evidently perfectible"** Cabet, "History and Constitution," *Iowa Journal of History and Politics*, 234.

304   **"entice us only to evil"** Fourier, "Of the Role of the Passions," https://www.marxists.org/reference/archive/fourier/works/ch01.htm.

304   **A Shaker theologian wrote** Bestor, *Backwoods Utopias*, 5.

305   **On a freezing Thursday evening** Parker, *Yankee Saint*, 21, 22.

305 **"He that committeth sin"** Ibid.

305 **"Three times in quick succession"** Sutton, *Communal Utopias*, 68.

306 **"the High Tide of the Spirit"** Robertson, *Oneida Community*, 102.

306 **"the climax of the flesh"** Seldes, *Stammering Century*, 161.

306 **The next morning, one of Noyes's classmates** John Humphrey Noyes, *Confessions* (1849), Syracuse University Library, Oneida Community Collection, https://library.syr.edu/digital/collections/c/ConfessionsOfJohnHNoyesPartI/.

306 **"Don't you commit sin?"** Ibid.

306 **"I have taken away their license"** Parker, *Yankee Saint*, 29.

306 **He took a room in a boardinghouse** Ibid., 30.

306 **Test-driving his newfound sanctity** Klaw, *Without Sin*, 32.

306 **He returned to the boardinghouse** Ibid.

307 **He later recalled that those three weeks** Ibid.

307 **At one point he walked for three days** Klaw, *Without Sin*, 37.

307 **"vagabond, incoherent service"** Dixon, *New America*, 367.

307 **Their mother held out for a while** Klaw, *Without Sin*, 38.

307 **When John Sr. died in 1841** Parker, *Yankee Saint*, 90.

308 **Even more than most of the ink-stained reformers** Ibid., 91.

308 **Noyes's decision to remain in Putney** Michael Barkun, "John Humphrey Noyes and Millennialism," *Syracuse University Library Associates Courier* 28, no. 2 (1993): 15.

308 **"permanent basis, not by preaching"** Seldes, *Stammering Century*, 167.

308 **By the winter of 1843, there were twenty-eight** Parker, *Yankee Saint*, 96.

308 **"the little church at Putney began cautiously"** Anthony Wonderley, "An Introduction," in Noyes, *Sexual Relations in the Oneida Community*, 15.

309 **"as appetite or fancy may suggest"** Parker, *Yankee Saint*, 97.

309 **"Health, Comfort, Economy"** Ibid.

309 **Later, when the Perfectionists had more money** Seldes, *Stammering Century*, 176.

309 **The Putney community was directly inspired** Noyes, *History of American Socialisms*, 61.

310 **"drank copiously of the spirit of"** Ibid.

310 **In the winter of 1846, two Brook Farmers visited** "Perfectionism the Antecedent of Communism," *Oneida Circular*, August 31, 1868.

310 **"well-meaning people, ardently longing"** Ibid.

310 **"On many points [Fourier's] philosophy"** Ibid.

310 **"trying to build a chimney by beginning"** Ibid.

310 **Noyes offered a surprising third option** Noyes, *Berean*, 276.

310 **The technical terms for these two views** Harrison, *Second Coming*, 4.

312 **"could face a battery of cannon"** Parker, *Yankee Saint*, 13.

312 **"kin of some degree"** Ibid., 6.

313 **Their spiritual connection was intense** Ibid., 28.

313 **When he came back to visit, she refused** Ibid., 34, 35.

313 **Even at the height** George Wallingford Noyes, *Free Love in Utopia*, 85.

313 **At the start of January 1837** Parker, *Yankee Saint*, 43.

313 **"I will write all that is in my heart"** John Humphrey Noyes, "The *Battle-axe* Letter," in *Putney Community*, Syracuse University Library, Oneida Community Collection, https://library.syr.edu/digital/collections/j/JohnHumphreyNoyes,ThePutneyCommunity/.

314 **David Harrison passed the letter on to Simon Lovett** Ibid.

314 **"Abigail Merwin's marriage stimulated"** George Wallingford Noyes, *Free Love in Utopia*, 105.

314 **"to defend and ultimately carry out"** Parker, *Yankee Saint*, 56.

314 **To prop up the concept of "communism in love"** Klaw, *Without Sin*, 41.

315 **"exclusiveness, jealousy, [and] quarreling"** John Humphrey Noyes, "The *Battle-axe* Letter," in *Putney Community*, Syracuse University Library, Oneida Community Collection, https://library.syr.edu/digital/collections/j/JohnHumphreyNoyes,ThePutneyCommunity.

315 **"Whoever has well studied"** Louis J. Kern, "Breaching the 'Wall of Partition Between the Male and the Female,'" *Syracuse University Library Associates Courier* 28, no. 2 (1993): 87.

316 **His starkly unromantic proposal** Foster, *Religion and Sexuality*, 83.

316 **"enter into no engagements with each other"** Ibid.

316 **The newlyweds spent their honeymoon** Parker, *Yankee Saint*, 64.

316 **"If we can raise up an army of effective writers"** Ibid., 106.

316 **George was a buttoned-up Grahamite** Ibid., 73.

317 **"a refinement of wickedness which puts papacy"** Ibid., 74.

317 **He called her a second Mary Magdalene** Ibid., 86.

317 **"Her spirit," he wrote, "[was] exceedingly intoxicating"** Klaw, *Without Sin*, 11.

317 **By 1846, Noyes had begun to wonder** Robertson, *Oneida Community*, 9.

317 **"All the circumstances invited advance"** John Humphrey Noyes, "My First Act in Sexual Freedom," in *Putney Community*, Syracuse University Library, Oneida Community Collection, https://library.syr .edu/digital/collections/j/JohnHumphreyNoyes,ThePutney Community/chap21.htm.

317 **Back at the main house** Ibid.

317 **"The last part of the interview was as amicable"** Ibid.

318 **To the small circle of initiates** Parker, *Yankee Saint*, 125.

318 **Like Ann Lee, who took up her "cross"** Foster, *Religion and Sexuality*, 93.

318 **In 1831, Robert Dale Owen** Ibid.

319 **Owen père, who had been greatly interested in Malthus** Owen, *New View of Society*, xiv.

319 **"It is as foolish and cruel"** Foster, *Religion and Sexuality*, 94.

319 **Along with coitus interruptus** George Wallingford Noyes, *Free Love in Utopia*, 4.

319 **"the most atrocious robbery"** Parker, *Yankee Saint*, 177.

319 **Along with Owen's pamphlet** Ibid., 178.

319 **"The 'system' of Male Continence"** Ibid.

319 **"The situation may be compared"** George Wallingford Noyes, *Free Love in Utopia*, xxxiii.

320 **Lingering in "the region of easy rowing"** Ellis, *Studies in the Psychology of Sex*, 553.

320 **According to one woman's recollection** Klaw, *Without Sin*, 178.

320 **"The Kingdom of God"** John Humphrey Noyes, "The Kingdom of God Has Come," in *Putney Community*, Syracuse University Library, Oneida Community Collection, https://library.syr.edu/digital/ collections/j/JohnHumphreyNoyes,ThePutneyCommunity/chap24 .htm.

320 **"We have been able to cut our way"** Ibid.

320 **"Is not now the time"** Ibid.

321 **A month later, a Putney woman named Harriet** Klaw, *Without Sin*, 63.

321 **He ordered her to sit up** Seldes, *Stammering Century*, 168, 169.

321 **Matters were made worse** Parker, *Yankee Saint*, 127.

321 **"a hideous monster of iniquity"** Eastman, *Noyesism Unveiled*, v.

322 **He tried to initiate Daniel Hall** Parker, *Yankee Saint*, 132.

322 **After freely admitting to having sex** Ibid., 133.

322 **Before the actual trial commenced** Klaw, *Without Sin*, 67.

322 **The land was part of a reserve** Parker, *Yankee Saint*, 166.

323 **There were a few small farms** Dixon, *New America*, 351.

322 **When Burt heard that the Putney community** Parker, *Yankee Saint*, 130.

323 **"There is some romance," he wrote** John Humphrey Noyes, "The Call to Oneida," in *Putney Community*, Syracuse University Library, Oneida Community Collection, https://library.syr.edu/digital/collections/j/JohnHumphreyNoyes,ThePutneyCommunity/chap35.htm.

323 **Over time, Noyes wrote, they could build** Ibid.

323 **As a heavy snow fell, they traveled the three miles** Klaw, *Without Sin*, 73.

323 **About 40 percent of the subscribers** Cross, *Burned-Over District*, 248.

324 **The majority entered the community** Parker, *Yankee Saint*, 169.

324 **While small utopias often suffocate** Noyes, *History of American Socialisms*, 619; Klaw, *Without Sin*, 223.

325 **By the start of 1849, the Oneida Association** George Wallingford Noyes, *Free Love in Utopia*, 22.

325 **Food—at first mostly coarse bread** Seldes, *Stammering Century*, 171.

325 **During the first summer, dysentery** Parker, *Yankee Saint*, 173.

325 **"The Oneida Community owes much"** John Humphrey Noyes, "American Socialisms," *Circular*, January 18, 1869.

326 **"Owen, Ripley, Fourier, [and] Cabet"** Dixon, *New America*, 394.

326 **"communism pure and simple"** Shaw, *Icaria*, 179.

326 **Even pocket watches belonged** Klaw, *Without Sin*, 1.

326 **Brisbane and Ripley claimed that the constraints** Codman, *Brook Farm*, 38.

326 **He called it the freedom of the porcupine** Noyes, *Berean*, 461.

327 **"liberty of communism"** Parker, *Yankee Saint*, 234.

327 **"The two great principles of human existence"** John Humphrey Noyes, "Analysis of Liberty," *Circular*, February 14, 1870.

327 **"When the Spirit of Truth pricked"** Noyes, *History of American Socialisms*, 26.

328 **In 1848, on a low knoll at the center of their estate** Robertson, *Oneida Community*, 13.

328 **After considering and rejecting the terms** *phalanstery* Ibid.

328 **Winter came before the Mansion House** Robertson, *Oneida Community*, 31.

328 **In 1860, the three-story building** Parker, *Yankee Saint*, 171, 175.

328 **They rearranged their estate with such frequency** Ibid., 175.

328 **Most adults slept in their own narrow** Wonderley, "An Introduction," in Noyes, *Sexual Relations in the Oneida Community*, 23.

329 **"the balance of inducement should always"** Janet White, "Building Perfection," *Syracuse University Library Associates Courier*, 28, no. 2 (1993): 35.

329 **In 1870, for the two hundred adults** Robertson, *Oneida Community*, 88.

329 **"Their coming together should not be to sleep"** Wonderley, "An Introduction," in Noyes, *Sexual Relations in the Oneida Community*, 23.

329 **Men ironed sheets in the laundry** Robertson, *Oneida Community*, 28.

330 **"a standing lie [that] proclaims"** George Wallingford Noyes, *Free Love in Utopia*, 333.

330 **"uniform of a vital society"** Robertson, *Oneida Community*, 294.

330 **This so-called short dress** Hayden, *Seven American Utopias*, 200.

330 **After a group of Perfectionist women were harassed** Fellman, *Unbounded Frame*, 56.

330 **"Any fashion which requires women to devote"** Robertson, *Oneida Community*, 298.

331 **"is not ornament but a covering"** Ibid., 298.

331 **While the community came under constant attack** Ibid., 294.

331 **"We women of thirty are"** Marlyn Klee-Hartzel, "Mingling the Sexes," Syracuse University Library, Oneida Community Collection, https://library.syr.edu/digital/collections/c/Courier/.

331 **When they read about the new trend of "enameling"** Parker, *Yankee Saint*, 243.

331 **"People sneer at our dress"** Robertson, *Oneida Community*, 307, 308.

332 **While tracts by the likes of Stanton and Susan B. Anthony** Ibid., 284.

332 **In the 1860s, a group of community women** Ibid., 300, 301.

332 **"'Woman's Rights,' is a term we always prefer"** Ibid.

332 **"the germ of falsity and immorality"** Fourier, *Harmonian Man*, 281.

332 **"women are not men's slaves"** Robertson, *Oneida Community*, 302.

333 **"We are not opposed, after the Shaker fashion"** Ibid., 207.

333 **"child-bearing, when it is undertaken, should be a voluntary affair"** Ibid., 341.

333 **Among roughly two hundred sexually busy** Foster, *Religion and Sexuality*, 95.

333 **"the sedative and relaxing seminal fluid"** Van de Warker, "A Gynecological Study of the Oneida Community," *American Journal of Obstetrics and Diseases of Women and Children*, 804.

333 **To refute these sorts of pseudoscientific claims** Robertson, *Oneida Community*, 271.

333 **The doctor was surprised to find** Ellis, *Studies in the Psychology of Sex*, 809.

333 **Those few men who were unable to master** Ibid., 803.

334 **"the increase of population by birth"** Robertson, *Oneida Community*, 274.

334 **Infants were reared and nursed** Ibid., 311; Parker, *Yankee Saint*, 176.

334 **"recognition of the Community sponsorship"** Robertson, *Oneida Community*, 79.

334 **"as blind a passion as ever [romantic] love"** Ibid., 318.

334 **"self-culture and the appetite for universal improvement"** Ibid., 319.

334 **To foster the "Pentecostal spirit"** Ibid., 324.

335 **"weekly ablution of the infantile population"** Ibid., 320.

335 **A large, steam-heated playroom** Ibid., 323.

335 **"fifteen willow whistles, blown in the most violent manner"** Ibid., 328.

335 **"This doll-spirit that seduces us"** Ibid., 332.

336 **"a more quiet place for reflection"** "Third Annual Report of the Oneida Association," https://library.syr.edu/digital/collections/t/ThirdAnnualReportOfTheOneidaAssociation/.

336 **"It is a business," Noyes wrote** Ibid.

336 **A fourth, smaller group shared a house** Ibid.

336 **In 1851, the fifth and largest satellite** George Wallingford Noyes, *Free Love in Utopia*, 93.

337 **Once in Brooklyn, Noyes quickly** Ibid., 72.

337 **George Ripley, by then resident in Flatbush** Ibid.

337   **He and Noyes discussed the woeful state of "civilization"** Ibid., 71.

337   **In 1851, Noyes learned that Greeley would be attending** Ibid., 91.

337   **"a Congress of all nations, and it seemed proper"** Ibid.

337   **Noyes found out which ship Greeley** Ibid.

337   **"a natural and favorable opportunity"** Ibid.

337   **Although they "crossed swords" over the merits** Ibid., 92.

338   **"disgusting order of united adulterers"** "Perfectionism and Polygamy," *New York Observer,* January 22, 1852.

338   **"the foulest days and darkest places"** Ibid.

338   **"plainly the germ of *bloomerism*!"** Ibid.

338   **The Perfectionists sent as much honest information** Robertson, *Oneida Community,* 273.

338   **"saturated all the time with worldly influences"** Ibid., 124.

338   **The community subscribed to 140 separate publications** Ibid., 187; Hayden, *Seven American Utopias,* 197.

338   **"well-aired and in rapport"** George Wallingford Noyes, *Free Love in Utopia,* 156.

338   **"The Oneida Associationists are honorably contrasted"** "Perfectionism and Polygamy," *New York Observer,* January 22, 1852.

339   **Support for the Perfectionists** George Wallingford Noyes, *Free Love in Utopia,* 71.

339   **Despite a tense exchange** Ibid.

339   **"It appears to me," James wrote** James, "To the Editor of the *New York Observer,*" *New-York Tribune,* November 15, 1852.

339   **In February 1850, the community bought a sloop** "Third Annual Report of the Oneida Association," https://library.syr.edu/digital/collections/t/ThirdAnnualReportOfTheOneidaAssociation/.

340   **"If Printing is the most important art"** Ibid.

340   **On a bright, warm day in late July 1851** George Wallingford Noyes, *Free Love in Utopia,* 103.

340   **When they docked at Kingston** Ibid.

340   **While they ate, a sudden gust filled the mainsail** Ibid.

340   **On the floor of the Hudson, the ship righted itself** Ibid., 109.

341   **After nineteen days, the sloop was raised** Ibid., 113.

341   **"[They have] the North River for a grave"** Ibid., 105.

341   **"There is no other woman I loved as I did her"** Ibid., xxvi.

341 **"see and show how much God can do"** Robertson, *Oneida Community*, 249.

341 **"Mrs. Cragin's death will lead me"** George Wallingford Noyes, *Free Love in Utopia*, xxxvii.

342 **The Perfectionists claimed to have introduced** Robertson, *Oneida Community*, 277.

342 **Later, the community disavowed the term** Ibid., 281.

342 **"In a holy community," Noyes wrote** John Humphrey Noyes, "The *Battle-axe* Letter," in *Putney Community*, Syracuse University Library, Oneida Community Collection, https://library.syr.edu/digital/collections/j/JohnHumphreyNoyes,ThePutneyCommunity.

342 **"a more perfect symbol of [a union with Christ]"** Anthony Wonderley, "Noyes on Sex," in Noyes, *Sexual Relations in the Oneida Community*, 48.

343 **"the highest instruments of praise and worship"** Wonderley, "Watervliet Shakers Through the Eyes of Oneida Perfectionists," *American Communal Societies Quarterly*.

343 **"making of twain one flesh"** Robertson, *Oneida Community*, 269.

343 **In practice, this meant that the young** Foster, *Religion and Sexuality*, 106.

343 **Noyes occupied the top of this pyramid** Ibid.

343 **For years, he considered it his duty** Klaw, *Without Sin*, 181.

343 **the mechanics of male continence** Van de Warker, "Gynecological Study of the Oneida Community," 789.

344 **"The new commandment," Noyes preached** Parker, *Yankee Saint*, 182.

344 **"Variety is, in the nature of all things"** Ibid.

344 **In extreme cases, one lover might be called away** Foster, *Religion and Sexuality*, 107.

344 **The usual procedure for initiating a tryst** Parker, *Yankee Saint*, 184.

344 **Everyone was theoretically free to decline any lover** Ibid., 183.

344 **"Let us consider whether we may not do good"** George Wallingford Noyes, *Free Love in Utopia*, 26.

344 **"Let us be heroes in love"** Ibid., 26.

345 **At one point, Noyes considered staging live sex shows** Klaw, *Without Sin*, 17.

345 **"museum orgies"** Beecher, *Charles Fourier*, 311.

346 **At Andover Theological Seminary** Parker, *Yankee Saint,* 19.

347 **Each man would sit silently** Ibid.

347 **"whipping enough to keep one man sober"** Ibid., 218.

347 **Praise, or "commendatory criticism"** Robertson, *Oneida Community,* 130.

347 **"sauciness of speech"** Dixon, *New America,* 96.

347 **"his whole manner is sensational"** *Mutual Criticism,* 61.

347 **"masculinity carried to excess"** Seldes, *Stammering Century,* 179.

347 **"too frequent mentions of Vermont"** Klaw, *Without Sin,* 114.

348 **"the four-year olds have had a round of criticism"** Robertson, *Oneida Community,* 147.

348 **When Francis Long, the young man whose inexperience** George Wallingford Noyes, *Free Love in Utopia,* 109.

348 **"It is Theocratic, for in recognizing the Truth"** *Mutual Criticism,* 94.

348 **"the real secret of the prolonged life"** Parker, *Yankee Saint,* 221.

349 **"It is our spiritual Turkish Bath"** *Mutual Criticism,* 87.

349 **"One secret of its efficacy"** Robertson, *Oneida Community,* 132.

349 **When an epidemic of croup broke out** Ibid.

349 **"to reduce sail and shift anchor"** George Wallingford Noyes, *Free Love in Utopia,* 167.

349 **"the disasters of Owenism and Fourierism"** Noyes, *History of American Socialisms,* iii.

350 **"It is certainly high time"** Ibid.

350 **"[We] are destined," wrote one colonist** Hayden, *Seven American Utopias,* 191.

350 **During their first year on Jonathan Burt's land** Klaw, *Without Sin,* 78.

350 **Sewell Newhouse, a trapper and blacksmith** Parker, *Yankee Saint,* 205.

350 **His traps were lighter and more reliable** Seldes, *Stammering Century,* 175.

350 **In short order, the community** Robertson, *Oneida Community,* 229; Parker, *Yankee Saint,* 207.

351 **While many Americans laughed** Robertson, *Oneida Community,* 217.

351 **One Oneidan, clearly channeling Fourier** Seldes, *Stammering Century,* 175.

351 **If, for instance, the Hudson's Bay Company** Robertson, *Oneida Community*, 305.

351 **They held bees for every large task** Ibid., 38, 48, 62, 81.

351 **The *Circular* regularly trumpeted** Ibid., 64.

352 **Laboring in "mixed company"** Ibid., 58.

352 **Under the influence of Fourier** Noyes, *History of American Socialisms*, 636.

352 **"We have lately found it pleasant and profitable"** Robertson, *Oneida Community*, 193, 194.

352 **Taking another suggestion from Fourier** Ibid., 300.

352 **A machinist requisitioned** Ibid., 86.

352 **After being thrown out of France** George Wallingford Noyes, *Free Love in Utopia*, 70.

352 **After his visit, a portrait of Fourier** Ibid., 74.

352 **"Amativeness," Noyes wrote, "is a mighty passion"** Ibid., 87.

352 **Even more than the Fourierists** Stein, *Shaker Experience in America*, 336.

353 **Relations were particularly friendly** Wonderley, "Watervliet Shakers Through the Eyes of Oneida Perfectionists," *American Communal Societies Quarterly*.

353 **Noyes, who borrowed liberally** Andrews, *People Called Shakers*, xiii.

353 **One Shaker elder wrote that the two sects** Wonderley, "Watervliet Shakers Through the Eyes of Oneida Perfectionists," *American Communal Societies Quarterly*.

353 **The soul might be perfected through faith** Robertson, *Oneida Community*, 58.

353 **"the tendency in living together"** Ibid., 74.

354 **The library in the Mansion House** Hayden, *Seven American Utopias*, 197.

354 **He favored poetry that did what he thought** Parker, *Yankee Saint*, 237.

354 **During the winter of 1863** Robertson, *Oneida Community*, 180.

354 **"If anything will arouse persons from their apathy"** Ibid., 183.

355 **"This caused a general laugh in the room"** Ibid.

355 **Much of this activity took place** Ibid., 35.

355 **At seven thirty each evening** Ibid., 46.

355 **"partly social, partly intellectual, partly industrial"** Ibid., 66.

355 **Afterward they might sing a few songs** Ibid., 59.

355 **"Enjoyment," he said, was "the very business"** Klaw, *Without Sin*, 89.

355 **In keeping with the "spirit of improvement"** Robertson, *Oneida Community*, 188.

355 **They formed bands and orchestras** Ibid., 180, 189.

355 **Staying impressively au courant** Klaw, *Without Sin*, 97.

356 **"a good medium of communism"** Ibid., 266.

356 **"The love of the beautiful could be made"** Robertson, *Oneida Community*, 177.

356 **Aside from complex marriage** Ibid., 189.

356 **"very hard striking of the balls"** Ibid., 202.

356 **"chain of redemption"** Oneida Community, *Bible Communism*, 42.

357 **"victory over death"** Robertson, *Oneida Community*, 108.

357 **"The thought occurred to me"** Ibid., 109.

357 **In light of this new thinking** Ibid., 145.

357 **In July 1852, at the height** Ibid., 193.

358 **"the people in this vicinity will not"** George Wallingford Noyes, *Free Love in Utopia*, 190.

358 **Around the increasingly luxurious Mansion House** Ibid., 29.

358 **"Few corners of America"** Dixon, *New America*, 351.

358 **On the Fourth of July, as many as fifteen hundred** Robertson, *Oneida Community*, 71.

358 **In 1870, a new rail spur** Parker, *Yankee Saint*, 241.

358 **The new line shortened the trip** Robertson, *Oneida Community*, 29.

358 **"Cars stop for fifteen minutes for stealing fruit"** Ibid., 39.

358 **Among the attractions at Oneida** Ibid., 40.

358 **So many tourists came** Ibid., 70.

359 **"Eggs," a sign in the refectory noted** Ibid.

359 **Some cornered Perfectionist children** Ibid., 67.

359 **Oneida women grew accustomed** Ibid.

359 **The press compared him with Brigham Young** Ibid., 273.

359 **"If Mr. Noyes takes a pinch of snuff"** Ibid., 260.

359 **Some visitors speculated** Ibid., 77.

360 **"there will normally be on earth thirty-seven million"** Manuel and Manuel, *Utopian Thought in the Western World*, 667.

360 **"desired to produce a Byron, a Napoleon"** Klaw, *Without Sin*, 118.

360 **"foster abnormal or excessive development"** Ibid.

360 **"is willing to learn little by little"** Robertson, *Oneida Community*, 58.

361 **"We believe that the time will come"** Ibid., 270.

361 **"promiscuous scrambling"** Ibid., 348.

361 **"thousands [who] are ready to rush in"** Ibid., 348.

361 **"Owenites, infidels, spiritualists, irresponsible free lovers"** Klaw, *Without Sin*, 194.

361 **"by another entrance"** Robertson, *Oneida Community*, 349.

361 **Mainstream enthusiasm would not peak** Rushby, *Paradise*, 192.

362 **"by weeding out its poorest stock"** Robertson, *Oneida Community*, 346.

362 **"The principles of natural selection"** Ibid.

362 **"the true handmaid of faith"** Ibid., 168.

362 **"I have followed . . . Darwin"** Parker, *Yankee Saint*, 262.

362 **"The Lord himself has exercised the herdsman's right"** Robertson, *Oneida Community*, 343.

363 **Ten long generations later** Ibid.

363 **Noyes carefully documented how God employed** Ibid., 346; Seldes, *Stammering Century*, 191.

363 **"the last citadel of social falsehood"** Klaw, *Without Sin*, 207.

363 **When the stirpiculture experiment began** Parker, *Yankee Saint*, 259.

363 **Like breeders of flowers or dogs** Robertson, *Oneida Community*, 342.

363 **"The existence of Noyes"** Parker, *Yankee Saint*, 253.

363 **Not surprisingly, Noyes personally fathered** Ibid., 257.

364 **Ultimately, a total of fifty-three women** Ibid.

364 **"'living sacrifices' to God and true Communism"** Ibid.

364 **Between 1869 and 1879, forty-five "stirpicults"** Foster, *Religion and Sexuality*, 119.

364 **The stated goal of the experiment was quality** Robertson, *Oneida Community*, 345.

364 **The experiment's rate of infant mortality** McGee, "An Experiment in Human Stirpiculture," *American Anthropologist*, 319.

364 **after the breakup of the community, Anita Newcomb McGee** Ibid., 319–27.

364 **Assuming that "inspiration" was somehow inheritable** Klaw, *Without Sin*, 191.

365 **At the time of McGee's study** McGee, "An Experiment in Human Stirpiculture," *American Anthropologist*, 319.

365 **By the middle 1870s, with stirpiculture in full swing** George Wallingford Noyes, *Life of John Humphrey Noyes*, Syracuse University Library, Oneida Community Collection, https://library.syr.edu/digital/collections/l/LifeOfJohnHumphreyNoyes/#11.

365 **"We are so near a second coming"** Ibid.

365 **It also dimmed the erotic magnetism** George Wallingford Noyes, *Free Love in Utopia*, xxiii.

366 **In 1874, James William Towner** Parker, *Yankee Saint*, 273.

366 **Two years after Towner's arrival** Ibid., 263.

366 **Theodore's skepticism did not extend** Klaw, *Without Sin*, 216.

366 **The community approved his promotion** Ibid., 225; Parker, *Yankee Saint*, 277.

367 **During his brief presidency** Klaw, *Without Sin*, 224.

367 **After eight months, Theodore resigned** Parker, *Yankee Saint*, 279.

367 **"the fading word of truth"** Fellman, *Unbounded Frame*, 3.

367 **When James Towner began to challenge Noyes's authority** Klaw, *Without Sin*, 237.

368 **"a means of keeping unwanted children"** Seldes, *Stammering Century*, 188.

368 **The same upwelling of conservative prudery** Robertson, *Oneida Community*, 288.

368 **"utopia of obscenity"** Parker, *Yankee Saint*, 268.

368 **"The people of Illinois could not endure"** Ibid.

368 **In a dismally familiar bit of reasoning** Ibid., 270.

368 **"In the Children's House"** Carmer, "Children of the Kingdom," *New Yorker*, 26.

368 **Some of the secular press** Robertson, *Oneida Community*, 290.

369 **"Oh, dreadful!"** *Puck* 4, no. 103 (February 26, 1879); Parker, *Yankee Saint*, 280.

369 **"were within [our] power to wipe"** *Israelite*, September 19, 1873.

369 ***persons living in concupiscence*** Klaw, *Without Sin*, 244; Parker, *Yankee Saint*, 279.

369 **"vastly purer than some of the most respectable marriages"** Stein, *Shaker Experience in America*, 336.

369 **When the legislature in Albany proved unwilling** Parker, *Yankee Saint*, 281.

369 **The real risk for Noyes** Ibid., 282.

369 **"COMMUNIST NOYES TO BE ARRESTED"** *New-York World,* June 29, 1879.

369 **The previous night, without telling anyone** Klaw, *Without Sin,* 2.

370 **Professor Mears's zeal was not satisfied** Parker, *Yankee Saint,* 285.

370 **Noyes's view was that for the community to continue** Klaw, *Without Sin,* 250.

370 **Others, especially younger communists** Parker, *Yankee Saint,* 284.

370 **"which allows marriage but prefers celibacy"** Ibid.

370 **On a hot afternoon in late August 1879** Ibid., 295.

370 **"sexual 'good-byes'"** Klaw, *Without Sin,* 254.

370 **Young women let their hair grow** Ibid., 249.

371 **Within four months of the vote** McGee, "An Experiment in Human Stirpiculture," *American Anthropologist,* 324.

371 **Professor Mears demanded to see** Parker, *Yankee Saint,* 285.

371 **"Our relations are no longer 'complex'"** Klaw, *Without Sin,* 256.

371 **a year after the first monogamous marriage** Ibid., 271.

371 **At midnight on the last day of 1880** Lawrence Foster, "Free Love and Community," in Pitzer, ed., *America's Communal Utopias,* 268.

371 **Six hundred thousand dollars' worth** Ibid., 266.

371 **Eighty-four of the 109 adults** Ibid., 261.

372 **Some of them had never once handled cash** Parker, *Yankee Saint,* 287.

372 **Towner and thirty-five of his supporters left Oneida** Ibid., 290.

372 **Although the Townerites continued to receive** Ibid.

373 **"We made a raid into an unknown country"** Robertson, *Oneida Community,* 26.

CONCLUSION: THE FUTURE AIN'T WHAT IT USED TO BE

375 **"Everyone forgets that Icarus also flew"** Gilbert, *Collected Poems,* 228.

375 **"I understand. You mean that [the just person will]"** Plato (*Republic* IX, 592b), *Complete Works,* 1199.

375 **At the teetering breakaway Icaria** Sutton, *Les Icariens,* 113.

376 **At the United Society's two villages** Stein, *Shaker Experience in America,* 202.

376 **"You ought to be made to fight"** Andrews, *People Called Shakers,* 216.

376 **At Oneida, a clerical error saved the Perfectionist men** Klaw, *Without Sin,* 195.

377 **"It is our Father's beautiful garden"** Codman, *Brook Farm,* 178.

378 **In the new, battle-born Republic, reformist causes** Seldes, *Stammering Century,* 202.

379 **"The nineteenth century," wrote the critic Greil Marcus** Ibid., viii.

381 **"There is a small number," wrote Horace Greeley** Rourke, *Trumpets of Jubilee,* 274.

381 **"When citizens are classed by rank"** Tocqueville, *Democracy in America,* 515.

383 **"Things are in the saddle, / And ride mankind"** Emerson, "Ode to William H. Channing," http://www.poetryfoundation.org/poem/175144.

383 **"While we are pouring ever increasing intellectual efforts"** Bertrand de Jouvenel, "Utopia for Practical Purposes," in Manuel, ed., *Utopias and Utopian Thought,* 225.

384 **"We all work with tireless zeal"** Sutton, *Les Icariens,* 99.

Bibliography

Adams, John Quincy. *Memoirs of John Quincy Adams*. Edited by Charles Francis Adams. Philadelphia: J. B. Lippincott & Co., 1877.

Andrews, Edward Deming. *The People Called Shakers*. New York: Dover Publications, 1953.

Aristotle. *The Politics*. Translated by Trevor J. Saunders. London: Penguin Books, 1992.

Barkun, Michael. *Crucible of the Millennium: The Burned-Over District of New York in the 1840s*. Syracuse, NY: Syracuse University Press, 1986.

Barthes, Roland. *A Barthes Reader*. Edited by Susan Sontag. New York: Hill and Wang, 1983.

Beecher, Jonathan. *Charles Fourier: The Visionary and His World*. Berkeley: University of California Press, 1986.

———. *Victor Considerant and the Rise and Fall of French Romantic Socialism*. Berkeley: University of California Press, 2001.

Bellow, Saul. *The Adventures of Augie March*. New York: Penguin Books, 1996.

Berlin, Isaiah. "A Message to the 21st Century." *New York Review of Books,* October 23, 2014, 37.

Bernhard, Karl, Duke of Saxe-Weimar Eisenach. *Travels Through North America, During the Years 1825 and 1826*. Vol. 1. Philadelphia: Carey, Lea & Carey, 1828.

Berry, Brian J. L. *America's Utopian Experiments: Communal Havens from Long-Wave Crises*. Hanover, NH: University Press of New England, 1992.

Berry, Lorraine Stephens. "A Granddaughter Reminisces on the Role the Dehay and Leroux Families Played in the Icaria-Speranza Colony." In *Icaria-Speranza: Final Utopian Experiment of Icarians in America: Proceedings of the 1989 Cours Icarien Symposium*. Edited by the National Icarian Heritage Society. Nauvoo, IL: National Icarian Heritage Society, 1995, 3–23.

Bestor, Arthur. *Backwoods Utopias: The Sectarian Origins and the Owenite Phase of Communitarian Socialism in America, 1663–1829*. 2nd ed. Philadelphia: University of Pennsylvania Press, 1970.

Brewer, Priscilla J. *Shaker Communities, Shaker Lives*. Hanover, NH: University Press of New England, 1986.

"Brisbane and Fourier." *Oneida Circular* 4 (October 1868): 253–54.

Brisbane, Albert. *Albert Brisbane, a Mental Biography: With a Character Study by His Wife, Redelia Brisbane*. Boston: Arena Publishing, 1893.

————. *Association: Or, A Concise Exposition of the Practical Part of Fourier's Social Science*. New York: Greeley & McElrath, 1843.

————. *Social Destiny of Man: Or, Association and Reorganization of Industry*. Philadelphia: C. F. Stollmeyer, 1840.

Brooks, Van Wyck. *The Flowering of New England, 1815–1865*. New York: E. P. Dutton & Co., 1937.

Brown, Paul. *Twelve Months in New Harmony*. Philadelphia: Porcupine Press, 1972.

Burks, Jean M., ed. *Shaker Design: Out of This World*. New Haven, CT: Yale University Press, 2008.

Burton, Katherine. *Paradise Planters*. New York: Longmans, Green and Co., 1939.

Cabet, Étienne. "History and Constitution of the Icarian Community." Translated by Thomas Teakle. *Iowa Journal of History and Politics* 15, no. 2 (April 1917): 214–86.

————. *Travels in Icaria*. Translated by Leslie J. Roberts. Syracuse, NY: Syracuse University Press, 2003.

_____. *Le vrai Christianisme suivant Jésus-Christ.* 2nd ed. Paris: Au Bureau du Populaire, 1846.

Campion, Nardi Reeder. *Mother Ann Lee: Morning Star of the Shakers.* Hanover, NH: University Press of New England, 1990.

Carlyle, Thomas. *Past and Present.* Boston: Estes and Lauriat, 1886.

Carmer, Carl. "Children of the Kingdom." *New Yorker,* March 21, 1936, 26–36.

Carmony, Donald F., and Josephine M. Elliott. "New Harmony, Indiana: Robert Owen's Seedbed for Utopia." *Indiana Magazine of History* 76, no. 3 (September 1980): 161–261.

Cavell, Stanley. *Cities of Words: Pedagogical Letters on a Register of the Moral Life.* Cambridge, MA: Belknap Press of Harvard University Press, 2004.

"Celebration of Fourier's Birthday at Brook Farm." *Phalanx* 1, no. 22 (May 1845): 336–37.

Chicoineau, Jacques C. "Etienne Cabet and His World." In *Humanistic Values of the Icarian Movement: Proceedings of the Symposium on the "Relevance of the Icarian Movement to Today's World."* Edited by Lillian M. Snyder. Nauvoo, IL: 1980, 7–14.

Codman, John Thomas. *Brook Farm: Historic and Personal Memoirs.* Boston: Arena Publishing, 1894.

Crain, Caleb. "Tea and Antipathy." *New Yorker,* December 20 and 27, 2010, 132–39.

Cross, Whitney R. *The Burned-Over District: The Social and Intellectual History of Enthusiastic Religion in Western New York, 1800–1850.* Ithaca, NY: Cornell University Press, 1950.

Crowe, Charles. *George Ripley: Transcendentalist and Utopian Socialist.* Athens, GA: University of Georgia Press, 1967.

Curtis, George William. *Early Letters of George Wm. Curtis to John S. Dwight: Brook Farm and Concord.* Edited by George Willis Cooke. New York: Harper & Bros., 1898.

Davenport, Guy. *Apples and Pears and Other Stories.* San Francisco: North Point Press, 1984.

Delano, Sterling F. "*The Harbinger* Reviews Its Transcendental 'Friends': Margaret Fuller, Theodore Parker, and Ralph Waldo Emerson." *Colby Library Quarterly* 17, no. 2 (June 1981): 74–84.

_____. *Brook Farm: The Dark Side of Utopia.* Cambridge, MA: Belknap Press of Harvard University Press, 2004.

Dixon, William Hepworth. *New America.* 8th ed. London: Hurst and Blackett, 1867.

————. *Spiritual Wives.* Vol. 1. London: Hurst and Blackett, 1868.

Doyle, William. *The Oxford History of the French Revolution.* 2nd ed. Oxford: Oxford University Press, 2002.

Eastman, Reverend Hubbard. *Noyesism Unveiled: A History of the Sect Self-Styled Perfectionists; with a Summary View of Their Leading Doctrines.* Brattleboro,VT: published by the author, 1849.

Ellis, Havelock. *Studies in the Psychology of Sex.* Vol. 6. Philadelphia: F. A. Davis Company, 1910.

Emerson, Ralph Waldo. *The Complete Works of Ralph Waldo Emerson.* Vol. 10. Boston: Houghton, Mifflin, and Co., 1883.

————. *The Essential Writings of Ralph Waldo Emerson.* Edited by Brooks Atkinson. New York: Modern Library, 2000.

Engels, Friedrich. *The Condition of the Working-Class in England in 1844.* London: S. Sonnenschein & Co., 1892.

————. *Socialism: Utopian and Scientific.* Translated by Edward Aveling. New York: Cosimo Classics, 2008.

Evans, Frederick. *Shaker Communism, or, Tests of Divine Inspiration.* London: James Burns, 1871.

Extract from an Unpublished Manuscript on Shaker History, by an Eyewitness Giving an Accurate Description of Their Songs, Dances, Marches, Visions, Visits to the Spirit Land, &c. Boston: E. K. Allen, 1850.

Feller, Daniel. *The Jacksonian Promise: America, 1815–1840.* Baltimore: Johns Hopkins University Press, 195.

Fellman, Michael. *The Unbounded Frame: Freedom and Community in Nineteenth Century American Utopianism.* Westport, CT: Greenwood Press, 1973.

FitzGerald, Frances. *Cities on a Hill: A Journey Through Contemporary American Cultures.* New York: Simon & Schuster, 1986.

Fitzgerald, F. Scott. *The Great Gatsby.* New York: Scribner, 2004.

Fluhman, J. Spencer. "Early Mormon and Shaker Visions of Sanctified Community." *BYU Studies Quarterly* 44, no. 1 (2005): 79–110.

Fogarty, Robert S. *American Utopianism.* Itasca, IL: F. E. Peacock Publishers, 1972.

————. *Desire and Duty at Oneida: Tirzah Miller's Intimate Memoir.* Bloomington: Indiana University Press, 2000.

————. *Dictionary of American Communal and Utopian History.* Westport, CT: Greenwood Press, 1980.

Foster, Lawrence. *Religion and Sexuality: Three American Communal Experiments of the Nineteenth Century.* New York: Oxford University Press, 1981.

Fourier, Charles. *Harmonian Man: Selected Writings of Charles Fourier.* Translated by Susan Hanson. Edited by Mark Poster. Garden City, NY: Anchor Books, 1971.

———. *The Hierarchies of Cuckoldry and Bankruptcy.* Translated by Geoffrey Longnecker. Cambridge, MA: Wakefield Press, 2011.

———. *The Theory of the Four Movements.* Edited by Gareth Stedman Jones and Ian Patterson. Cambridge, UK: Cambridge University Press, 1996.

Francis, Richard. *Ann the Word: The Story of Ann Lee, Female Messiah, Mother of the Shakers, the Woman Clothed with the Sun.* New York: Arcade Publishing, 2000.

———. *Transcendental Utopias: Individual and Community at Brook Farm, Fruitlands, and Walden.* Ithaca, NY: Cornell University Press, 1997.

Frothingham, Octavius Brooks. *George Ripley.* Boston: Houghton, Mifflin and Co., 1883.

Gauthier, Paul S. *Quest for Utopia: The Icarians of Adams County.* Corning, IA: Gauthier Publishing, 1992.

Gilbert, Jack. *Collected Poems.* New York: Alfred A. Knopf, 2012.

Godwin, Parke. *A Popular View of the Doctrines of Charles Fourier.* 2nd ed. New York: J. S. Redfield, 1844.

Greaves, Alexander (under the name Philalethes). *Reflections on the Statements and Opinions Published in the* Free Enquirer, *edited by Frances Wright, Robert Dale Owen, and Robert L. Jennings.* New York: Greaves, 1829.

Guarneri, Carl J. *The Utopian Alternative: Fourierism in Nineteenth-Century America.* Ithaca, NY: Cornell University Press, 1991.

Gundy, Lloyd W. "Glimpses of the Immigration of French Icarians to America." In *Immigration of the Icarians to Illinois: Proceedings of the Icarian Weekend in Nauvoo, Illinois, July 19 and 20, 1986.* Edited by Lillian M. Snyder and Robert P. Sutton. Macomb, IL: 1987, 23–38.

———. "Liberty, Equality and Fraternity in Butter Rights: Icarian Rules Can't Govern Everything." In *Culture and Colony Life of the Icarians: Proceedings of the 1994–97 Cours Icarien Symposia.* Edited by the National Icarian Heritage Society. Nauvoo, IL: National Icarian Heritage Society, 1998, 11–19.

Harrison, John F. C. *Quest for the New Moral World: Robert Owen and the Owenites in Britain and America.* New York: Charles Scribner's Sons, 1969.

———. *The Second Coming: Popular Millenarianism, 1780–1850.* London: Routledge & Kegan Paul, 1979.

Hawthorne, Nathaniel. *Tales and Sketches.* New York: Library of America, 1982.

————. *The Blithedale Romance*. Gloucester, UK: Dodo Press, 2012.

Hayden, Dolores. *Seven American Utopias: The Architecture of Communitarian Socialism, 1790–1975*. Cambridge, MA: MIT Press, 1976.

Hazlitt, William. *The Collected Works of William Hazlitt*. London: J. M. Dent & Co., 1902.

Hinds, Alfred William. *American Communities: Brief Sketches of Economy, Zoar, Bethel, Aurora, Amana, Icaria, the Shakers, Oneida, Wallingford, and the Brotherhood of the New Life*. Oneida, NY: Office of the American Socialist, 1878.

Hinton, Mary Beth, ed. *Syracuse University Library Associates Courier* 28, no. 2 (1993).

Hobsbawm, Eric. *How to Change the World: Marx and Marxism 1840–2011*. London: Little, Brown, 2011.

————. *The Age of Revolution: Europe, 1789–1848*. London: Weidenfeld & Nicolson, 1975.

Holloway, Mark. *Heavens on Earth: Utopian Communities in America, 1680–1880*. New York: Dover Publications, 1966.

Holy Bible, King James Version. Nashville, TN: Holman Bible Publishers, 1973.

Howe, Daniel Walker. *What Hath God Wrought: The Transformation of America, 1815–1848*. Oxford: Oxford University Press, 2007.

James, Henry. "To the Editor of the *New York Observer*." *New-York Tribune*, November 15, 1852.

Johnson, Christopher H. *Utopian Communism in France: Cabet and the Icarians 1839–1851*. Ithaca, NY: Cornell University Press, 1974.

Johnson, Oakley C. *Robert Owen in the United States*. New York: Humanities Press for the American Institute for Marxist Studies, 1970.

Judt, Tony. *Thinking the Twentieth Century*. New York: Penguin Press, 2012.

Kanter, Rosabeth Moss. *Commitment and Community: Communes and Utopias in Sociological Perspective*. Cambridge, MA: Harvard University Press, 1972.

Klaw, Spencer. *Without Sin: The Life and Death of the Oneida Community*. New York: Viking, 1993.

Lane, Charles. "Brook Farm." *Dial* 4, no. 3 (January 1844): 45.

Lane, Margaret. *Frances Wright and the "Great Experiment."* Manchester, UK: Manchester University Press, 1972.

Lester, Toby. "A New Geography." In *A New Literary History of America*. Edited by Greil Marcus and Werner Sollors. Cambridge, MA: Belknap Press of Harvard University Press, 2009.

Linn, William Alexander. *Horace Greeley: Founder and Editor of the* New York Tribune. New York: D. Appleton and Co., 1912.

Locke, John. *Two Treatises on Government.* London: Whitmore and Fenn, 1821.

Lockwood, George B. *The New Harmony Movement.* New York: D. Appleton and Co., 1905.

Lossing, Benjamin J. "The Shakers." *Harper's New Monthly Magazine* 15, no. 86 (July 1857): 164–77.

Macdonald, Dwight. *Masscult and Midcult: Essays Against the American Grain.* New York: New York Review of Books, 2011.

Mackie, Alexander. *The Gift of Tongues: A Study in Pathological Aspects of Christianity.* New York: George H. Doran Co., 1921.

MacLean, John Peterson. *A Sketch of the Life and Labors of Richard McNemar.* Franklin, OH: Franklin Chronicle, 1905.

The Manifesto. Vol. 22. East Canterbury, NH: United Society, 1892.

Mannhein, Karl. *Ideology and Utopia: An Introduction to the Sociology of Knowledge.* New York: Harcourt, Brace & Co., 1936.

Manuel, Frank E., ed. *Utopias and Utopian Thought.* Boston: Houghton Mifflin, 1966.

Manuel, Frank Edward, and Fritzie P. Manuel. *Utopian Thought in the Western World.* Cambridge, MA: Belknap Press of Harvard University Press, 1979.

Marchand, Ernest Leroy. "Homesteading in the Big Bend." *Assimilation of Icarians into American Life: Proceedings of the 1988 Cours Icarien.* Edited by Lillian M. Snyder. Nauvoo, IL: National Icarian Heritage Society, 1994, 20–27.

Marcus, Greil. *The Shape of Things to Come: Prophecy and the American Voice.* New York: Farrar, Straus and Giroux, 2006.

Marini, Stephen A. *Radical Sects of Revolutionary New England.* Cambridge, MA: Harvard University Press, 1982.

Marshall, Mary. *The Rise and Progress of the Serpent from the Garden of Eden, to the Present Day: With a Disclosure of Shakerism Exhibiting a General View of Their Real Character and Conduct from the First Appearance of Ann Lee. Also, the Life and Sufferings of the Author, Who Was Mary M. Dyer but Now Is Mary Marshall.* Concord, NH: printed for the author, 1847.

Marx, Karl. *Karl Marx: Selected Writings.* 2nd ed. Edited by David McLellan. Oxford: Oxford University Press, 2000.

McCarthy, Mary. *The Oasis.* Brooklyn, NY: Melville House Publishing, 2013.

McGee, Anita Newcomb. "An Experiment in Human Stirpiculture." *American Anthropologist* 4, no. 4 (October 1891): 319–26.

McLaren, Donald Campbell. *Boa Constrictor, or, Fourier Association Self-Exposed as to Its Principles and Aims.* Rochester, NY: Canfield & Warren, 1844.

McNemar, Richard. *The Kentucky Revival, or, A Short History of the Late Extraordinary Out-pouring of the Spirit of God, in the Western United States of America.* Albany, NY: E. and E. Hosford, 1808.

Medlicott, Carol. *Issachar Bates: A Shaker's Journey.* Hanover, NH: University Press of New England, 2013.

Menand, Louis. *The Metaphysical Club: A Story of Ideas in America.* New York: Farrar, Straus and Giroux, 2001.

Mill, John Stuart. *Principles of Political Economy.* New York: Colonial Press, 1899.

Miscellaneous Selections, Published as a Supplement to the Connecticut Courant. Vol. 3. Hartford, CT: Godwin & Co., 1832.

More, Thomas. *Utopia.* Translated by Paul Turner. London: Penguin Books, 1965.

Morell, John Reynell. *Sketch of the Life of Charles Fourier, Introductory to His Treatise on the Human Soul.* London: J. Watson, 1849.

Morin, France, ed. *Heavenly Visions: Shaker Gift Drawings and Gift Songs.* Minneapolis: University of Minnesota Press, 2001.

Morse, Flo. *The Shakers and the World's People.* Hanover, NH: University Press of New England, 1980.

Morton, A. L. *The Life and Ideas of Robert Owen.* New York: International Publishers, 1978.

Mumford, Lewis. *The Story of Utopias.* Charleston, SC: BiblioBazaar, 2008.

Muravchik, Joshua. *Heaven on Earth: The Rise and Fall of Socialism.* San Francisco: Encounter Books, 2002.

Mutual Criticism. Oneida, NY: Office of the American Socialist, 1876.

Nordhoff, Charles. *American Utopias.* Stockbridge, MA: Berkshire House Publishers, 1993. (Originally published 1875 as *The Communistic Societies of the United States.*)

Noyes, George Wallingford. *Free Love in Utopia: John Humphrey Noyes and the Origin of the Oneida Community.* Edited by Lawrence Foster. Urbana: University of Illinois Press, 2001.

Noyes, John Humphrey. *The Berean: A Manual for the Help of Those Who Seek the Faith of the Primitive Church.* Putney, VT: Office of the Spiritual Magazine, 1847.

————. *History of American Socialisms.* Philadelphia: J. B. Lippincott & Co., 1870.

————. *John Humphrey Noyes on Sexual Relations in the Oneida Community: Four Essential Texts.* Edited by Anthony Wonderley. Clinton, NY: Richard W. Couper Press, 2012.

Nozick, Robert. *Anarchy, State, and Utopia.* New York: Basic Books, 1974.

Ohio History. Columbus: Ohio Archaeological and Historical Publications, 1904.

Oneida Community. *Bible Communism: A Compilation from the Annual Reports and Other Publications of the Oneida Association and Its Branches.* Philadelphia: Porcupine Press, 1972.

Orvis, Marianne Dwight. *Letters from Brook Farm, 1841–1847.* Edited by Amy L. Reed. Philadelphia: Porcupine Press, 1972.

Oved, Yaacov. *Two Hundred Years of American Communes.* New Brunswick, NJ: Transaction Publishers, 1993.

Owen, Robert. *A Development of the Principles and Plans on Which to Establish Self-Supporting Home Colonies.* London: Home Colonization Society, 1841.

————. *The Future of the Human Race; Or, A Great, Glorious, and Peaceful Revolution, Near at Hand, to Be Effected Through the Agency of Departed Spirits of Good and Superior Men and Women.* London: Effingham Wilson, 1854.

————. *A New View of Society and Other Writings.* Edited by Gregory Claeys. New York: Penguin Books, 1991.

————. *Lectures on an Entire New State of Society: Comprehending an Analysis of British Society, Relative to the Production and Distribution of Wealth, the Formation of Character, and Government, Domestic and Foreign.* London: J. Brooks, 1830.

————. *The Life of Robert Owen, Written by Himself.* Vols. 1 and 1.A. London: Effingham Wilson, 1857–1858.

Owen, Robert Dale. *Threading My Way.* New York: G. W. Carleton & Co., 1874.

————. *To Holland and to New Harmony: Robert Dale Owen's Travel Journal 1825–1826.* Edited by Josephine M. Elliott. Indianapolis: Indiana Historical Society, 1969.

————. "The Social Experiment at New Harmony: A Chapter of Autobiography." *Atlantic Monthly* 32, no. 190 (August 1873): 224–36.

Owen, William. *Diary of William Owen, November 10, 1824, to April 20, 1825.* Edited by Joel W. Hiatt. Indianapolis, IN: Bobbs-Merrill, 1906.

Packard, Frederick Adolphus. *Life of Robert Owen.* Philadelphia: Ashmead & Evans, 1866.

Paine, Thomas. *Common Sense: Addressed to the Inhabitants of America*. London: H. D. Symonds, 1792.

Parish, Charles T. "Who Were the Icarians?" In *Immigration of the Icarians to Illinois: Proceedings of the Icarian Weekend in Nauvoo, Illinois, July 19 and 20, 1986*. Edited by Lillian M. Snyder and Robert P. Sutton. Macomb, IL: 1987, 4–6.

Parker, Robert Allerton. *A Yankee Saint: John Humphrey Noyes and the Oneida Community*. New York: G. P. Putnam's Sons, 1935.

Pellarin, C. H. *The Life of Charles Fourier*. 2nd ed. Translated by Francis G. Shaw. New York: William H. Graham, 1848.

Piotrowski, Sylvester A. *Étienne Cabet and the* Voyage en Icarie. Westport, CT: Hyperion Press, 1975.

Pitzer, Donald E., ed. *America's Communal Utopias*. Chapel Hill: University of North Carolina Press, 1997.

Pitzer, Donald E., and Darryl D. Jones. *New Harmony Then and Now*. Bloomington, IN: Quarry Books, 2012.

Plato: Complete Works. Edited by John M. Cooper. Indianapolis, IN: Hackett Publishing, 1997.

Promey, Sally M. *Spiritual Spectacles: Vision and Image in Mid-Nineteenth-Century Shakerism*. Bloomington: Indiana University Press, 1993.

Raffles, Thomas. *Memoir of the Life and Public Services of Sir Thomas Stamford Raffles, F.R.S. &c*. Edited by Sophia Raffles. London: John Murray, 1830.

Rancière, Jacques. "Why did the Icarians Leave France?" In *Immigration of the Icarians to Illinois: Proceedings of the Icarian Weekend in Nauvoo, Illinois, July 19 and 20, 1986*. Edited by Lillian M. Snyder and Robert P. Sutton. Macomb, IL: 1987, 6–17.

Rexroth, Kenneth. *Communalism: From Its Origins to the Twentieth Century*. London: Peter Owen, 1975.

Ripley, Sophia. "Letter from Zoar." *Dial* 2 (August 1838): 129.

Robertson, Constance Noyes. *Oneida Community Profiles*. Syracuse, NY: Syracuse University Press, 1977.

———. *The Oneida Community: An Autobiography, 1851–1876*. Syracuse, NY: Syracuse University Press, 1970.

Ross, Dale W. "One's Man's Voyage to Icaria." In *Immigration of the Icarians to Illinois: Proceedings of the Icarian Weekend in Nauvoo, Illinois, July 19 and 20, 1986*. Edited by Lillian M. Snyder and Robert P. Sutton. Macomb, IL: 1987, 43–50.

Ross, Marie Marchand. *Child of Icaria*. Westport, CT: Hyperion Press, 1976.

Rourke, Constance Mayfield. *Trumpets of Jubilee: Henry Ward Beecher, Harriet Beecher Stowe, Lyman Beecher, Horace Greeley, P. T. Barnum*. New York: Harcourt, Brace & Co., 1927.

Rushby, Kevin. *Paradise: A History of the Idea That Rules the World*. New York: Basic Books, 2006.

Sargent, Lyman Tower, Roland Schaer, and Gregory Claeys, eds. *Utopia: The Search for the Ideal Society in the Western World*. New York: Oxford University Press, 2000.

Schama, Simon. *Citizens: A Chronicle of the French Revolution*. New York: Vintage Books, 1989.

Sears, Clara Endicott, ed. *Gleanings from Old Shaker Journals*. Westport, CT: Hyperion Press, 1975.

Seldes, Gilbert. *The Stammering Century*. New York: New York Review of Books, 2012.

Shaw, Albert. *Icaria: A Chapter in the History of Communism*. New York: G. P. Putnam's Sons, 1884.

Snyder, Lillian M. "A Day in the Life of Emile Baxter." In *Adaptation of the Icarians to America: Proceedings of the 1987 Cours Icarien Symposium*. Edited by Robert Sutton. Corning, IA: 1987, 14–25.

———. *The Search for Brotherhood, Peace, and Justice: The Story of Icaria*. Deep River, IA: Brennan Printing, 1996.

Soldiers of Humanity: A History and Census of the Icarian Communities. Edited by Dale Larsen. Nauvoo, IL: National Icarian Heritage Society, 1998.

Special Love/Special Sex: An Oneida Community Diary. Edited by Robert S. Fogarty. Syracuse, NY: Syracuse University Press, 1994.

Stein, Stephen J. *The Shaker Experience in America: A History of the United Society of Believers*. New Haven, CT: Yale University Press, 1992.

A Summary View of the Millennial Church, or United Society of Believers (Commonly Called Shakers). Albany, NY: Packard & Van Benthuysen, 1823.

Sutton, Robert P. *Communal Utopias and the American Experience: Secular Communities, 1824–2000*. Westport, CT: Praeger Publishers, 2004.

———. "Cabetian Orthodoxy Asserted: Past Practices and *Voyage en Icarie* in Icaria-Speranza." In *Icaria-Speranza, Final Utopian Experiment of Icarians in America: Proceedings of the 1989 Cours Icarien Symposium*. Edited by the National Icarian Heritage Society. Nauvoo, IL: 1995, 31–42.

———. *Les Icariens: The Utopian Dream in Europe and America*. Urbana: University of Illinois Press, 1994.

———. "Voyage to Icaria: A Message to the World." In *Humanistic Values of* the Icarian Movement: Proceedings of the Symposium on the "Relevance of the Icarian Movement to Today's World." Edited by Lillian M. Snyder. Nauvoo, IL: 1980, 14–26.

———. "The Icarians of Corning, Iowa." In *Adaptation of the Icarians to America: Proceedings of the 1987 Cours Icarien Symposium.* Edited by Robert Sutton. Corning, IA: 1987, 3–14.

Swift, Lindsay. *Brook Farm: Its Members, Scholars, and Visitors.* New York: Macmillan Company, 1900.

"Third Annual Report of the Oneida Association: Exhibiting Its Progress to February 20, 1851." Oneida, NY: Oneida Association, 1851. https://library.syr.edu/digital/collections/t/ThirdAnnualReportOfTheOneidaAssociation/.

Thoreau, Henry David. *The Writings of Henry David Thoreau.* Vol. 6, *Familiar Letters.* Edited by F. B. Sanborn. Boston: Houghton Mifflin and Company, 1906.

———. *Walden and Civil Disobedience.* New York: Penguin Books, 1983.

Tocqueville, Alexis de. *Democracy in America.* Translated by Arthur Goldhammer. New York: Library of America, 2004.

Trollope, Frances. *Domestic Manners of the Americans.* London: Whittaker, Treacher, & Co., 1832.

Vallet, Emile. *An Icarian Communist in Nauvoo.* Springfield: Illinois State Historical Society, 1971.

Van de Warker, Ely. "A Gynecological Study of the Oneida Community." *American Journal of Obstetrics and Diseases of Women and Children* 17, no. 8 (1884): 786–810.

Visiting the Shakers 1778–1849. Edited by Glendyne R. Wergland. Clinton, NY: Richard W. Couper Press, 2007.

Warren, Josiah. *True Civilization: An Immediate Necessity, and the Last Ground of Hope for Mankind.* Boston: J. Warren, 1863.

Wiener, Philip P., ed. *Dictionary of the History of Ideas: Studies of Selected Pivotal Ideas.* New York: Charles Scribner's Sons, 1973.

Wilde, Oscar. *The Soul of Man Under Socialism.* Portland, ME: Thomas B. Mosher, 1905.

Williams, Robert Chadwell. *Horace Greeley: Champion of American Freedom.* New York: New York University Press, 2006.

Wilson, Edmund. *Patriotic Gore: Studies in the Literature of the American Civil War.* New York: Oxford University Press, 1962.

———. *To the Finland Station.* New York: New York Review of Books, 2003.

Wilson, James Harrison. *The Life of Charles A. Dana*. New York: Harper & Brothers, 1907.

Wilson, William E. *The Angel and the Serpent: The Story of New Harmony*. Bloomington: Indiana University Press, 1964.

Wonderley, Anthony. "Watervliet Shakers Through the Eyes of Oneida Perfectionists, 1863–1875." *American Communal Studies Quarterly* 3, no. 2 (April 2009): 51–65.

———. "Making the Bible Argument: John H. Noyes' Mission Statement for the Oneida Community." *American Communal Studies Quarterly* 5, no. 3 (July 2011): 148–74.

———. "Oneida Community Gender Relations—in Context and Over Time." *American Communal Studies Quarterly* 7, no. 1 (January 2013): 3–28.

Wright, Frances. *Views of Society and Manners in America*. London: Longman, Hurst, Rees, Orme, and Brown, 1821.

———. "Establishment at Nashoba, West Tennessee, for the Benefit of the Negro Race." *New Harmony Gazette* 2, no. 21 (February 1827): 164–65.

Young, Marguerite. *Angel in the Forest: An Epic of Two Utopias*. New York: Charles Scribner's Sons, 1945.

Youngs, Benjamin Seth. *The Testimony of Christ's Second Appearing*. 2nd ed. Albany, NY: E. and E. Hosford, 1810.

The Youth's Guide to Zion, and Holy Mother's Promises. Given by Inspiration at New Lebanon, N.Y., January 5, 1842. Canterbury, NH: United Society, 1842.

Index

Note: Page numbers followed by *f* indicate a figure.

CHRIS JENNINGS grew up in New York City. He graduated from Deep Springs College and Wesleyan University. He lives in Northern California.

ABOUT THE TYPE

This book was set in Baskerville, a typeface designed by John Baskerville (1706–75), an amateur printer and type-founder, and cut for him by John Handy in 1750. The type became popular again when the Lanston Monotype Corporation of London revived the classic roman face in 1923. The Mergenthaler Linotype Company in England and the United States cut a version of Baskerville in 1931, making it one of the most widely used typefaces today.